LIVING SYSTEMS

principles and relationships

Canfield Press, San Francisco

a department of Harper & Row, Publishers, Inc.

New York   Evanston   London

LIVING SYSTEMS

principles and relationships

James M. Ford

James E. Monroe

Biological illustrations by Laney Hicks

Chapter Opening Photographs

Editorial and design supervision : *Ken Burke*

Design : *Michael Rogondino*

Graphic illustration : *Douglas Luna*

Cover photographs : *Tom Tracy*

LIVING SYSTEMS : *Principles and Relationships*

Copyright © 1971 by James M. Ford and James E. Monroe.

Standard Book Number : 06—382700—X

Library of Congress Catalog Card Number : 78—148575

Fourth Printing

To Our Families

Preface

One of the most exciting and relevant experiences of education can be the study of life—what it is, how it functions, and how knowledge of it can affect our everyday existence. The discoveries of modern science have enabled us to make successful organ transplants, consider genetic manipulation, vastly improve crop yields, and even send man to the moon. But our very existence may be threatened by the activities of life itself. For example, the side effects of some insecticides may cancel the desired benefits, modern technology often pollutes the environment, and the rapidly increasing human population strains our basic resources. A study of biology thus is necessary for a rational and intelligent consideration of the many medical and ecological issues of our day.

It is important that students have an understanding of all fields of biology, not just the areas in which exciting developments are occurring today. In this book, therefore, we have attempted to present a balance between the classical aspects of the biological sciences and the areas of recent research. Moreover, historical perspective often accompanies explanation of the development of a principle to show how a scientific concept evolves. And since it is also important for students to appreciate and understand the nature of science, scientific methodology, and the analysis of data in biology, these are stressed throughout the book.

Designed for an introductory course in the life sciences for either general education students or biology majors, this book presents the important principles and concepts of biology through the use of selected examples. The book is organized into eleven chapters and an appendix, which perhaps forms one of the strongest features of the book. For example, the chemistry of life is included in one chapter, the structure and function of the cell constitutes a chapter, and energy relationships, such as photosynthesis and respiration, are also in one chapter. The classification and major characteristics of organisms appear in the appendix for use and reference when desired. We feel that this method of organization best illustrates and presents the fundamental principles of biology.

Each chapter concludes with summarizing principles which outline the major points in the chapter. Thought-provoking review questions are provided for each chapter. Up-to-date supplementary readings encourage the student to study a particular subject in more detail. And an extensive glossary is available and should be consulted frequently as the book is used.

Since modern biology relies heavily on a knowledge of chemistry and cells, the first three chapters should be read in order. After that, if preferred, the chapters may be studied in a somewhat different order. For example, the chapters on reproduction and genetics could readily follow the chapter on cell structure.

A textbook cannot be developed by the authors alone. The completion of this book depended on the contributions and hard work of many people, and we wish to gratefully acknowledge the following: Kenneth Burke for his tireless and devoted efforts in the editing of this book, Laney Hicks for her excellent illustrations, Jan Allen for her efficient typing and most helpful secretarial services, Dr. John Smith of Grays Harbor College and Richard Nowadnick of Skagit Valley College for their helpful classroom testing of the manuscript, Dr. James Newstead of the University of Saskatchewan for supplying original electronmicrographs, T. Leslie Elliott of Harper and Row for his encouragement and guidance, Dr. Ernst Dornfeld and Dr. Alfred Owczarzak of Oregon State University for their example as master teachers, and finally, the many reviewers for their helpful suggestions and advice.

James Ford
James Monroe

Skagit Valley College
Mount Vernon, Washington
April 1971

Contents

1

SCIENCE AND BIOLOGY: PERSPECTIVE 1

2

CHEMISTRY AND LIFE 17

3

BIOLOGICAL ARCHITECTURE: CELLS 59

4

BIOLOGICAL ARCHITECTURE: TISSUES, ORGANS, AND ORGANISMS 81

5

THE LIVING COMMUNITY 111

6

ENERGY 167

7

SUPPORTING PROCESSES OF LIFE 195

11

EVOLUTION AND NATURAL SELECTION 351

LIVING SYSTEMS

principles and relationships

1

Science and Biology: Perspective

Most of us at some time have been irresistibly drawn to investigate a bee hive or a wasp nest; this attraction no doubt stems from the living activity around these insect homes. Often our observations lead to further investigation and, eventually, inspection of the contents of the hive, exposing the inhabitants and their way of life. What were these activities that stimulated our curiosity? First of all we saw the movement and the characteristic structure of these animals. We could see bees collecting nectar from flowers to make honey, and if we looked closer we saw eggs and various growth and developmental stages. More subtle than these obvious characteristics are the social structure and the communication among members of the society. The well-developed communication system employed by these organisms permits the exchange of important information on the location and source of food. Actually all the characteristics of life—movement, responsiveness, reproduction, growth and development, structure and organization, and metabolism and adaptation—occur in a bee hive.

Through curiosity and experimentation with nature, man has been able to modify much of his environment to suit his needs. For example, man has derived great benefit from the discovery of better medical techniques and better agricultural practices. Man's eagerness to investigate and manipulate his environment, however, has produced some damaging results to the balance of nature. Some of these, such as air and water pollution, are among the most serious problems in biology today.

The problems and achievements of biology affect all human beings, and therefore a knowledge of the principles of biology is important to all of us. Today this knowledge is even more important since the biological achievements are more numerous and the problems more serious. The accomplishments of biology have resulted, for the most part, from orderly *scientific* studies and experimentation.

WHAT IS A SCIENCE?

THE NATURAL SCIENCES

When the term *science* is used, we frequently think of one of the natural sciences. The natural sciences (physics, chemistry, and biology) deal with matter, energy, and their interactions. Most fields of study are interdisciplinary—that is, understanding them involves knowledge of more than one of these general areas. For example, geology, the study of the earth, must utilize knowledge and concepts from both chemistry and physics. Oceanography is an excellent example of interdisciplinary study, since its subject matter spans every area of the sciences. It is concerned not only with the physical structure and chemical composition of the oceans but also with the life found there. Biochemistry, a relatively new interdisciplinary field, concerns the chemistry of organisms, and biophysics deals with the physics of life. In fact, all of modern biology requires some background in physics and chemistry. Science, as we will use the term, seeks to investigate matter and its properties and to explain nature. Stated another way, the goal of science is to derive meaningful concepts about nature.

THE METHODS OF SCIENCE

Most scientists agree that no single method really exists for scientific investigation, and some contend that there are perhaps as many methods as there are problems in science. What is characteristic of science, however, is the attitude and the general approach to problems. This logical, systematic approach might really be used by anyone in problem solving. A person contemplating the purchase of an automobile, a homeowner attempting to discover why the light doesn't burn when he flips the switch, or a mechanic trying to figure out why your automobile won't start are all approaching their problems in a general systematic manner. But each is using specific methods unique to his field or to the solution of his problem. Objectivity, maintaining an open mind, hard work, honesty, and critical thinking are all characteristics of a scientific attitude. What we have in science then, rather than a rigid "scientific method," is a general scheme of inquiry or approach. This general scheme can be outlined as follows:

1   An unexplained phenomenon exists.
2   A tentative explanation, or *hypothesis*, is selected to be tested.
3   Experiments designed to test the hypothesis are set up and data are collected.
4   These data are analyzed.
5   The hypothesis is either supported by the data or it is not. If it is, then further experimentation determines the *probability* or degree of certainty to which the hypothesis explains the phenomenon.
6   If the probability is high, the hypothesis can be considered to be a reliable explanation. It then becomes a *theory*.
7   If the hypothesis turns out to have a low probability, then a new hypothesis is sought and tested by experimentation.

An application of this scientific approach is diagrammed in Figure 1-1, which illustrates a test of the hypothesis that light is necessary for the making of food, in the form of starch, in plants. Two plants that were taken as cuttings from the same plant were used in the experiment. Both plants were given equal amounts of water and the same exposure to

STEP I

Plant in light   Plant in dark
(for 48 hours)

STEP II

Plant in light   Plant in dark
(remove leaf from each)

Leaf from "light" plant   Leaf from "dark" plant
(test for presence of food—starch)

STEP III

Leaf from "light" plant   Leaf from "dark" plant
(starch present)   (no starch present)

STEP IV

Figure 1·1   An example of how scientific procedure can be employed to test a hypothesis.

air (oxygen, carbon dioxide, etc.). Their treatment was varied, however, in one respect only—exposure to light. The diagrams in Figure 1–1 illustrate the experimental procedure. Thus the original hypothesis that light is necessary for food production in plants appears to be true; that is, it has high probability. This experiment could lead to further questions and hypotheses about the light factor involved in the food-making process. For example, is all the light that falls on the plant necessary for food making? In what part of the food-production process is light required? (These questions will be considered later in Chapter 6.)

The importance of using a *control* was introduced in this experiment. A control is used as a standard against which the effects of the experimental conditions are compared. Since exposure to periods of light is a normal condition for plants, the light-exposed plant served as a control.

Probability, Hypothesis, Theory, Law

Note that the solution to the foregoing problem was stated in terms of *probability*. The suggested hypothesis may not be correct 100 percent of the time (few answers or explanations hold true in all cases), but it may be correct 90 percent of the time. Modern science therefore seeks the answers and explanations to natural phenomena in terms of probability. The greater the probability of a solution to a problem, the greater its value to scientific prediction.

Besides the term *hypothesis*, you have no doubt also heard the terms *theory* and *law* and wonder where they fit into this scheme. In order of importance they can be defined as follows. A *hypothesis* implies present insufficiency of evidence and therefore is only a tentative explanation. A *theory* implies a greater range of evidence and greater likelihood of truth. And, finally, a *law* implies a statement of order and relation in nature that has been found to be invariable under the same conditions.

Any explanation or interpretation of natural phenomena must be viewed in light of the available evidence. New evidence may be obtained through the use of new instruments and techniques, and we may find that the old explanation does not hold true. Even the use of the term *law* therefore should be regarded as somewhat tentative, since new evidence may show the relations explained by that law to be variable under different conditions.

Models

When scientists seek an explanation of some natural process or event they often use a physical *model*. This model may be very tentative at first until it is tested further; thus models serve as working hypotheses with varying degrees of probability. One biological model, proposed by Watson and Crick to explain the structure of the hereditary material DNA, will be presented in Chapter 2. We will encounter other models in our study of biology, such as the one currently used to explain the structure of the cell membrane.

SCIENCE AS A SELF-CORRECTING SYSTEM

Since science deals with the material world and involves experimentation, any theory proposed by one scientist can be tested by others. A scientist is forced to report his findings honestly, since it is possible for another scientist to check his results. Thus science is characterized as a *self-correcting system*.

This self-correcting characteristic is unique to science, and the same principle cannot be applied to problems in the humanities or philosophy. This of course does not mean that a scientist cannot make a mistake. They are as vulnerable to human error as anyone. A scientist may approach his work with the same deep feelings and emotions that any other professional individual may have. In fact, a researcher may select a hypothesis on the basis of a "hunch" that it might be the right solution to a problem. In doing so, however, the scientist is drawing on his background and experience in his field.

THE MECHANISTIC NATURE OF SCIENCE AND ITS LIMITATIONS

The attitude of science is often referred to as *mechanistic*. The concept of mechanism holds that natural phenomena are due to the properties of matter; that is, all events can be explained in physical and chemical terms. An alternative to the mechanistic viewpoint is the doctrine of *vitalism*, which relies on supernatural explanations. Vitalists often refer to a "vital force" as causing natural events or processes.

Just as vitalism impedes the progress of science, so does *teleology*, the belief that all natural phenomena have a definite purpose and thus are in some way preordained. Teleology is actually a form of vitalism, since it suggests a "divine plan" in nature. Statements such as "some plants have developed thorns to protect themselves" or "some worms have light-sensitive cells so that they can orient themselves to light" suggests that these organisms have consciously developed these structures for a purpose. It would be more scientifically correct to state that "some plants have thorns and as a result they have some protection" and "some worms have light-sensitive cells and as a result they can orient themselves to light."

Science is limited, however, to the study of the properties and interactions of matter and therefore cannot be effective in certain areas such as philosophy, theology, and politics. It is presently impossible to test certain questions and problems that arise in these fields. Social scientists, working in the fields of psychology and sociology, have utilized the methods of science in their work. Since these researchers are dealing with total human beings, the application of scientific methods has been helpful in limiting and controlling many variable factors. The use of experimentation in the fields of learning and memory has been noteworthy, but the complexity of living material and especially the complex structure of the human brain make it extremely difficult to isolate individual aspects of human behavior for study and experimentation.

BIOLOGY AS A SCIENCE

Biology encompasses all aspects of the study of life. If biological knowledge is to be acquired and recorded in a usable manner and if meaningful concepts are to be synthesized about the living world, organized studies must be conducted. In most studies of organisms it is possible to apply the methods of science.

It should be quite evident that science must seek its explanations in the material substance. Advances have been made in medicine and agriculture, for example, because research has followed mechanistic procedure. A patient would have little faith in modern medicine if it attributed his diseased condition to a vital spirit or demon. Although science cannot yet explain the causes of all natural phenomena, such as specific diseases or how certain minerals are taken in by plants, it cannot simply ascribe such unexplained phenomena to some mysterious force.

Knowledge in biology has grown tremendously in the past thirty years and this "knowledge explosion" is likely to continue. At the same time, discoveries that were made a hundred years ago are still important to our understanding of certain concepts. To understand the growth of biology we will look at some of the important developments that have led to the existing study we call the modern biological sciences. Like the other sciences, biology has a long history during which many false starts were made and progress was slow. A brief review of this history will illustrate the problems faced by the early researchers and to a great extent by their modern counterparts. Although we often give credit to one or two individuals for a major discovery, their achievement would not have been possible without the contributions of earlier researchers. It does require ingenuity and imagination, however, to tie isolated and often seemingly unrelated bits of knowledge together into a meaningful concept.

EARLY DEVELOPMENTS IN BIOLOGY

THE GREEKS

We might say that man first showed interest in biology when he learned to identify the plants and animals that supplied his food. His descendants no doubt later practiced selective breedings and crossings of certain plant groups in an effort to obtain better crops. The historical records of this activity are fragmentary, and we can only conclude that the biological activity was essentially practical. Since the Greeks left some of the earliest records of their activity, discussions of biological history usually begin with them. The speculations and interpretations of nature that the Greeks recorded show that they did attempt to see relationships in the natural world.

Although there were several distinct periods of Greek civilization dating back to around 3000 B.C., perhaps the greatest contributions to science were made during the Hellenic and Hellenistic periods (about 750–31 B.C.). Driven by an insatiable curiosity, the desire to observe nature carefully, and the ability to reason both inductively and deductively, Greek scholars formulated many concepts about their natural environment. *Inductive* reasoning involves the formulation of general conclusions from individual facts; *deductive* reasoning is the process of utilizing a general premise to explain a specific case. Both types of reasoning are useful to scientific thought. The Greeks were good observers but they were primarily philosophers and often arrived at philosophical explanations for natural phenomena. It was Hippocrates, known today as the "father of medicine," who stressed the importance of careful observation. In his school, which he founded in 420 B.C., the notion originated that all diseases have natural causes and that "divine diseases" do not exist.

Figure 1·2 Aristotle, often known as the "father of natural history." (Bettmann Archives.)

Figure 1·3 Galen, physician, and anatomist. (Bettmann Archives.)

Aristotle

No doubt the greatest Greek scientist was Aristotle (384–322 B.C.), a student of Plato. Aristotle (Figure 1–2) was a truly great natural historian who obviously possessed a very keen power of observation. Many of his descriptions of certain animals, their characteristics, and their behavior, were accurate even by modern standards. For example, Aristotle recognized that mammals (animals that are "hair-coated," as he referred to them) gave birth to young that were attached to the mother by an umbilical cord. He also realized that although most fish lay eggs from which the young hatch, others (the shark group) released live offspring. He knew, however, that these young were not attached to an umbilical cord except in the case of the dogfish shark, in which the young carry a yolk sac for some time after birth. The remarkable thing here is that zoologists paid little attention to this account until it was confirmed about 1850. Aristotle was shown to be correct even though the cord has a different origin in the dogfish than in mammals.

On the organization and complexity of life, Aristotle placed plants as the "lowest form" of life, animals higher, and man, since he possessed a "rational soul," as the most complex organism. The Aristotelian system of classification, often known as the "scala naturae," was utilized for approximately 2,000 years. In matters concerning the complexity and the nature of life we would term Aristotle a vitalist.

Although Aristotle was a good observer, he unfortunately relied heavily on second-hand information, much of which was faulty. Thus many of his interpretations and pronouncements were incorrect, but most of these were accepted as facts long into the 1800s merely because Aristotle had stated them. For example, he claimed that plants did not have sexual organs. Aristotle's ideas on sex determination in humans were nonsensical, since he taught that if the father were weak, his child would be a girl, whereas a strong father would produce a son. His teachings on the human circulatory system also showed a lack of close observation or experimentation. Aristotle believed that the heart was the center of intelligence and sensations and that the arteries contained blood and air while the veins carried only blood.

6

THE ROMANS AND THE MIDDLE AGES

Science under the Romans did not flourish as it had in Grecian times. The Greeks were curious about their natural environment, but the Romans showed little concern except in matters that pertained directly to the practical aspects of life, such as government, engineering, and warfare. Two scientists of this era are often referred to—Pliny (first century A.D.) and Galen (second century A.D.). The former was a natural historian and the latter, a Greek anatomist and physician. Many of Pliny's works were not original but rather collections of tales he had heard and recounted in his books.

Galen

Although Galen (Figure 1–3) was considered a great physician of his time, it is doubtful that he went so far as to perform dissections on the human body. Many of his interpretations of the function of organs, such as the heart and the lungs, were wrong, and these were perpetuated for many centuries because of the respect in which he was held. Most of Galen's writings were based on his dissections of the Old World Monkey and he seemed to be preoccupied with the spiritual nature of the blood. For example, he wrote that the forming blood receives "natural" spirits in the liver, "vital" spirits in the left ventricle of the heart, and "animal" spirits in the brain. Another erroneous belief concerning the blood was that it ebbed and flowed through the body (rather than circulated). He also supposed that the blood in the heart passed from the right side to the left side through tiny pores in the ventricular septum.

Although some chemical elements and compounds were discovered by alchemists in the period we call the Middle Ages, substantial advances in biology did not take place. New concepts and discoveries in science were to come later in a period that embraced new philosophies.

Figure 1·4 Leonardo da Vinci, Renaissance artist and scientist. (Photo courtesy of Biblioteca Reale di Torino.)

THE RENAISSANCE

The general climate of this era can be characterized by two important developments. First, there was a great resurgence of interest in the Greeks and their intellectual accomplishments; and second, and perhaps more important, a new spirit developed embracing a questioning attitude. The social and religious systems of medieval Europe were questioned, and the freedom of the individual was proclaimed. This then offered an atmosphere in which science could again flourish.

Art also blossomed along with the natural sciences during the Renaissance. The most famous artist-naturalist was Leonardo da Vinci (1452–1519) (Figure 1-4). His interest in science certainly went beyond biology as is evident from his engineering accomplish-

Figure 1·5 Andreas Vesalius, Renaissance anatomist. (Bettmann Archives.)

Figure 1·6 William Harvey, English physician and physiologist, who traced the circulation of the blood. (Bettmann Archives.)

ments. Another important scientist of this era was the anatomist Andreas Vesalius (1514–1564) (Figure 1-5) who, as a most careful dissector, challenged much of the work of Galen, who was still the accepted authority.

Perhaps the most characteristic feature of da Vinci and Vesalius, and other scientists of this time, was their insistence on the importance of first-hand observations in the study of nature. Certainly, it was this factor plus the general spirit of the Renaissance that led to the development of important concepts about the living world.

SEVENTEENTH- AND EIGHTEENTH-CENTURY DISCOVERIES

EARLY STUDIES IN PHYSIOLOGY

Harvey and Hales

Modern biology had its inception when William Harvey (1576–1657) (Figure 1-6), an English physician and physiologist, traced the pattern of the circulation of blood in man. Aristotle's and Galen's incorrect theories on the mechanism of blood circulation were still respected when Harvey set out to solve

the problem in an experimental manner. He realized, as his calculations showed, that the blood had to travel through the arteries and veins in a circular pattern in one direction. Moreover, Harvey was a careful observer and he studied the heart cavities, the valves between the cavities, and the vessels entering and leaving the heart. Where Galen had believed that the blood passed from the right side of the heart through the wall to the left side, Harvey concluded that the blood moved from the right side of the heart, to the lungs, and then to the left side, to be circulated through the body. Harvey did not fully understand how the blood passed from arteries to veins. This discovery was to be made later by those who had access to microscopes.

Another pioneer in physiology of the next generation was the Reverend Stephen Hales (1677–1761) of England. He conducted many experiments on plants and demonstrated such basic functions as water intake and its loss by transpiration. Hales was also interested in animal physiology and he successfully measured blood pressure in mammals. His work was always characterized by his concern for quantitative measurements. This was a new

Figure 1·7 A microscope used by Robert Hooke. (Photo courtesy of Bausch and Lomb.)

concept in science at this time, but its importance was soon to be recognized.

THE DEVELOPMENT OF THE MICROSCOPE

About 1590 the Dutch lens maker Zacharias Janssens developed the first compound microscope by placing a lens at each end of a long tube. In this same manner, Galileo Galilei (1564–1642), the great Italian scientist and philosopher, constructed a telescope with which he studied the planets and stars. Later more efficient microscopes were produced when lenses were ground to provide shorter focal lengths. The value of the microscope to the study of biology is probably obvious. It has made possible the observation of cellular structure in larger organisms as well as the study of minute living organisms such as protozoa and bacteria.

Hooke and Leeuwenhoek

Two men, Robert Hooke (1635–1703), an Englishman, and Anton van Leeuwenhoek (1632–1723), a Dutchman, pioneered the field of microscopy. It was Hooke who used the word *cell* to describe the "honeycomb" appearance of a thin section of cork he observed under his microscope (Figure 1-7). Leeuwenhoek (Figure 1-8) made excellent microscopes for his day and vigorously observed almost anything that suited his fancy. Several of his discoveries were outstanding. He discovered bacteria, differentiated them from other single-celled forms, and described spermatozoa. Another contribution was his detailed description of the capillary bed between arteries and veins. This filled in the remaining information to complete Harvey's partial description of the pattern of circulation.

Figure 1·8 Anton van Leeuwenhoek, the great Dutch microscopist. (Bettmann Archives.)

Figure 1·9 Carolus Linnaeus, who laid the framework for the classification system we use today. (Bettmann Archives.)

THE DEVELOPMENT OF CLASSIFICATION SYSTEMS

Ray and Linnaeus

A major accomplishment of this period was the recognition of the need for some classification schemes to deal with the diversity of living things. Such a system is indispensable both for an orderly study and for communication. Aristotle's system, which was based more on function and reproduction than on structure, was essentially too simple to handle the many different kinds of organisms known today. John Ray (1627–1705), an English naturalist, devised a classification scheme for both plants and animals, based on structure, and he classified the plants as herbs, shrubs, and trees. Later in his study of animals, Ray differentiated between vertebrates and invertebrates.

In the eighteenth century, classification was further developed by the work of Carolus Linnaeus (1707–1778), who laid the basic foundation for the system we use today. Linnaeus (Figure 1-9), a Swede, attempted to classify every known plant and animal, assigning a *genus* and *species* name to each. Thus every living organism is known by two names, the genus and the species. (For example, the dog is called *Canis familiaris*.) Furthermore these names are in Latin or Greek and therefore are the same in any country regardless of the spoken language.

Linnaeus used the sexual organs of flowers to classify them and this method is still used today. Perhaps his greatest single contribution was his *Systema Naturae*, published in 1735. Linnaeus used the concept of the species as the basis for classification and at first felt that a species was a fixed, unchanging unit created in nature. He apparently questioned this concept of the permanency of a species later in his work.

THE SYNTHESES OF THE NINETEENTH CENTURY

The 1800s can be regarded as one of the most important periods in the history of biology when some of the most significant concepts of biology were developed. These significant concepts were made possible no doubt through specialized studies in such fields as embryology, the study of development, and cytology, the study of cells. Even though specialization was an important aspect of nineteenth-century biology, many unifying themes that span the entire field of biology were formulated.

THE CELL THEORY

The idea that the cell is the structural and functional unit of life gained acceptance at this time. Cells were first observed in the 1600s and 1700s when microscopes became available. As improvements in microscope construction advanced, cellular studies also advanced and a great deal of information about cells was gradually accumulated. Based on these observations, M. J. Schleiden and Theodor Schwann, in 1838 and 1839, were able to formulate a "cell theory" for the structure of living things—that is, all organisms are composed of cells.

HEREDITY

The nineteenth century also saw remarkable accomplishments in the study of *heredity*. Most significant were the findings of Gregor Mendel in 1866, which dealt with the basic mechanisms of inheritance. These events are described in Chapter 10.

EMBRYOLOGY

Many important concepts in embryology emerged during this period. At the same time, however, many erroneous ideas were formulated as biologists sought to explain how an individual organism develops from a single cell into a mature adult. The idea of *preformation*, which supposed that all adult structures were present in the egg and merely grew larger and developed to produce an adult individual, was widely held. Those biologists who believed these structures to be present in the egg were called "ovists," while others, known as "spermists," contended that the immature structures were all present in the sperm. A controversy thus developed between the two schools. Some spermists even claimed that they could see in sperm cells a

Figure 1·10 The homunculus, a tiny, fully formed individual supposedly found in sperm cells.

tiny, undeveloped individual whom they called a "homunculus" (Figure 1-10). The idea of preformation was dealt a severe blow late in the eighteenth century by C. F. Wolff who proposed the concept of *epigenesis* based on his research on developing root and shoot tips in plants. Epigenesis refers to the formation of completely new parts as an organism grows and develops. Karl von Baer's "germ layer theory" in the 1800s strengthened the idea of epigenesis over preformation. It was von Baer who followed the development of the fertilized egg into three distinct germ layers and the subsequent development of tissues and organs from these germ layers. Another important discovery in embryology was made by Oscar Hertwig, who in 1875 proved that one nucleus in the fertilized egg came from the egg and the other nucleus from the sperm.

Figure 1·11 Louis Pasteur, the great French chemist. (Bettmann Archives.)

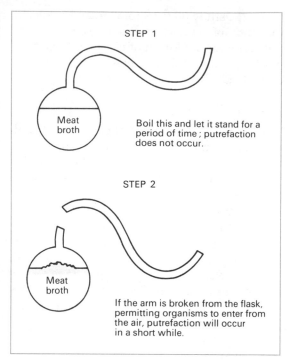

STEP 1

Meat broth

Boil this and let it stand for a period of time; putrefaction does not occur.

STEP 2

Meat broth

If the arm is broken from the flask, permitting organisms to enter from the air, putrefaction will occur in a short while.

Figure 1·12 An experiment by Pasteur to show that putrefaction is caused by organisms from the air.

SPONTANEOUS GENERATION

A very controversial topic was the idea of "spontaneous generation." Proponents of this concept believed that life could arise from putrifying or decaying organic matter. Francesco Redi in 1668 and Lazzaro Spallanzani in 1766 demonstrated that spontaneous generation did not occur under their experimental conditions. Other experimenters had arrived at an opposite conclusion and so the controversy continued into the nineteenth century. Louis Pasteur (Figure 1-11), the great French chemist, performed the conclusive experiments to adequately prove to the scientific world that spontaneous generation does not take place if existing life such as spores, eggs, and bacteria are excluded from a growth medium (Figure 1-12).

EVOLUTION

An outstanding step in the 1800s was the introduction of the concept of *evolution*, the theory that all existing types of animals and plants are derived from preexisting types. The Darwin and Wallace theory proposed around 1859 provided a fundamental framework and unifying theme for the study of biology. This theory, based on *natural selection*, also provided for the first time a logical explanation of how the diversity of life arose on our planet. Natural selection explains how some organisms survive and reproduce better than others because of favorable hereditary characteristics that occur by chance. Although evolution will be discussed in detail in a later chapter, it will be referred to in many places throughout this book.

TWENTIETH-CENTURY BIOLOGY

With the development of new chemical and physical techniques, more refined studies on the chemical composition of life have become possible. New, more powerful electron microscopes have revealed parts of the cell hitherto unknown. Modern genetics is no longer concerned only with the transmission of heredity from generation to generation but also with the structure and function of the hereditary material. Embryologists are devising experiments to determine how cells differentiate in the development of an organism—that is, why one cell becomes a muscle cell and another, a nerve cell. The term *molecular biology* has been applied to some of the newer aspects of the biological sciences which are concerned with structure and function at the level of molecules. Learning and memory are being approached from this viewpoint today. Many of the new findings will be discussed in this book and woven in with the important knowledge gained in earlier times in an attempt to present a clear picture of biology.

SUMMARIZING PRINCIPLES

Science is an organized study of the material world; the methods of science provide an orderly and systematic approach to problems dealing with matter; since any proposed theory can be subjected to experimentation, science is a self-correcting system.

Science is based on the mechanistic concept that all natural phenomena can be explained in terms of physics and chemistry; biology therefore is mechanistic in its approach.

Most concepts in the biological sciences have been developed over a long period of time; recent discoveries generally have been made possible through observations and experiments of earlier workers.

Because of their ability to observe and reason, the Greeks made many discoveries in the biological sciences; most important among them was Aristotle.

Under the Romans and during the Middle Ages science did not progress as it had with the Greeks; Galen was an outstanding physician and anatomist of this era but he made many errors concerning the functioning of certain parts of the body.

The Renaissance was a period when observation was again stressed and a time when the status quo was questioned; this attitude provided an atmosphere in which science could advance.

During the seventeenth and eighteenth centuries important foundations were laid in many fields of biology: in physiology, William Harvey traced the circulation of blood; Hooke and Leeuwenhoek developed microscopy; a classification scheme for the living world was worked out by Ray and Linnaeus.

The nineteenth century was a period when important concepts in biology were clearly synthesized. The cell theory by Schleiden and Schwann was prominent among these concepts; Mendel's studies were extremely important in understanding the mechanism involved in inheritance; in embryology the theory of epigenesis replaced the old idea of preformation; the principle of spontaneous generation was disproved by Pasteur's experiments; perhaps the greatest synthesis of this period was the theory of evolution proposed by Darwin and Wallace.

Provided with such tools as the electron microscope, chemical analyses, and electronic instrumentation, twentieth-century biologists are able to study life at finer dimensions—the cellular and molecular levels.

REVIEW QUESTIONS

1 Using the scientific approach, design an experiment to test the hypothesis that:
   (*a*) light is necessary for the production of green pigment (chlorophyll) in plants.
   (*b*) moths are attracted to specific wavelengths of light.

2 What is the importance of a "control" in each experiment above?

3 It has been argued that religion has impeded the progress of science through the ages. List reasons why this might be true.

4 List some examples of explanations that show elements of vitalism in our modern thought.

5 What is your personal viewpoint on the role of scientists in modern society? Must they assume responsibility for the use of their discoveries?

6 How did the work of Galen, Vesalius, and Harvey contribute to the ability of modern medicine to transplant human organs?

7 In what ways can chemistry, physics, and social science contribute to the study of biology?

8 We often speak of the great synthesis of biology in the nineteenth century. What were some of the major ideas formulated during this period?

9 What were some of the attitudes and technological advances that led to the resurgence of scientific study during the Renaissance?

10 Is it reasonable to assume that one can apply scientific methods in the selection of a mate? Discuss the advantages and limitations involved in doing so.

SUPPLEMENTARY READINGS

Asimov, Isaac, *View from a Height,* Garden City, N.Y., Doubleday, 1963.

Bronowski, J., *Science and Human Values,* New York, Harper & Row, 1959.

Brooks, Harvey, and Raymond Bowers, "The Assessment of Technology," *Scientific American,* February, 1970.

Eiseley, Loren, *The Firmament of Time,* New York, Atheneum, 1962.

Grobstein, C., *The Strategy of Life,* San Francisco, Freeman, 1965.

Hoyle, Fred, *Of Men and Galaxies,* Seattle, University of Washington Press, 1964.

Huxley, Thomas H., *On a Piece of Chalk,* New York, Charles Scribner's Sons, 1967. (A lecture delivered in 1868.)

Lenhoff, E. S., *Tools of Biology,* New York, Macmillan, 1966.

McCain, Garvin, and E. M. Segal, *The Game of Science,* Belmont, Calif., Brooks/Cole, 1969.

Morowitz, Harold J., and Mark E. Touretellotte, "The Smallest Living Cells," *Scientific American,* March, 1962.

Platt, J. R., *The Excitement of Science,* Boston, Houghton Mifflin, 1962.

Russell, Bertrand, *The Future of Science,* New York, Philosophical Library, 1959.

Sarton, George, *The Life of Science,* Bloomington, Indiana University Press, 1960.

Shapley, H., *The View from a Distant Star,* New York, Basic Books, 1963.

Singer, Charles, *A History of Biology,* New York, Abelard-Schuman, 1959.

The following list of several short reference books relates closely to the subjects discussed in this textbook. Each book contains a series of short readings about the principles and ideas of biology. These interesting readings by many great biologists will enrich your study of life.

Bonner, John T., *The Ideas of Biology,* New York, Harper & Row, 1962.

Gabriel, M., and S. Fogel, eds., *Great Experiments in Biology,* Englewood Cliffs, N.J., Prentice-Hall, 1955.

Johnson, W., and W. Steere, eds., *This is Life,* New York, Holt, Rinehart and Winston, 1962.

Moment, Gairdner, ed., *Frontiers of Modern Biology,* Boston, Houghton Mifflin, 1962.

Rapport, S., and H. Wright, eds., *Biology,* New York, New York University Press, 1969.

Waddington, C. H., *The Nature of Life,* New York, Atheneum, 1962.

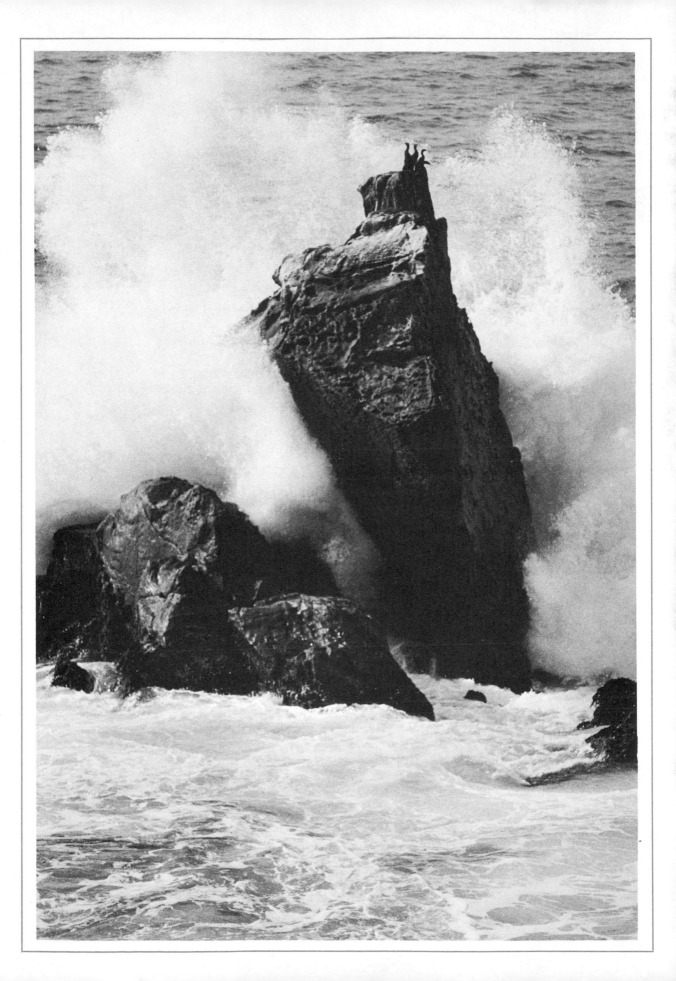

2

Chemistry and Life

The sight of hundreds of fireflies on a summer evening is an experience not easily forgotten. A curious observer undoubtedly wonders how this light is produced. It is now known that the glow is the result of a complex series of chemical reactions that transform chemical energy into light energy. But before we can thoroughly understand this and other biological processes, some knowledge of chemistry is necessary.

Since living things are composed of matter and involve the interactions of matter, we should first attempt to answer the questions: what is matter and where does it come from? This will ultimately lead us to the bigger question of the possible origin of the earth and the universe.

Throughout this study we will be concerned with the structure of chemical compounds and how they react in living systems.

MATTER AND ELEMENTS

The first philosophical thoughts on the origin and structure of matter are attributed to the early Greeks. In the sixth century B.C., Thales of Miletus reasoned that water must be the "mother

17

element" of all matter, whereas Anaximenes of Miletus, later in the same century, proposed that it was air. Heraclitus of Ephesus, about 500 B.C., considered change to be the only reality and fire the primary substance. Finally, Empedocles of Agrigentum, about 450 B.C., summarized the primary substances as water, air, fire, and earth. A different materialistic approach to the universe was taken by a group generally referred to as the atomists. Democritus (460–370 B.C.) felt that matter consisted of small, indivisible particles which he called *atomos*. Further, he considered these atomos, or *atoms* as we would call them, to be different for each kind of matter. These differences, he thought, were the cause of the different physical properties of matter.

During the period of the first century A.D. through the seventeenth century, much of the scientific activity was devoted to alchemy—the transmutation of elements such as iron and lead into gold and silver. Many basic elements and compounds were discovered and named by these sometimes mystic experimenters. Among these were mercury, sulfur, lead acetate, zinc, acetic acid, nitric acid, sulfuric acid, and hydrochloric acid.

Following a renewed interest in chemistry, the Englishman Robert Boyle, in 1661, defined the known chemical elements as substances that could not be further broken down by chemical means. In 1808, another English chemist, John Dalton, proposed a modern atomic theory and used the term *atom* after the earlier atomos of Democritus. This theory

gave rise to the concept that atoms were tiny, indivisible spheres that could not be destroyed. (We now know, however, that atoms can be broken into subparts.)

We will have more to say about the developments that lead to the modern atomic theory in the next section. For the present only a brief description of atomic structure will be presented in order to discuss some of the theories of cosmic evolution.

ATOMS AND MOLECULES

The smallest building blocks of nature that can be practically studied are the components of atoms, and we refer to these as subatomic particles, electrons, protons, and neutrons. Actually, other subatomic particles are known, but they are not essential to a basic understanding of the atom. The three particles we have named are organized into atoms as shown below.

The protons and neutrons form a compact nucleus around which the electrons move in specific energy levels. A collection of one type of atoms is known as an *element*; therefore we speak of the elements hydrogen, helium, carbon, oxygen, etc. Although over a hundred such elements are known, only about sixteen of these are present in abundance and are important to life. Elements range in complexity from hydrogen with one proton and one electron to lawrencium with 103 protons, 154 neutrons, and 103 electrons. When atoms of two or more elements unite, a *compound* is

p = proton
e = electron
n = neutron

1 proton and 1 electron

Hydrogen atom

2 protons, 2 neutrons, and 2 electrons

Helium atom

18

formed and the fundamental unit of this compound is called a *molecule*. For example, when four hydrogen atoms combine with one carbon atom, the compound methane (CH_4) is formed. Thus a molecule of methane is composed of five atoms, four hydrogen and one carbon.

THE ORIGIN OF THE UNIVERSE

EXPLOSION THEORY

One popular theory on the origin of the universe holds that an original concentration of matter exploded about ten billion years ago. This theory is often referred to as the "explosion" or "big bang theory." This theory assumes that, in the original concentration of matter, there were protons, neutrons, and electrons (or perhaps only neutrons, from which protons and electrons were derived). These subatomic particles rather randomly formed atoms of the chemical elements we know today. Since hydrogen is the simplest element and probably would have formed first, it is considered the parent element by those who accept this theory. That is, hydrogen came first and through subsequent additions of subatomic particles the other elements were formed. This process would require a vast amount of energy, which could have been furnished in the interior of stars, where element formation may be still going on. Some credence is granted to the explosion theory because several of the 103 elements have been artificially produced by the addition of subatomic particles to existing atoms.

STEADY-STATE THEORY

Another popular theory, the "steady-state theory," of the origin of the universe states that the universe has no beginning and no end. Matter is constantly being formed and converted from one form to another and energy—in other words, creative forces are continuously at work.

STARS, GALAXIES, AND OUR SOLAR SYSTEM

Whichever theory of the universe we accept, it is apparent that matter became organized into masses called *stars*. The star, then, becomes the fundamental unit in the universe. In addition, stars are found in large clusters called *galaxies* of which approximately 260,000,000 are visible from the Mount Palomar telescope in California. Each galaxy is composed of approximately ten billion stars, and all galaxies are similar in appearance. The distances between galaxies are continuously increasing, indicating that they are swiftly moving farther and farther apart and expanding into space.

Stars apparently are born when cosmic dust and gases concentrate into large masses within a galactic formation. Matter does exist between stars and galaxies as dust and gases, but it is very minute when compared to the density of a star, being on the order of about one atom per cubic centimeter. At sea level on our planet the atmosphere is composed of about ten million million million atoms per cubic centimeter.

OUR SOLAR SYSTEM

Our sun, with its solar system, is part of the Milky Way galaxy (Figure 2–1). Evidence indicates that our solar system was formed seven to ten billion years ago and, according to the "explosion theory," this would also be the time of the formation of the other galactic systems in the universe. Various theories have also been proposed to account for the origin of our solar system. One of the first, and quite plausible, was put forth by the philosopher-astronomer Laplace in 1796. According to his theory, the solar system was formed from a hot, swirling ball of gases that condensed, with the core forming the sun. Circling this mass was a belt of gases in which centers of condensation also occurred and the centers became solid bodies which are now the planets. Since Laplace a more refined theory has been advanced by several modern astronomers.

Figure 2·1*a* The view of the rising earth as it greeted the Apollo 8 astronauts. On the earth, 240,000 miles away, the sunset terminator bisects Africa. (NASA photo.)

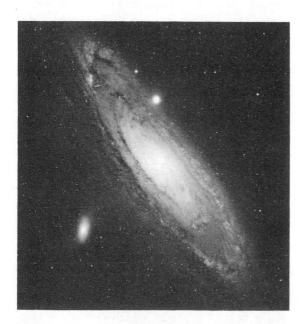

Figure 2·1*b* The Great Spiral Galaxy in the constellation Andromeda. This galaxy, about two billion light years away, is the nearest one to our galaxy. (Mount Wilson and Palomar Observatories.)

This theory incorporates some features of the Laplace theory but differs radically by suggesting that the gaseous atomic mixture was cold rather than hot. This theory proposes that cosmic dust and gases came together in a swirling mass to form the sun while secondary condensations occurred outside of this mass to form the planets. The planets then were held in orbits by the gravitational influence of the sun. Elements were formed during the origin of the planets, and molecules later formed from these elements. We have evidence from the decay of radioactive elements that the earth originated about five billion years ago.

This completes a brief sketch of cosmic evolution and we should now turn our attention to a more detailed discussion of matter. The concept of how atoms unite to form molecules will be important when we consider the diverse chemical compounds and chemical reactions that occur in life.

ATOMIC STRUCTURE OF MATTER

SOME EARLY STUDIES

Experiments by Englishmen Davy and Faraday about 1800 demonstrated that certain compounds in solution could be separated into their component elements when an electric current was passed through them. If atoms and electricity could interact then atoms must possess electrical charges. This discovery of charged particles in the atom prompted J. J. Thompson to theorize erroneously that the atom was a uniformly positive sphere in which negative electrons were distributed throughout like the seeds of a watermelon, and this "watermelon or plum pudding" model was accepted by many as a working theory of atomic structure for many years.

About 1911, Rutherford, Geiger, and Marsden performed a unique and valuable series of experiments. Using a radioactive element that emitted heavy particles, known as alpha particles (helium nuclei), they bombarded a thin piece of gold foil (Figure 2–2). To their surprise, most of the particles passed straight through the foil, but a few were diverted from their normal course into angular paths (Figure 2–3).

Rutherford decided that the individual atoms in the gold foil must contain areas of unequal mass. He therefore proposed that most of the mass of the atom is squeezed into a small, dense, central nucleus that carries a positive charge. The negatively charged particles or electrons he believed to be distributed throughout the remaining atomic space. Since he knew that like charges repel each other, he assumed that the positively charged alpha particles had come into close association with positively charged gold atomic nuclei and were repulsed into new paths.

PROTONS AND NEUTRONS

Further research showed that the nuclei of atoms of all elements except hydrogen are composed of positively charged protons and uncharged neutrons (hydrogen has only a single proton). Each proton and neutron possesses nearly equal mass and thus each is assigned a mass unit of one. Hydrogen, with its single proton, is the simplest element, and the single proton has an atomic mass of one, whereas helium, which has two protons and two neutrons, has an atomic mass of four.

The number of protons (positive charges) in the nucleus of an atom determines the characteristic number of electrons (negative charges) for that atom, and in a neutral atom there are an equal number of negative and positive charges. Neutrons, as mentioned above, are electrically neutral and thus contribute only to the mass of the atom. Since the mass of a proton or a neutron is about 1840 times greater than that of an electron, the total mass of the atom, for all intents and purposes, is determined by the number of protons and neutrons in the nucleus. This mass is also called the *atomic weight* of the atom. In addition, the atom is assigned an *atomic number*, which is simply the number of protons in the nucleus.

THE PERIODIC TABLE

For easy reference in scientific work, chemical elements are arranged in a *periodic table* on the basis of their atomic number and chemical

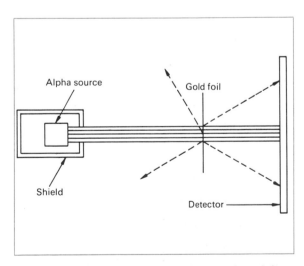

Figure 2·2 Rutherford's experiment using alpha particles and gold foil. Most of the positively charged alpha particles passed through the gold foil, but a few were deflected away from the beam in angular paths.

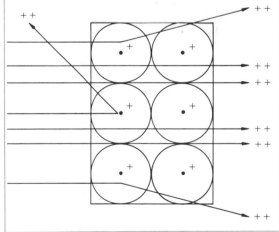

Figure 2·3 A diagram of the atomic structure of gold foil showing the divergence of some of the alpha particles from the normal path due to the presence of dense, positively charged nuclei.

Ia	IIa	IIIb	IVb	Vb	VIb	VIIb	VIIIb			IB	IIB	IIIa	IVa	Va	VIa	VIIa	O
1 H 1.008																	2 He 4.00
3 Li 6.94	4 Be 9.01											5 B 10.81	6 C 12.01	7 N 14.00	8 O 15.99	9 F 18.99	10 Ne 20.18
11 Na 22.99	12 Mg 24.31											13 Al 26.98	14 Si 28.09	15 P 30.97	16 S 32.06	17 Cl 35.45	18 Ar 39.95
19 K 39.10	20 Ca 40.08	21 Sc 44.96	22 Ti 47.90	23 V 50.94	24 Cr 51.99	25 Mn 54.94	26 Fe 55.85	27 Co 58.93	28 Ni 58.71	29 Cu 63.54	30 Zn 65.37	31 Ga 69.72	32 Ge 72.59	33 As 74.92	34 Se 78.96	35 Br 79.91	36 Kr 83.80
37 Rb 85.47	38 Sr 87.62	39 Y 88.91	40 Zr 91.22	41 Nb 92.91	42 Mo 95.94	43 Tc (99)	44 Ru 101.07	45 Rh 102.91	46 Pd 106.4	47 Ag 107.87	48 Cd 112.40	49 In 114.82	50 Sn 118.69	51 Sb 121.75	52 Te 127.60	53 I 126.90	54 Xe 131.30
55 Cs 132.91	56 Ba 137.34	see below 57–71	72 Hf 178.49	73 Ta 180.95	74 W 183.85	75 Re 186.2	76 Os 190.2	77 Ir 192.2	78 Pt 195.09	79 Au 196.97	80 Hg 200.59	81 Tl 204.37	82 Pb 207.19	83 Bi 208.98	84 Po (210)	85 At (210)	86 Rn (222)
87 Fr (223)	88 Ra (226)	see below 89–103	104 Rf (261)	105 Ha (260)													

57 La 138.91	58 Ce 140.12	59 Pr 140.91	60 Nd 144.24	61 Pm (147)	62 Sm 150.35	63 Eu 151.96	64 Gd 157.25	65 Tb 158.92	66 Dy 162.50	67 Ho 164.93	68 Er 167.26	69 Tm 168.93	70 Yb 173.04	71 Lu 174.97
89 Ac (227)	90 Th 232.04	91 Pa (231)	92 U 238.03	93 Np (237)	94 Pu (242)	95 Am (243)	96 Cm (247)	97 Bk (247)	98 Cf (251)	99 Es (254)	100 Fm (253)	101 Md (256)	102 No (254)	103 Lw (257)

Figure 2-4 The periodic table of the elements.

properties. The first listing of the elements according to their relative weights, using hydrogen as the base 1, was proposed by John Dalton in 1803. The forerunner of the modern periodic chart of the elements (Figure 2–4) was developed in 1869 by the Russian chemist Mendeleev, who realized that the elements could be arranged in the order of increasing atomic weights and related chemical properties.

The vertical columns in the table are called *groups* and represent elements that react similarly. For example, group 1 elements (the alkali metals) all react violently with water and, furthermore, the degree of reaction increases with increased atomic weight. Therefore the order of the elements within a group also provides important information that can be used to predict chemical reactions.

The horizontal rows on the chart, called *periods*, generally show decreasing reaction activity from left to right. For example, sodium, magnesium, and aluminum are all metals but have different chemical properties —aluminum being the least reactive. Argon, at the far right, is in the group known as "inert gases" and is extremely nonreactive as are all other members of this group.

If we examine the periodic chart, we notice that the atomic weights given underneath each chemical symbol are not whole numbers as might be expected. In order to understand this we must realize that the atomic weights are relative weights and not actual weights such as one might obtain by weighing. That is, one element has been assigned a certain weight arbitrarily, and all other elements are compared with this reference weight. It is known that not all atoms of an element have exactly the same weight. These variations are caused by varying numbers of neutrons above and below the number in most atoms of that element. Remember that the type of atom (element) is determined by the atomic number, which is the number of protons contained in the nucleus. It thus makes no difference to an atom's identity whether it has more or fewer neutrons, although it does change the atomic weight. Elements having the same number of protons but varying numbers of neutrons are termed *isotopes*. For example, there are four isotopes of the element carbon —carbon-12, 13, 14, and 15—all of which have six protons and six electrons but differ in the number of neutrons (Figure 2–5). The reason then that the atomic weights given in the chart are not whole numbers is that these weights are averages of the weights of all the isotopes of a given element. Many isotopes are unstable, and may be in the process of breaking down into a more stable state—that is, they may give up a neutron by emitting it in the form of energetic particles. Isotopes of this type are said to be *radioactive*. Originally all atomic weights were based on oxygen-16 as the reference weight, but in 1963 the most abundant isotope of carbon, carbon-12, became the new standard.

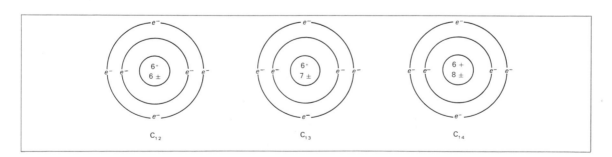

Figure 2·5 Three isotopes of carbon. Note that only the number of neutrons change. Each neutron represents one mass unit.

ELECTRON DISTRIBUTION IN THE ATOM

A good approximation to atomic structure, and one that we will use in our discussion of atoms, is the so-called "planetary" or *Bohr model*. Niels Bohr, the Danish physicist, proposed this atomic model in which the electrons move around the nucleus in orbits corresponding to specific energies possessed by the particular electrons. The more energetic electrons move in larger orbits and the least energetic are closest to the nucleus. Each orbit, also called a "shell" or "energy level," can accommodate only a certain number of electrons. Today we know that the electrons do not actually travel around the nucleus in specific orbits but are located in certain probable areas called *clouds*. Reported distances of an electron from the nucleus are based on the highest probability of finding the electron in that position.

Bohr designed this model to account for the characteristic spectra he observed around various atoms. Spectra are light emissions by the atom at specific frequencies, which vary for different atoms, and Bohr theorized that these light emissions correspond to the energy given up by an electron as it falls from a higher to lower orbit. Since these energies could be measured, he was able to determine the diameters of the possible orbits which are generally similar for all atoms. If an atom has few electrons, its higher energy orbits will be empty. An electron can be moved to a higher orbit by pushing energy into an atom, but after a very short time it falls back to its original level and releases the excess energy in the process.

To keep this discussion brief, we will give the arrangement of electrons for only a few elements, namely those for the first eleven elements in the periodic chart (Figure 2–6). There are seven principal energy levels or shells labeled 1, 2, 3, 4, 5, 6, 7. Although each of these is further divided into sublevels, we need not concern ourselves with that refinement. Again, each of the principal levels can accommodate only a certain number of elec-

Element	Symbol	Atomic Number	Electron Distribution in Shells		
			1	2	3
Hydrogen	H	1	1		
Helium	He	2	2		
Lithium	Li	3	2	1	
Beryllium	Be	4	2	2	
Boron	B	5	2	3	
Carbon	C	6	2	4	
Nitrogen	N	7	2	5	
Oxygen	O	8	2	6	
Fluorine	F	9	2	7	
Neon	Ne	10	2	8	
Sodium	Na	11	2	8	1

Figure 2.6 The electron distribution of the first eleven elements in the periodic chart.

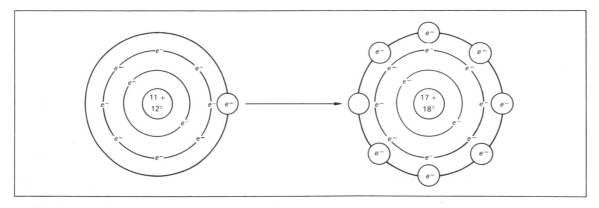

Figure 2·7 The Bohr structure of sodium and chlorine. Note that the outer electron shell of sodium has only one electron whereas the outer shell of chlorine has seven. When sodium and chlorine combine to form sodium chloride, the outer electron of sodium is transferred to chlorine.

trons. The stable number of electrons in the outer shell of an element appears to be eight except in the case of hydrogen which is stable with two. One clue to this stable configuration is that all of the chemically unreactive elements have eight outermost electrons (the inert gases).

An atom that has less than eight electrons in its outer shell may transfer or take up or share electrons with another atom to complete its electron shell. Either way, both atoms achieve a stable configuration which provides a strong force of attraction between the atoms.

CHEMICAL BONDING

Whenever two or more atoms combine they are held together by a chemical bond. There are several kinds of chemical bonds, and they all depend on the electron distribution of the atoms. We will discuss three of the most important types of bonds—electrovalent, covalent, and hydrogen.

ELECTROVALENT BONDS

When atoms of two or more elements combine to form a compound by an exchange of electrons, they are strongly held together by an electrostatic force of attraction. Such a bond is termed an *electrovalent bond*. Sodium chloride offers an excellent example of electrovalent

bonding (Figure 2–7). The atomic number of sodium is 11 and thus it has eleven electrons. When these are distributed in the shells we see that the outer, or *valence*, shell contains only one electron. Chlorine, atomic number 17, has seven electrons in its valence shell— one less than required for a complete shell. When sodium and chlorine come into close contact, one electron is transferred from sodium to chlorine, leaving sodium positively charged, since it now has one less electron than protons, and giving the chlorine atom a negative charge, since it has gained an electron. The resulting charged particles are called *ions*. Both ions now have a stable electronic configuration and, due to the formation of positive and negative charges, there is an attraction between them. This force forms the electrovalent or *ionic bond*. Figure 2–8 illustrates the result of this electron transfer. It should be noted that atoms possessing more than four valence electrons tend to take up electrons, whereas atoms with fewer than four outermost electrons generally transfer those electrons in bonding reactions. Therefore the number of electrons in the valence shells determine which atoms will react with one another.

COVALENT BONDS

If we examine the atomic structure of the element carbon, we note that its valence shell contains four electrons and this number of

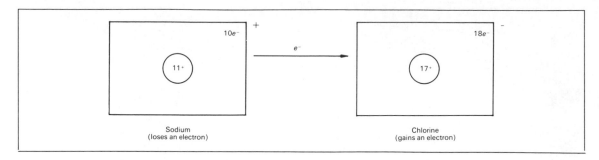

Chlorine
(gains an electron)

Figure 2·8 A diagram to illustrate the ions produced when sodium transfers an electron to chlorine in solution. Note that sodium now has one more proton than it has electrons, thus acquiring a positive charge. Chlorine has one more electron than it has protons, therefore it possesses a negative charge.

electrons is just one-half the number required for completion. In addition to electron transfer it is also possible for electrons to be shared between atoms, and the resulting bond when this occurs is called *covalent*. For example, it is possible for carbon to share its four electrons with the four electrons of four hydrogen atoms to form methane, CH_4 (Figure 2–9). In fact, many atoms, other than hydrogen, are capable of sharing electrons with carbon: oxygen, phosphorus, nitrogen, chlorine, and calcium are among the most common. Perhaps the most important characteristic of carbon is its ability to share electrons with other carbon atoms. In this manner, carbon atoms may form

long chains or complicated ring structures. Later in this chapter we will discuss the structure of several types of carbon molecules.

The four valence electrons of a carbon atom are located at an equidistant 109.5° from each other. The resulting structure is similar to a regular tetrahedron (Figure 2–10). We stated earlier that it is impossible to locate the exact position of an electron at any given instant, but in order to locate the electrons, it is necessary to conceive of the electron moving in a cloud rather than in precise orbits. It is possible, however, to calculate the density of the cloud and find out where the electron is most likely to be in terms of its

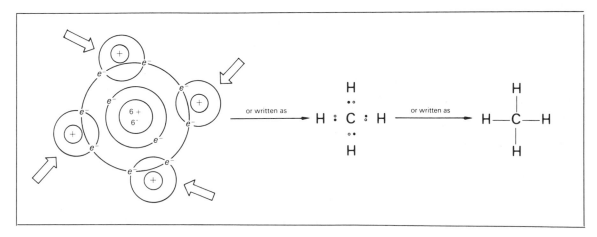

Figure 2·9 The covalent bonding of four hydrogen atoms to carbon. Each hydrogen atom shares a pair of electrons with carbon to complete the shell of each atom.

26

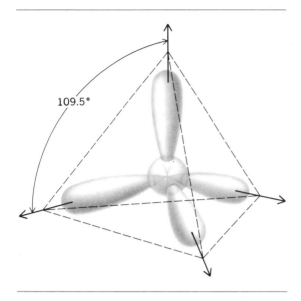

Figure 2·10 The tetrahedral configuration of the valence electrons of carbon. The long axis of each of the four electron clouds is oriented toward one corner of the tetrahedron, thus forming the bond angles.

distribution whether they are in long chains or rings (Figure 2–12). Between two carbon atoms two pairs of electrons may be shared, and when this occurs it is termed a *double covalent bond* (Figure 2–12b). Covalent bonds are the most common bonds found in the molecules of living organisms.

HYDROGEN BONDS

A bond weaker than either ionic or covalent is formed when hydrogen is bonded simultaneously between two other atoms. This results when the positive charge of an already bonded hydrogen proton attracts a negatively charged atom. This attraction is known as a *hydrogen bond* and is demonstrated in the association of water molecules (Figure 2–13). Hydrogen bonding helps explain some of the unique properties of water, such as its resistance to temperature change and its ability to exist in three states—liquid, steam, or ice.

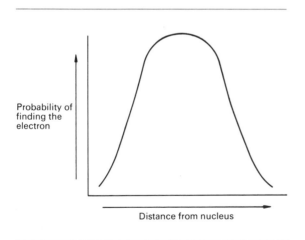

Figure 2·11 A graph showing the probability of finding an electron at a particular distance from the nucleus.

distance from the nucleus (Figure 2–11). All bonds in carbon compounds must closely conform to the angles formed by the electron

Carbon-to-carbon chain
(a)

Carbon-to-carbon ring (benzene ring)
(b)

Figure 2·12 Two common types of carbon-to-carbon bonding: (a) a straight chain; and (b) a six-carbon ring, the benzene ring.

27

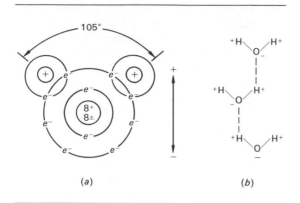

(a)   (b)

Figure 2·13   (a) The molecular structure of the water molecule. Because the electrons of hydrogen are primarily associated with the oxygen atom, this produces a dipolar molecule with negative and positive ends. (b) The hydrogen bonding found between water molecules. The dashed lines represent the hydrogen bonds. Since the electrons of hydrogen are associated with the oxygen valence shell, the positive charge of the proton attracts the negatively charged region of other water molecules, thus forming the hydrogen bond.

ELECTROLYTES AND NONELECTROLYTES

Ionically bonded compounds, such as sodium chloride, that readily separate into charged particles in water are called *electrolytes* because, as charged particles, they will conduct an electric current (Figure 2–14). Covalently bonded compounds, such as sucrose (table sugar, $C_{12}H_{22}O_{11}$), on the other hand, do not dissociate in water to any appreciable degree. Sucrose therefore is a *nonelectrolyte*.

COMPOUNDS IN NATURE

Chemical compounds that contain the element carbon are called *organic*, and all other compounds are classified as *inorganic*. The early chemists were convinced that carbon compounds could be produced only by living organisms, yet today we know that organic compounds can be synthesized. For example, all of our modern synthetic fabrics and plastics are organic compounds.

Figure 2·14   An experiment showing the ability of dissociated ions (Na^+Cl^-) to conduct electricity. Sucrose is a nonelectrolyte. The bulb in the NaCl solution is the only one which lights.

Distilled water

$Na^+ + Cl^-$ in distilled water

INORGANIC COMPOUNDS
Water, Acids, and Bases

Water is an important component in all living organisms. The exact content varies greatly from one organism to another. Jellyfish are made up of nearly 99 percent water, whereas the human body is composed of an average of 67 percent water. Within an organism, some tissues contain more water than others; for example, the gray matter of the brain is about 80 percent water, whereas compact bone contains only 25 percent. Recent evidence suggests that water is associated with the structure and function of proteins and other cellular components. Albert Szent-Gyorgyi, one of the world's foremost biologists, has said "Biology has forgotten water as a deep sea fish may forget about it. . . . Water may be important for biological happenings both by its presence and its absence."

Most of us are familiar with several common acids and bases that are used routinely in our homes or jobs. In general we know that strong acids and strong bases burn the skin and injure the eyes, but the question we want to consider here is what causes these caustic properties.

A good way to begin is with a neutral molecule—that is, one that is neither acid nor base. One such substance is pure water. The formula for water, H_2O, can also be written as H–OH or, in its ionized form, H^+ (hydrogen ion) and OH^- (hydroxyl ion). A small number of water molecules actually dissociate into these ions. Ionic concentrations may be expressed in terms of the *gram-atomic weight* of the ions present in one liter of solution. (One liter equals 1000 cubic centimeters.) A gram-atomic weight is simply the atomic weight of the substance measured in grams. Another useful unit for expressing the amount of a substance is the *mole*. One mole is the amount of a substance equal to its *molecular weight* in grams. Molecular weight is the sum of the atomic weights of all atoms in a molecule. For example, the molecular weight of sodium chloride is 58 (Na = 23 + Cl = 35); of glucose, 180 (C_6 = 72 + H_{12} = 12 + O_6 = 96). A *molar solution* is one that contains the molecular weight in grams of a substance dissolved in a solvent such as water which yields a total volume of one liter.

Careful measurements have shown that one liter of pure water contains 0.0000007 (10^{-7}) gram of hydrogen ions, and since the ratio of hydrogen ions to hydroxyl ions in water is 1:1, there is also 10^{-7} mole of hydroxyl ions in the same water. The ionic concentration of water may be expressed in terms of the ratio of ionized water to nonionized water. This ratio is known as the *dissociation constant*, K. Since the overwhelming majority of water molecules do not dissociate, we can consider the concentration of HOH to be 1. The dissociation constant then is calculated as follows:

$$K = \frac{[H^+]\,[OH]}{[HOH]} = \frac{[10^{-7}]\,[10^{-7}]}{[1]} = 10^{-14}$$

where the brackets denote ionic concentrations.

Sucrose in distilled water

Some common acids and bases are listed in the table in Figure 2-15. Note that the hydrogen ion (or proton) is always present in acids and that a hydroxyl ion (OH^-) is common to the bases. All of these compounds dissociate in water. The "strength" of an acid or base is directly proportional to the degree of dissociation. In comparison to the strong inorganic acids and bases listed in Figure 2-15, the organic acid known as acetic acid, CH_3COOH (vinegar), is quite weak. The hydrogen covalently bonded to oxygen in the COOH part of the molecule does not dissociate to the extent of the H^+ in inorganic hydrochloric acid (HCl). Since dissociation of H^+ in organic acids occurs as $COO^- + H^+$, its dissociation constant is determined to be:

$$K = \frac{[CH_3COO^-] \, [H^+]}{[CH_3COOH]} = 1.8 \times 10^{-5}$$

This is much smaller than that for hydrochloric acid which is almost 100% ionized:

$$K = \frac{[H^+] \, [Cl^-]}{[HCl]} = 10^7$$

pH. In pure water the product of the ionic concentration of H^+ and OH^- is always constant—that is, 10^{-14}, since pure water has an equal number of hydrogen and hydroxyl ions. If a solution contains more H^+ than OH^-, it is acidic; if more OH^-, it is basic

or *alkaline*. To describe the acidity or alkalinity of a solution, it is sufficient therefore to state only the hydrogen-ion concentration. This concentration is commonly expressed in terms of pH, which is defined as:

$$pH = \log \frac{1}{[H^+]} = -\log [H^+]$$

Since pH is a *reciprocal* (a number divided into one), the low pH values stand for greater H^+. The acid range is then located between 0 and 7 on a scale (Figure 2-16). For example, if the H^+ concentration of a solution is 10^{-4} gram per liter, the pH is 4. Since pH is expressed on a logarithmic scale the numerical values are based on powers of ten and pH 3 represents ten times more H^+ than pH 4 and pH 2, a hundred times more than four.

There are also compounds that show basic properties even though they contain no hydroxyl ions. This fact led to a slightly different definition for both acids and bases. An acid is said to be any compound that can *donate* protons (H^+) to a solution and, conversely, a base is any compound that can *accept* protons.

One example is NH_3, which accepts a proton to form NH_4. The OH^- group is a very strong proton acceptor and the addition of a single proton to an OH^- ion forms neutral HOH. This reaction is called a *neutralization reaction*.

Salts. A salt is a compound containing a positive ion other than H^+ and a negative ion other than OH^-.

Acid		K	Base		K
Hydrochloric	H^+Cl^-	10^7	K^+OH^-	Potassium hydroxide	Very large
Sulfuric	$2H^+SO_4^=$	10^2	Na^+OH^-	Sodium hydroxide	Very large
Phosphoric	$3H^+PO_4^=$	7.5×10^{-3}	$NH_4^+OH^-$	Ammonium hydroxide	1.8×10^{-5}

Figure 2-15 A table of common acids and bases and their dissociation constants. All K values are calculated from solutions of the same concentrations, 0.1 molar.

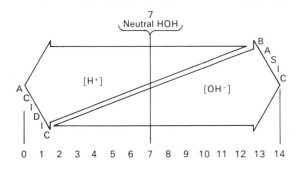

Figure 2·16 The pH scale. Equal concentrations of $[H^+]$ and $[OH^-]$ are considered to be neutral and are represented by pH 7.

HCl—a strong acid   Carbonic acid— a weak acid

Figure 2·17 Buffering action of $NaHCO_3$. Note how a weak acid can be formed from a strong acid through the action of the buffer, $NaHCO_3$.

The reaction between a strong acid and a strong base produces a *salt* and water.

$$HCl + NaOH \longrightarrow NaCl + H_2O$$
$$Acid + base \longrightarrow Salt + water$$

The NaCl in the following system will ionize almost completely as $Na^+ + Cl^-$.

Buffers. In living systems the pH value must be maintained within strict limits (pH balance is also discussed in Chapter 7). If the blood becomes too acidic, for instance, certain chemical reactions in the cells will cease to take place and the equilibrium of the body will be upset. Compounds known as *buffers* are found in the animal bloodstream which help to combat a sudden increase in acidity. Buffers, as implied in their name, act as a cushion for pH changes. One of the most common buffering compounds is sodium bicarbonate ($NaHCO_3$), which dissociates into Na^+ and $HCO_3{}^-$. Excess protons in the blood plasma are quickly picked up by the bicarbonate ion to form a weak acid, carbonic acid (H_2CO_3). Through the buffering action of the bicarbonate ion on hydrochloric acid, a strong acid is converted into a weak acid and a salt (Figure 2–17).

The formation of carbonic acid in the blood is a key reaction in biology. For example, carbon dioxide is combined with water to produce carbonic acid in the following reactions:

$$CO_2 + H_2O \rightleftharpoons H_2CO_3 \rightleftharpoons H^+ + HCO_3^-$$

This simple reaction which provides a source for the bicarbonate ion is involved in many important biological processes such as gas exchange and photosynthesis.

ORGANIC COMPOUNDS

Carbon compounds such as sugars, amino acids, fatty acids, and glycerine are all essential to the organism. Each of these basic molecules may combine with similar or other molecules to form more complex structures. In this section we will discuss the chemical structure and function of carbohydrates, fats, proteins, nucleic acids, and porphyrins.

Carbohydrates

This important class of organic compounds includes the various types of sugars. Sugars are compounds that contain from three to as many as twelve carbon atoms. Glucose, a *monosaccharide* and a major biological energy source, contains six carbon atoms arranged with hydrogen and oxygen in the following way:

If we add the components of this structure, we obtain the formula $C_6H_{12}O_6$. In this structural formula, the heavy lines are used to help us visualize a three-dimensional model. Ribose, a five-carbon sugar, $C_5H_{10}O_5$, may be written similarly:

Ribose is a very important structural component of compounds involved in energy processes (ATP) and heredity (DNA). Both ATP and DNA will be discussed at length later in the book. It should be noted that whereas six-carbon sugars are commonly utilized as fuel molecules, the five-carbon sugars are involved in the structure of molecules such as the nucleic acids.

Two monosaccharides linked together are called a *disaccharide* and more than two linked monosaccharides are known as *polysaccharide* compounds. Maltose is one example of a disaccharide, and it is formed by the union of two glucose molecules (Figure 2–18).

In this *synthesis* reaction of joining two molecules of glucose to form maltose, one molecule of water is lost. Since water is given off in this reaction it is known as a *dehydration* synthesis and the resulting formula for maltose is $C_{12}H_{22}O_{11}$. The linkage between the number 1 carbon of one molecule and the number 4 carbon of the other is simply an oxygen bridge (C—O—C) and the specific linkage described for maltose is an *alpha 1, 4 glucoside*. Alpha is used here to indicate that the two hydrogen atoms attached to the oxygen bridge are in the same plane. Many glucose units linked in this manner into a long chain compose the polysaccharide called *starch*. In the liver a glucose storage product, *glycogen*, is formed which is structurally similar to starch in that it is linked by alpha 1, 4 glucosides. It differs, however, in also having alpha 1, 6 glucoside linkages that give a branched structure to the molecule. Glycogen, which provides a ready source of glucose for the blood, is also stored in the muscles.

Another important type of polysaccharide is *cellulose,* in which the 1, 4 glucoside linkage is formed in a slightly different manner (one hydrogen is away from you and the other is toward you). This produces the "twisted" configuration called a *beta linkage* (Figure 2–19). One important result of this different linkage is that digestive juices, which split starch into glucose units, will not work on beta glucosides. One test for distinguishing starch from cellulose is simply to incubate the sample with saliva and test for the presence of glucose. When starch is broken down into glucose molecules during digestion, water is added at the linkage. This hydration reaction, often called *hydrolytic cleavage,* is the opposite of synthesis. We will return to this process in Chapter 7 when digestion is discussed.

Fats

Fats, often referred to as *lipids*, are important compounds since they store energy, provide protection for the internal organs, and are essential constituents of more complex molecules. The two components of a fat molecule are glycerine and fatty acids. Glycerine is a

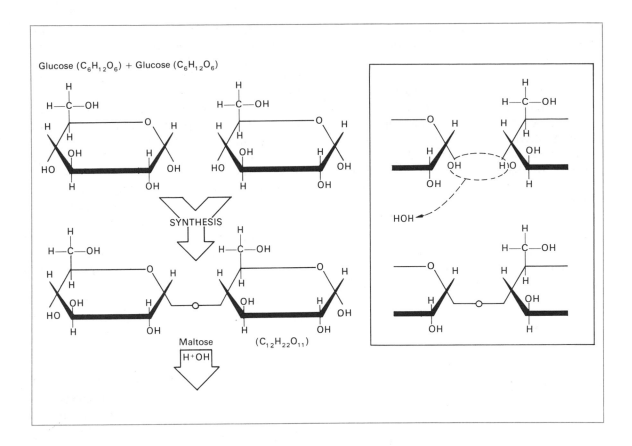

Glucose ($C_6H_{12}O_6$) + Glucose ($C_6H_{12}O_6$)

SYNTHESIS

Maltose ($C_{12}H_{22}O_{11}$)

H⁺OH

HOH

Figure 2·18 The synthesis of the disaccharide maltose from two glucose molecules. The linkage formed is the alpha 1-4 glucoside. Note that the two hydrogen atoms in the linkage are away from the viewer and the oxygen is oriented toward the viewer.

Figure 2·19 The beta 1-4 glucoside linkage of cellulose. The hydrogen atom in bold type is oriented toward you. Note that as a matter of convenience the carbons in the ring structure have been omitted.

three-carbon molecule that contains three hydroxyl groups (OH). In this case the hydroxyl group is simply an oxygen atom that shares one pair of electrons with carbon and another pair with hydrogen (Figure 2–20).

Fatty acids are straight chains of carbon which have most of their bonding sites occupied by hydrogen. If some of the hydrogens of the fatty acid are removed, the carbon atoms may share two or even three pairs of electrons to form —C = C or —C ≡ C— bonds (double and triple bonds). A fatty acid in which all available bonding sites are occupied by hydrogen is said to be *saturated* with hydrogen and when some hydrogen is removed, usually forming double bonds, *unsaturation* is produced. You may be familiar

with certain brands of vegetable oil that are advertised as *polyunsaturated*, which means that the carbons share most of the available bonds and very few hydrogen atoms occur along the chain.

One end of the fatty-acid molecule contains an acid or *carboxyl* group which is formed when carbon shares two pairs of electrons with oxygen to form a double bond and one pair of electrons with a hydroxyl. The carboxyl group is an acid because the hydrogen of the hydroxyl will dissociate to donate a proton to a solution. When it occurs as part of an organic acid group, the carboxyl end of the fatty acid may be linked to one of the hydroxyls of glycerine to form an *ester* linkage (Figure 2-20).

In this synthesis water is removed in much the same way as it was in the formation of maltose and starch. Three fatty acids attached to a glycerine molecule form a fat.

Proteins

Proteins are produced in every living cell in many sizes and shapes. Moreover, each cellular protein fulfills a specific function and is specifically synthesized according to the heredity of the cell. A protein, regardless of its size, is composed of smaller units called *amino acids* which are carbon compounds that possess an acid carboxyl at one end and a nitrogen-containing amino group on the same carbon. The two simplest amino acids are glycine and alanine (Figure 2-21). Histidine and tryp-

GLYCINE
(a two-carbon amino acid)

ALANINE
(a three-carbon amino acid)

Figure 2·20 The formation of an ester linkage between a fatty acid and glycerine.

Figure 2·21 Two simple amino acids.

tophane, which incorporate ring structures, are more complex amino acids than glycine and alanine (Figure 2-22), but the amino and carboxyl groups are still present. Some amino acids also contain sulfur and there are approximately 23 different types of amino acids.

When amino acids are linked together, the resulting linkage is called a *peptide*. Two amino acids linked by one peptide is called a *dipeptide*; more than two linked amino acids produce a *polypeptide*. The peptide linkage is formed in an interaction between the amino group of one amino acid and the carboxyl group of another (Figure 2–23). The nitrogen unites with the carboxyl carbon, with the resultant loss of one water molecule.

Simple proteins are composed of only amino acids. In nature proteins can combine with other substances such as carbohydrates, fats, or inorganic ions and such proteins are said to be *conjugated*. Rather large amounts of conjugated proteins may be found in brain and nerve tissues, mucous secretions, egg white,

Figure 2·23 The synthesis of the dipeptide alanyl-histidine. Note that the structure of histidine here is reversed from that shown in Figure 2-22.

Figure 2·22 Diagram of two amino-acid molecules—histidine and tryptophane.

and in all cells. In the cell, proteins provide the fundamental structure for all major structural components. One very special class of proteins, vital to life, are *enzymes* which speed up chemical reactions in an organism. Tendons, hair, fingernails, blood globulins, and skin are other examples of structures in which proteins are the major component.

The primary linkage group in a protein is the peptide, which holds the amino acids in specific polypeptide chains. Since most proteins are made up of more than one polypeptide, other secondary bonds must also be present to maintain a spiral structure of the complex molecule. Hydrogen bonds are the most common in this secondary role, and these hydrogen bonds usually occur between adja-

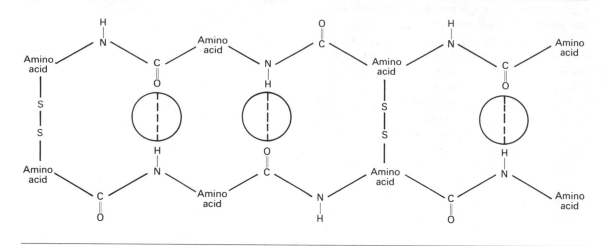

Figure 2·24 Two adjacent polypeptide chains connected by hydrogen bonds (circled) and disulfide bridges.

cent peptide linkages (Figure 2–24). In addition, disulfide bridges (— S — S —) formed between certain amino acids can maintain the protein in a folded pattern (Figure 2–25). Owing to these various types of bonds, proteins may occur in many structural forms, such as globular, sheetlike, or long spiraled fibers. The ability of protein molecules to function as enzymes is related to the fact that they can be structured into specific configurations.

ADENINE
(a purine)

THYMINE
(a pyrimidine)

Figure 2·26 Chemical diagrams of two nitrogen bases to illustrate purine and pyrimidine structures.

Nucleic Acids

Nucleic acids are macromolecules that are essential to all living things because they are indispensable to the heredity and the protein synthesis of every cell. Two types of nucleic acids are known, *ribonucleic acid* (RNA) and *deoxyribonucleic acid* (DNA). Each of these molecules is made up of subunits called *nucleotides* which are strung together (polymerized) to form long chains. Nucleotides are always composed of three basic parts: first, nitrogenous bases (either purine or pyrimidine); second, a five-carbon sugar [either ribose ($C_5H_{10}O_5$) or deoxyribose ($C_5H_{10}O_4$]; and the third, phosphoric acid. The structures of a purine and a pyrimidine are shown in Figure 2–26 and the composition of an adenine nucleotide is diagrammed in Figure 2–27. There are four kinds of nitrogenous bases in nucleic acids: two purines, adenine and guanine; and two kinds of pyrimidines, cytosine and thymine, or uracil. In RNA, uracil is present, whereas DNA contains thymine.

The nucleotides of DNA always contain deoxyribose sugar (similar to ribose but having

Figure 2·25 The three structural levels found in proteins. (*a*) Primary: peptide linkages between amino acids in a chain. (*b*) Secondary: hydrogen bonds hold the spiraled chain in an alpha helix. (*c*) Tertiary: disulfide bonds maintain the complex three-dimensional shape of a protein.

37

PHOSPHATE | SUGAR | NITROGENOUS BASE

Figure 2·27 A structural diagram of an adenine nucleotide showing the three basic components: adenine, deoxyribose sugar, and phosphate.

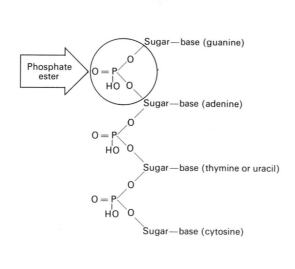

Figure 2·28 The phosphate ester linkages that link sugars and nitrogen bases into nucleic-acid chains.

one less oxygen atom), one of the nitrogen bases mentioned above, and phosphoric acid. This means there are four kinds of DNA nucleotides. For example, the deoxyribose sugar and phosphoric acid may unite with adenine, guanine, cytosine, or thymine.

Simple phosphate ester linkages can hook the sugars and their attached nitrogen bases into a long nucleotide chain by attaching alternately to the number 3 and 5 carbons of the sugars (Figure 2–28). This single-stranded molecule is representative of the structure of RNA, which is usually single stranded. In RNA thymine is replaced by the pyrimidine, uracil, and since uracil is found only in RNA, it is sometimes helpful to use it as a "marker base" to determine the location of RNA in the cell.

The Structure of DNA. In the structure of DNA purine nucleotides always pair with

ADENINE   THYMINE

Figure 2·29   The chemical structure of an adenine-thymine base pair. Note the hydrogen bonds, represented by dashed lines, and the 3-5 phosphate esters that link the sugars into a polymeric chain.

pyrimidine nucleotides to form a long *double-stranded molecule.* Furthermore, certain types of purines and pyrimidines pair only with each other. For instance, adenine (a purine) pairs only with thymine (a pyrimidine), and guanine (a purine) pairs only with cytosine (a pyrimidine) (Figure 2–29).

In 1953, F. H. C. Crick of Cambridge University and J. D. Watson of Harvard University (Figure 2–30) proposed a model to account for the structure of the DNA molecule. This model, based on chemical analyses and x-ray diffraction studies, also accounts for the unique activities of DNA such as reproduction and the coding of hereditary information. The double-stranded DNA molecule is believed to be twisted into a spiral or helical shape (Figure 2–31). If it were not twisted the molecule would look something like a ladder, in which the rails of the ladder correspond to the sugar and phosphate and the steps to the sequence of paired nitrogenous bases.

Figure 2·30   Dr. James D. Watson, recipient of the Nobel Prize in 1962 for his role in the discovery of the molecular structure of DNA.

39

plementary polynucleotide chain (Figure 2–32). The significance of base pairing in reproduction, genetic coding, and protein synthesis will be discussed further in Chapter 3.

Porphyrins

Porphyrins are the fundamental structural units in pigments such as chlorophyll, hemoglobin, and cytochromes. The basic porphyrin structure is a unique configuration of carbon, nitrogen, and metallic ions. This basic structure (Figure 2–33), is composed of four *pyrrole rings* and is commonly called a *tetrapyrrole-ring compound*. Each carbon atom around the periphery of the tetrapyrrole structure may be bonded to specific side chains such as alcohols or proteins. The most important aspect of the molecule, to living systems, is its ability through its metallic ions (magnesium in chlorophyll, iron in hemoglobin and cytochromes) to gain or lose electrons. Chlorophyll and cytochromes, in the process of trapping and transfer of energy, provide a mechanism for the transfer of electrons in living systems.

CHEMICAL REACTIONS

Chemical compounds may react with one another to form new compounds. For these new compounds to be formed, chemical bonds must be broken and reformed and this rearrangement of bonds always involves energy changes.

ENERGY

Some chemicals react spontaneously—that is, the reaction proceeds without an external energy source. Such spontaneous reactions are called *exergonic,* and they generally produce heat. One such reaction is the violent one that occurs when metallic sodium comes in contact with water. This is a rapidly completed reaction that produces both heat and light. Reactions that require external energy for

Figure 2·31 The spiral structure of DNA as proposed by Watson and Crick.

The two strands of DNA are held together by hydrogen bonds between the bases (Figure 2–29). Since the hydrogen bonds are relatively weak they may be broken, thereby resulting in two distinct half-chains. Each half of the molecule can then reproduce a new com-

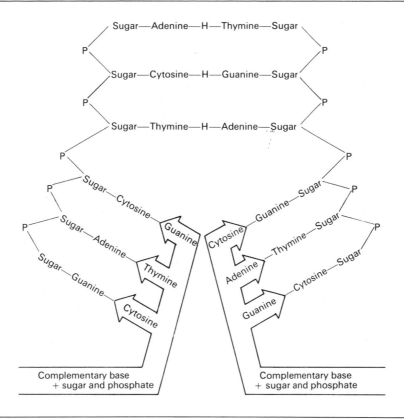

Figure 2·32 The process of reproduction of the DNA molecule. Two identical strands will be formed.

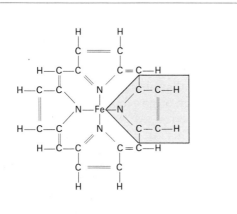

Figure 2·33 The basic structure of an iron-containing porphyrin. The shaded area represents one pyrrole ring.

their activation are known as *endergonic*. (It should also be noted that some exergonic reactions require energy to get them started.) Light, heat, and pressure are possible sources of the *activation energy* needed to start a chemical reaction. Once started, a reaction may or may not be self-sustaining. If it is not, small amounts of *continuation energy* may be needed to keep it going.

CONCENTRATION AND MASS ACTION

In many instances where chemical reactions, for one reason or another, do not go to completion, the products formed may react in a reverse direction as their concentration increases. This is known as a *reversible chemical*

41

reaction and may be stated generally in terms of the ratio of the reactants to the products:

$$A + B \rightleftharpoons C + D$$

Reactants   Products

As the reactants are gradually used up and the products accumulate, the rate of the reaction to the right is slowed down and an equilibrium may finally be established. The *law of mass action* states that the rate of a reaction is directly proportional to the concentration of the reactants. In the case of hydrogen and iodine, the reaction proceeds to the right until

$$H_2 + I_2 \rightleftharpoons 2HI$$

the product concentration reaches an equilibrium with the reactants. The addition of more hydrogen and iodine, however, will increase the reaction to the right to produce more HI.

In some chemical reactions the product is constantly removed through the formation of an insoluble precipitate or a volatile gas. For example, in the reaction between silver nitrate and sodium chloride, the precipitated silver chloride cannot take part in a reverse reaction.

$$AgNO_3 + NaCl \xrightarrow{H_2O} \overset{\text{Insoluble precipitate}}{AgCl} + NaNO_3$$

| Silver nitrate | Sodium chloride | Silver chloride | Sodium nitrate |

The law of mass action then enables us to predict not only the rate of a reaction but also its direction and duration.

ENZYME ACTION

The energy requirement in chemical reactions is chiefly needed to increase the thermal agitation of the atoms. With higher temperature and consequently greater movement, the atoms bump into each other with greater frequency, and the probability of reactions among these atoms is greatly increased. Organisms must sustain a large number of chemical reactions, and most of them require energy. For instance, how is it that, in cells, chemical reactions can occur that ordinarily would require enough heat to literally burn up the cells. Clearly some mechanism is needed, and it is provided by biological catalysts called *enzymes*. Although all enzymes are composed primarily of protein, the polypeptide chains are linked together in various ways to form specific structures that are specialized for catalyzing a certain reaction. That is, the enzyme appears to actually "fit" the reactants into its structure in order to bring them close together and thus increase the probability of the reaction. The function of enzymes thus is similar to that of heat—namely, to get the reactants together. The action of an enzyme in lowering the activation energy of a biochemical reaction is illustrated in Figure 2–34.

Active Sites

The catalytic action of enzyme molecules is located at specific *active sites*, which can react with specific regions of the reactant molecules. The specific geometry of the active site therefore is important, and any change in the molecule that alters the active site structure will change or possibly inactivate the enzyme. A hypothetical synthesis catalyzed by an enzyme is illustrated in Figure 2–35. Note that the enzyme does not appear in the product and thus is capable of participating in further reactions.

Ribonuclease, an enzyme capable of catalyzing the hydrolysis of nucleic acids, was the first enzyme for which the amino-acid se-

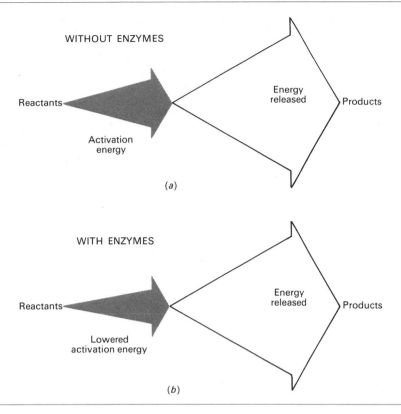

WITHOUT ENZYMES

Reactants

Activation
energy

Energy
released

Products

(a)

WITH ENZYMES

Reactants

Lowered
activation energy

Energy
released

Products

(b)

Figure 2·34 Diagrams of the energy relationships in two chemical reactions. In (a) the activation energy is much greater than that in (b) owing to the action of enzymes.

Reactants + Enzyme   ⟶   Enzyme-reactant complex   ⟶   Product

Figure 2·35 A proposed model for the action of an enzyme in a synthesis reaction. The reactants form a complex with the active sites of the enzyme, complete their reaction, and are released as product.

43

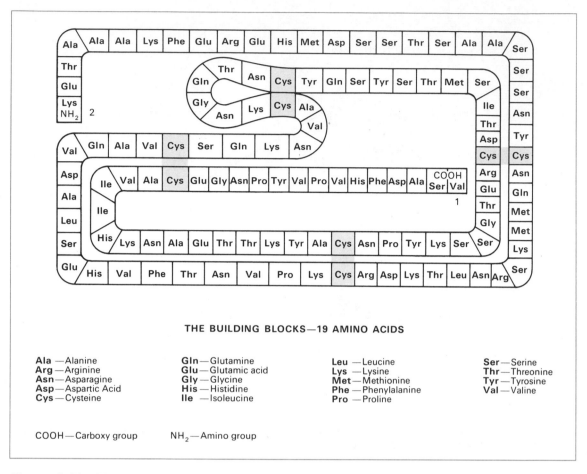

THE BUILDING BLOCKS—19 AMINO ACIDS

Ala —Alanine   Gln—Glutamine   Leu —Leucine   Ser —Serine
Arg —Arginine   Glu—Glutamic acid   Lys —Lysine   Thr —Threonine
Asn—Asparagine   Gly —Glycine   Met —Methionine   Tyr —Tyrosine
Asp—Aspartic Acid   His —Histidine   Phe —Phenylalanine   Val —Valine
Cys—Cysteine   Ile —Isoleucine   Pro —Proline

COOH—Carboxy group   NH₂—Amino group

Figure 2·36 The amino-acid sequence of ribonuclease. In the synthesis of this enzyme by R. B. Merrifield and B. Gutte, reported in 1969, the carboxy-terminal amino acid valine (1) was attached to a solid polymer resin. Then the residual 123 amino acids were coupled one at a time, the last one being the amino-terminal lysine (2). (Redrawn by permission of B. Gutte.)

quence was determined (Figure 2–36). Ribonuclease is structured in a long, folded chain of 124 amino acids of 19 different types. At four spots along the folded molecule disulfide linkages hold the molecule in its specific shape. Recently scientists at Rockefeller University and Merck, Sharp and Dohme Research Laboratories have synthesized active forms of ribonuclease. Not only is this the first enzyme to be synthesized but it is also the largest protein thus far assembled outside of a living system.

Entirely different techniques were utilized by the two research teams to accomplish ribonuclease synthesis. The Rockefeller team, headed by R. B. Merrifield and B. Gutte, began with the terminal amino acid, valine, and added the remaining 123 amino acids in a process much like coupling a string of railroad cars together one at a time. The chain assemblage was constructed on a solid resin support; after the 124 units were coupled, it was placed in solution and allowed to fold into the characteristic three-dimensional structure of the active enzyme. It is also possible to construct small peptide groups composed of approximately three to twenty amino acids each and join these together to form the enzyme. This was the approach utilized by the Merck group led by R. G. Denkewalter and R. F. Hirschmann. They assembled an active ribonuclease from twenty different fragments.

Influences on Enzyme Action

Enzyme action may be influenced by pH, temperature, and concentration; optimal activity for each enzyme depends on a combination of these. In general, an increase in temperature or enzyme concentration increases reaction rates, whereas lower temperatures slow down reactions. Deviation from the optimum pH will also slow a reaction. Extreme deviation from the normal temperature of pH causes *denaturation* of the protein structure and inactivation of the enzyme. Denaturation refers to a structural change produced in a protein and will be further considered in Chapter 3.

A summary of our discussion on chemical compounds and reactions might well be done by returning to the firefly example given at the beginning of this chapter. Light, or bioluminescence, is produced in a series of chemical reactions involving at least three organic compounds—ATP, luciferin, and luciferase. It should be noted again that ATP is involved in all energy reactions in all living forms. Luciferin is an organic compound produced by the firefly (and many other bioluminescent organisms) and luciferase is the principal enzyme involved in the reaction. The first reaction in this process apparently links luciferin and ATP. Light energy then can be released when a solution of luciferase and some inorganic ion, such as Mg^{++} in the presence of oxygen, is added to the luciferin-ATP complex. The final reaction in the process may be summarized as:

$$\text{Luciferin-ATP} \xrightarrow[\substack{Mg^{++}, O_2 \\ H_2O}]{\text{luciferase}} \text{light} + \text{luciferin} + \text{ADP}$$

(Note the ATP is changed to ADP in this reaction and the reason for this will be given in Chapter 6 when energy is discussed.) In this process we can see a chemical change that releases light energy and occurs in the presence of an enzyme.

ENTROPY

Living systems are characterized by highly ordered atomic structures and chemical reactions. The extent of disorder in any chemical system can be measured and is known as *entropy*. In our universe, as we know it, all atomic combinations tend toward a state of complete disorder—that is, high entropy (the second law of thermodynamics). A highly organized chemical combination, therefore, possesses less entropy than a more disorganized one. Since living systems reproduce and maintain an orderly state, they appear to defy the universal law defined above.

Living things, however, are not closed systems; they require large amounts of fuel either from the sun and photosynthesis or energy-rich molecules from other organisms. Life, in its ordered state, possesses low entropy and thus has the energy necessary to perform biological work. It might be said that an increase in entropy actually drives the energy-requiring reactions of life. Or, in the total picture, then, entropy is increasing in the universe and the living system is only a brief interlude along the course to disorder.

CHEMICAL DEVELOPMENT AND THE ORIGIN OF LIFE

Before we begin our discussion of the structure and function of living systems, a most fundamental question should be explored—the problem of the origin of life on our planet. Since all organisms are composed of chemical compounds, we must first look at some of the basic chemical principles involved. It is perhaps more realistic to think of the origin of life as a twofold process: first, the development or formation of very large molecules whose special duplicating and coding features are characteristic of life; and second, the organization of these molecules into cells. Let us now consider the proposed evolutionary developments necessary for this process to come about.

SMALL MOLECULES TO LARGE MOLECULES

As the earth formed and heavy elements such as iron and nickel sank to the center of the earth, the lighter gases collected in the atmosphere. The Russian scientist Oparin suggested that this primitive atmosphere contained little or no oxygen but was composed mainly of hydrogen and nitrogen. Most of the oxygen probably escaped into space or was tied up in oxides of metals in the earth's crust (iron oxide, for example). The primitive atmosphere also could have contained methane (CH_4), ammonia (NH_3), hydrogen cyanide (HCN), and some water vapor (H_2O).

The fundamental problem in explaining the origin of life in a mechanistic manner lies in the interesting fact that the organic molecules we know today are essentially synthesized by living organisms. We must show that these molecules could have been produced outside of living systems under conditions which are believed to have existed in the early development of our planet.

We know that energy is required to form molecules from atoms and energy is also necessary to construct larger molecules from smaller ones. Sources of energy probably available on the primitive earth were ultraviolet light, electric discharges (lightning), cosmic radiation, and heat from volcanoes. It has been postulated that the molecules of this early atmosphere, under the stimulation of a source of energy, could have formed many of the simpler organic molecules such as amino acids (Figure 2–37).

In 1953, at the University of Chicago, Stanley Miller performed an experiment to test this hypothesis. His apparatus is shown and discussed in Figure 2–38. Essentially he circulated the gases NH_3, CH_4, H_2, and H_2O

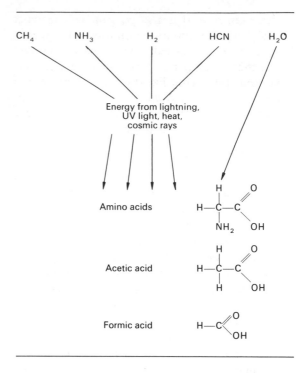

Figure 2·37 Formation of simple organic molecules from a hypothetical primitive atmosphere.

past an electric discharge and examined the resulting mixture. Among the products were amino acids, a fatty acid, and formic acid! The study of the origin of organic molecules with electric discharge apparatus is still going on. One particular experimenter in this field is Dr. Cyril A. Ponnamperuma of Ames Research Center (Figure 2–39). This experiment proved that the process proposed by Oparin and others was possible and experiments by other investigators have yielded similar results. An interesting report in 1970 by Sidney W. Fox and Charles Windsor showed that seven different amino acids could be synthesized from the heating of ammonia and formaldehyde. This is especially significant since these two simple molecules are present in galactic space and could certainly be precursors of amino acids. Configurations such as carbon chains, carbon rings, NH_2 groups, $—C = O$) and $—C—OH$ are important parts of molecules associated with life.

46

Figure 2·38 The laboratory apparatus set up by Stanley Miller to simulate the chemical and physical conditions on the primitive earth. Water vapor produced in flask 2 is mixed with the gases in flask 1, passed through an electric discharge, and condensed in the U tube at the bottom. After the gases had circulated for one week, samples of the water were analyzed for organic compounds and several simple amino acids were found.

LARGE MOLECULES TO LARGER MOLECULES

The next logical step in the formation of molecules required for life would be the production of still larger molecules such as proteins. Proteins are large molecules that result when many amino acids combine. Sidney W. Fox and several of his coworkers at Florida State University have shown that such a process is possible. By subjecting a mixture of amino acids (including an abundance of glutamic and aspartic acids) to intense heat (160–200° C) for several hours they were able

Figure 2·39 Working with the electric discharge apparatus for the study of the origin of organic molecules is Dr. Cyril A. Ponnamperuma, chief of the Chemical Evolution Branch at NASA-Ames Research Center. (Photo courtesy of NASA.)

47

Figure 2·40 Microspheres produced by combining water with hot proteinoids. The spheres range in size from 1 to 3 microns. (Courtesy of the Institute of Molecular Evolution, University of Miami.)

to produce proteinlike compounds which they called *proteinoids*. Other experiments have produced similar polymerizations.

By pouring water over a mixture of hot proteinoids, Fox produced tiny spherical bodies which he termed "microspheres (Figure 2–40). These can be seen under the light microscope and, when observed with the electron microscope, a double-walled membrane, typical of living cells, is apparent. These microspheres, however, cannot be considered to be cells, but this experiment demonstrated that proteinoids could form membranelike structures that are characteristic of cells.

Certainly, compounds other than proteins are necessary for life, and among these are sugars, purines, pyrimidines, and fatty acids. It seems quite likely that molecules of these compounds could have been produced early in the total series of events leading up to life. Simple sugars have indeed been produced by irradiating solutions of formaldehyde ($H_2C = O$) with ultraviolet or gamma rays, and larger sugar molecules have also been produced by heating mixtures of simple sugars. Fats, as we learned earlier, are formed from one glycerine molecule and three molecules of fatty acids. The glycerine molecule is a rather simple three-carbon structure, whereas fatty acids may be long carbon chains. It is conceivable that these molecules could have come together in the presence of an energy source to produce the large fat molecules. Purines and pyrimidines are ring compounds of carbon and nitrogen which are necessary for the heredity and reproductive processes in all

Figure 2·41a Electron micrograph of the polio virus magnified X 230,000, representing the polyhedral type. See next page for Figure 2·41b.

organisms (Figure 2–26). The purine adenine has been synthesized in several different ways and in one experiment it was produced when HCN and NH_3 were heated together at 100°C. In other experiments purines and pyrimidines were produced from mixtures of methane, ammonia, hydrogen, and water.

Compounds such as purines and sugars frequently combine to form even larger molecules. This combination has also been duplicated in laboratory conditions paralleling those of the primitive earth. Recently at Ames Research Center, sponsored by NASA, a large molecule known as a nucleotide was produced when a solution of ribose sugar, adenine, and phosphoric acid was irradiated with ultraviolet light. This was an important step in the confirmation of the theory of the origin of life as outlined here, since nucleotides are inseparably linked with life's functions. The nucleotide synthesized at Ames was adenosine triphosphate, commonly known as ATP, which functions as the basic energy carrier for all life (Figure 6–1*b*).

SELF-DUPLICATING, CODING MOLECULES

Life requires even larger molecules than the nucleotide structure, and further polymerization or construction of larger molecules from smaller units must have somehow occurred. We know that nucleotides can unite in living systems in the presence of an enzyme to form some of the largest natural molecules known, the nucleic acids. Two of these are known, ribonucleic acid (RNA) and deoxyribonucleic

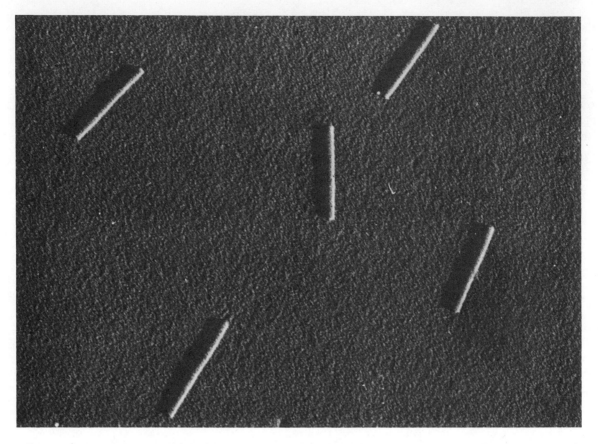

Figure 2·41b Electron micrograph of the tobacco mosaic virus, a rod-shaped type, magnified X 100,000. (Courtesy of Virus Laboratory, University of California at Berkeley.)

acid (DNA). As was noted earlier in this chapter, RNA is a long single chain of nucleotides, and DNA is a long double chain of nucleotides. The sugar in DNA, deoxyribose, is slightly different than the ribose in RNA. You may also recall that both RNA and DNA contain one unique pyrimidine that does not occur in the other—uracil in RNA and thymine in DNA. The basic structure of these macromolecules was illustrated in Figures 2–28, 2–29, 2–31, and 2–32. Efforts to synthesize these nucleic acids under the hypothetical primitive earth conditions have not been completely successful. Large nucleic-acid structures have been approximated, however, by mixing high concentrations of nucleotides at temperatures of around 60°C.

The chromosomes of living cells, to be dis-

cussed in detail later, are composed of nucleic acids (essentially DNA) and protein. Viruses (Figure 2–41) have a similar composition, that is, either RNA or DNA, and protein, and it is tempting to speculate that they are similar to the early structures formed when the nucleic acid and protein molecules first evolved. This is only one hypothesis, however, to explain the existence of viruses. Some biologists believe that viruses have evolved to an extreme state of parasitism, with the gradual loss of all cellular structures except nucleic acid and protein. Since viruses do not possess the necessary cell parts for reproduction and other life processes, they must invade living cells and utilize the host's cellular machinery.

The important point to note at this stage of our discussion is that DNA is a molecule that can divide and reproduce another molecule exactly like itself as well as provide a code system of information for the cell. These are two basic requirements for living systems. The DNA molecule shown in Figure 2–32 splits down the middle and each half constructs another half exactly like the one it lost. All living organisms must be capable of reproduction in order to survive.

In DNA, adenine can combine only with thymine, and guanine can combine only with cytosine. A code based on various linear combinations of these bases can exist along the molecule as in the following example:

Code
Sequence

Figure 2·42 Dr. Arthur Kornberg was awarded a Nobel Prize in 1959 for his work in DNA synthesis. (Courtesy of Stanford University Photographic Department.)

This code, which is a precise sequence of nitrogen bases, can be organized in a great variety of combinations and can control the cellular synthesis of compounds such as proteins. We will discuss the information code of DNA in greater detail in Chapter 3.

Following the introduction in 1953 of the three-dimensional model of DNA by Watson and Crick, many scientists turned to the task of synthesizing DNA. Since we know that DNA is the basis of heredity, a complete understanding of the components of this molecule would have great genetic and medical significance. In 1958 Arthur Kornberg (Figure 2–42) succeeded in isolating the enzyme DNA polymerase which links individual nucleotides into long DNA molecules if a strand of "natural" DNA is added as a template. This test-tube synthesis constituted a great advance in biochemistry for which Kornberg was awarded the Nobel Prize in medicine in 1959.

The synthetic DNA produced by Kornberg was not, however, exactly like "normal" DNA. The new chains were branched and exhibited no biological activity. If a biologically active DNA could be produced, it would prove that a molecule could be synthesized which could perform the essential functions of life. In 1967 Kornberg announced a new synthesis. In his laboratory at Stanford University he and his associates had synthesized a viral DNA that was capable of invading bacterial cells to produce a new generation of normal viruses. Kornberg used the virus ΦX174, which is unique because its DNA is single stranded and circular. He was able to isolate the viral DNA, copy it in a test tube, and finally copy

ΦX174 DNA   Nucleotides   DNA Polymerase   Joining Enzyme   DNase and Denaturation

Figure 2·43 The various steps in the synthesis of complete, biologically active, viral DNA are schematically represented here. The circular DNA of ϕ X 174 virus is used as a template. Nucleotides containing adenine, thymine, guanine, and cytosine are then added, along with DNA polymerase. The enzyme causes formation of a synthetic polypeptide circle complementary to the template DNA. However, the synthetic circle is incomplete and therefore not biologically active. Completion of the complementary circle is accomplished by the polynucleotide-joining enzyme, and a semisynthetic covalent duplex circle is formed. DNAase treatment and denaturation permit separation of the two circles and of linear forms of both template and synthetic origin. Various techniques have been employed along the way to create density differences and exploit shape differences so that the template and synthetic linears, the template and synthetic circles, and the semisynthetic duplexes can be segregated as shown. The synthetic circles can then be employed as templates for the formation of a second complementary synthetic circle, using the same procedures as before. The result is a completely synthetic viral DNA in its biologically active replicating form. (Courtesy of Hospital Practice Company.)

the copy (Figure 2–43). A photograph of the duplicating DNA of step 3 is shown in Figure 2–44. This amounted to a completely extracellular synthesis of DNA. When the artificial DNA was introduced into a specially prepared culture of *Escherichia coli* bacteria, the copy DNA entered the cells and produced normal viruses. Although the DNA in this case was single stranded, the biological activity demonstrated indicates that scientists have moved a step nearer to an understanding of the origin of life and genetic mechanisms.

Later, in 1970, H. G. Khorana of the University of Wisconsin successfully synthesized the basic code unit for the production of a yeast enzyme. In this experiment he joined

77 nucleotides into double-stranded DNA, which constitutes the laboratory synthesis of a unit of heredity, the *gene*.

CELLULAR DEVELOPMENT

Most of the basic molecules necessary for life have been discussed in this chapter, but we know that these molecules must be enclosed in cells. How then were the first cells formed? Fox's experiments demonstrated a possible way in which cells could have been formed with protein membranes. Other possibilities have been suggested, however, and the truth is that, at this stage, we do not really know how the first cells were formed. We do know

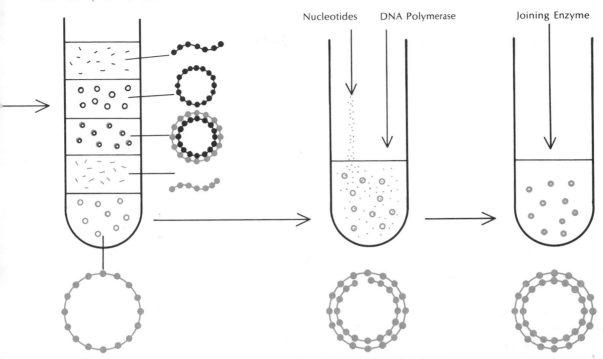

that cells have membranes composed of protein and fat and possess chromosomes containing DNA which seem to control the activities of the cell. With the development of additional cell structures, the processes of *respiration* (which provide energy to the cell) and *photosynthesis* (food making) could have evolved. In cellular respiration, carbon dioxide is given off while oxygen is used. In food making the reverse is true—that is, oxygen is released and carbon dioxide is used. These processes probably played a significant role in the conversion of the primitive reducing atmosphere to the present state which contains a considerable amount of oxygen.

WHAT IS LIFE?

Perhaps the best summarizing statements about life involve cellular structure and the chemical compounds contained within the cell. That is, life can be simply defined as "cells containing nucleic acids." Inherent in this definition is the ability of life to reproduce, code messages, and change (mutate), since nucleic acids can perform these three functions.

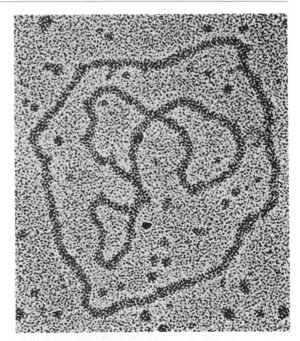

Figure 2·44 Two duplex circles of partially synthetic ϕ X DNA are shown in electron micrograph (X 310,000); one duplex happens to lie inside the other. Each consists of a template of natural virus with a complete synthetic complementary circle. (Courtesy of Hospital Practice Company.)

Usually life is defined in terms of the characteristics of the living material (sometimes known as *protoplasm*). The structural characteristics have already been mentioned and we emphasize again that all life is composed of cells. All living material exhibits *sensitivity* and living things respond to their environment. *Movement* is yet another characteristic of the living substance. Further, all life must constantly undergo chemical reactions for nourishment and the construction of new protoplasm. In this process, *ingestion* of food, *secretion,* and *excretion* of wastes occur. All of the chemical reactions necessary for life are often summarized with the term *metabolism.* Living cells and organisms must also *reproduce* and undergo an orderly process of *growth.* Each living organism must ultimately die, decay, and decompose to return the living substance to nonliving material. Finally, the important characteristic of *adaptation* is exhibited by all forms of life and all of the other functions certainly contribute to the ability of an organism to adapt. Actually, these fundamental characteristics form the framework for the rest of this book.

WHERE IS LIFE GOING?

NATURAL SELECTION

The explanation for the diversity of life found on our planet is based on the concept of *natural selection.* In its simplest form natural selection is the effect of the environment upon the different coding combinations of DNA. We can assume that various code arrangements (A-T, G-C, etc.) developed and environments must have varied in the early days of our earth just as they do today. Certain codes then could produce cells varying in their abilities to cope with the various environments. Perhaps many different coded cells were produced in a specific environment but only those suited to that environment could live there. These "favored" cells could divide and produce others like themselves.

Natural selection is a fundamental concept that should be kept in mind throughout your study of biology, for it is a mechanism that can explain the diversity of life. Natural selection therefore is considered to be the force that determines the type of life that inhabits the earth.

SUMMARIZING PRINCIPLES

All material substance of the universe is known as matter, and each chemically different type of matter is termed an element; the fundamental unit of matter is the atom, which is composed principally of protons, neutrons, and electrons.

Theories of the origin of the universe include: (1) the explosion theory which proposes that the universe was formed by the explosion of a concentration of matter some seven to ten billion years ago; and (2) the steady-state theory which holds that the universe has always existed and thus has no beginning and no end.

One of the most useful models of the structure of the atom is the Bohr planetary model which depicts the electrons moving about a central nucleus in shells corresponding to the specific energies of the electrons.

The forces that hold atoms together to form molecules are chemical bonds; the most common bonds are electrovalent or ionic, covalent, and hydrogen.

Compounds may be divided into two groups, organic and inorganic. Organic compounds always contain the element carbon; common organic compounds of life are carbohydrates, fats or lipids, proteins, and nucleic acids.

Chemical reactions occur when atoms or compounds interact to form other compounds, called products. These reactions always involve energy changes and rearrangement of bonds. The rate, duration, and direction of a chemical reaction is directly proportional to the concentration of the reactants; practically all biological reactions are accelerated by enzymes.

The proposed chemical events leading to the development of life are summarized as follows:

Primitive atmosphere NH_3, CH_4, HCN, H_2O

Small organic molecules   Amino acids, glycerin, fatty acids, 5-C sugars, 6-C sugars, purines, and pyrimidines

Large organic molecules   proteins, fats, compound sugars, nucleotides

Larger organic molecules   Nucleic acids (DNA and RNA)

Macromolecules   Chromosomes

Life   Chromosomes in cells

Diversity of life   Natural selection and the variety of cells produced

Life may be defined essentially as "cells containing nucleic acids." The characteristics of living organisms include: sensitivity, movement, metabolism, reproduction, growth, and adaptation. The most plausible explanation for the direction of the development of life lies in the concept of natural selection.

REVIEW QUESTIONS

1   Outline the development of the modern concept of atomic structure. How does atomic structure relate to bonding potential?

2   Name and illustrate the basic structures of five different organic compounds and explain how each might be utilized in living systems.

3   Why is hydrochloric acid a stronger acid than acetic acid?

4   Explain the organization of the periodic table as you would to a nonscience major. In your explanation include the terms groups, periods, isotopes, atomic number, and atomic weight. How is this chart useful to chemists?

5   Describe how electrovalent or ionic compounds can be separated by the use of an electric current.

6   How does sodium bicarbonate ($NaHCO_3$) alleviate the condition of stomach hyperacidity?

7   What role does water play in the synthesis and cleavage of organic molecules such as glucose, maltose, glycerin, and fatty acids?

8   How is it possible for cows to digest cellulose (split the molecules) while human beings cannot?

9   A nucleotide is composed of a purine or pyrimidine, a ribose sugar, and a phosphate ester. Show by a diagram how nucleotides can be strung together to form a nucleic acid. Distinguish between the structures of DNA and RNA. What are some of the biological implications of these structures?

10 Of the organic molecules discussed in this chapter, protein can assume the most complex and varied structures. What is the chemical basis for this ability? Why do you suppose all known enzymes are proteins?

11 Why do chemical reactions occur? What is the activation energy in the lighting of a match? How do biological reactions differ in terms of activation energy? Why do chemical reactions generally occur faster with increasing temperature?

12 If you were asked to defend the theory that life arose from nonliving matter, how would you organize your presentation? Note any experimental evidence that would strengthen your case.

SUPPLEMENTARY READINGS

Alder, Irving, *How Life Began,* New York, New American Library (Signet Books), 1957.

Allen, Robert D., "Amoeboid Movement," *Scientific American,* February, 1962.

Baker, J. J. W., and G. E. Allen, *Matter, Energy, and Life,* Reading, Mass., Addison-Wesley, 1965.

Borek, E., *The Atoms Within Us,* New York, Columbia University Press, 1961.

Calvin, M., and J. A. Bassham, *The Photosynthesis of Carbon Compounds,* New York, Benjamin, 1962.

Crick, F. H. C., "Nucleic Acids," *Scientific American,* September, 1957.

Edelman, Gerald M., "The Structure and Function of Antibodies," *Scientific American,* August, 1970.

Eglinton, Geoffrey, and Melvin Calvin, "Chemical Fossils," *Scientific American*, January, 1967.

Fowler, William A., "The Origin of the Elements," *Scientific American*, September, 1956.

Gamow, George, "The Evolutionary Universe," *Scientific American*, September, 1956.

Hoyle, Fred, "The Steady-State Universe," *Scientific American*, September, 1956.

Keosian, John, *The Origin of Life*, New York, Reinhold, 1964.

Kornberg, Arthur, "The Synthesis of DNA," *Scientific American*, October, 1968.

Locke, David, M., *Enzymes—The Agents of Life*, New York, Crown, 1969.

McElroy, W. D., *Cellular Physiology and Biochemistry*, 2nd ed., Englewood Cliffs, N.J., Prentice-Hall, 1964.

Merrifield, R. B., "The Automatic Synthesis of Proteins," *Scientific American*, March, 1968.

Miller, Stanley L., "The Origin of Life," in W. Johnson and W. Steere, eds., *This Is Life*, New York, Holt, Rinehart and Winston, 1962.

Mirsky, Alfred E., "The Discovery of DNA," *Scientific American*, June, 1968.

Oparin, A. I., *Origin of Life*, New York, Dover, 1953.

Ovenden, Michael W., *Life in the Universe*, Garden City, N.Y., Doubleday (Anchor Books), 1962.

Patton, Stuart, "Milk," *Scientific American*, July, 1969.

Pryor, William A., "Free Radicals in Biological Systems," *Scientific American*, August, 1970.

Schrödinger, Erwin, *What Is Life?*, London, Cambridge University Press, 1944.

Schrödinger, Erwin, "What Is Matter?" *Scientific American*, September, 1953.

Sinsheimer, Robert L., "Single-Stranded DNA," *Scientific American*, July, 1962.

Stein, William H., and Stanford Moore, "The Chemical Structure of Proteins," *Scientific American*, February, 1961.

Urey, Harold C., "The Origin of the Earth," *Scientific American*, October, 1952.

Wald, George, "The Origin of Life," *Scientific American*, August, 1954.

White, E. H., *Chemical Background for the Biological Sciences*, Englewood Cliffs, N.J., Prentice-Hall, 1964.

Young, R. S., and Cyril Ponnamperuma, *Early Evolution of Life*, BSCS Pamphlet No. 11, American Institute of Biological Sciences, Boston, Heath, 1964.

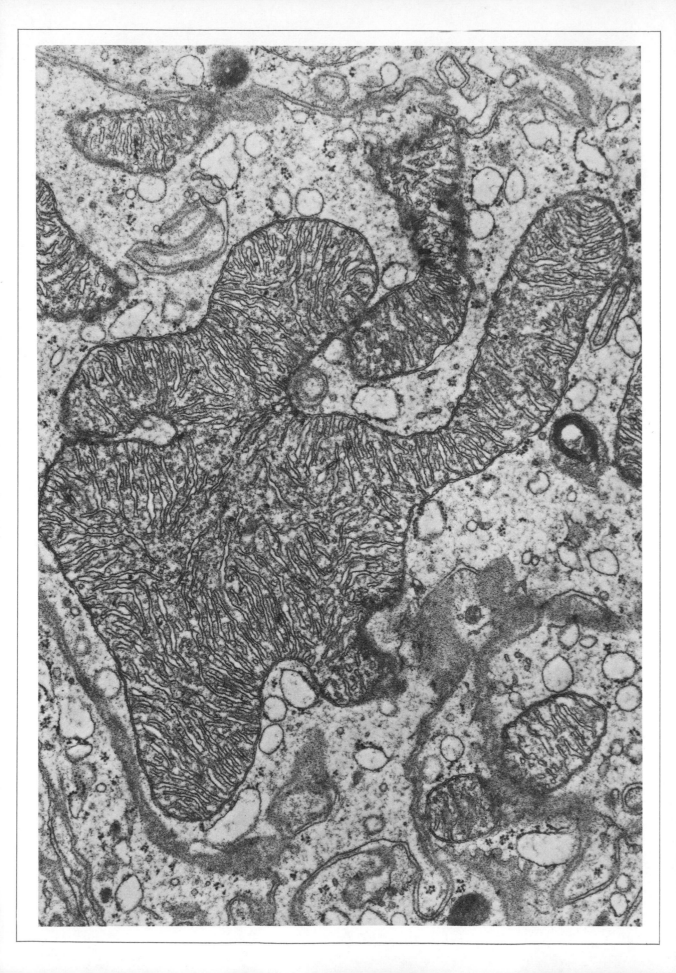

3

Biological Architecture: Cells

Cells have sometimes been compared with architectural bricks. The various sizes, shapes, and strengths of bricks permit the design of many different functional structures, and although the bricks differ, still they are easily recognized as bricks. This is also true of living cells. For decades now biologists have labored to understand life and its processes primarily by studying the structure and function of cells.

Consider the mushrooms in their multitude of sizes, shapes, and colors. What are they, where did they come from, and what are they made of? Perhaps you know the answer to most of these questions. A dictionary might say mushrooms are the fruiting bodies of certain fungi that arise from the soil each year to produce reproductive spores, but a microscopic examination reveals much more. All parts of the mushroom are composed of small cells, but these remarkably similar cells give rise to strikingly different structures such as a stalk, gill filaments, and a cap. Furthermore, different fungi produce structurally unique mushrooms.

The term *cell* was first used by Robert Hooke in 1665 to describe the small chambers he had observed in cork. Much later, in 1838, the German botanist M. J. Schleiden recognized the aggregation of cells in *tissues* of plants. This observation was extended to animals and developed more fully about a year later by Theodor Schwann, a German zoologist. The cell theory proposed

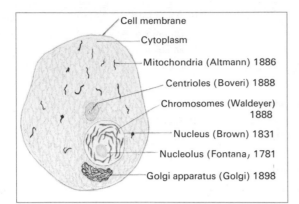

Cell membrane
Cytoplasm
Mitochondria (Altmann) 1886
Centrioles (Boveri) 1888
Chromosomes (Waldeyer) 1888
Nucleus (Brown) 1831
Nucleolus (Fontana) 1781
Golgi apparatus (Golgi) 1898

Figure 3·1 A summary of cell structures before the introduction of the electron microscope.

Figure 3·2 Modern electron microscope. This Elmiskop 101 with a point resolution of 3.5 Angstrom units and a magnification range of X 285 to 280,000 provides excellent high-resolution microscopy. (Courtesy of Siemens America, Inc.)

by Schleiden and Schwann became a basic concept in biology and is one of the most significant generalizations ever made in the field. According to this theory all living organisms are composed of cells, and the cell may be considered to be the fundamental unit of all life.

THE CELL AND ITS PARTS

The discoveries of the various parts of the cell were made over a period of 300 years by many men. In 1835 Dujardin described the contents of cells from his studies on certain protozoa as a "perfectly homogeneous, elastic, contractile, diaphanous, gelatinous substance, insoluble in water and without traces of organization." In 1839 Purkinje and von Mohl adopted the term *protoplasm* for this substance so articulately described by Dujardin. But today, owing to our finer microscopes, we know more about the organization and structure of cells. Consequently the term protoplasm is used currently only as a generalized description of living materials. Cytoplasm is another general term used to describe the living material between the outer limits of the cell (the cell membrane) and the nucleus.

By 1900 the structures shown in Figure 3–1 had been observed and described. Robert Brown discovered the nucleus in 1831 while examining the cells of orchids. He described it as an opaque spot and demonstrated its presence in most of the plant's cells. The original observation of the nucleus and a smaller body within it called the *nucleolus* had been made by Fontana in 1781. It was Brown, however, who proposed that they were characteristic structures of all cells. Flemming and Strasburger (1882) showed that the nuclear material produced long threads which split lengthwise and passed into the daughter cells during cell division. In 1888 Waldeyer named these threads *chromosomes* because they became much more visible when dyes were added to the cell, a technique called *staining*.

Altmann, in 1886, suggested that the long

60

Figure 3·3 An electron micrograph of a section of rat kidney tubule cell. Note that the structures are labeled on the micrograph and the diagrammatic inset. C, chromosome material; ER, endoplasmic reticulum; M, mitochondrion; NM, nuclear membrane; NP, nuclear pore; G, Golgi apparatus. (Courtesy of James D. Newstead.)

filaments he observed in the cytoplasm under a light microscope might have something to do with the energy production in cells. He called the filaments *mitochondria*. Biochemists have now proved that mitochondria produce most molecules for storing and delivering energy. In 1898 Camillo Golgi reported a network of material in nerve-cell cytoplasm which stained heavily with silver nitrate. The *Golgi apparatus* was hotly disputed by many biologists to be a product resulting from the staining techniques. After many years of controversy, the validity of Golgi's observations was confirmed, and today we know that these structures perform an important function in cellular secretion.

The cytoplasm of all animal and some protist cells contains two small structures that function in cell division. Boveri in 1888 referred to these as "central bodies," but they are now known as *centrioles*. The role of the centrioles in cell division will be discussed later in this chapter.

As improved lenses became available, it was

found that the limiting factor in light microscopy was the wavelength of light itself. The most important aspect of microscopy is the capability to distinguish between two structures. This characteristic is termed *resolution*. The greatest practical resolution with a light microscope is about 0.25 micron. (A micron is 1/1000 of a mm.)

In 1940 a revolutionary type of microscope was produced. It utilized a beam of high-speed electrons of extremely short wavelength and electromagnetic "lenses" to focus the electrons onto a photographic plate. Today, through perfected electron microscopes, resolution is routinely possible to less than 10 angstrom units ($1 \text{ Å} = 10^{-8}$ cm), and magnification may approach 300,000 times (Figure 3–2). With the advantages of this greater resolution, many cellular components have been discovered in recent years. Moreover, a more thorough investigation of the structure of all parts of cells is now possible.

In an electron micrograph of a thin section of a rat kidney (Figure 3–3), several new struc-

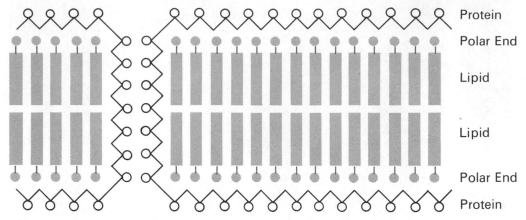

Figure 3.4 A schematic drawing of the molecular structure of a membrane (sometimes called the Danielli model).

tures such as the *endoplasmic reticulum, ribosomes,* and *lysosomes* can be seen in addition to the previously known components. Since it is generally believed that structure and function are closely related, the ability to observe subcellular components in almost molecular detail has enabled scientists to formulate theories about the function of each part in the cell. We shall now turn to a detailed discussion of the structure and function of these subcellular components.

THE CELL MEMBRANE

One structure common to all living cells is the *cell membrane,* the molecular boundary between the cell and its immediate environment. This living membrane not only provides a physical containment for the cell but also produces a large surface area on which many chemical reactions occur. The Danielli model of these cell membranes (Figure 3–4) represents a theoretical molecular arrangement of proteins and lipids that agrees with biochemical and electron-microscope observations. Essentially, the structure is a sandwich of proteins and lipids with two protein layers enclosing a double layer of lipids. One end of the lipid molecules found in the membrane is water soluble and associates with the protein layer (Figure 3–4).

If the cell is so securely bounded by a structural membrane, one might ask how water and nutrients get inside. All living cells require that water and minerals be able to enter through the membrane. Membrane permeability therefore is of extreme interest.

THE MOVEMENT OF MATERIALS INTO CELLS

It is highly probable that cell membranes contain pores that allow the passage of water and certain ions into and out of the cell. It is also probable that these pores are protein lined as shown in Figure 3–4. Since the free amino and carboxyl groups of the amino acids of the protein can take either a negative or positive charge and since like charges repel, it would be possible for specific charged ions to be attracted or rejected according to the immediate physiological state of the cell. This theory also helps to explain the high degree of selectivity shown by these semipermeable membranes for certain ions even when others may exist in greater concentrations. A semipermeable membrane allows certain materials to pass through, but excludes others. Most membranes, for instance, are permeable to water in either direction but vary in their degrees of permeability for other substances.

A second possibility is that the ability of a substance to penetrate a cell depends largely on its solubility in lipids. For instance, large

Figure 3·5 Phagocytosis: white blood cell engulfing bacteria.

molecules having high fat solubility pass relatively easily into a cell. According to this theory, molecules may actually dissolve their way through the lipid layers.

Phagocytosis and Pinocytosis

Like the amoeba, most cells can actively ingest nutrients. The engulfment of solid materials is known as *phagocytosis*—a process employed by human white blood cells to rid the body of bacteria and waste. Another process is *pinocytosis* or "cell drinking." In either case the cell membrane encircles the particle or droplet and forms a small membranous pouch. Once inside the cell the droplet is pinched off to become a pinocytotic vesicle or, as it is commonly known, a *vacuole* (Figure 3–5).

Diffusion and Osmosis

In 1827 Robert Brown noted that tiny particles suspended in water collide with one another and move in random zigzag patterns. Although Brown thought that the plant spores he had observed under the microscope were capable of independent movement, it was soon demonstrated by other scientists that a similar movement occurred with nonliving particles in liquid or gas. This phenomenon, known as *Brownian motion*, has been observed in all states of matter—solid, liquid, and gas. The theory that all matter is in constant motion is known as the *kinetic theory*. Heat is the measurable result of this bombardment among atoms and molecules.

Traditionally the study of the interchange of substances between the cell and its environment was approached as some aspect of diffusion or osmosis. It must be noted, however, that these processes are not specifically cellular mechanisms and do not explain how materials get into and out of cells. Diffusion is often defined as the movement of particles through a medium from a greater concentration toward a lesser concentration. For example, if a bottle of ammonia is opened in a classroom, the first students to detect the odoriferous molecules are those seated nearest the demonstration. Within a short time, however, the molecules distribute themselves so that even those in the back row can detect the smell of ammonia in the air.

It is possible for particles in a water medium to diffuse through a membrane if they are small enough to pass through the membrane pores. The particles on the left side of the membrane represented in Figure 3–6 are in constant motion and move through the membrane pores from a greater to a lesser concentration until an equilibrium is reached—that is, after equilibrium is reached particles will continue to move in equal numbers back and forth across the membrane.

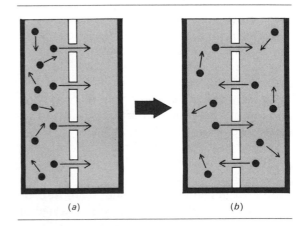

(a) (b)

Figure 3·6 Diffusion of particles through a membrane. In (*a*), particles move from a greater to a lesser concentration until an equal number of particles are present on each side of the membrane as shown in (*b*). The short arrows indicate random movement.

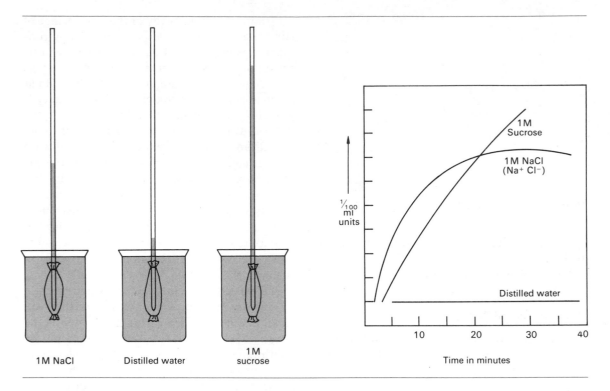

Figure 3·7 Demonstration of osmosis across semipermeable membrane using sausage-skin bags. The bag at the left contains 1 M NaCl; the center bag, distilled water; the right bag, 1 M sucrose.

The term *osmosis* is used to denote the passage of water across a semipermeable membrane from a region of greater concentration of water to a region of lesser concentration of water. The side of the membrane that contains the greatest number of dissolved particles then is the side that has proportionally less water. Thus the passage of water may be controlled by the concentration of particles dissolved on either side of the membrane.

Figure 3–7 illustrates three conditions that affect the osmotic process. In this demonstration, cellulose sausage skins were used for the semipermeable membrane, since cellulose contains many small holes that permit water to pass through the membrane but block the passage of large particles such as sucrose. Three such bags were prepared and filled with the following solutions: (1) 1 M NaCl, (2) distilled water, and (3) 1 M sucrose. Each bag then was tied tightly to a 1/10 ml pipette that

extended into the bag. The pipettes were secured to a holder and the bags were immersed in three beakers of distilled water. Within a few minutes it was noted that the solution in pipette number 1 (NaCl) was rising rapidly. After about 25 minutes, however, the sucrose solution in pipette number 3 equaled that of number 1 and gradually surpassed number 1 until it spilled over the top of the pipette.

Since NaCl ionizes in solution, nearly twice as many particles were present in the NaCl bag as were in the sucrose bag. For this reason water moved into the NaCl bag faster than into the sucrose bag. In this simple experiment, however, particles of dissociated Na^+Cl^- eventually will pass through the holes and the solutions will attain equilibrium —that is, an equal number of particles will be found on each side. Because the sucrose molecules are too large to move through the bag, equilibrium cannot be reached. In the bag

64

containing distilled water, equilibrium was present from the beginning with an equal number of water molecules moving into and out of the bag. The distilled water bag thus represents a "control" in this experiment.

Active Transport

It has been found that the movement of materials into certain cells does not always follow the principles of diffusion or osmosis. The absorptive cells of the small intestine, for example, are capable of taking in large amounts of glucose liberated by the digestive process. Even though the bloodstream may contain many more glucose molecules than are found inside the intestine, glucose is still moved into the bloodstream. Since this violates the principle of diffusion, we refer to it as an absorption against a concentration gradient, concentration gradient being that tendency for molecules to move from higher to lower concentration. This very necessary and important process is called *active transport* and requires the expenditure of energy by the cell. For some sub-

stances it is the only means of entering a cell. At this time the exact details of the process are not understood, but experiments have shown that a carrier molecule and energy (ATP) are probably involved. Figure 3–8 illustrates the movement of glucose across the intestinal cells into the bloodstream against a high concentration gradient. Part c of Figure 3–8 presents a hypothetical mechanism to account for this movement which involves the expenditure of energy and the use of a carrier. The carrier molecule is released when the glucose is "delivered" to the bloodstream. A detailed discussion of ATP will be presented in Chapter 5. At this point it is only necessary to note that ATP (a complex organic molecule) stores and delivers the energy utilized by living organisms. In all cases of active transport that have been studied, the addition of a poison, to stop the production of ATP, inhibits the transport mechanism.

Large molecules like glucose are not the only materials that may be taken into cells against a concentration gradient. Ions such as

(a) (b) (c)

Figure 3·8 Schematic diagram of the absorption of glucose from the intestine into the bloodstream. Shortly after a meal, high concentration of glucose is present in the lumen of the intestine (a). As glucose is absorbed, a higher concentration results in the bloodstream (b). At this stage, glucose is moving from a region of low concentration to a region of high concentration. Part (c) represents a hypothetical mechanism to explain the movement of glucose against the concentration gradient. A carrier molecule is represented by the letter C. Energy in the form of ATP and enzymes is also required.

Vacuole

Nitella cell

Pond water

Ca⁺⁺	260	Ca⁺⁺	26 mg/liter

Ca^{++} 260 Ca^{++} 26 mg/liter
Na^+ 1147.7 Na^+ 27.6
K^+ 1922.7 K^+ 19.89
Cl^- 3538.5 Cl^- 35.0
$SO_4^=$ 208.0 $SO_4^=$ 10.7

Nucleus

Figure 3·9 A comparison of the ionic concentration in the vacuolar sap of *Nitella* and the pond water in which it lives. The higher concentration of ions in the cell sap is a result of active transport. The data are expressed in milligrams per liter.

sodium (Na^+), potassium (K^+), calcium (Ca^{++}), chloride (Cl^-), and sulfate ($SO_4^=$) are also transported by many cells. The cells that form the tubules of the kidneys actively reclaim ions and glucose from the forming urine. The freshwater alga *Nitella* concentrates large amounts of certain ions in its sap. A comparison of the ionic concentration in the sap and in pond water is shown in Figure 3–9. Note particularly that the concentration of chloride ion (Cl^-) in the cell sap is a hundred times greater than in pond water.

CYTOPLASMIC ORGANELLES

It has been suggested recently that the small structures, known as organelles, located in the cytoplasm may have derived from the cell membrane through an evolutionary process of infolding and adaptation to specific functions. This suggestion is supported by evidence that mitochondria, the Golgi apparatus, and the nuclear membrane are essentially double membrane structures. If the cell membrane is considered to be a single-unit membrane as represented in Figure 3–4, these organelles should be thought of as double-unit membrane structures.

ENDOPLASMIC RETICULUM AND RIBOSOMES

Early electron micrographs clearly showed that an extensive system of tubules and membranous plates extend throughout the supposedly homogeneous area called cytoplasm. These structures, known as the *endoplasmic reticulum* (ER), generally have small particles called *ribosomes* attached to their surfaces. If the ER has no ribosomes, it is called *smooth ER*. Ribosomes were discovered by George Palade of the Rockefeller Institute, who also found that they contain protein and particulate RNA. Ribosomes, as we shall see later, are the sites of protein synthesis. It is thought that these structures function primarily to increase the surface area within the cell.

GOLGI APPARATUS

The basketlike system of silver-stained fibers observed by Camillo Golgi is actually a series of membranous, laminar tubules very closely related to the endoplasmic reticulum. There are, however, no ribosome particles on their surfaces. The function of the Golgi apparatus appears to be the storage and release of cellular secretions. Cells that are very active in producing secretions always contain large amounts of Golgi structure. The larger lamellae appear to break up into smaller vesicles that eventually reach the cell membrane to be expelled as secretion droplets. Cells of the pancreas, which secrete digestive enzymes, are an excellent example of this process. Since enzymes are composed of protein, studies using radioactive-labeled amino acids such as leucine have enabled scientists to trace the formation, storage, and release of cellular secretions.

MITOCHONDRIA

When Richard Altmann observed tiny threadlike bodies in the cytoplasm of stained cells, he named them "bioblasts," thinking that they might be the elementary living particles. The name *mitochondrion*, suggested by Benda in 1897, corresponds to the two principal shapes

66

←180 Å

Inner membrane

Crista

Outer membrane

Figure 3·10 A cutaway view of a mitochondrion showing the relationship between the inner cristae membrane and the outer membrane. An enlargement of these membranes is shown upper left. (From John M. Allen, editor; *Molecular Organization and Biological Function. Harper & Row.*

he had observed (*mito*, meaning "thread" and *chondrion*, meaning "granule").

Through biochemical studies and electron microscopy, we know today that the mitochondrion is an essential organelle and is not caused by chemical treatment, a bacterium, or a parasite within the cell. It is the principal site of energy production in every cell and often has been called the "powerhouse of the cell." A look at an electron micrograph (Figure 3–3) shows that the mitochondrion is made up of two membranes: an outer membrane and a greatly folded inner membrane. The folds of the inner membrane are called *cristae*, and the increased surface area provided by the cristae folds is believed to permit the attachment of extensive enzyme systems.

Energy-rich compounds are produced within the mitochondrion through two enzyme-catalyzed processes. The enzymes for the first series of reactions (the Krebs cycle, Chapter 6) are located in the mitochondrial fluid between the cristae; the enzymes for the second series are attached to the crista membrane itself (Figure 3–10).

Even when the mitochondria are removed from cells by centrifugation, the energy-producing reactions still operate. Indeed, if the mitochondria are broken up into small fragments, certain fragments are still capable of producing energy, if incubated in the proper medium. The cristae, therefore, must contain many functional areas along their surfaces. A detailed study of these enzyme reactions will be presented in Chapter 6.

Recently it was discovered that mitochondria contain a small amount of DNA and ribosomal RNA and therefore have the system necessary for the production of specific proteins. Mitochondrial DNA occurs as naked fibers—that is, the DNA is not associated with protein as it is in a nucleus. Although the information necessary for the synthesis of most of the mitochondrial enzymes is probably contained in nuclear DNA, the nucleic acid system of mitochondria is apparently responsible for the synthesis of some proteins necessary for the structure and function of mitochondrial membranes. It has long been known that mitochondria are capable of dividing but the discovery of DNA has also raised the question of their origin. One hypothesis suggests their possible origin in cells from endoplasmic reticulum or nuclear membrane. Another hypothesis holds that mitochondria were once free-living organisms similar to modern bacteria. These entered other cells and subsequently became part of the host cell's machinery.

CENTRIOLES

The area that includes the centrioles was described and named the *centrosome* by Walther Flemming in 1875. Through the light microscope the centrioles appear as two dark granules embedded in a heterogeneous matrix, but electron micrographs show their structure in much greater detail. They are cylindrical and contain numerous fibrils arranged in a very precise pattern. Nine sets of one to three fibrils or tubules are spaced around the periphery of the cylinder. It has been observed

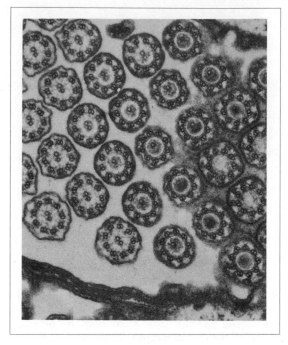

Figure 3·11 Electron micrographs of centrioles from rat kidney. (*a*) Longitudinal and cross section, X 73,000.

(*b*) Cross section of cilia from the ciliate, *Trichodina*, X 35,000. (Courtesy of James D. Newstead)

that the basal part of *flagella* and *cilia*, which are organelles specialized for locomotion, have a similar structure. This similarity in structure suggests that centrioles may have given rise to both flagella and cilia. Figure 3–11*a* shows the centriole fibril arrangement in a longitudinal and cross section. In cilia and flagella two additional fibrils appear in the center, known as the 9 + 2 fibril arrangement (Figure 3–11*b*). The centriole pattern is described as 9 + 0.

During cell division, centrioles split away from the centrosome area and move to positions on opposite sides of the nucleus. By this time many protein fibers have radiated from each centriole to form an aster, and other fibrils have connected centrioles to the chromosomes. It is believed that these protein fibers or spindle fibers play a major role in the separation of the chromosomes and the formation of daughter cells.

At the end of cell division each daughter cell contains one centriole. The centrioles are capable of reproduction and a duplication occurs before the next cell division. It is interesting, however, that the centrioles do not occur in many algae and never in higher plants. In these species the spindle fibers form just before the separation of the chromosomes. Since spindle fibers may form in the absence of centrioles, the relationship between the two is still uncertain.

LYSOSOMES

Contained in a single membrane, the lysosome (splitting body) appears in electron micrographs as a nearly homogeneous vacuole. The name *lysosome* was used to describe the great hydrolytic power of the enzymes contained within its structure. Among the enzymes present are those that digest protein, polysaccharides, nucleic acids, and those that permit the release of energy from ATP. These enzymes could be very destructive to the cell if released into the cytoplasm; for this reason they have sometimes been called "suicide bags." We do not yet know how the enzymes are retained within the membrane. It has been successfully demonstrated that the lysosomes have an important function in the digestion of materials taken into individual cells through the cell membrane, since the breakdown of lysosome membranes by injury or toxic agents causes the death of that particular cell. It is also likely that the lysosomes normally digest dead structures within the cell, thus ridding the cell of waste and providing an additional source of energy. One interesting example of how lysosomes function is the absorption of the tadpole tail in frog development. In this case entire cells are digested by the lysosomes in a controlled manner until the tail disappears. The products of this digestion will be translocated to other areas and used to fabricate new tissue in the developing frog. Figure 3–12 depicts the stages of lysosome function in the digestive gland cells of snails.

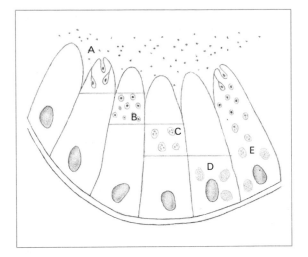

Figure 3-12 A diagrammatic representation of the functional stages of lysosome digestion found in the digestive gland cells of snails. (*a*) Small granules of food are taken into the cell by pinocytosis at the free end. (*b*) Enzyme action occurs within the vacuoles. (*c*) Small vacuoles unite to form larger vacuoles and food products are absorbed by the cell. (*d*) At the completion of enzyme digestion, large vacuoles are formed near the base of the cell and are finally excreted from the cell. (*e*) The entire process is shown as it occurs in one cell.

PLASTIDS

In plant and algae cells there are three types of cytoplasmic bodies known generally as *plastids*. These three types of plastids are *leucoplasts*, which contain no pigments but are generally the site of starch formation and storage; *chromoplasts*, which contain pigments other than chlorophyll; and *chloroplasts*, which are complex membranous structures and contain chlorophyll. Chloroplasts are highly specialized for the production of food and will be described in detail in Chapter 5.

THE COLLOIDAL NATURE OF PROTOPLASM

So far in our discussion of subcellular structure, we have stressed the importance of the membranous organelles and the relationship of structure to function. Of equal importance, however, is the chemical nature of the watery fluids within these structures. Again, the term "protoplasm," which was once used to define living substance, is entirely inadequate in the light of modern biochemistry. Today we know that the cells of various tissues contain unique concentrations of suspended and dissolved materials. Each functional area of a cell contains its own special "protoplasmic" composition. The nonmembranous contents of the cell cytoplasm, the fluid portion, is called *ground cytoplasm*. Like protoplasm, however, this term is hardly adequate to describe the complex composition and functions of this material. In order to understand this we need to look at the various ways in which particles may be dispersed in liquid.

MIXTURES, COLLOIDS, AND SOLUTIONS

From a chemical standpoint, fluids containing particles may be classed in three systems:

simple suspension or mixture, colloidal suspension, and true solution. Larger particles that settle out of a mixture in a very short time illustrate a simple suspension—for example, suspension of fine sand grains in water. Very small particles such as table salt or sugar remain suspended in water almost indefinitely and form a true solution. One must consider, however, that 100 ml of cold water holds only about 36 grams of NaCl—after this amount has been added, the solution becomes saturated and salt crystals form on the bottom of the container.

When relatively large particles remain suspended in a medium over long periods, we call this a colloidal suspension. In colloidal suspensions the fluid part of the system (which is commonly water) is termed the *dispersion phase,* and the suspended particles are collectively termed the *dispersed phase.* Other terms that correspond to these phases are *solvent* and *solute,* respectively. The most important factor determining dispersions is simply the size of the suspended particles. Droplets of water suspended in air to form clouds are a common example. Homogenized milk in which the fat droplets are extremely small is also a type of colloidal suspension.

Figure 3·13 The beam of light in the bottle on the left is bright because of scattering in the colloidal particles of egg white. The bottle on the right is a sodium chloride solution in which the beam is barely visible. This is known as the Tyndall effect.

One method used to distinguish between a colloidal suspension and a true solution is simply to pass a strong beam of light through the liquid. In a true solution the light passes invisibly through the liquid; in a colloidal suspension, however, the particles are large enough to scatter the light, thus forming a cloudy cone known as a Tyndall beam. This is similar to the beam produced by automobile headlamps in fog (Figure 3–13).

It is necessary to stress here the importance of colloids in living systems. All chemical and physical reactions depend on surface contact, and a colloidal suspension—with its great surface area provided by the suspended particles—certainly is the ideal medium. The colloidal state is the matrix in which all life processes occur.

THE MAINTENANCE OF COLLOIDAL SUSPENSIONS

Since colloidal particles are large enough to defract a beam of light, we might wonder what keeps them in suspension. In biological systems the most important component of the dispersed phase is protein. Remember that proteins are large molecules made up of numerous amino acids joined together by peptide bonds (Chapter 2). The amino acids that make up this structure impart a charge to the protein. We know that like charges repel one another and that unlike charges attract. In a colloid, all particles have the same charge, hence they all repel one another. This charge relationship is very important in maintaining the colloidal suspension. If the charges are changed by the addition of certain chemicals, the proteins will clump together in semisolid form. In the process, most of the water is trapped inside the protein mass (Figure 3–14). A second factor responsible for the maintenance of the suspension is the random movement of the water molecules, which constantly bombard the suspended particles. This agitation, known as *Brownian motion,* tends to prevent the settling of the particles.

Sol state   Gel state

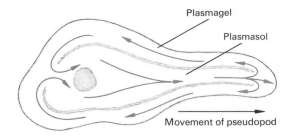

Plasmagel

Plasmasol

Movement of pseudopod

Figure 3·14 Diagram of the dispersed and dispersion phases of a colloid in sol and gel states. Protein molecules are represented by irregular blocks and water by gray shading.

Figure 3·15 Fountain-streaming of amoeboid movement. At the tip of the advancing pseudopod, the sol turns to gel.

SOLS, GELS, AND DENATURATION

Collodial suspensions may exist in two forms —the watery, fluid state or sol, and the more solid state known as a gel. Sometimes the change in state from sol to gel is irreversible, such as the boiling of egg white. When this occurs the permanent change is known as *denaturation* of the protein. In some cells, however, a temporary change occurs naturally and often, as in the movement of the unicellular amoeba where the internal cell fluids flow into an extending foot or pseudopod. This is one of the latest theories of amoeboid movement and is shown in Figure 3–15. The plasmasol streams out into the developing pseudopod somewhat like a fountain. As it reaches the tip it is converted into the gel state. At the same time plasmasol is being re-formed from plasmagel at the opposite end.

Changes in the colloidal state may be produced by several means. We have already discussed the charges carried by the dispersed particles. In addition, high temperatures may break down the large organic molecules and bring about denaturation. The same result may be effected by adding a strong acid or base (changing the pH).

THE NUCLEUS

Up to this point we have discussed only the membranes and membranous organelles of the cytoplasm. The nucleus, with its inclu-

sions, is also extremely important to the functions of the cell. Of course, not all cells contain a well-defined nucleus with a surrounding membrane, but even such cells as bacteria and blue-green algae do have masses of nucleoprotein that function in place of the organized nucleus of more complex organisms.

Many experiments have shown that the nucleus is necessary for the continuation of life activities in a cell. With a very fine glass needle mounted on a microscope, it is possible to remove the nucleus from an amoeba. The resulting enucleate cell is incapable of reproduction or digestion and can make only sluggish movements. An enucleate amoeba usually will die within three weeks. If a new nucleus from the same species is transplanted back into the cell within a few days, however, normal functions will return.

One interesting aspect of this enucleate amoeba is its inability to digest foods. Digestion is accomplished by enzymes, which are specific proteins, and when these important proteins are lacking, digestion cannot take place. This supports the theory that the nucleus contains the information necessary for the cell to synthesize specific proteins.

The nuclear membrane actually contains many small pores (Figure 3–3) which are passageways for the exchange of materials between the nuclear and cytoplasmic regions. These pores are roughly 400 Å in diameter and appear to be evenly distributed over the membrane.

CHROMOSOMES

The nucleus contains a fluid (nucleoplasm) similar to the watery, nonmembranous cytoplasm. Long, threadlike chromosomes composed of DNA and protein are suspended in this nuclear sap. When observed under a light microscope, the chromosomes appear to be a network of fibers; the original term "chromatin network" was based on this observation. This term is still used occasionally, but we know today that the DNA-protein threads are simple uncoiled chromosomes of quite definite individual structure.

As described in Chapter 2, the chromosomes contain the genetic information necessary for the development and maintenance of each cell in the organism. Chapter 9 will deal specifically with the genetic mechanism of inheritance. At this point it is important to know only that the DNA in the chromosomes contains coded information that assures the proper organization and continuation of life processes.

NUCLEOLUS

In addition to the chromosomes, the nucleus of most cells contains one or more smaller bodies called nucleoli. Each nucleolus is produced by a specific chromosome after cell division and contains a large amount of RNA. The function of the nucleolus was not understood for over a hundred years after its discovery. We know today that the nucleolus stores ribosomal RNA which is transported to the endoplasmic reticulum and functions in the synthesis of specific proteins.

DNA AND THE CODE

DNA is a molecule composed of repeating pairs of nucleotides. It is believed that nitrogen base pairs are arranged in some meaningful code that can be transcribed by the cell at the time of protein synthesis. It is further hypothesized that a linear sequence of nucleotides provides protein synthesis information. The question then is how many nucleotides are involved in each "unit" of information. Since proteins are made up of different combinations of about 23 different amino acids, a workable code must be capable of "recognizing" each of these amino acids. If the code were "one nucleotide—one amino acid," only four amino acids could be coded, because there are only four different DNA nucleotides. If a sequence of two nucleotides were used, 16 amino acids could be recognized ($4^2 = 16$). Sequences of three nucleotides could handle the operation ($4^3 = 64$) with some to spare. If the code were analogous to a language of letters and words, it would not be unreasonable to have some *triplet nucleotides* for use as synonyms and punctuation. The unit of genetic information, known as a *codon*, is composed of three nucleotides and specifies one particular amino acid. This is referred to as *triplet coding,* and has been verified in the laboratory using the nucleic acids of bacteria. Investigators are presently working to learn the full details of the code and its transcription.

PROTEIN SYNTHESIS

The synthesis of proteins within the cell illustrates the important relationship between the nucleus and the cytoplasm. This relationship involves the chromosomes (DNA), the various types of RNA, and the ribosomes in the cytoplasm. The production of specific proteins begins with DNA, which contains the "master blueprint" or the original code. The RNA, known as *messenger RNA* (mRNA), is synthesized in certain areas of the chromosomal DNA and is ordered according to a specific nucleotide sequence. Thus the coded message is transferred from DNA to the single-stranded messenger RNA. Coded mRNA leaves the nucleus and attaches to the polyribosome complex in the cytoplasm. At this point another type of RNA known as *transfer RNA* (tRNA) is attracted to the messenger RNA. Transfer RNA, which is synthesized in the nucleus, appears to be a folded chain that contains four areas of unpaired nitrogen bases (Figure 3–16, part 5). A set of three unpaired bases at one end recognizes and at-

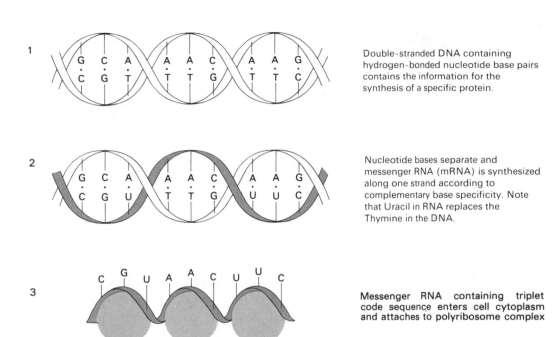

1   Double-stranded DNA containing hydrogen-bonded nucleotide base pairs contains the information for the synthesis of a specific protein.

2   Nucleotide bases separate and messenger RNA (mRNA) is synthesized along one strand according to complementary base specificity. Note that Uracil in RNA replaces the Thymine in the DNA.

3   Messenger RNA containing triplet code sequence enters cell cytoplasm and attaches to polyribosome complex

Transfer RNA attaches to specific amino acids in the cytoplasm. ATP is required to form the linkage. One phosphate is lost from ATP during the energy transfer and ADP is formed. tRNA brings the amino acids into position along the mRNA and the three unpaired bases "recognize" the mRNA codon.

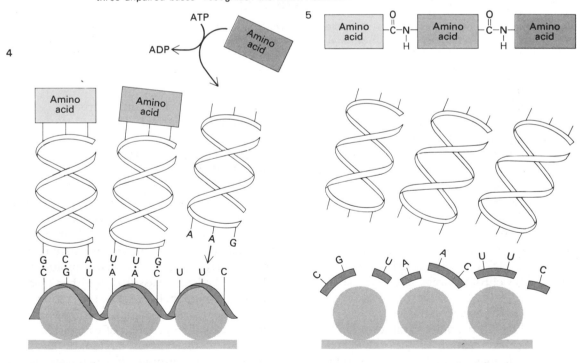

Figure 3·16   An outline of the individual steps involved in the synthesis of a polypeptide.

73

Figure 3·17 Electron micrograph of nucleolar DNA from a salamander egg synthesizing precursor molecules of ribosomal RNA. The long axial filaments are composed of DNA and the lateral fibrils are RNA molecules coated with protein. This is apparently the first photograph of DNA-directed synthesis of RNA and protein. Magnification X 25,000. (Courtesy of O. L. Miller, Jr., and Barbara R. Beatty, Biology Division, Oak Ridge National Laboratory.)

taches to a specific amino acid while the unpaired bases at the other end recognize the mRNA triplet codon. A different set of bases corresponds to each amino acid. ATP is required at this point to activate the amino acids for attachment to the tRNA. The mRNA and tRNA now come together on the surfaces of the ribosomes on the endoplasmic reticulum (polyribosome complex) and peptide bonds are formed between the ordered amino acids. Ribosomal RNA is synthesized in the nucleolar area of the chromosomes and may be stored in the nucleolus for some time before its attachment to the endoplasmic reticulum (Figure 3–17). The important "transcription" between the information in the codon and the proper sequence of amino acids is thus accomplished. The individual steps are outlined in Figure 3–16. The entire process is summarized in Figure 3–18.

TYPES OF CELLS—PROTISTS, PLANTS, AND ANIMALS

In the foregoing description of cell structure and function we were concerned with a general understanding of living cells. It is impossible to speak of a typical cell. Generalizations have been made, however, by many biologists in which all cells are classified as either plant or animal. Others believe this separation into two groups to be inadequate to present the true picture. The problem of categorizing cell types can be solved to some extent by considering three main groups of organisms rather than two.

tRNA synthesized by
DNA in the nucleus

④ tRNA pick
up specific
amino acids

ATP
ADP

ATP
ADP

nuclear pore

③ mRNA moves
to polyribosomes

⑤ amino acids into position along
the mRNA

⑥ polypeptide synthesis

rRNA
synthesized by
DNA in nucleus

tRNA released

Figure 3·18   A diagrammatic summary of protein synthesis in the cell. The numbered steps are the same as those described in Figure 3·16.

PROTISTAN CELLS

Many organisms exist in nature as single cells (*Euglena,* Appendix). Some organisms are simply aggregations of similar cells—that is, a cellular colony (*Volvox,* Appendix), and many organisms are constructed of a body of rather similar cells (fungi; and brown, red, and green algae, Appendix). The cells in all these examples often have a mixture of the characteristics we generally associate with either plant or animal cells. In other words, a large group of living forms cannot be called true plants or animals. For convenience, and for a clearer understanding of evolution, these organisms can be classified as a category or a *kingdom* known as *protista* (from the Greek word, *protistos,* meaning "first").

A good example of a protist is the green unicellular *Euglena.* It moves with a whiplike flagellum and sometimes ingests food like an animal cell. But, since *Euglena* contains chlorophyll, it has the ability to synthesize food like a typical green plant cell. Most authorities agree that the flagellate protistans are living examples of some of the earliest forms of life. In other words, it is thought that the ancestors of cells which possess both animal and plant characteristics probably gave rise to the plant and animal groups.

PLANT AND ANIMAL CELLS

On higher levels of development organisms are commonly classified either as plant or animal. Plant cells generally have cell walls, large central vacuoles, and contain chlorophyll but lack centrioles. Animals, on the other hand, have cells that contain centrioles, lack cell walls and chlorophyll, but are capable of locomotion. It can be assumed that animal cells have lost chlorophyll and thus the ability to make their own food. Plant cells, on the other hand, have lost centrioles and, generally, the ability to move.

A summary of the characteristics of the cells of organisms is presented in Figure 3–19. This method of grouping the cells of organ-

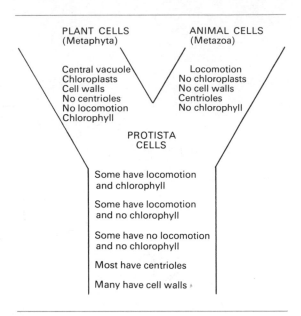

Figure 3·19 Summary of the characteristics of the cells of the three kingdoms of living organisms and their possible evolutionary relationships.

isms into three kingdoms (Protista, Metaphyta, and Metazoa) is also used in the classification section in the Appendix.

The Plant Cell

The plant cell commonly has an outer wall that is hardened and nonliving. Unlike the cell membrane, plant walls have no selective permeability. Any substance that can pass through the cell wall approaches the cell membrane which lies just inside the wall. Since the cell wall is nonliving, most substances pass through it. It is composed of two layers, an outer primary wall, which is the first to be formed, and an inner secondary wall. The major structural component of these walls is cellulose (1,4 beta-linked glucose units, Chapter 2). An additional layer may be produced when two cells lie closely adjacent. A thin middle lamella is formed between the primary walls of the two cells and contains a colloidal substance called pectin (polymers of the six-carbon sugar galactose). Powdered pectin is the familiar substance added to fruits to make jellies. In older tissues the soft

Figure 3·20 A diagram of the microscopic structure of the cell walls of four adjacent plant cells.

Figure 3·21 A diagram of a leaf cell of *Elodea*, a common aquarium plant, showing the major structural components.

pectin may become hardened by the accumulation of calcium to form calcium pectate. Evidently the middle lamella is important in holding cells together. In woody plants a tough, gluelike substance called *lignin* is impregnated in the cellulose walls. Lignin helps to bind the wood-fiber cells together to form a solid material. Figure 3–20 shows the microscopic structure of cell walls.

The central vacuole is very common in plant cells and is functional in the cell's water balance. Since the nonliving cell wall produces a rigid framework for the cell's contents, the cell is unable to swell to accommodate changes in osmotic conditions. The central vacuole therefore is important in regulating the osmotic pressure balance by losing or gaining water. The vacuole contains a slightly viscous colloid which may include salts, mineral ions, proteins, sugars, and pigments. The typical structure of a plant cell is shown in Figure 3–21.

SUMMARIZING PRINCIPLES

All organisms are composed of individual units called cells. A cell is divided into two regions—the cytoplasm and the nucleus. Cytoplasmic cell parts include: cell membrane, centrioles, golgi apparatus, mitochondria, endoplasmic reticulum, lysosomes, and ribosomes. The nucleus includes the nuclear membrane, chromosomes, and nucleoli.

The movement of materials into cells may occur in the following ways: phagocytosis, pinocytosis, diffusion, osmosis, and active transport.

The fundamental physical state of the cell cytoplasm is a colloidal suspension which can exist in sol or gel states.

The nucleus is the functional control center for all cell activities. The DNA of the chromosomes provides the information necessary for the production of specific proteins, some of which function as enzymes. The actual synthesis of proteins occurs in the cytoplasm on the ribosomes. The transcription of the DNA code into specific proteins involves mRNA and tRNA.

Plant and animal cells can be compared in the following ways: Plant cells have cell walls, large central vacuoles, generally contain chlorophyll, and lack centrioles. Animal cells contain centrioles and lack cell walls and chlorophyll. Many protistan cells show combinations and variations of these characteristics.

REVIEW QUESTIONS

1. How has the electron microscope assisted biologists in determining the construction and function of cells? What advantages does the electron microscope offer over the light microscope? What advantages does the light microscope provide?

2. The cells of the pancreas contain large numbers of golgi apparatus. What might you conclude about the function of these cells?

3. Describe the structural features of the cell membrane or the process which might account for each of the following:
   (a) glucose molecules pass into intestinal cells
   (b) alcohol molecules pass quickly into cells lining the stomach
   (c) positively or negatively charged particles may be selectively taken into certain cells
   (d) white blood cells engulf and destroy bacteria

4. When sea urchin eggs are placed in distilled water they swell and burst. Explain why.

5. Centrioles, cilia, and flagella show a similar structural organization. What evolutionary or developmental relationships does this suggest?

6. Why don't the large molecules and organelles within a living cell settle out in response to gravity?

7. When the nucleus is removed from a cell it survives only a short time. Discounting its inability to reproduce, why does the cell die?

8. Sketch an original diagram which shows the relationship between DNA and RNA in the synthesis of specific proteins. Include the roles of mRNA, tRNA, and rRNA and indicate their location in the cell.

9. In humans wide variations occur in the types and amounts of blood plasma proteins among individuals. From your knowledge of the total process of protein synthesis explain why this is so.

10. Compare the structural characteristics of plant, animal, and protistan cells.

SUPPLEMENTARY READINGS

Agranoff, Bernard W., "Memory and Protein Synthesis," *Scientific American*, June, 1967.

Allfrey, Vincent G., and Alfred E. Mirsky, "How Cells Make Molecules," *Scientific American*, September, 1961.

Allison, Anthony, "Lysosomes and Disease," *Scientific American*, November, 1967.

Brachet, Jean, "The Living Cell," *Scientific American*, September, 1961.

Clowes, Royston, *The Structure of Life*, Baltimore, Penguin, 1967.

Crick, F. H. C., "The Genetic Code," *Scientific American*, October, 1962.

Crick, F. H. C., "The Genetic Code: III," *Scientific American*, October, 1966.

Dippell, Ruth V., "Ultrastructure and Function," in W. H. Johnson and W. C. Steere, eds., *This Is Life*, New York, Holt, Rinehart and Winston, 1962.

Gorini, Luigi, "Antibiotics and the Genetic Code," *Scientific American*, April, 1966.

Grimstone, A. V., *The Electron Microscope in Biology*, New York, St. Martin's Press, 1968.

Hayashi, Teru, "How Cells Move," *Scientific American*, September, 1961.

Hayflick, Leonard, "Human Cells and Aging," *Scientific American*, March, 1968.

Hokin, Lowell E., and Mabel R. Hokin, "The Chemistry of Cell Membranes," *Scientific American*, October, 1965.

Holter, Heinz, "How Things Get into Cells," *Scientific American*, September, 1961.

Hurwitz, Jerard, and J. J. Furth, "Messenger RNA," *Scientific American*, February, 1962.

Mercer, E. A., *Cells, Their Structure and Function*, New York, Natural History Press, 1962.

Neutra, Marian, and C. P. Leblond, "The Golgi Apparatus," *Scientific American*, February, 1969.

Nomura, Masayasu, "Ribosomes," *Scientific American*, October, 1969.

Paul, John, *Cell Biology*, Stanford, Calif., Stanford University Press, 1966.

Rich, Alexander, "Polyribosomes," *Scientific American*, December, 1963.

Satir, Peter, "Cilia," *Scientific American*, February, 1961.

Sharon, Nathan, "The Bacterial Cell Wall," *Scientific American*, May, 1969.

Siekevitz, Philip, "Powerhouse of the Cell," *Scientific American*, July, 1957.

Solomon, Arthur K., "Pores in the Cell Membrane," *Scientific American*, December, 1960.

Swanson, C. P., *The Cell*, 2nd ed., Englewood Cliffs, N.J., Prentice-Hall, 1964.

Wilson, G. B., and J. H. Morrison, *Cytology*, New York, Reinhold, 1966.

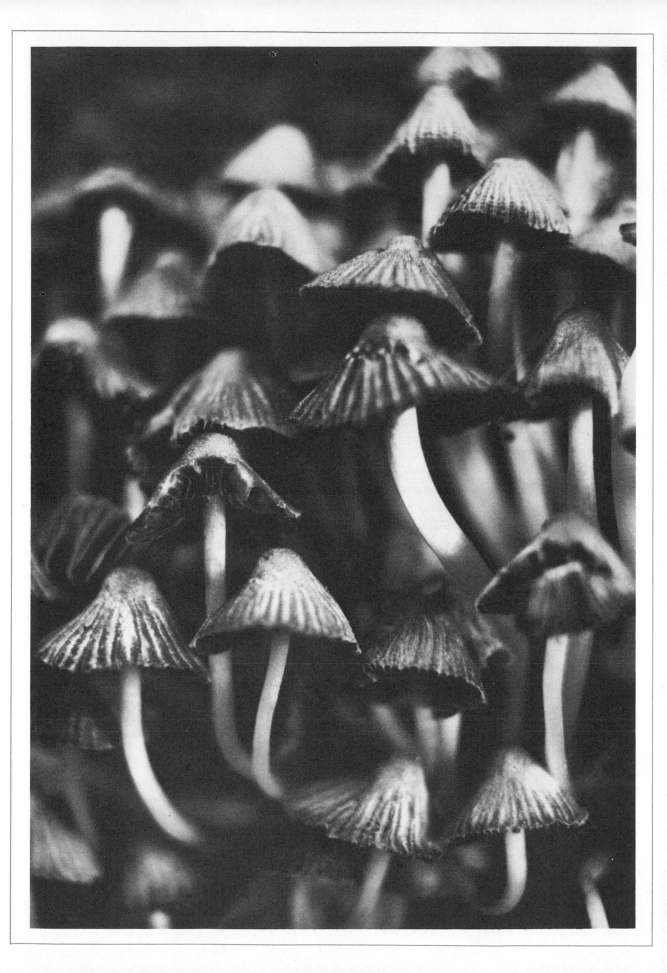

4

Biological Architecture: Tissues, Organs, and Organisms

In the preceding chapter an analogy was drawn between cells and bricks as building blocks. Like individual bricks, cells are ultimately organized into functional structures such as walls. Groups of similar cells working together to perform specific functions are called *tissues*. Since there are several different types of tissues, it is necessary to discuss the major types in order to understand their function. With tissues, as with cells, scientists frequently distinguish between plant and animal. Even though each group has developed tissues to serve common functions, the differences are sufficient to warrant separate discussion. Some of the common functions of tissues include (1) protection, (2) support, (3) circulation, (4) growth, and (5) reproduction.

PLANT TISSUES

Plant tissues are identified and named primarily according to their location and function. The four basic types of plant tissues are meristematic (growth), vascular (conduction), fundamental (storage and support), and epidermal (protection).

Before discussing specific examples of higher plant tissues, we should consider briefly their general organization and evolutionary pattern. The classification system used today is an attempt to demonstrate the probable evolutionary relationships among organisms (see Appendix). In plants these evolutionary relationships are most evident in the cellular structure and reproductive cycles.

Although mosses do not possess roots, stems, or leaves homologous to the higher plants, they do have simple tissue organizations that perform functions similar to those of the higher plants. For example, small hairlike *rhizoids* serve to anchor the plant and absorb water, and the "stem" provides the rigidity necessary for erect growth. The leafy outgrowths contain chloroplasts for making food and the areas at the tips of stems form sex organs. The complexity in tissue organization increases from the mosses through the ferns to the conifers and flowering plants. Since the distribution of the basic tissues varies greatly throughout the plant kingdom, we will limit our observations to the more familiar seed plants that possess true roots, stems, and leaves—the *gymnosperms* (conifers) and the *angiosperms* (flowering plants).

Angiosperms may be divided into the orders Dicotyledonae and Monocotyledonae. Dicots are characterized by having (1) two "seed leaves" or *cotyledons* upon germination, (2) net-veined leaves, (3) flower parts in fours or fives, and (4) fibrovascular tissue arranged in concentric rings. Dicots may be herbaceous (they generally lack lignin) like the pansy or they may be woody like the apple tree. Monocots, on the other hand, possess (1) a single cotyledon, (2) parallel-veined leaves, (3) flower parts in threes, and (4) scattered fibrovascular bundles. Typical examples are the lily and corn plants.

MERISTEMATIC TISSUES

These tissues provide for growth in plants. All the tissues of seed plants differentiate from a rapidly dividing group of cells known as the *apical meristem.* The subsequent development and growth of a maturing plant is due primarily

Figure 4·1   Location of tissues in a mature stem of elderberry, a woody angiosperm. (Courtesy of Eliott Weier.)

to these apical meristems, stem and root tip, and the lateral cambiums, vascular and cork. The vascular cambium is one of several tissue types found in a gymnosperm or a woody dicot stem (Figure 4–1). The cellular regions of a growing root tip and an apical meristem are illustrated in Figure 4–2.

The cambium layer, which is present as a complete ring of tissue in gymnosperms and woody dicots, gives rise to the vascular tissues. This complete cambium sheath is sometimes absent in herbaceous dicots and is always absent in monocots.

VASCULAR TISSUE

The vascular tissues of plants are the *xylem* and *phloem.* The structure of the monocot

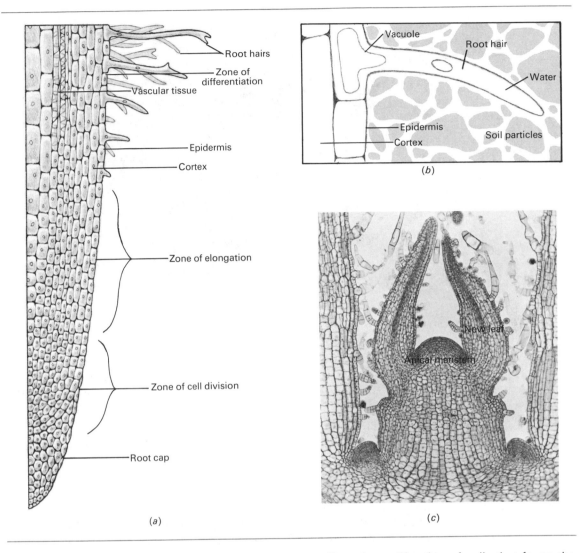

Labels in figure (a):
- Root hairs
- Zone of differentiation
- Vascular tissue
- Epidermis
- Cortex
- Zone of elongation
- Zone of cell division
- Root cap

(a)

Labels in figure (b):
- Vacuole
- Root hair
- Water
- Epidermis
- Cortex
- Soil particles

(b)

Labels in figure (c):
- New leaf
- Apical meristem

(c)

Figure 4·2 (a) Longitudinal section of a growing root. Note the proliferation of cells that forms the root cap. (b) A diagram of a root hair in soil. (c) Growing stem tip of *Coleus* showing meristematic tissue. (Courtesy of Triarch, Inc., Ripon, Wis.)

stem, such as corn, is perhaps the most graphic example of the location of the xylem and phloem. The vascular bundles, which are groups of xylem and phloem, are scattered throughout the supportive tissue of the stem. The arrangement of the vascular bundles resembles a monkey face. The brow is composed of thin-walled phloem cells (sieve tubes) and companion cells, and the eyes and nose are vessel tubes of xylem. What appears as the mouth is a ruptured xylem vessel, resulting from stem growth that forms an air space (Figure 4–3).

In woody plants the cambium produces at its inner surface, the xylem cells, which conduct water and minerals, and toward the outside, the cambium produces phloem, the food-transporting tissue (Figure 4–1). Each

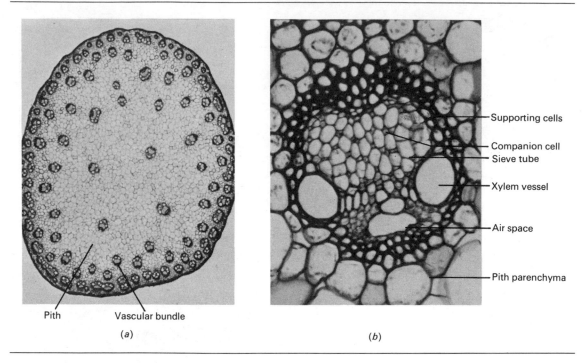

Pith   Vascular bundle

(a)   (b)

Figure 4·3 (a) Cross section of a corn stem showing scattered vascular bundles; magnification about X 20. Note that the "monkey faces" all look toward the center of the stem; therefore the phloem is external to the xylem. (b) A single vascular bundle similar to those in (a); magnification about X 350. (Photo courtesy of Eliott Weier.)

year following the spring and summer growth, the old phloem layer dies and is pushed outward by the new spring phloem where it remains as bark. The xylem layers are left on the inside as wood. Thus the rings of xylem present in a stem indicate the age of the plant. It must be noted, however, that a year's growth of xylem shows two bands—an inner band of large vessels known as spring wood and an adjacent outer band of smaller vessels of summer wood. The greater availability of water in the spring allows faster growth and the formation of larger cells than during the summer.

Xylem

Water and minerals are conducted upward through the xylem from the roots. The leaves thus receive raw materials to use in photosynthesis. Sugar-laden sap moves primarily downward in the phloem to the actively absorbing and growing roots. In the early spring, sap also may rise in the plant to nourish developing buds and flowers.

Xylem tissues in general are composed of two types of conducting tubes: tracheids and vessels. Gymnosperms possess only tracheids, whereas angiosperms contain both tracheids and vessels. The tracheids are elongate cells and somewhat narrowed at the ends. At maturity, in some cells, the nucleus and the cell contents die leaving a large lumen. Thin spots, called pits, along the cell walls allow water and minerals to pass from cell to cell. Thickenings of lignified cellulose along the secondary cell walls form annular reticulated or spiral rings (Figure 4–4).

Although vessel cells found in flowering plants also contain pits, small openings or pores occur at the ends to form a continuous open tube. Vessels have a larger diameter than

84

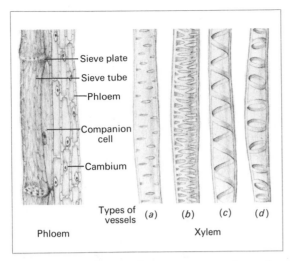

Figure 4·4 Conducting structures of angio-sperms. *Left*, longitudinal section of phloem and cambium; *right*, longitudinal section of xylem vessels: (*a*) pitted, (*b*) reticulated, (*c*) spiral, and (*d*) annular.

tracheids, thus allowing easier passage of fluids. Not all the cells in the xylem are dead. Living xylem parenchyma cells are located in rays throughout the wood and function in food storage and lateral conduction.

Phloem

Living phloem tissue is easily observed as the slick, glistening layer just beneath the bark of a tree. The cells of these food-transporting tissues are unique in that they possess end walls that are perforated with many small pores (Figure 4–4). These end walls are called *sieve plates*. Phloem cells are stacked end to end like xylem cells. Unlike xylem cells, however, phloem cells contain slimy strands of proto-plasm that appear to stretch from cell to cell through the pores of the sieve plates. It is believed that the phloem cell which has no nucleus at maturity is controlled by adjacent, nucleated companion cells through cyto-plasmic connections.

FUNDAMENTAL TISSUES

The regions of the plant stem that are utilized specifically for support and storage are the *pith* and *cortex*. Although the xylem is ob-viously an important supporting tissue in wood plants, its primary function is that of conduction. The three tissues that are col-lectively termed *fundamental* include the *parenchyma, collenchyma,* and *sclerenchyma.*

Parenchyma

This is a thin-walled, living tissue found in the unspecialized regions of all parts of a plant. Parenchyma cells vary in shape, generally contain a central vacuole, and retain their capacity for cell division. These cells function in various ways such as food making, storage, and support.

Collenchyma

Collenchyma is a living tissue that has tough cell walls and often contains chloroplasts in the cytoplasm. The pectin compounds in the cell walls give this tissue strength and elasticity. The cortex cylinder of growing stems and roots often contains this special support tissue.

Sclerenchyma

Sclerenchyma is much less flexible than collenchyma. The secondary cell walls in these tissues become very hard at maturity, and the cells always die at maturity and lose their cytoplasm. Both collenchyma and scleren-chyma may occur in long bundles or sheaths in the cortex and pith. The hard shells of nuts and the gritty texture of pears are due to sclerenchyma cells.

EPIDERMAL TISSUE

The protective outer covering of plant struc-tures is termed the *epidermis* (outer skin). The cells of this tissue are generally one layer and organized into a thin sheath. The shape of epidermal cells is generally polyhedral—having more than four sides.

The epidermis of plants, especially leaves, shows several functional adaptations. The upper and lower epidermis of a leaf usually has a secreted cuticle of a waxy substance

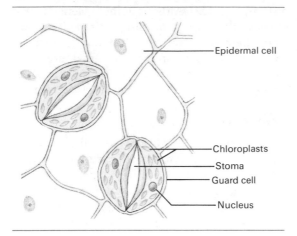

Figure 4·5 Stomata in the epidermis of a leaf.

Labels: Epidermal cell, Chloroplasts, Stoma, Guard cell, Nucleus

known as *cutin* which helps the leaf retain water. Many stems and leaves possess tiny hairs which also reduce evaporation. Perhaps the most unique epidermal structures are the tiny openings principally on the underside of leaves that regulate the exchange of water and gases. These openings, called *stomata,* are actively controlled by the swelling or shrinking of two adjacent *guard cells* (Figure 4–5). The action of the guard cells appears to be controlled by osmotic pressure. When the osmotic pressure is high and more water moves into the guard cells, the stomata open. The loss of water to adjacent epidermal cells causes the guard cells to become limp and the openings to close. In general, the production of sugar by the guard-cell chloroplasts during daylight causes increased osmotic pressure and swelling. At night the osmotic pressure decreases due to the utilization of sugar for energy and its conversion to larger starch molecules. Recall that osmotic conditions are determined by the number of dissolved particles. In mature woody stems, the original epidermis has been destroyed by the developing bark, which is continuously being pushed outward and eroded.

We have seen that plants possess tissues which are related to their particular needs: epidermal for protection, meristematic for growth, fundamental for support, and vas-cular for conduction. Not all plants contain all these tissues and certainly not in the same ratio. For example, the most simple land plants, such as mosses and liverworts, do not contain vascular tissues at all.

ANIMAL TISSUES

Animals possess unique tissues because they have the complex characteristics of locomotion and nervous systems. Again these tissues can be organized along functional lines. The basic animal tissues include epithelial (protection), connective (support), muscle (locomotion), nerve (communication), and blood (circulation).

EPITHELIAL TISSUE

These tissues cover the structures of the body or line the cavities. At this point we should add that the cells of epithelial tissues may also function in secretion or absorption. Certain glands such as the intestinal glands, which lie beneath the inner intestinal lining, empty secretions into the gut through special ducts. Nutrients provided through the action of digestive enzymes are actively absorbed into the

Figure 4·6 Examples of epithelial types: (*a*) squamous, (*b*) cuboidal, (*c*) columnar, (*d*) ciliated columnar.

(a)   (b)

(c)   (d)

Figure 4·7 Stratified squamous epithelium of the human hand; magnification X 500. Note the sloughing of dead cells.

circulatory system through the intestinal lining. The primary function of the epithelial tissues, however, is protection. The shapes of epithelial cells may be *squamous, cuboidal,* or *columnar* (Figure 4–6).

Squamous Cells

Squamous or "pavement" epithelium is composed of extremely thin cells. In most cases, the cells are so thin that the nucleus bulges out when viewed from the edge. This type of tissue lines the inside of the mouth, the inside body cavity, and also covers the body as skin epidermis. In the skin, these cells are stacked in thick layers called stratified squamous epithelium (Figure 4–7).

Cuboidal Cells

Cuboidal epithelium cells, as the name indicates, are cube-shaped and make up the

87

Figure 4·8 Cuboidal epithelium of the collecting tubules of the mammalian kidney; magnification X 500.

tissues found as the lining of special ducts. Particularly important are the urine-collecting tubules in the kidneys (Figure 4–8).

Columnar Cells

Columnar cells are taller than cuboidal and form the lining tissue of many organs. The most common example is the lining of the small intestine (Figure 4–9). Both columnar and cuboidal cells can possess tiny hairlike structures called *cilia* (Figure 4–6). Cilia have the ability to move in a whiplike, rhythmical motion. Ducts that require a continuous clearing of foreign particles, such as the nasal passages or trachea, contain many ciliated cells. Recent research suggests that the movement of a cilium is due to contractile proteins in the cilium itself. It is not yet clear just how the contraction is initiated or how the regular rhythm is coordinated.

Figure 4·9 Columnar epithelium lining the small intestine of the dog; magnification X 500. The large cells are mucus-secreting goblet cells.

CONNECTIVE TISSUE

The tissues responsible for support in animal bodies fall into several categories: loose or areolar connective tissue, tendon, cartilage, bone, and fat-storing or adipose tissue. The connective tissues contain tough white fibers of a protein called *collagen* and sometimes yellow elastic fibers also made of protein.

Depending on the location and function of these tissues, the arrangement may be loose as in the mesenteries which support internal organs (Figure 4–10) or more compact as in the underlying layers of the skin. The loose connective tissue allows for movement and pliability in an organ. This is especially important in the digestive tract, since the food must be moved through the tube by rhythmic muscular contractions (peristalsis). Dense con-

Figure 4·10   Loose areolar connective tissue from the mesentery of a cat; magnification X 1000.

nective tissues such as tendon, cartilage, and bone are found where structural strength is required.

Loose or Areolar Tissue

This type of tissue forms the *mesentery* membranes that hold the organs of the body cavities in place, and through its elastic properties it also helps hold the skin to the muscles. Undifferentiated cells called *fibroblasts* are the most common in this tissue, and next in number are large phagocytic cells known as *macrophages*. The fibroblasts synthesize collagenous and elastic fibers and the macrophages ingest foreign substances (refer to Figure 3–5). Figure 4–10 is a photograph of cat mesentery.

Cartilage

The function of cartilage is to give firm support without rigidity. Basically, the various types of cartilage are similar in cellular detail. The

90

Figure 4·11 Hyaline cartilage from the trachea of a cat; magnification X 1000. M, matrix; C, chondrocyte.

living cartilage cells, or *chondrocytes*, secrete a matrix material around themselves that is composed of a polysaccharide and protein material. All cartilage contains protein fibrils to a greater or lesser degree and thus is classified as a fibrous connective tissue. The hyaline cartilage in the end of the nose, lining the joints between bones and forming the tracheal rings, is tough but flexible, whereas the outer ear cartilage contains springy elastic fibers and is known as elastic cartilage. Figure 4–11 is a photograph of hyaline cartilage from a tracheal ring. A very strong cartilage, fibrocartilage, contains a dense network of protein fibers and is found between the vertebrae as intervertebral discs.

Adipose Tissue

Adipose tissue is composed of special cells that store fat. The nuclei of the mature cells are always pushed up against one side of the cell membrane by the accumulation of fats in the

Figure 4·12 Adipose (fat) tissue; magnification X 500. The central portion of the cell is filled with fat, which forces the nucleus (N) to the periphery of the cells.

cytoplasm (Figure 4–12). Adipose tissues function in support (packing), protection (overlying organs), and food storage.

Bone

We are all familiar with bone and its function of structural support. A thin section of bone shows a complicated pattern of cells and canals (Figure 4–13). The living bone cells or *osteocytes* are located in tiny chambers called *lacunae* in the compact, calcified bone. The cells are interconnected and also are connected to the central marrow cavity by a network of tiny canals called *canaliculi*. All the nutrients that reach these cells must pass through these tiny channels by way of the main nutrient canal, known as the *Haversian canal*, which brings blood and nerves into the compact bone from the outer covering.

Essentially there are two types of bone tissue, that which develops from an original cartilage "model" (endochondrial ossification) and that which replaces a membrane (intra-

membranous ossification). The long bones of the arms and legs, for example, develop slowly from cartilage whereas some bones of the cranium form within a special membrane.

MUSCLE TISSUE

Three types of muscle tissue may be recognized: smooth, striated, and cardiac. Although all of these have a contractile function, each is highly specialized.

Smooth Muscle

These muscle tissues have the simplest cells of the three types. An individual muscle cell is called a *fiber* and is capable of independent contraction. The muscle cytoplasm, or *sarcoplasm,* of each spindle-shaped cell contains contractile protein fibers called *myofibrils*. A smooth muscle is composed of many cells grouped into a bundle (Figure 4–14). Smooth muscles are sometimes called *involuntary* muscles because their action is not directly

Figure 4·13 Photomicrograph of a thin section of ground bone; X 1000. H, Haversian canal (main nutrient canal). (Courtesy of Triarch, Inc., Ripon, Wis.)

under conscious control. They are located in the visceral organs and are responsible for such movements as *peristalsis*. Smooth muscle fibers are also found in the walls of blood vessels and the uterus.

Striated Muscle

Movement of striated or skeletal muscle tissues is primarily under conscious direction. The term *striated* comes from the observation of large numbers of crossbands along the fibers under the microscope. Careful observation with the electron microscope coupled with chemical analysis has demonstrated that the

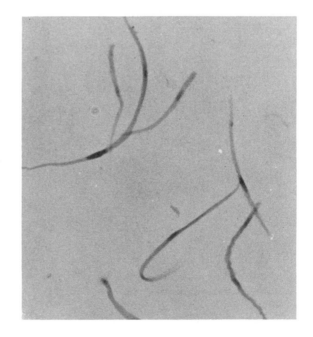

Figure 4·14 Smooth muscle fibers teased from the intestine wall; X 450. These fibers are generally spindle-shaped and have no striations.

Figure 4·15 Striated muscle fibers from the tongue of a rat. The banded pattern is due to the arrangement of the actin and myosin protein fibrils as shown in Figure 4·16; X 500.

striation patterns are produced by specific arrangements of two protein fibrils—actin and myosin. As in smooth muscle the myofibrils compose the contractile elements of the muscle fiber. A striated muscle fiber (cell) contains several nuclei, all of which are located near the membrane, and therefore is termed *multinucleate* (Figure 4–15). The contractile myofibrils within each fiber show a definite banded pattern or striations, which are set off by dark-staining bands called Z lines (Figure 4–16). The banded area between the Z lines is termed a *sarcomere*. The overlapping arrangement of myosin (thick filament) and actin (thin filament) proteins produces the bands of differing density within the sarco-

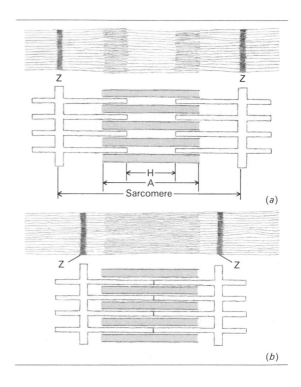

Figure 4·16 A model of striated muscle. Myosin is shown in color. The regions of crossbanding are lettered as they appear in relaxed muscle in (*a*). Part (*b*) illustrates the contracted state.

Figure 4·17 Photomicrograph of cardiac muscle of a dog showing intercalated discs; X 500.

mere. In cross section, the filaments are arranged in hexagonal patterns.

The picture of the muscle we have presented so far is that of the tissue at rest. What happens when the muscle contracts? A nerve impulse or mild electric shock will cause a certain number of muscle fibers to contract depending on the strength of the stimulus. Physiological studies have shown that increasing the strength of the stimulus causes a corresponding increase in the strength of muscle contraction. In vertebrate muscle, each fiber contracts to its greatest extent when it is stimulated; thus muscle contractions of varied strengths depend on the number of fibers that are stimulated.

At the moment of contraction, the actin filaments move together in a horizontal sliding action. This action changes the pattern (Figure 4–16) as follows: the Z bands are brought closer together, since the actin filaments are anchored to these bands, and the H zones, which represent the spaces between the actin

filaments, disappear. Because this shortening occurs throughout the entire muscle, a great contraction can be accomplished. Following the contraction phase, the actin filaments return to their original relaxed condition.

Cardiac Muscle

Cardiac or heart muscle is a unique tissue that begins regular rhythmic contractions during embryonic development and continues to beat throughout the lifetime of an organism. In vertebrates the control of the heartbeat rhythm is principally through nerve impulses originating in the *medulla* of the brain. The contractility of the muscle itself, however, appears to be inherent in the tissue. The fine structure of the myofibrils of cardiac muscle is similar to that described for skeletal muscle. The nucleus of a cardiac muscle cell, however, is located in the center of the fiber rather than along the outer membrane. Each cardiac muscle fiber contains only one nucleus.

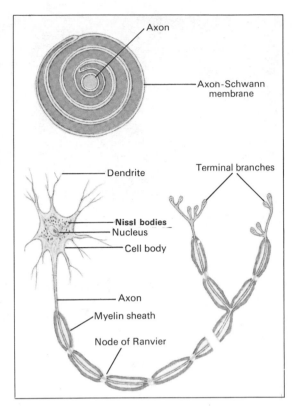

Figure 4·18 Multipolar neurons from the cerebellum of a rat; X 350. (From Hild.)

Figure 4·19 Diagram of a myelinated neuron. At upper left is an enlarged view of a cross section of an axon and the myelin sheath.

Cardiac muscle is oriented in flat, overlapping sheets and surrounds the heart cavities. The individual fibers are broad and many-sided in shape—that is, the cell membranes are irregular and branching. Early investigators observed dark-staining transverse bands in the muscle. It was once thought that these bands were in some way related to the heartbeat and apparent tirelessness of the muscle. The bands were called *intercalated discs* but are now known to be only the thickened, adjacent cell membranes of individual muscle cells (Figure 4–17).

NERVE TISSUE

The tissues that provide for communication and integration in animals are found in the brain, spinal cord, peripheral nerves, and nerve endings. The fundamental element of nerve tissue is the nerve cell or *neuron*. Although several other specialized cell types are also found in this tissue, the neuron is the "functional unit."

A typical neuron is composed of a cell body and filamentous extensions. These extensions associate with similar ones from other neurons to form a communication "chain" (Figure 4–18). The cytoplasm of a neuron contains a nucleus, nucleolus, mitochondria, Golgi apparatus, and many small particles of RNA and protein known as Nissl bodies (Figure 4–19). Cellular extensions, *axons* and *dendrites*, extend from the cell body. In some cases these extensions may reach over a meter in length. A nerve impulse travels along the cell membrane from a dendrite toward the axon. In this manner the axon of one cell excites one or several

96

dendrites of the next cell and the impulse is carried the length of the neuron "chain." (The formation and propagation of the nerve impulse will be explained in detail in Chapter 9.) In other words, the nerve impulse travels toward the cell body along the dendrites and away from the cell body along the axon. Where the axon connects with a dendrite, small bulbous structures are found which are known as *synaptic knobs* (Figure 4–20). A small space of approximately 200 Å, called a *synaptic cleft,* lies between these endings. The traveling nerve impulse triggers tiny vesicles in the synaptic knob to secrete *acetylcholine,* which in turn excites the adjacent dendrites. The chemical reactions at the synapse keep nerve impulses flowing in a specific direction (axons to dendrites). This is possible, since only the dendrite membrane has chemically sensitive receptor sites. Immediately following the production of acetylcholine, an enzyme splits the chemical into nonreactive components. The synapse thus is prepared to transfer a new impulse.

The Nissl bodies, first described in 1876, were thought to be related to the nuclear material, since they were stained by nuclear dyes. It was supposed that the Nissl substance somehow supplemented the nuclear function during nerve activity. Using modern techniques, however, it has been learned that the Nissl substance corresponds to the ribosomal parts of other cells. It is understandable, then, that a concentrated complex of protein-producing organelles are needed for these cells that contain such large amounts of cytoplasm and undergo intense activity.

The central area of the spinal cord of vertebrates is gray in color, shaped like a butterfly, and is composed of nerve cell bodies. The peripheral areas of the cord, however, are composed of white, glistening nerve tracts known as the white matter. The white appearance is due to myelin sheaths that surround the axon (Figure 4–19). Gaps which expose the axon membrane occur at intervals along the myelin sheath and are called *nodes of Ranvier.* This special fatty sheath is formed

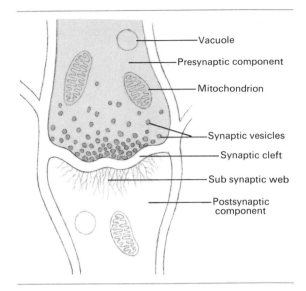

Figure 4·20 Diagram of the synaptic region between a dendrite and an axon showing a synaptic cleft and a synaptic knob. (Redrawn with permission from De Robertis.)

around the axon by nearby Schwann cells. During development, these cells actually wrap themselves around the axon to form a spiral layer of membrane and myelin. It has been discovered that the speed of impulse transmission in myelinated nerves is about four times as great as in nonmyelinated nerves. At first it was thought that the fatty sheath only protected the cell membrane like the insulation on an electric wire, but it was later theorized that the impulse jumps along the axon from node to node. In this event, impulses would not have to pass through the entire length of the axon membrane, and the time required to reach the synapse would be greatly shortened. The gray-matter neurons have no myelin sheaths and are sometimes referred to as "naked."

BLOOD TISSUE

Tissues, then, are made up of various kinds of cells, and these cells must be nourished. In vertebrates and most higher animals the blood, within a circulating system, serves many important functions such as transportation for

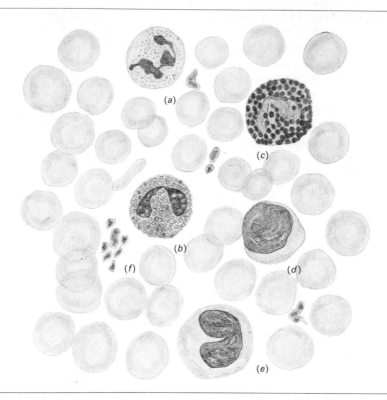

Figure 4·21   Cellular components of human blood: (*a*) neutrophils with multilobed nuclei; (*b*) eosinophils with large red granules; (*c*) basophils with large purple-staining granules; (*d*) lymphocytes with large nuclei; (*e*) monocytes; and (*f*) platelets. The numerous enucleate corpuscles in each plate are erythrocytes.

nutrients, oxygen, carbon dioxide, metabolic wastes, hormones, and proteins. Blood is composed of several cell types carried in a fluid matrix or *plasma*. Oxygen-transporting pigments may be dissolved in the plasma, as in the earthworm, or they may be contained in cells.

In man, the cellular components make up about 45 percent of the blood, and all that remains is generally called plasma. Noncellular plasma contains water, dissolved salts and nutrients, hormones, gases, and antibodies. In addition, certain proteins such as serum albumin, serum globulin, and fibrinogen (necessary for clotting) are also present.

The cells found in the blood are derived form the same cells that form bone, muscle, and cartilage. This process of the differentia-

tion of early cells into basic tissues will be discussed in Chapter 9.

Red Blood Cells

In vertebrates the oxygen-carrying cells are called red blood cells (RBCs) or *erythrocytes*, due to the presence of the pigment *hemoglobin* which is red. Not all erythrocytes are the same size or shape. For example, the nucleated erythrocytes of amphibian blood are very large and elongated when compared to those of a mammal (24 microns for a frog to 7.7 microns for man). The red blood cells of man, produced in the red bone marrow, are small, biconcave discs which lose their nuclei at maturity (Figure 4–21). The average life span of an enucleate RBC is about 120 days, after which destruction occurs in the spleen or liver.

The red blood cells of all vertebrates, except mammals, possess nuclei.

White Blood Cells

The blood of man and other vertebrates also contains colorless white blood cells (WBCs), or *leucocytes*. The leucocytes are larger than the erythrocytes (10–12 microns) and can be identified by their characteristically shaped nuclei. The function of the leucocytes is primarily the ingestion (phagocytosis) of bacteria and particulate wastes in the bloodstream and tissue fluids.

Classification of WBCs

Leucocytes, most of which are produced in the red bone marrow (Figure 4–21), are classified in two general groups, granular and agranular, depending on the presence or absence of stainable granules in the cytoplasm.

1 Granular
   (a) *Neutrophils* (about 65 percent of all WBCs) possess fine cytoplasmic granules and a multilobed nucleus. These are phagocytic cells which may pass in and out of capillaries to ingest foreign particles.
   (b) *Eosinophils* (about 3 percent of all WBCs) contain very large red-staining cytoplasmic granules and possibly function in antigen-antibody immune reactions (asthma, hayfever, and parasite infections). The nucleus is usually bilobed at maturity.
   (c) *Basophils* (about 1 percent of all WBCs resemble eosinophils in having large cytoplasmic granules. However, the granules stain dark purple and the nucleus may have several lobes. Their function is unknown.
2 Agranular
   (a) *Lymphocytes* (25 percent of all WBCs) have a large nucleus that occupies almost the entire cell. Lymphocytes are produced in lymphoid tissue (lymph nodes and spleen) and function in the production of antibodies.
   (b) *Monocytes* (6 percent of all WBCs) also possess a large nucleus which is kidney shaped. They function in phagocytosis and some enter the connective tissues to become giant macrophage cells that ingest foreign substances.

PLATELETS

Platelets are fragments of large cells, megakaryocytes, which are produced in the bone marrow. These fragments contain the enzyme *thromboplastin*, which is essential for initiating blood clotting (Figure 4–22). A

Figure 4·22 A diagram of the interacting substances and their sources in blood clotting. Prothrombin and fibrinogen are soluble blood proteins produced in the liver. Vitamin K is necessary for the synthesis of prothrombin. A deficiency of Vitamin K will produce symptoms similar to bleeders' disease.

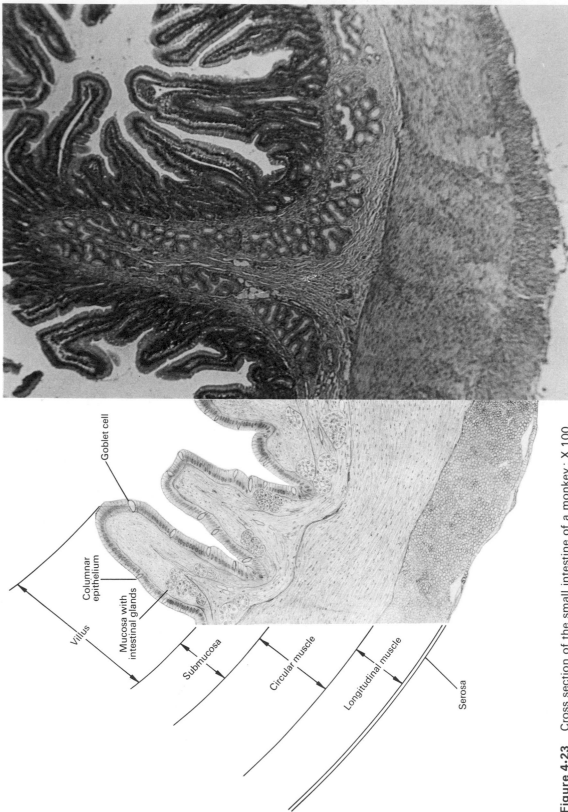

Figure 4·23 Cross section of the small intestine of a monkey; X 100.

blood clot is essentially a meshwork of insoluble fibrin that traps all the nearby blood cells and platelets. The remaining fluid is called blood serum.

GROUPING OF TISSUES INTO ORGANS

To continue our earlier analogy of biological structure to architecture, we must now turn our attention to the specific structures that are formed by the association of various types of tissues. Functional structures made up of different tissues are called *organs*. The small intestine of a vertebrate is a good example of an organ. A photograph of a cross section of the small intestine of a monkey shows four major regions: mucosa, submucosa, muscularis, and serosa (Figure 4–23).

The mucosa consists of a columnar epithelial lining, some glands, and the loose connective tissues that support the villi (finger-like projections on the inner surface of the intestine). Immediately beneath the mucosa lies the submucosa, a region of more closely packed connective tissues, intestinal glands, arterioles and venules, lymphatic vessels, and nerve fibers. The muscularis is composed of an inner layer of circular smooth muscle and a thinner external band of longitudinal fibers, and the organ is covered externally with a thin layer of squamous epithelium called the serosa.

The principle of *division of labor* is clearly illustrated in an organ since each tissue has a specific function in that organ. For example, the epithelial cells of the mucosa layer form a lining, whereas the muscle tissue of the muscularis provides movement of the organ. An organ consequently is capable of doing a job which could not be accomplished by each tissue functioning independently.

THE ORGANISM

To complete our concept of biological architecture we must recognize that all organs are finally organized into functional *systems*. For example, the mouth, esophagus, stomach, small intestine, and large intestine form the digestive system in higher animals. Other systems include the respiratory, circulatory, reproductive, excretory, muscular, skeletal, endocrine, and nervous systems. Some organs actually contribute to more than one system. The liver, for example, participates in digestion, excretion, and circulation. All systems are organized into a functional *organism* by nervous and hormonal control. The success of the organism therefore depends on the orderly coordination and organization of all organs as they function together to meet the demands of the environment.

THE SPECIES CONCEPT

An organism constitutes a living unit in nature, and many different types of organisms exist. Similarities within the diversity are evident, however, and organisms can be placed in specific groups. This grouping, which is generally based on external characteristics (though others are often needed), forms a classification system. One category of organisms, for instance, is known as sparrows. Within this general group of sparrows is a distinct subgroup known as English sparrows which are identified by their coloration and song. A group of similar organisms is called a *species* and forms the fundamental category of classification. For example, one variety of clams, the butter clam, lives in the gravel and sand along certain regions of the West coast (Figure 4–24). These clams live in close association, and potentially the sperm cells of any male butter clam can fertilize the eggs of any female butter clam, and we say that they can interbreed. The definition of a species thus should include the principle of reproduction, and species definitions always include interbreeding groups. Ernst Mayr, in 1942, very aptly defined the species as "a group of actually or potentially interbreeding populations that are reproductively isolated from other such groups." The species name for the

Figure 4·24 *Saxidomus giganteus*, the butter or Washington clam.

butter clam is *giganteus*. It is always stated with the genus name, however, and the total specific designation for the organism is *Saxidomus giganteus*. The term species is both singular and plural.

The concept of a species, however, has much greater significance than merely a classification group. The fact that sexual reproduction is involved in the definition implies that organisms can be formed which differ from the parents. Consequently, species can change. Although regarded as a fixed unit in nature, for the purpose of classification we must treat them as variable, dynamic, and alterable

groups. As a result of changes, some members of the once interbreeding group would be incapable of mating with other members of the original species. The process by which a species may change and become two species is discussed under "speciation" in Chapter 11.

CLASSIFICATION OF ORGANISMS

Since there are many different organisms on our planet, some type of organizational system is required to deal with this diversity. Organisms may be classified in several different ways. Some textbooks use a basic scheme of

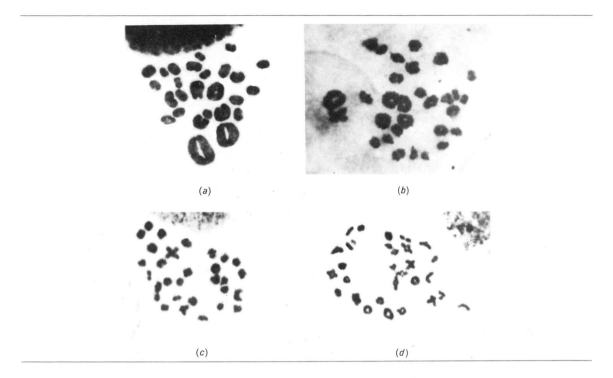

(a)   (b)

(c)   (d)

Figure 4·25   Four sets of chromosomes from four closely related pulmonate snails. Parts (a) and (b) are from the same family, Polygyridae, but represent two different genera. Parts (c) and (d) are from the family Haplotrematidae and are members of the same genus. Part (c) is *Haplotrema vancouverense* (n = 30) and (d) is *Haplotrema sportella* (n = 29).

two *kingdoms*, whereas others recognize three or four fundamental kingdoms. Authorities seldom agree on every detail of classification. Any system of classification should be as natural as possible—that is, it should reflect the way organisms have developed and, as far as possible, their relationships to one another. We have used a system of three kingdoms in this book, and although it may not represent the exact pattern by which life evolved on our planet, it seems more natural than a system that recognizes only plant and animal categories. It should be noted, however, that any system of classification is man-made and represents man's attempts to categorize nature into specific groups.

Organisms were at first classified on the basis of the only characteristics available to man—their gross visible features. With the development of the microscope and other instruments, it has been possible to use other characteristics such as microscopic structures, chromosome comparisons, and protein comparisons (serum analyses). The use of these various techniques should help biologists arrive at a more accurate classification system —that is, one that more closely parallels nature. We often refer to the field of biology that employs these techniques in classification as *biosystematics*.

Four sets of chromosomes from four closely related snails of the subclass Pulmonata are shown in Figure 4–25. Two families of snails are represented here and family characteristics in chromosome structure are apparent. This comparative chromosome study supports the present classification system for these snails.

As we stated in Chapter 3, the justification for using a three-kingdom system of classification, *Protista*, *Metaphyta* (plants), and

103

Metazoa (animals) is based primarily on two points. First, many organisms exist which do not fit neatly into the plant or animal group; and second, organisms did not originate or evolve directly as plants or animals—there probably were many "experiments in nature" involving organisms with a variety and mixture of characteristics.

Kingdoms are further divided into *phyla* (singular = phylum). Additional subclassification categories are used and these are noted in the Appendix. The general characteristics of the three kingdoms are given below, and some of the important phyla in each kingdom are presented with a brief summary of their characteristics. For a more complete classification scheme of the living world, see the Appendix.

KINGDOM PROTISTA

This large and diverse kingdom includes organisms with varying characteristics. Many of the members that do not immediately seem to be related to each other represent rather specialized groups. The criteria for this kingdom often vary among biologists and thus the boundaries are not clear cut. For example, algae and fungi may or may not be placed in this kingdom depending on the specific characteristics used. The general characteristics that differentiate protists from plants and animals are (1) unicellular or a simple, undifferentiated body (except in some algae); (2) unicellular reproductive structures; (3) mostly aquatic; and (4) some have chlorophyll (plantlike) while others do not (animallike).

PHYLUM SCHIZOPHYTA (BACTERIA)

These tiny organisms (the smallest cells known) differ from most of the other protists in not having a well-defined nucleus. Although many bacteria produce diseases in man and other organisms, they are necessary for life on our planet because they play a vital role in nitrogen metabolism and the decay process.

These processes will be discussed in the next chapter.

PHYLUM CHLOROPHYTA (GREEN ALGAE)

Green algae are widespread and can be found in most bodies of water and on moist soils. These organisms contain the two types of chlorophyll found in plants, chlorophyll a and b. For this reason, as well as others, it is believed the members of the plant kingdom have evolved from the green algae.

Although members of this phylum do not show a high degree of differentiation, three basic structural plans are evident, namely the single cell, filamentous colonies, and nonfilamentous colonies. Within the colonies it is important to note the specialization of some cells as reproductive cells.

PHYLUM MASTIGOPHORA

This large and varied phylum consists of unicellular or colonial organisms that possess one to several flagella. The group is often divided into three classes: (1) photosynthetic flagellates that contain chlorophyll, (2) dinoflagellates that also contain chlorophyll and have two flagella; these are important as one of the primary food sources in the ocean and some species can produce the toxic condition known as "red tide"; and (3) animallike flagellates, many of which are parasitic and cause diseases in vertebrates such as sleeping sickness in man.

PHYLUM EUMYCOPHYTA (FUNGI)

Since these organisms lack chlorophyll, they cannot manufacture their own food and consequently must obtain nutrients from sources of already synthesized foodstuffs, such as decaying matter or another living organism. These generally multicellular organisms show little differentiation and are usually composed of filaments. The fungi probably represent a specialized side line in the evolutionary process.

PHYLA SARCODINA, SPOROZOA, CILIOPHORA

These single-celled forms do not contain chlorophyll and are sometimes grouped into the single phylum Protozoa. Many of the members of these phyla exhibit a high degree of specialization within a single cell and possess organelles specialized for feeding, excretion, water balance, and protection. Locomotion is accomplished in Sarcodina by extensions of the cell cytoplasm known as "pseudopodia," whereas ciliophorans move by cilia. Sporozoans are all parasitic in the blood or tissues of animals (some cause malaria) and produce spores at some stage of their life cycles.

KINGDOM METAPHYTA

PHYLUM BRYOPHYTA (MOSSES AND LIVERWORTS)

Bryophytes are land plants that can live only under moist conditions, since water is required for completion of one stage of their life cycle. They contain chlorophyll but lack true leaves, stems, and roots. Vascular tissue (xylem and phloem), necessary in tall plants for the conduction of water and food, is also absent in the bryophytes.

PHYLUM TRACHEOPHYTA (VASCULAR PLANTS)

These organisms are the familiar land plants and have the typical plant plan of leaves, stems, and roots. The possession of vascular tissue has permitted many of these plants to grow tall and inhabit most environments on the earth. The ferns are primitive members of this group but probably the most familiar are the seed-producing tracheophytes—the gymnosperms and the angiosperms.

KINGDOM METAZOA

Many structural features of animals are determined by the fact that animals cannot manufacture food. The muscle tissue provides locomotion, and nervous tissue permits the coordination of muscle action and senses to aid in obtaining food.

One method of discussing and differentiating the several body plans that have evolved in animals is to consider the presence or absence of a body cavity between the internal organs and the body wall. Those animals without such a cavity have a rather solid type of body construction. Some of the advantages of having a body cavity are:

1. More space and freer movement is provided for coiled and folded internal organs.
2. A certain degree of protection is afforded for internal organs that are not connected directly to the body wall.
3. Fluid is present in the cavity and can assist in the circulation of gases and foods as well as help remove wastes.
4. Overall increase in size of animals would probably not have been possible without a body cavity to facilitate the physiological and anatomical adaptations necessary for larger animals.

These body cavities are of two types—*coelom* and *pseudocoelom*. A coelom is a cavity in which the internal organs and the inside surface of the body wall are lined with an epithelial tissue. This tissue is known as the *peritoneum* and, in addition to serving as a lining, it forms part of the mesenteries that hold the internal organs in place. This lining forms from the embryonic tissue called the mesoderm, which will be discussed in Chapter 9. A cavity which is not completely lined with a mesodermal tissue is a pseudocoelom. Figure 4–26 compares the major coelomic conditions.

It is possible to use this distinguishing characteristic as a basis for classification. Thus we find animals without body cavity or coelom, the *Acoelomata*; animals with a body cavity but without a true coelom, the *Pseudocoelomata*; and animals with a coelom, the *Coelomata*. Coelomic animals can be further divided on the basis of the manner in which the coelom develops from the mesoderm. In some animals, notably the earthworms, molluscs, and arthropods, a group of mesoderm

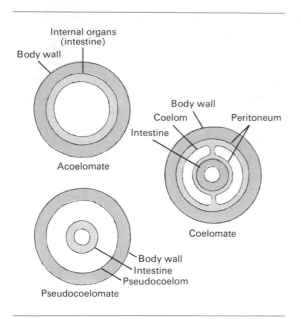

Figure 4·26 The three major coelomic conditions—acoelomate, pseudocoelomate, and coelomate. The diagrams represent cross sections of generalized animal bodies.

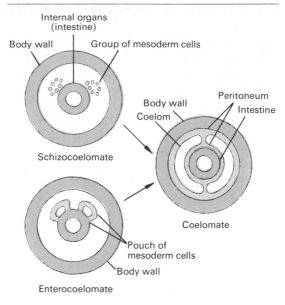

Figure 4·27 Schizocoelomate and enterocoelomate development of the coelomate body plan. The diagrams represent cross sections of generalized animal bodies.

cells separate with one group forming a lining for internal organs and the other a lining for the body wall. These animals are in the subclass *schizocoelomates* (*schizo* referring to the splitting of the group of mesodermal cells). In other animals, among these are the chordates and echinoderms, the coelom develops as a pouch with one side of the pouch lining the internal organs and the other side lining the body wall. This group of animals is referred to as the *enterocoelomates* (*entero* denoting the formation of the pouches from the enteron which is the developing intestine). These two types (schizo and entero) of coelom development are shown in Figure 4–27. The metazoans or animals therefore can be divided into four subgroups—Acoelomata, Pseudocoelomata, Schizocoelomata, and Enterocoelomata.

The acoelomate condition is believed to be the most primitive. Although the pseudocoelomates do have the advantage of a body

cavity, the organs are free within the cavity and are not lined with a peritoneum. The coelomate body plan is considered to be the highest level of development.

Another important characteristic in the animal kingdom is that of body symmetry. Some animals such as amoebae and certain sponges have no definite body shape and are classified as *asymmetrical*. Body plans that appear to radiate from a central area like the spokes of a wheel are termed *radially symmetrical* (jellyfish are a good example). Most animals are *bilaterally symmetrical*, which means that the body may be cut into two halves along one plane only so that the halves are mirror images.

ACOELOMATA

Phylum Coelenterata

This is a large group of chiefly marine animals constructed of essentially two layers of tissues.

A *gastrovascular* cavity with only one opening, a mouth, provides for digestion and circulation. Tentacles, with stinging cells that assist in the capturing of food, surround the mouth in some forms. The characteristics stated above can be manifested into two basic types of body plans: (1) the *polyp*, a usually sedentary form; or (2) the *medusa*, a free-swimming or floating form. Freshwater hydras, jellyfish, and sea anemones are members of this group.

Phylum Platyhelminthes (Flatworms)

Some organ development is shown in the members of this phylum, but a gastrovascular cavity with only one opening still exists. The small, freshwater planaria, for instance, shows characteristics of the flatworms. Many parasitic forms, among them the flukes and tapeworms, are in this phylum.

PSEUDOCOELOMATA

Phylum Aschelminthes

This phylum shows a significant evolutionary advancement in its complete intestinal tract with two openings—a mouth and an anus. The body form is generally slender and tubular. Both parasitic and free-living forms are members of this group. The abundant roundworms (nematodes) are members of this phylum.

SCHIZOCOELOMATA

Phylum Mollusca

This large group of animals has a general body plan of the following characteristics: (1) a muscular foot, (2) a soft body, and (3) usually a shell around the soft body secreted by a *mantle*. Common members of this phylum are snails, clams, and the octopus. Many mollusks are important as food for man.

Phylum Annelida (Segmented Worms)

The members of this phylum are wormlike and have a body composed of a series of segments. Although the segments may appear similar externally, considerable differentiation and specialization occurs internally. For example, the intestinal tract has many specialized regions. Annelids, like the animals already mentioned, still depend on an aquatic environment even though it may be only moist soil. The earthworm is the most familiar example of this phylum. Leeches and many marine worms are also annelids.

Phylum Arthropoda

The arthropods are the largest and most successful (biologically speaking) phylum. It is a very diverse group including insects, crustaceans, spiders, millipedes, and centipedes. Among the characteristics of this phylum are a hard skeleton on the outside of the body; paired, jointed appendages; body usually divided into a head, thorax, and abdomen. The insects make up the largest group of animals known.

ENTEROCOELOMATA

Phylum Echinodermata

Echinoderms possess an internal skeleton of calcium plates embedded in their skin. A unique characteristic of this group is tube feet, which are operated by a water vascular system. These animals show a closer relationship to the chordates (the most highly developed phylum) than any other group. Starfish, sea cucumbers, and sea urchins are members of this phylum.

Phylum Chordata

Although this phylum contains some relatively primitive-appearing forms, it also contains some of the most highly developed animals. Characteristics such as similarity in early development (embryological development) and the possession of a hollow nerve cord down the back are reasons for placing these diverse-appearing animals in this phylum. A large subphylum, Vertebrata, includes animals with backbones, such as fish, frogs, snakes, birds, and mammals.

SUMMARIZING PRINCIPLES

Groups of cells which perform specific functions are known as tissues and may be identified according to their structure and function. Functions common to both plants and animals include protection, support, circulation, growth, and reproduction.

The principle plant tissues are: meristematic (cambium), vascular (xylem and phloem), fundamental (parenchyma, collenchyma, and sclerenchyma) and epidermal (epidermis).

The principle animal tissues are: epithelial (squamous, cuboidal, and columnar), connective (areolar, cartilage, adipose, and bone), muscle (smooth, striated, and cardiac), nerve, and blood. Blood cells originate from the same cells that produce cartilage and bone and therefore may be considered to be a connective tissue.

Functional structures composed of more than one tissue are known as organs. Examples of organs in man include the heart, lungs, pancreas, stomach, and intestines. Each of these organs contains structural components of nearly all tissue types. The principle of division of labor is evidenced in organs since each tissue performs specific functions.

Organs are interrelated in functional organ systems which comprise the organism. Examples include respiratory, circulatory, digestive, excretory, reproductive, muscular, skeletal, nervous, and endocrine systems.

The living unit in nature is the organism and each unique type is referred to as a species. Usually, individual species may be identified by their different structures. Technically, however, the definition must include the fact that species are interbreeding groups.

In order to handle the many diverse species, all organisms are placed into broad categories called kingdoms. Three to five kingdoms are generally recognized, and Protista, Metaphyta and Metazoa are used throughout this book. Each kingdom is further subdivided into more and more specific groups including phylum, class, order, family, genus, and species.

Animals which possess a body cavity (coelom) show adaptive advantages over those without a cavity (acoelomates). The type and development of the body cavity is helpful in classification.

REVIEW QUESTIONS

1   What are some of the advantages of cellular construction to life? What are some advantages of tissue construction?

2   What structural characteristics would you use to identify microscopic sections of the following plant tissues: meristematic, xylem, phloem, and epidermal.

3   How does the arrangement of vascular tissue differ in monocot, dicot and gymnosperm stems?

4   What structural and functional characteristics are common to all animal connective tissues?

5   Skeletal muscles show striated patterns which change when the muscle contracts and relaxes. How can these pattern changes be explained?

6 What are the unique characteristics of nerve cells? How is the nerve impulse passed from neuron to neuron?

7 Compare the cellular components of human blood with respect to size, shape, nucleus, relative numbers, and function.

8 In an organ such as the small intestine several tissue types are present. Describe the specific functions of each of the following: serosa layer, smooth muscle, nerve fibers, and epithelial lining.

9 What is the value of the term species? Why must reproduction be considered in a definition of a species?

10 How has the concept and use of the kingdom Protista facilitated the classification of the living world? Can you see how this kingdom could be further divided into additional kingdoms?

11 How are the structural variations of the animal body cavity, or coelom, of value in classifying animals? Define acoelomate, pseudocoelomate, schizocoelomate, and enterocoelomate.

SUPPLEMENTARY READINGS

Bold, H. C., *The Plant Kingdom*, Englewood Cliffs, N.J., Prentice-Hall, 1960.

Buchsbaum, R., *Animals Without Backbones*, Chicago, University of Chicago Press, 1948.

Eccles, Sir John, "The Synapse," *Scientific American*, January, 1965.

Echlin, Patrick, "The Blue-Green Algae," *Scientific American*, June, 1966.

Goodenough, U. W., and R. P. Levine, "The Genetic Activity of Mitochondria and Chloroplasts," *Scientific American*, November, 1970.

Gross, Jerome, "Collagen," *Scientific American*, May, 1961.

Huxley, H. E., "The Contraction of Muscle," *Scientific American*, November, 1958.

Huxley, H. E., "The Mechanism of Muscular Contraction," *Scientific American*, December, 1965.

Jaques, H. E., *Living Things, How to Know Them*, Dubuque, Iowa, Wm. C. Brown, 1960.

Laki, K., "The Clotting of Fibrinogen," *Scientific American*, March, 1962.

Patt, Donald I., and Gail R. Patt, *Comparative Vertebrate Histology*, New York, Harper & Row, 1969.

Szent-Györgyi, A., "Muscle Research," *Scientific American*, June, 1949.

Wilkie, D. R., *Muscle*, New York, St. Martin's Press, 1968.

Zucker, M. B., "Blood Platelets," *Scientific American*, February, 1961.

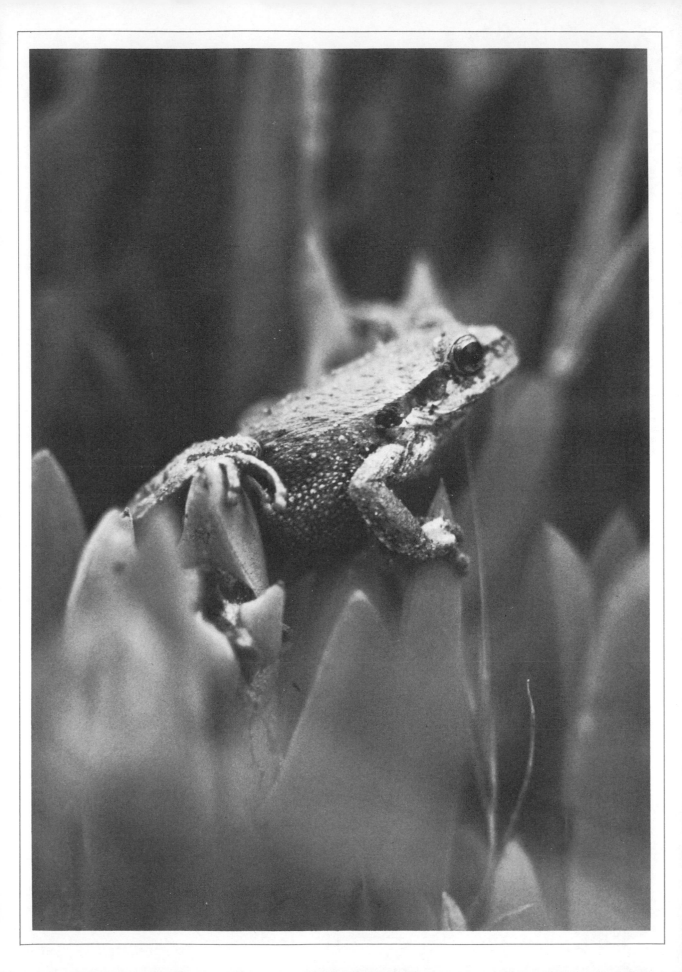

5

The Living Community

An individual organism does not live alone. Each living thing is part of a *biotic community*, a group of organisms inhabiting a common environment and interacting with each other. Each species, moreover, fits into its community in a unique functional way—it has a specific *niche*. The specific part of a biotic community in which each organism lives is called a *habitat*. Between the seashore and high mountain peaks (Figure 5-1), we can observe many different communities such as ponds, forests, lakes, and deserts.

One example of a biotic community is a quiet ocean tidepool. Although a casual observation frequently will permit us to identify specific organisms, it will not help us to understand the interactions of these organisms or their relationships and contributions to their environment. This understanding comes only with close study and time. One obvious member of the tidepool is usually the sea anemone (Figure 5-2). Patient observation might show the anemone devouring a fish, which had probably just eaten tiny microcrustaceans. The microcrustaceans might have just fed on certain algae cells that manufacture their food by trapping sunlight and using raw materials from the environment. We might see a chiton rasping algae from a rock or mussels passively filtering water over their gills to remove tiny food particles. Any barnacles in the water would show rhythmical beating of their appendages as they capture food. Some worms

Figure 5·1 Examples of two living communities, seashore and alpine forest. (Part *b* courtesy of Eliott Weier.)

112

Figure 5·2 A tidepool community showing green sea anemones and purple sea urchins. (Courtesy of Helen Dillon.)

and crabs would find temporary homes under rocks and in crevices while others were sheltered under large filaments of algae.

If newcomers, say a particular species of snails, join this community, we might see the *population* of this species undergo a specific growth pattern over a period of time. If the tide is out for quite a while and the sun is bright, the water becomes several degrees warmer. This condition is most unfavorable for study; in fact, activity may virtually cease. When the tide flows again, however, it brings cooler water, oxygen, chemical nutrients, and provides transportation into and out of the community for certain organisms. If we were to microscopically examine the water periodically, we could detect special sex cells from some of the organisms, such as the anemones. These appear at approximately the same time each year, and some of the sex cells unite for fertilization, thus producing new organisms.

All members of the community ultimately, of course, will die and even though parts of their bodies may be eaten by scavengers such as crabs, bacteria will also assist in the decomposition process. Thus the tidepool, like all communities, shows a definite organization with each organism contributing in an indispensable way. Cyclical patterns are also evident even though many of the individual chemical cycles, such as nitrogen and phosphorus, are not as obvious as those of the salinity and tide.

Although many relationships have been discussed in this brief account of the tidepool community, it is much more complex. A better understanding of a community can be gained by examining some of the associations and processes in detail. The area of science concerned with the relationships of organisms to one another and to their environments is known as *ecology*.

113

ENERGY FLOW AND CHEMICAL CYCLING

THE ECOSYSTEM

Each living community depends on energy for its structure and function, and these energy relationships follow a similar pattern in each community. The flow of energy is always in one direction, whereas the chemical materials involved circulate in cycles. Energy flows from organism to organism whereas the cycling of chemicals involves not only living forms (the biotic) but also the nonliving (the abiotic) environment. The biotic and the abiotic together form an *ecosystem*, and through this integrated system of energy flow and the cycling of materials the ecosystem is maintained.

ENERGY FLOW

In any ecosystem chemicals must be converted into living matter and energy storage products. In general, large molecules, such as $C_6H_{12}O_6$, are synthesized from smaller molecules found in soil, air, and water. Organisms capable of performing these syntheses are referred to as the *producers*—such as plants on land and plants and algae in aquatic environments. Although the flow of energy is not

Figure 5.4   The basic scheme of photosynthesis.

cyclical in a community, the sun provides a continuing source of energy (Figure 5-3). Producers or *autotrophs* (self-feeding) always contain chlorophyll and/or other light-trapping compounds that permit the utilization of the sun's energy. Simply stated, the basic process called *photosynthesis* (Figure 5-4) is one in which solar energy is converted to chemical energy in the form of simple carbohydrates. After photosynthesis takes place,

Figure 5.3   The electromagnetic spectrum. Wavelengths are given in millimicrons (1/1000 of a micron). Visible light is used in photosynthesis, thus only a small part of the sun's energy (about 2 percent) can be used by producers.

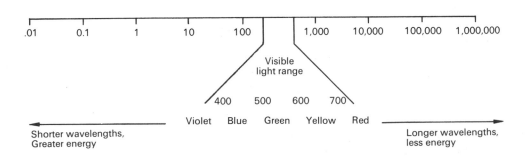

metabolic processes convert these simple sugars into more complex sugars, proteins, and fats. In these forms, energy and material stored by producers are then transferred to *consumers*—first to the plant-eating herbivores and through them to the carnivores. These *heterotrophs* (other-feeding) are also known as primary and secondary consumers.

Although we have a constant source of energy from the sun, the chemical elements are not in such constant supply. Therefore a very important element of any ecosystem is the group of bacteria and fungi, known as *decomposers*, that break down and decompose dead organisms. It is through decomposition that the necessary chemical nutrients are returned to the environment, and without it all life would eventually cease to exist. The important decomposers are found in the organic layer of the soil and at the bottom of ponds and lakes.

Thus we see a structural and functional organization within an ecosystem that begins with the producers, which provide food (and energy) for the consumers. The consumers, as well as many producers, are broken down by decomposers which return raw materials to the producers. Each group of organisms in the community derives energy from the group preceding it in this chain of events (Figure 5-5), and these represent *trophic levels*. The principal trophic levels in two ecosystems, a fresh water lake and a deciduous forest illustrate trophic levels and their relationship to the abiotic (Figure 5-6a). A pyramid is frequently used to show the relative masses of the various components of an ecosystem (Figure 5-6b). In the movement from one trophic level to another, 100 percent efficiency is not achieved and energy is lost from the system along the way. For example, a specific mass of plants will support a group of herbivores much smaller in mass than the plants and fewer carnivores in turn will be supported by the herbivores.

A specific structural organization as described here can be observed in a forest where the trees and shrubs are the primary pro-

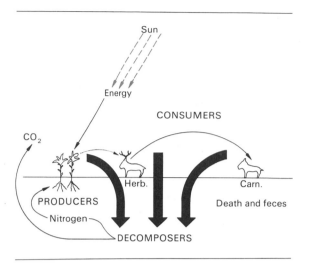

Figure 5·5 Relationships among members of an ecosystem.

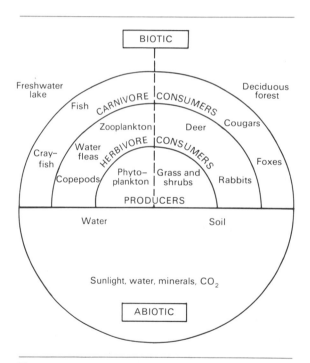

Figure 5·6 (*a*) Principal trophic levels in two ecosystems, freshwater and terrestrial.

ducers. Plants supply food to deer and other herbivores who in turn are eaten by the carnivores such as cougars, wolves, and coyotes.

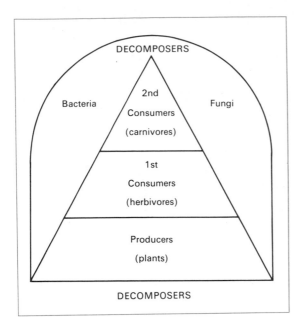

Figure 5·6 (b) The biomass relationships in an ecosystem.

FOOD CHAINS AND WEBS

The flow of energy from one trophic level to another is called a *food chain*. For example, the following food relationship is important to game-management experts:

Plants → Deer → Cougars

To farmers in some areas the following food chain is recognized:

Crops → Field mice → Hawks and/or coyotes

Serious results can occur when one element of a food chain is disturbed. If bounties permit excessive cougar hunting, a deer population in a specific area may increase to the point where insufficient food is available to sustain the herd. Nutritional problems and crowding result so that a large herd of deer is produced which contains mostly weak and emaciated members. If the coyotes around a farming area

are poisoned because they have killed a few sheep, the field mice population may increase to the point where they severely damage the grain crop, which may cause the death of many more sheep.

Many instances are known in which man has imported a predator to control nuisance animals such as rats. Soon the predator may destroy the pests to the point that he must feed on some of the more desirable animals. Man must be very careful when he interferes with a natural order and must realize that it is possible to change the entire ecological relationship by tampering with one element of a particular ecosystem. It is often necessary to take steps to correct a situation in which the activities of man and perhaps some of his domesticated animals have disturbed what were once natural conditions.

Most animals do not rely on one species for their food source but usually feed on several different organisms. A hawk, for example, will eat squirrels, mice, rabbits, and large insects. Because consumers do not rely solely on one plant or animal for food, there are many interrelated food chains. These make up a *food web* which can be very complex (Figure 5-7).

CHEMICAL CYCLES

In addition to the one-way flow of energy through the ecosystem (from producers through consumers to decomposers), life also depends on nutrients and other chemical compounds that are cycled from the soil, through atmosphere and living organisms, and back to the soil. Perhaps the best known and most studied of these are water, oxygen, carbon, nitrogen, phosphorus, sulfur, and calcium. Some of these will be discussed here to show how they are made available to living organisms.

Oxygen

Oxygen is important not only as a structural component of sugar, fat, and protein molecules but also as a necessary agent for the process,

116

Figure 5·7 Part of a food web in a forest community.

called oxidation, by which energy is released from foods. We know that oxygen is released as green plants manufacture food. It can be demonstrated that this oxygen comes from water taken in by the plant. Oxygen from the atmosphere (or from water in the case of aquatic forms) is used in the process of respiration by living organisms. Within cells the oxygen unites with hydrogen from sugar molecules to produce water. This water can be used again by green plants in photosyn-

thesis and the cycle continues. The details of photosynthesis and respiration will be discussed in Chapter 6. The general events of the oxygen cycle are summarized in Figure 5-8.

Carbon

The general pattern of the movement of carbon is from the atmosphere to green plants, where organic carbon compounds are produced and used by both plants and animals,

117

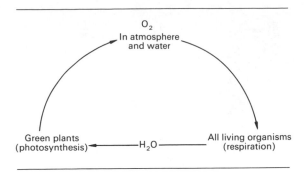

Figure 5·8 Simplified schematic of the oxygen cycle.

then back to the atmosphere as a by-product of respiration from plants and animals (Figure 5-9). Carbon dioxide (CO_2) is the form in which the carbon circulates in most phases of the cycle. Through decomposition of dead organisms and the waste products of plants and animals, some carbon dioxide is returned to the atmosphere. In addition, the burning of coal and other fossil fuels releases considerable quantities of CO_2. In this process carbon may be stored for some time before it is returned to the cycle via the atmosphere or water. Note in Figure 5-9 that the carbon used by green

Figure 5·9 The carbon cycle.

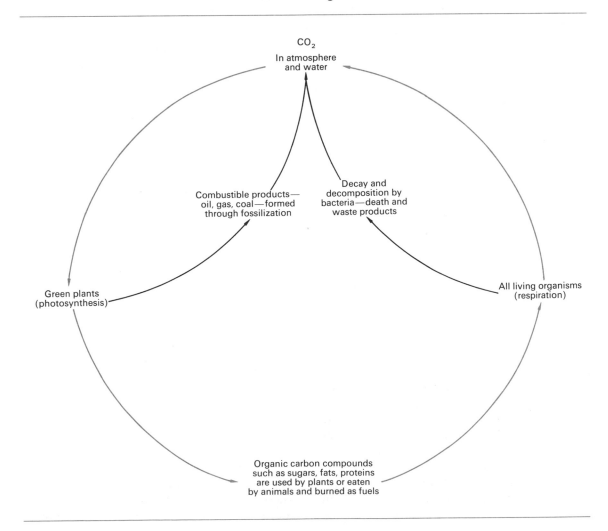

plants must come directly from CO_2 in the atmosphere or water.

In recent times considerable amounts of CO_2 as well as highly toxic compounds such as sulfur dioxide are being added to the environment by industry and automobiles. The consequences of this are quite dramatic in the smog-filled atmospheres of most major cities. In fact, even CO_2 may be hazardous in excessive amounts since many control centers in living systems are dependent on a balance between CO_2 and O_2.

Nitrogen

The process by which nitrogen is made available to living organisms is somewhat more complex than the oxygen and carbon cycles. Nitrogen is an essential element in such compounds as amino acids, purines, and pyrimidines. These compounds are usually produced first in green plants and then made available to animals. Although nitrogen makes up 78 percent of the atmosphere, it is not directly available to the majority of living organisms since much of the nitrogen used by green plants must be in the form of nitrates. A slight amount of direct *nitrogen fixing* does take place, however, in a small number of organisms in some groups of bacteria, blue-green algae, and fungi. Lightning can also fix a small amount of nitrogen. Most of the nitrogen made available to living organisms originates through two principal routes—(1) through the production of *nitrate* and (2) through the action of *nodule bacteria* on the roots of certain plants (Figure 5-10).

Some free-living microorganisms in the soil and water can convert atmospheric nitrogen to ammonia (NH_3). This ammonia is either used by these organisms or given off to the environment. Another group of bacteria can convert the ammonia to *nitrite* (NO_2), and a third group can convert the nitrite to *nitrate* (NO_3). In the form of nitrates, nitrogen can be used by green plants. The ammonia, nitrites, and nitrates are usually present as ions (NH_4^+, NO_2^-, NO_3^-) which can unite with other ions of opposite charges to produce

Figure 5-10 Roots of birdsfoot trefoil, a legume, with nodules containing bacteria. (Courtesy of The Nitragin Co., Inc., Milwaukee, Wis.)

salts. Other sources of ammonia are also available to nitrite-forming bacteria such as the ammonia produced in animal wastes (urine) and in decomposition. This sequence may be summarized as follows:

$$
\begin{array}{c}
\text{Decomposing organisms} \\
\text{N}_2\text{-fixing bacteria} \longrightarrow \text{NH}_3 \to \text{NO}_2 \to \text{NO}_3 \\
\text{Waste products} \longrightarrow \quad\quad \left(\begin{array}{l}\text{available to}\\\text{green plants}\end{array}\right)
\end{array}
$$

Certain plants, such as members of the pea family (legumes) and alder trees, have bacteria attached to nodules on the root structure which can take free nitrogen directly from the soil and convert it into organic nitrogen (Figure 5-10). This nitrogen, in the form of amino

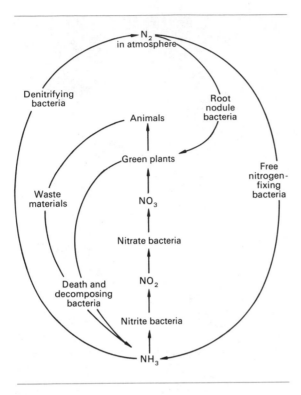

Figure 5·11 The nitrogen cycle.

acids, can be passed directly into the plants possessing these nodules. Thus legumes and alders can grow in soil that lacks usable nitrogen.

Although some bacteria are required for supplying nitrogen in usable form to living organisms, others are responsible for an opposite process known as *denitrification.* These bacteria can convert ammonia, nitrites, and nitrates to free nitrogen which is released to the atmosphere. Although it is unnecessary for nitrogen to return to the atmosphere to complete its cycle (as in the carbon cycle), some, nevertheless, is released as free nitrogen. Figure 5-11 is an attempt to summarize the complex details involved in the circulation of nitrogen in an ecosystem.

Phosphorus

The major reservoirs of phosphorus are the rock formations of the earth's crust. Slowly, through the processes of weathering and leaching, phosphates are returned to the soil and the sea. Dissolved phosphate can be incorporated into living organisms, usually into plants and then into animals.

Phosphorus, in this form, is essential to the functioning of the metabolic processes that convert food to usable energy, energy transfer, and the structure of the hereditary material. In addition it is a major component of bones and teeth. In some aquatic environments, phosphates may be the "limiting factor" for growth and reproduction at certain times of the year. Since phosphorus is eroded away, phosphates are often added to lawns and farmland when the soil has become depleted.

When organisms excrete or decompose, phosphates are put back into circulation. Some phosphate, however, is deposited in sediments, and the deep, rather insoluble sediments are lost to living organisms until an upheaval occurs. Eventually these will be returned to the cycle, although some concern has been expressed that gradually we are permanently losing more phosphates to the deep sediments. Shallow sediments often redissolve and may be brought up by the currents and waves of the oceans. Land-dwelling organisms contribute to the terrestrial phosphate deposits and thereby assist in maintaining the cycle. Fish eaten by man and birds help to return phosphorus from the sea to the land. The events of the phosphorus cycle are shown in Figure 5-12.

CHANGES IN A COMMUNITY— SUCCESSION

All environments change constantly. In addition to the many daily and yearly changes, every ecosystem undergoes a definite series of biological changes related to climate, parent soil material, and organisms living in adjacent areas. The home gardener, for instance, knows that weeds will soon overtake his garden if it is left unattended. A familiar sight in certain regions of the western United States is the swath cut through the evergeen forests for power lines (Figure 5-13). In this

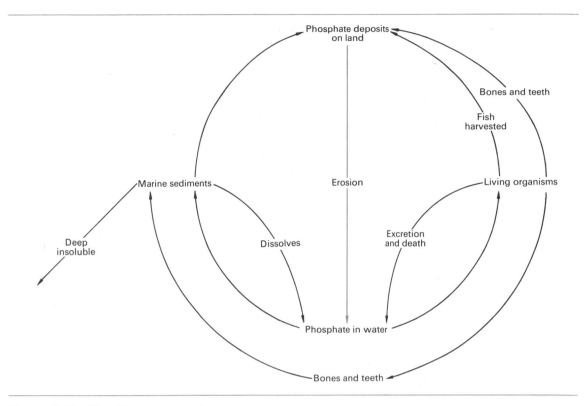

Figure 5·12   The phosphorus cycle.

Figure 5·13   The right-of-way beneath this power line was cleared of all vegetation. This photograph illustrates the successive reforestation of the area as described in the text.

Figure 5·14 Early stage of primary succession in which rock is broken into soil by plants. The plants are primarily lichens and mosses. (Courtesy of U. S. Forest Service; photo by Russell K. LeBarron.)

process all vegetation is removed from a strip that is 50 to 100 feet wide and may extend for miles in length. Within a short time herbaceous plants, such as grasses and fireweed, cover the strip and are soon followed by blackberry, salmon berry, currant, and other shrubs. Mingling with these plants and even replacing them in time are the deciduous alder and willow trees. But after a few years these trees will be crowded out by evergreen species such as Douglas fir, western hemlock, or western red cedar, which occupied these areas before the clearing was done. Over a

period of years, therefore, one community will replace another until a relatively stable community, the evergreen forest, again inhabits these strips.

Analysis shows these events to be an orderly and sequential pattern that would repeat itself if the trees were again removed. Such a series of uniform vegetational changes through these several stages is known as ecological *succession*. The final occupants of an area make up a stable, essentially self-reproducing community called the *climax*. One group of plants prepares the way, chemically and physically, for the next group until this climax is attained. The series of changes that occurred in the cleared forest areas is an example of *secondary* succession since the land was previously occupied by plants. Succession in a new environment or on any area devoid of organisms is called *primary* succession. Although we are concerned here mostly with the plants involved in succession, we should note that the animal population in a particular area is determined in part by the plants.

One primary succession site is on bare rock, and this is generally a slow process depending on the hardness of the rock and the water available. The first occupants of the area are usually lichens and mosses, which contribute to the actual breakdown of the rock and the preparation of the area for later colonization (Figure 5-14). Soil collects in crevices permitting seeds from nearby herbaceous plants to gain a foothold, and the establishment of a rather specific type of vegetation begins (Figure 5-15). Grasses then can move in, followed by small shrubs, then larger shrubs, and eventually trees. When this process occurs along the western coast of the United States, deciduous, broad-leaved trees usually move in first to be succeeded later by evergreen, cone-bearing trees. In the Midwest, on the East Coast, and in other parts of the United States, the climax vegetation will be different, depending on the soil, the climate, and the specific plants in the various areas (Figure 5-17). These climax communities will be discussed later in this section.

Another succession pattern is shown by a lake or pond. All lakes theoretically are in the process of being converted to land and the time required for this conversion will vary. As streams carry soil into a lake, the bottom begins to build up and change. Also plants, such as tussock sedges, cattails, rushes, or sphagnum moss, may grow out from the shore over the water's edge to form a mat. All of these plants, through the intertwining of their roots, can collect soil and hold humus material in place. Soon the way is prepared for other plants such as shrubs of the heath

Pioneers in the form of lichens and mosses begin the succession on a rocky hillside

More soil is produced and larger plants (herbs) can move in

Next, shrubs requiring more soil can grow here

Finally, dedicuous, broad-leaved trees inhabit the area

Figure 5-15 Ecological succession on a rocky hill side.

family to gain a foothold. At the same time a buildup is occurring from the bottom as the deposition of soil and dead plants and animals continues. After a time, larger shrubs and trees can move into this newly formed land

123

Deposition begins and encroachment from the edges by sphagnum moss, the pioneer

Deposition continues and a mat of mutual support from the moss, sedges, and trailing heaths forms

The lake has been completely succeeded and a bog remains in the middle; soon this will be succeeded by shrubs and trees

Figure 5·16   Succession of a lake by land.

area (Figure 5-16). Peat bogs in the northern United States and Canada are the result of this type of succession (Figure 5-17). If you have never done so, you should visit a peat

bog to witness this striking example of succession. The quaking, resilient floating border of the bog presents an interesting environment. Owing to the incomplete decay of organic

Figure 5·17 A lake in a stage of succession by sphagnum moss in the northwestern United States.

matter, nitrogen in a usable form is insufficient. A variety of insectivorous plants such as the sundew, pitcher plant, and Venus's-flytrap inhabit bog communities. These plants trap insects to obtain nitrogen from the animal's proteins (Figure 5-18).

Although the basic patterns of succession are similar, different plant species are involved in different geographical areas. Certain stages may be accelerated or arrested in a successional series when man interferes or pollutes the environment. For example, mining, farming, and logging may seriously alter the environment from the natural state.

THE MAJOR COMMUNITIES OF THE WORLD

BIOMES

The terrestrial regions of the earth are sometimes classified according to the dominant plant and animal life inhabiting them. Each

Figure 5·18 The pitcher plant from a peat bog. These plants trap insects.

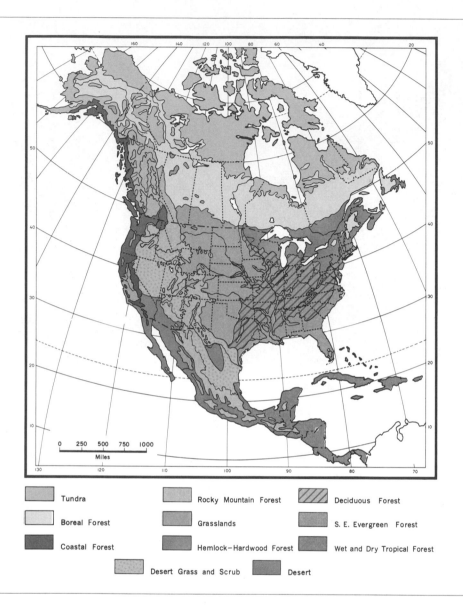

Figure 5·19 Climax vegetation zones of North America. Note that a specific type of vegetation develops in a specific climatic zone. (Map by Robert Winter.)

area, with a unique group of climax plants and related animal species, is termed a *biome*. Generally, six principal biomes may be recognized: tundra, northern coniferous forest, deciduous forest, tropical forest, grassland, and desert (Figure 5-19). An over-all view of the major biomes is presented in Figure 5-63.

Tundra

This biome stretches across the continents generally above 60 degrees north latitude. Since it is characterized by snow, ice, and frozen soil most of the year, the plants and animals that live here must have high resistance to cold. The tundra is virtually treeless and

Figure 5·20 Tundra of northern Alaska showing an isolated group of spruce trees growing on a protected slope. (Courtesy of Paul Heilman.)

consists primarily of lichens, low shrubs, and a few grasses. Caribou, arctic hares, foxes, lemmings, and migratory birds are common (Figure 5-20).

Northern Coniferous Forest

This area stretches across North America and Eurasia below the tundra. The major vegetation consists of evergreen trees such as pine, fir, cedar, and spruce. Many shade-resistant, broadleaf plants such as maple are also found here. The coniferous forest is an excellent habitat for elk, deer, grouse, rabbits, squirrels, mountain lions, and birds (Figure 5-21). In areas such as Washington's Olympic Peninsula and eastern Asia, high annual rainfall allows

the growth of lush vegetation. These areas are generally termed *rain forests* (Figure 5-22).

Deciduous Forest

The dominant tree is the deciduous hardwood, found largely in north-central Europe, the eastern United States, and eastern Asia. Hickory, oak, elm, beech, and maple are typical of the large variety of the broadleaf species that inhabit these regions. Annual rainfall (usually 30–60 inches) and a temperate climate are critical factors in this biome. The trees and shrubs lose their leaves annually when the temperature drops in the autumn. Deer, squirrels, foxes, song birds, rabbits, and

127

Figure 5·21 Northern coniferous forest in Idaho: alpine fir, Engelmann spruce, and whitebark pine. (Courtesy of U. S. Forest Service; photo by A. T. Boisen.)

raccoons are representative animals (Figure 5-23).

Tropical Forest

The tropical forest is characterized by high rainfall during most of the year (up to 100 inches). The major regions include central Africa, southern Asia, and northern Central America. The warm, humid climate supports broadleaf evergreen plants, and we generally refer to this area as a *jungle*. The animals may include monkeys, various snakes, anteaters, tropical birds, and large carnivores such as lions, tigers, and leopards (Figure 5-24).

Figure 5·22 Rain forest in Olympic National Park. Note the lush moss growth on the vine maple. Spruce and hemlock are in the background. (Courtesy of U. S. Dept. of the Interior; National Park Service photo.)

Figure 5·23 Deciduous oak-hickory forest in Virginia. (Courtesy of U. S. Forest Service; photo by E. S. Shipp.)

Figure 5·24 Tropical forest in Hawaii. (Courtesy of U. S. Forest Service; photo by R. E. Nelson.)

129

Figure 5·25 Mixed-grass prairie in Nebraska. (Courtesy of U. S. Forest Service; photo by Bluford W. Muir.)

Grassland

Grassland covers much of the world extending through north central Eurasia, north central and southern Africa, central United States, central South America, and the northern half of Australia. The irregular rainfall of this region averages between 10 and 30 inches annually. The grasslands of Africa, commonly known as *savannah*, undergo a period of high rainfall, but several months of severe drought limit the establishment of trees (Figure 5-25). Grazing animals dominate in this biome, and other common species include jack rabbits, antelope, and prairie dogs. A variety of animals is characteristic of the African grassland.

Desert

Deserts occur in any area of low annual rainfall (less than 10 inches) and show extreme temperature fluctuations. The major deserts are found in North Africa, southern Europe, the southern half of Australia, the southwestern United States, and Mexico. When vegetation occurs it is principally cacti, greasewood, sagebrush, and yucca; a common tree is the green-barked paloverde. Seasonal spring rainfall may produce a bloom of many varieties of colorful flowers. Typical animals found in the Arizona desert include rabbits, quail, doves, rattlesnakes, scorpions, lizards, and coyotes (Figure 5-26).

Figure 5·26 The Arizona desert near Tucson. The Saguaro cactus is characteristic of this Sonoran desert. (Photo by H. L. Parent from National Audubon Society.)

LIFE ZONES

In addition to the biomes another classification system for the distribution of plants and animals is sometimes used. This system is especially useful in the mountainous regions of western North America. In the 1890s, C. Hart Merriam, working in the San Francisco Peaks area of northern Arizona, recognized a definite distribution range according to altitude among the plants and animals. He further recognized the correlation between the altitudinal pattern and the north-south distribution of similar species according to latitude. For example, Merriam recognized the similarities between plant species living in the alpine mountain regions and those in the Arctic. Using North America as a model, he designated the Arctic-Alpine, Hudsonian, Canadian, transitional, and upper and lower Sonoran (Mexico) *life zones*. Merriam was convinced that the major factor in this distribution was temperature. Although most ecologists today feel that temperature alone is not a sufficient basis for the stratigraphy of plants and animals, the Merriam life zones are still useful in the western, mountainous states.

A comparison can be made between the vegetation on the eastern and western slopes of the North Cascade Range and the vegetation distributed according to north latitude (Figure 5-27). On the western slopes, which receive

131

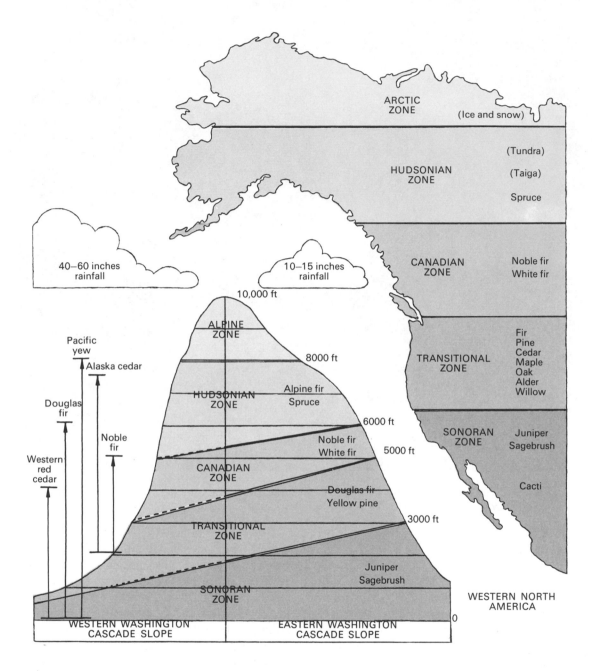

Figure 5·27 A comparison of the vegetation zones of the eastern and western slopes of the North Cascade Mountains. The eastern slope is further compared to the continental north-south distribution.

40–60 inches of annual precipitation, the typical life-zone pattern is not as distinct as on the eastern side. Although certain species of conifers show definite altitudinal preferences —western red cedar (0–4000 feet), noble fir (2000–5000 feet), Douglas fir (0–6000 feet), and Alaska cedar (2000–7500 feet)—the Pacific yew occurs from 0–8000 feet (treeline). This

Figure 5·28 Lake Chelan in eastern Washington. This lake is 55 miles long and has a maximum depth of 1500 feet. (Courtesy of H. R. Dursch.)

coastal slope distribution is apparently produced by high rainfall, generally cooler temperatures, and an ability to withstand "snow load." The distribution of plants on the eastern slopes, however, shows a definite correlation with the north-south plant distribution on the continent in accordance with Merriam's scheme.

THE FRESHWATER ENVIRONMENT— LAKES AND PONDS

Lakes and ponds are familiar features of the landscape and occur in practically every biome (Figure 5-28). They vary in size from less than an acre to many miles, and in depth from several feet to almost a mile. The origins of lakes are varied. Many are the direct or indirect result of glaciers, whereas natural or man-made dams may cause depressions to fill

with water. And parts of meandering rivers, cut off from the main stream, can also result in lakes. Lakes are often classified on the basis of the amount of organic matter they contain. *Eutrophic* lakes are relatively shallow with a rich accumulation of organic products. *Oligotrophic* lakes, on the other hand, are generally deep and often have rocky, steep sides. The supply of circulating nutrients, such as phosphates, is often low in these lakes and the ratio of organic materials to the volume of water is also very low. Additional characteristics of these two types of lakes will be given in the following topical discussions on lakes.

Almost every biology class has access to a body of fresh water which can be observed, and considerable amount of fundamental biology can be learned from the study of a lake. Moreover, such an ecosystem provides an excellent opportunity to correlate biological information with physical and chemical data.

LIGHT IN LAKES

The degree to which producers (algae) can photosynthesize depends on the amount of light entering the lake and the depth to which it penetrates. Several methods have been devised to determine the depth of the penetration of light in a body of water. Photoelectric cells and light-sensitive film are two of the more refined methods. A rather simple method from which comparative data can be obtained is to determine the greatest depth at which the observer can see a round, black and white disc. This disc, known as a Secchi disc, provides only a rough estimate of visibility, however, and does not give an actual measurement of light penetration. The amount of organic particles in a lake affects the depth to which the disc can be seen. On the same day, under similar weather conditions, the light penetration in an oligotrophic lake and a eutrophic lake was studied; the Secchi disc was visible to 14 meters in the first lake but could be seen only to 1.5 meters in the second.

TEMPERATURE OF LAKES

The temperature of a lake is affected by solar radiation, thus every temperate lake, whether it is deep or shallow, undergoes a definite cycle of events during a year. In the late winter or early spring when conditions become warmer, the ice, if present that year, melts and the upper waters warm slightly. The water warms to about 4°C and produces a rather uniform temperature situation from the top to the bottom of the lake. Since water reaches its maximum density at 4°C, the water on the bottom of the lake would be 4°C; ice, at 0°C, is lighter and floats on top. Moreover, the water at the bottom of any deep lake is generally 4°C throughout the year. Currents and waves generated by the wind can bring about a thorough mixing of the water, the spring turnover, since the body of water is generally unstable. Soon the warmth of summer produces a warm layer of water on the surface while the lower water remains colder.

Figure 5·29 Summer temperatures structures in two different lakes in Washington.

A sharp drop in temperature often develops at a particular depth in many lakes during the summer period. This region of rapid temperature drop with depth is known as the *thermocline*. In the deep lake mentioned previously, the thermocline was found to lie between 30 and 45 meters, whereas in the shallower lake it occurred between 3.5 and 4.5 meters (Figure 5-29). The body of water above the thermocline is known as the *epilimnion* and that below, the *hypolimnion*. The formation of a thermocline, which produces layering, prevents mixing of these two bodies of water, thereby causing a summer stagnation.

The autumn of the year brings cooler temperatures and the surface waters begin to cool, thus bringing about a uniform temperature structure again. At this time mixing can again take place through the currents and waves produced by the wind, causing an autumn turnover. As winter begins, an ice layer may form to produce a winter stagnation period. If ice does not form, some mixing of the water may continue throughout the winter since the temperature remains fairly uniform from the top to the bottom of the lake. The general sequence of temperature changes throughout

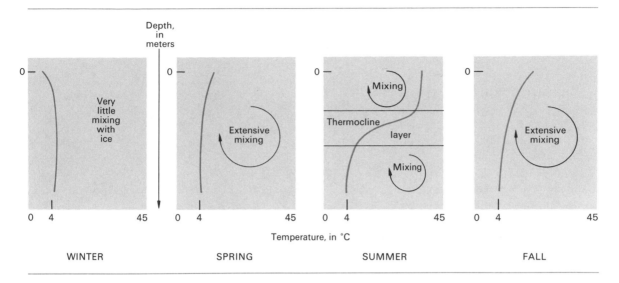

Temperature, in °C

WINTER   SPRING   SUMMER   FALL

Figure 5·30 Four graphs representing the general temperature structure of most lakes throughout the year.

the year is summarized in Figure 5-30. If movement of the water from top to bottom of a lake did not occur, materials could not be circulated and interchanged within the total body of water. Seasonal turnovers provide the opportunity for mixing so that nutrients can be moved up from the bottom while oxygen can be transported to the lower layers. In addition, certain organisms can be distributed about the lake through overturning.

OXYGEN IN LAKES

The oxygen content at the various depths in a lake provides some indication of the *productivity* of that lake. Productivity here refers to the ability of the lake to produce organic material from inorganic substances. The upper part of a lake is usually the region for autotrophism, while heterotrophism occurs in the lower part (where light does not penetrate). Systematic oxygen determinations often reveal this, especially in eutrophic lakes.

Oxygen content in lakes can be determined readily by taking samples from different depths and subjecting them to a chemical technique known as the Winkler method. Oxygen levels are usually given in terms of

milliliters or milligrams of oxygen per liter of water (ml/l or mg/l). The temperature structure may have a great deal to do with the amount of oxygen in certain parts of a lake especially during the summer when the hypolimnion is not in circulation with the epilimnion. Whether a lake is oligotrophic or eutrophic (high rate of photosynthesis) also determines how much oxygen is available and how it is distributed (Figure 5-31).

Figure 5·31 Summer temperatures and oxygen levels in two different lakes in Washington: (*a*) Cranberry Lake is eutrophic; (*b*) Lake Chelan is oligotrophic.

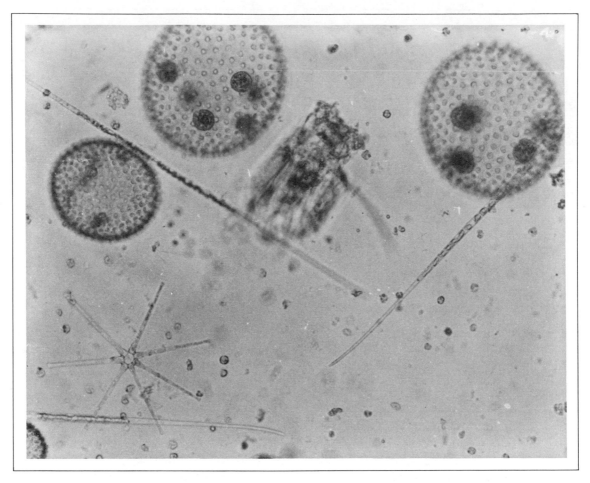

Figure 5·32 Common freshwater plankton: *Volvox*, a rotifer, and diatoms. Magnification about X 400.

Dissolved oxygen in bodies of water comes essentially from two sources—(1) the atmosphere, by mixing when surface disturbances occur; and (2) from photosynthesis, by producers (algae). Anything that enhances mixing, such as winds, will increase the oxygen content of a lake. The temperature of the water is also involved since cold water can hold more oxygen than warm water.

OTHER CHEMICAL COMPOUNDS IN A LAKE

Some of the carbon dioxide in a lake is present as the bicarbonate ion since CO_2 readily unites with water. The entire relationship is:

$$CO_2 + H_2O \rightleftharpoons H_2CO_3 \rightleftharpoons HCO_3^- + H^+$$

Large amounts of CO_2 thus can increase the acidity of a body of water. This can happen at certain times of the year when consumer organisms increase in numbers and release large amounts of CO_2 through respiration.

Nitrates and phosphates are also important to the productivity of any ecosystem as was mentioned earlier. Since ammonia is the chief product of protein decomposition in plants and animals, it can be the source of nitrates if the proper bacteria are present. Phosphates, on the other hand, can be a limiting factor especially in oligotrophic lakes where they

136

(a)

(b)

Figure 5·33 Common freshwater plankton: (a) the microcrustaceans *Daphnia*, and (b) *Diaptomus*. Magnified about X 50.

may be insoluble and unavailable. Some algae can concentrate phosphorus in their systems by the active-transport process even when its concentration is extremely low in the water.

FOOD RELATIONSHIPS

The same food relationships exist in an aquatic community as in a terrestrial system:

Producers → Consumers → Decomposers

A special group of organisms found in aquatic environments is the *plankton*, a large and varied group of mostly small, free-floating organisms. Some plankton, the *phytoplankton*, contain chlorophyll and therefore are capable of synthesizing food. Other types of plankton, the *zooplankton*, must depend on the phyto-

plankton as their food source. The plankton are essential members of all aquatic food chains since they are the producers and primary consumers. One common chain found in many lakes is:

Phytoplankton → Zooplankton →
Small fish → Large fish

Diatoms are one of the important members of the phytoplankton group, and it has been said that "all flesh in a body of water is diatoms." Although the statement probably exaggerates the condition, it does stress the importance of these producers to the overall system. Some of the common plankton members found in lakes are shown in Figures 5-32, 5-33 and 5-34.

Figure 5·34 Top and side views of a diatom, an important member of the phytoplankton. Magnification about X 1350. (Courtesy of General Biological Supply House.)

THE MARINE ENVIRONMENT

Today more and more attention is being focused on the sea, not only as a biome of interesting plants and animals but also as a source of food, minerals, petroleum, and even as a habitat for mankind's booming population.

The study of the sea is known as *oceanography* and encompasses all branches of science.

Perhaps the most well-known characteristic of the ocean is its high concentration of salt and mineral ions. The most abundant ions in seawater are sodium and chlorine followed by sulfur, magnesium, and calcium. In addition,

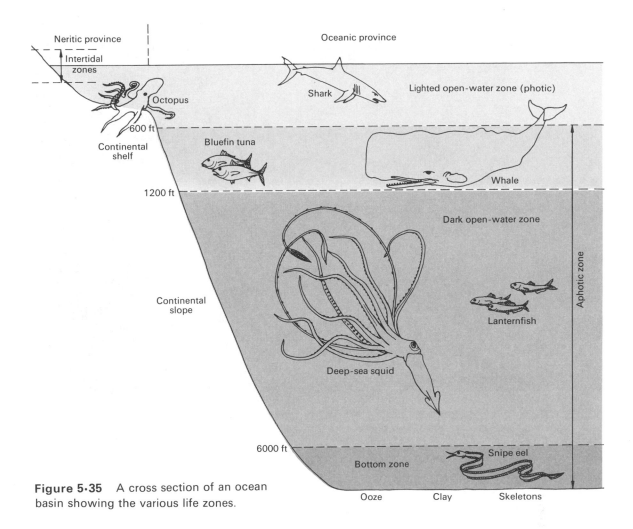

Figure 5·35 A cross section of an ocean basin showing the various life zones.

all the naturally occurring elements known to man are found in the sea.

The most common ions occurring in sea-water, expressed as grams per kilogram, are listed below.

		grams/kilogram
Chloride	Cl^-	19.4
Sodium	Na^+	10.7
Sulfate	$SO_4^=$	2.7
Magnesium	Mg^{++}	1.3
Calcium	Ca^{++}	0.4
Potassium	K^+	0.39
Bicarbonate	HCO_3^-	0.14
Bromide	Br^-	0.065

The dissolved ions in seawater occur in very stable proportions, and the total salinity often is calculated from the determination of the amount of chloride ion. The total salt concentration or salinity is considered to be the total grams of solids, excluding organic material, found in one kilogram of seawater. Salinity of the oceans averages 35 parts per thousand (g/kg). Salinity varies greatest in the surface water which is affected by land runoff, precipitation, evaporation, and melting polar ice. Salinity is highest in the tropical regions owing to the greater rate of evaporation.

The five major oceans of the earth are the Pacific, Atlantic, Indian, Arctic, and the

Figure 5·36   Modern methods utilized in the study of ocean-bottom life. Woods Hole oceanographers lowering a deep-sea camera from the research vessel Atlantis. (Courtesy of R. G. Munns and David Owen.)

Antarctic. The oceans are shaped generally like a wash basin in which the rim of the basin represents the continental shelf or the edge of the continents. A relatively shallow area of water, the *neritic province*, covers the continental shelf. The *oceanic province*, the deeper region of the sea, lies off the continental shelf (the major portion of the wash basin in our analogy). The continental shelves extend from the shore an average of 100 miles and form the continental slope, a gradual slope downward to the ocean bottom. The profiles of the Pacific and Atlantic show an irregular topography of ridges, basins, and deep trenches. The Mariana trench, believed to be the deepest, is located east of the Philippine Islands in the Pacific. In 1960 the manned bathyscaph Trieste II descended to a depth of 35,802 feet, man's deepest penetration. Although there are several deep trenches, the average depth of the oceans is two and a half miles (12,000 feet).

Since the amount of photosynthesis is determined by the availability of light, the ocean is often zoned according to light penetration (Figure 5-35). The upper 600 feet, the lighted open-water or *photic* zone, contains the largest number of organisms, and plankton are especially abundant in this zone. The phytoplankton are essentially algal organisms with diatoms, dinoflagellates, blue-green algae, and green algae as the important groups. Although zooplankton species contain representatives from many animal phyla, the crustaceans are easily the most predominant in both total numbers and species. Another category of organisms, the *necton*, are free-swimming organisms such as fish, squid, and whales which live not only in the photic zone but in all parts of the ocean. Below the depth of photosynthetic activity, the rate of food utilization is greater than food production and consequently more oxygen is consumed than is produced by photosynthesis. The depth at

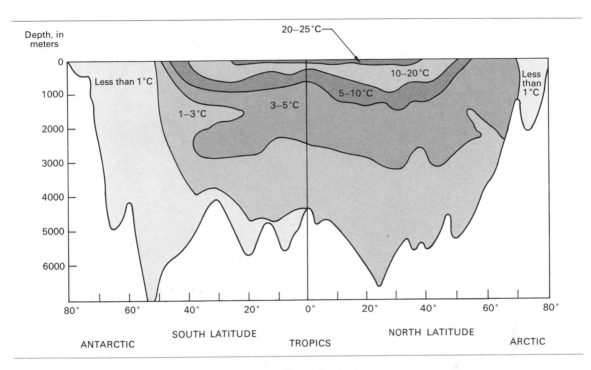

Depth, in meters

20–25°C

Less than 1°C

10–20°C

Less than 1°C

1–3°C

3–5°C

5–10°C

80° 60° 40° 20° 0° 20° 40° 60° 80°

SOUTH LATITUDE   NORTH LATITUDE

ANTARCTIC   TROPICS   ARCTIC

Figure 5·37 Generalized temperature profile of the Atlantic Ocean.

which the respiratory and photosynthetic rates are equal is termed the *compensation depth*.

Although the upper 600 feet of the ocean is generally referred to as the photic zone, some light does penetrate to 1200 feet. The light between 600 and 1200 feet is insufficient for photosynthesis, however, and thus the area below 600 feet is generally called *aphotic*. Below 1200 feet is the dark open-water zone which is a region of perpetual darkness. The animals living here are primarily predators that feed on smaller forms and exhibit interesting adaptations. Some, such as the viperfish and pelican fish, possess enormous jaws and sharp teeth, whereas others utilize luminescent organs to attract prey. Below 6000 feet is the bottom or *benthic* zone. Samples brought to the surface by dredging and net trawling from this depth include such organisms as bacteria, silicious sponges, sea cucumbers, bivalves, polychaete worms, various crustaceans, and brittle stars. Perhaps the newest and most efficient method of surveying benthic life is that of closed-circuit television (Figure 5-36).

Temperature in the ocean also limits the growth and respiration of both plants and animals. Many organisms are distributed according to their ability to withstand extreme temperatures. In general, however, the necessity for adaptation to great fluctuations in temperature is small when compared to that required in the land environment.

The major temperature variations in the ocean occur in the upper 3000 feet. The Arctic and Antarctic regions are always near 0°C, the Antarctic being somewhat colder. Although certain seas such as the Red Sea reach surface temperatures above 30°C, the major expanse of ocean surface is 15–27°C. Since seawater freezes at −1.9°C, the range of surface water is approximately −1.9°C to 30°C. The deeper water below 6000 feet between the two poles varies only 2 to 3 degrees throughout the seasons of the year. These temperature relationships are illustrated in Figure 5-37, which represents a section of the Atlantic Ocean between the Arctic and Antarctic poles.

141

High-tide zone

Mid-tide zone

Low-tide zone

Figure 5·38 Zonation on a rocky west coast. Note the vertical rock which shows the tide zones and some of the typical organisms found there. The holes in the rock were bored by piddock clams. (Courtesy of Helen Dillon.)

A seasonal thermocline also can exist in the oceans, but it is less pronounced than that in freshwater lakes. Several factors that may contribute to this include: (1) the influence of warm or cold currents; (2) the geographical location—tropical, temperate, or polar; (3) and the amount of mixing produced by wave action and upwelling. Because the surface

(a)   *(b)*

Figure 5·39 West Coast rocky beach. (*a*) This rocky reef is exposed only at very low tides. It abounds with both algal and animal life. (*b*) A close-up view showing various algae. (Courtesy of Sally Reid.)

water of the tropical regions is consistently warm, little mixing occurs and a thermocline persists there throughout the year. In temperate and northern latitudes where surface cooling does occur, cyclic temperature profiles may be established similar to those of freshwater lakes. Vertical mixing and upwelling allows a recirculation of minerals necessary to maintain the phytoplankton. Consequently the greatest amount of plankton and therefore the best fishing are found in the higher northern and southern latitudes.

THE INTERTIDAL ZONES

Tide refers to the vertical rise and fall of coastal waters resulting primarily from the gravitational effects of the moon and sun. The horizontal movements of water, the currents, are a consequence of tide, wind, temperature, and salinity. Plants and animals that live in the intertidal zones are repeatedly covered and uncovered by the cyclical tides. In general, four intertidal life zones may be recognized: (1) spray zone, (2) high-tide zone, (3) mid-tide zone, and (4) low-tide zone (Figure 5-38). (Tides are designated from a zero point that is calculated as the average of

the low tides. This average is indicated as zero on a tide table and consequently a range occurs on each side of this zero reference. Fluctuations above zero are plus tides and those below are minus tides.) The spray zone is never covered by water except during severe storms. The high-tide zone is above tide table zero, mid-tide represents the normal zero range, and the low-tide zone is uncovered only by minus tides (0 to -3).

The physical nature of the beach is significant in determining which species of plants and animals can survive there. The most common beach types are rocky, sandy, and mud flat (Figures 5–39, 5–40, and 5–41). In many areas, nearby freshwater sources may produce brackish or estuarine conditions. Organisms living in the estuarine habitat must be able to withstand extreme fluctuations in salinity. Several mechanisms exist in the organism for the regulation of internal salt concentration when the salt concentration changes in the environment. Some specific examples will be discussed in Chapter 7 under the topic of osmoregulation. Other determining factors of the population of a beach include the amount of protection available from the pounding surf and the length of tidal exposure.

Figure 5·40 West Coast sandy beach. (Courtesy of H. R. Dursch.)

The animals living in the tide zones show definite zone preferences and often specific physiological adaptions for living in these particular zones. On the rocky, unprotected beaches of the Pacific Northwest, for example, the air-breathing isopod (*Ligyda*) and the small periwinkle snail (*Littorina*) live on the rocks and in the crevices in the spray zone; the acorn barnacle (*Balanus*) and the shore crab (*Hemigrapsus*) inhabit the high-tide zone; the purple and green sea urchins (*Strongylocentrotus*), green anemone (*Anthopleura*), and the black turban snail (*Tegula*) are common in the midtide zone; the giant red sea urchin (*Strongylocentrotus franciscanus*) and the gum boot chiton (*Cryptochiton*) live in the low-tide zone (Figure 5–42a). By far the greatest number and variety of plants and animals are found on the rocky beaches. Fragile organisms such as worms and sea cucumbers find shelter in crevices and under large rocks. Some animals, such as the sea urchins and piddock clams, actually burrow into hard sandstone in the numerous tide pools left by the receding tide. Other hardy individuals such as the barnacles, mussels, starfish, chitons, snails, and anemones cling to the rocks under the full force of the surf.

Sandy beaches may abound with clams, worms, sand dollars, and certain crabs (Figure 5–42b). Since distribution of life on the sandy beach is limited principally by the lack of shelter, attachment sites, and permanent tide pools, the burrowing animals are best suited to this environment. Zonation is also evident. On the Atlantic and Gulf coasts, the ghost shrimp and ghost crab can live quite high on the beach with their burrows reaching down to the low-tide level. The entire beach usually abounds with the small variable clam (*Donax*). Other common species include the edible venus clam (*Mercenaria*), the cockle (*Dinocardium*), arc shells (*Arca*), jackknife clams (*Ensis*), scallops (*Aequipecten*), and the edible blue crab (*Callinectes*). On the West Coast, the sandy

(a)

(b)

Figure 5·41 West Coast mud flat. (a) Tide in ; (b) tide out. (Courtesy of Sally Reid.)

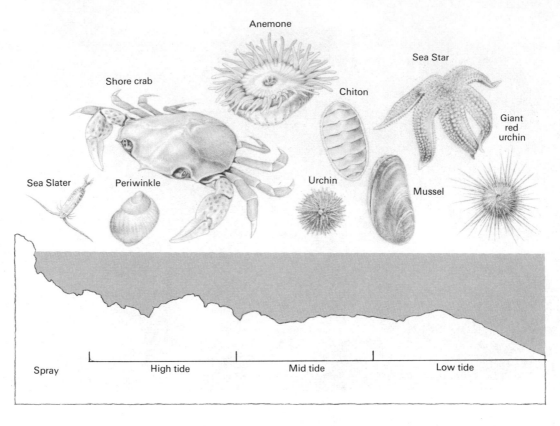

Spray   High tide   Mid tide   Low tide

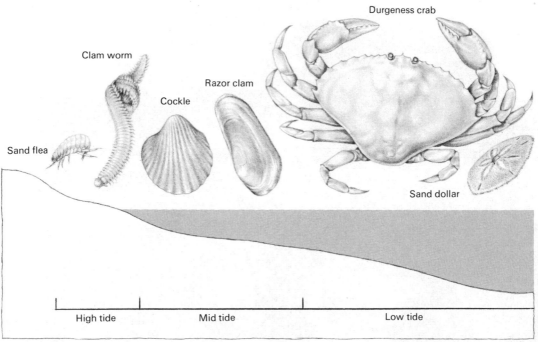

High tide   Mid tide   Low tide

Figure 5·42 (*a*) Representative animals found in the tide zones on a rocky west coast beach. (*b*) Representative animals found in the tide zones on a sandy west coast beach.

146

beaches support such edible varieties as the razor clam (*Siliqua*), butter clam (*Saxidomus*), steamer or little-neck clam (*Protothaca*), and the scallop (*Pecten*).

In the mud-flat habitat large expanses of mud and green eel grass may be exposed by even minor tidal fluctuations. Clams, worms, snails, crabs, shrimps, and isopods are the most common organisms. The muddy bottom is characteristic of shallow, protected bays that lack circulation and wave action. A rotten-egg stench of hydrogen sulfide gas from decaying organic matter is quite common when the tide is out. The mud is mixed with fine organic debris which provides excellent food for burrowing filter feeders and scavengers. On West Coast sand and mud flats, the large, edible geoduck clam (*Panope*) sometimes reaches a weight of six pounds. The Dungeness crab (*Cancer*), important for its food value, also thrives here.

POPULATIONS

POPULATION GROWTH

The members of a species form a *population* in a community. All populations possess certain characteristics such as birth rate, relative age structure, numbers (density), distribution pattern, and death rate. Once a population is established, it undergoes a rather specific growth pattern if conditions remain favorable and the habitat is not occupied by a competitor (Figure 5-43). Although population growth may be slow at first, it soon increases as more individuals mature and reproduce. Expansion is geometrical and fairly steady, until a population reaches *carrying capacity*. This capacity of any particular habitat depends not only on the amount of food available but also on the nutritional value of the food (Figure 5-44), which in turn depends on the nature of the soil and adequate amounts of water. The shelter or cover provided by a habitat for animals is also an aspect of the carrying capacity. When this limit has been reached, the population density usually fluctuates about

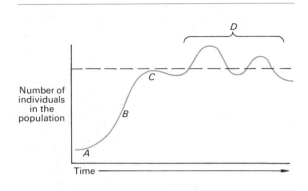

Figure 5·43 A graph illustrating the growth curve of a population. At *A*, the population is growing slowly because few members are present for reproduction. Soon, however, numbers have increased (*B*) to the point where many mates are present and a rapid increase occurs. Line *C* represents the carrying capacity of the environment. At *D* the population growth has reached a plateau since the carrying capacity has been exceeded; consequently, food and shelter are lacking to support any further increase in population numbers.

this level (Figure 5–43). If the carrying capacity is exceeded and the population becomes too dense, many harmful physiological and psychological effects may occur.

Much concern has been expressed recently that the human population may soon outgrow the carrying capacity of our planet. Others believe that modern technology can extend the carrying capacity to take care of our increasing population. It is true that better yields per acre are being achieved, and man is attempting to harvest the seas as well as raise crops in water. Man is also constructing high-rise apartments to provide shelter for the many world inhabitants. It is hoped, however, that man can adequately control the environmental pollution that results from the increased population. Even if man can solve the technological problems of providing basic needs for a greater world population, there are still the psychological and emotional considerations. The bulk of the human population now lives in cities. Can a human being withstand the stresses and strains produced by constant

147

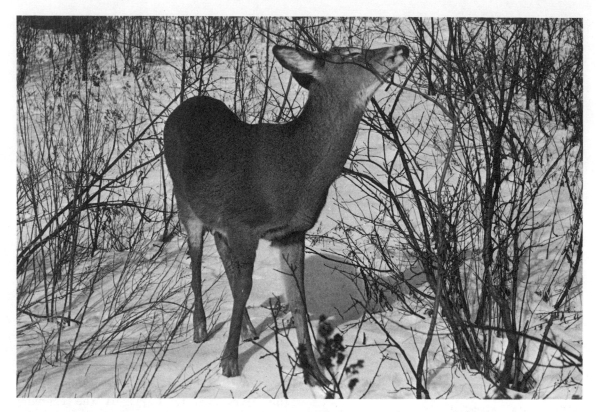

Figure 5·44 A deer browsing. The quality and availability of food determines the success of the population in an area. (Courtesy of New York State Conservation Dept.; photo by Nick Drakos.)

close contacts with other human beings? Will there be no recreational areas to which man can retreat if all of the land must be used either for living space or food supply? Desmond Morris has drawn an analogy between cities and zoos to more accurately define man's life in the "concrete jungle."

In 1962, John B. Calhoun reported in *Scientific American* that rats living under crowded conditions developed serious abnormal behavior patterns. In addition, the reproductive capabilities were reduced in these "stressed" animals. Calhoun expressed the belief that the colony eventually would perish from the failure to reproduce. In another experiment on crowding, published in 1964 by F. H. Bronson, the adrenal glands of crowded and fighting mice were found to be abnormally enlarged. The increased adrenal secre-

tions had caused an imbalance of certain body chemicals and finally affected the function of other glands and organs. Most ecologists feel that results and methods learned from the study of animal populations will assist in the solution of human population problems.

REGULATION OF POPULATIONS

Natural populations generally reach a balance of numbers based largely on the carrying capacity, relationships within the population, and outside forces.

Predation

One important force operating outside the population can be *predation*, in which one organism (prey) is eaten by another (predator).

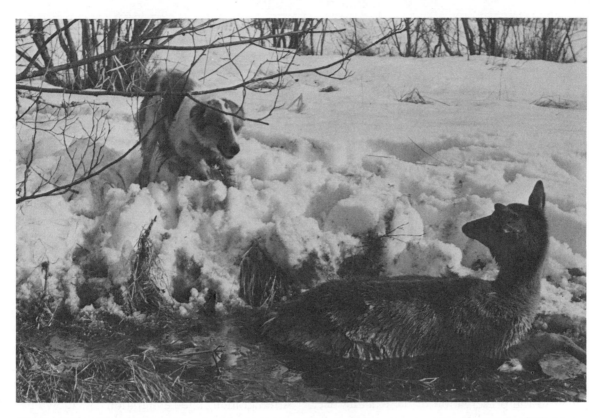

Figure 5·45 Dogs have replaced cougars as predators on deer in some areas. (Courtesy of Michigan Department of Natural Resources.)

In some forest communities, for example, deer are specific prey for cougars or dogs (Figure 5–45), and the size of the population of one species is affected by the population size of the other species. The snowshoe hare on the tundra is preyed upon by the lynx and its population cycles reflects this relationship; the lynx population increases as the snowshoe hare population decreases and vice versa. The general fluctuations in population density that exist between a predator and its prey are shown in Figure 5–46. The situation is usually more complicated than the simple relationships shown in this graph, since most organisms are part of a complex food web.

One well-known example of herbivore-predator imbalance is that of the deer population of the north rim of Arizona's Grand Canyon. The north rim area is a large plateau of approximately 10,000 square miles. This plateau, known as the Kaibab Plateau, is bounded on all sides by deep canyons that effectively isolate the animal populations.

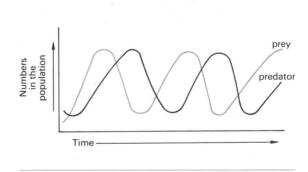

Figure 5·46 Simplified schematic showing fluctuations in population density of a predator and its prey. Note that the predator population reaches a peak after the prey population attains its peak.

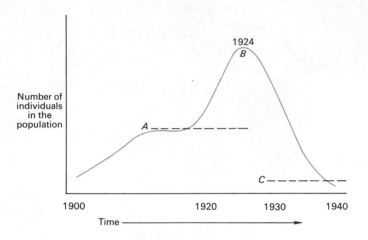

Figure 5·47 A graph representing the increased deer population on Kaibab Plateau after removal of natural predators. *A*, normal carrying capacity; *B*, peak population; *C*, decreased carrying capacity caused by overgrazing. (Redrawn from Dasman.)

In 1906, when the Grand Canyon was declared a national park, special attention was given to the preservation of the existing deer herd. Professional hunters and trappers were brought in to trap and kill the natural predators. By 1931, over 9000 predators had been removed including cougars, coyotes, bobcats, and wolves. The virtual absence of natural predators allowed the deer to flourish and the herd increased by about 20 percent each year. Although the Kaibab Plateau was rich in meadows, aspen groves, and ponderosa pine forest, it became apparent by 1920 that the area was overgrazed. By 1924 the deer population was estimated to be 100,000, over three times the carrying capacity (Figure 5–47).

During the next five years the Forest Service issued hunting permits but only 5000 animals were taken. Meanwhile, over 60 percent of the population died of starvation. By 1930 the herd had been lowered by hunting and starvation to about 20,000. Further hunting and deaths finally brought the herd back into a balance with the environment, and by 1940 the herd numbered approximately 10,000.

Migration

Immigration and emigration of individual members of a population also may regulate the density of that population. An interesting example of this is a population of lemmings, mouselike rodents, living in the Scandinavian countries. The lemming species has a peculiar cyclic increase and decrease in population. In most lemming groups, fluctuations occur every three to four years. Apparently ample food and increased litter size cause the increased population.

During the peak of the population cycle, however, large numbers of these small animals leave their home ground in mass migrations. For many years these "suicide marches" (so-called because many drown in streams and in the sea) were believed to be simply a quest for food. The leading proponent of this theory is Dr. Olavi Kalela of Finland. Independent studies by Garrett Clough and J. J. Christian of the United States indicate that there may be additional causes for these migrations. Christian has proposed the theory that increases in population density cause social

Figure 5·48 An early stage in a lemming fight. (Courtesy of Garrett C. Clough.)

stresses that result in lower birth rates. Earlier in our discussion it was mentioned that stress could bring about increased adrenal-gland secretion which influenced other organs. In this case, the control of egg production by the ovary and normal maternal functions could be altered.

Field observations by Clough in 1963 and 1964 indicate that lemmings show unusual intolerance for others of their species. As the population and social stresses increase, fighting and avoidance may trigger the migrations (Figure 5–48). According to Clough, the middle-sized lemmings leave the home territory first, leaving the older breeding population and the young behind. Many move into less favorable marsh and field areas and usually perish during the first winter. The very aggressive lemmings also appear to move away from high-density areas. Some scientists believe that this reaction to social stress is an innate mechanism that keeps these rodents from eating all the available food in an area and thus destroying the entire species through starvation.

Territoriality

Populations of most wild animals show distinct behavioral patterns that relate directly to the "ownership" of particular areas. This *territoriality* has been noted among both vertebrate and invertebrate animals. The concept of territoriality has recently been popularized by such writers as Konrad Lorenz, Robert Audrey, Desmond Morris, and Farley Mowat. Although most authors take an individual approach, it is now well established that the claiming and defense of territory plays an important role in animal populations.

The territoriality exhibited by wolves, rabbits, mice, sea lions, and other animals demonstrates that some wild populations can and do regulate themselves in nature. Territories are staked out by animals on both permanent and seasonal bases. Rabbits, for example, construct a permanent burrow-filled warren with established trails and warning signs surrounding the area. Many of the mechanisms utilized by rabbits to mark and protect their territory are now known. Roman

Myktowycz, in working with the wild Australian rabbit, has found two glands that produce marking secretions, an anal gland and a chin gland. The anal gland coats fecal pellets with a secretion easily recognized by other rabbits. When a warren is established, the male rabbits excrete pellets in mounds and urinate around the circumference, thereby warning any intruder that the area is occupied. The chin-gland secretions are utilized in marking twigs and grass for the same purpose.

Song birds establish a temporary territory early in the spring for breeding and nesting. The male flies from tree to tree around his area singing, repulsing intruding males, and attempting to attract a mate. The bird that sings the loudest and most often commonly occupies the largest territory.

Birds are perhaps more practical than lemmings, and confrontations over territory seldom involve serious fighting or death. In general, an intruder respects the line drawn by the occupants. If the intruder is larger and stronger than the defender, the defender usually retreats and gives up part of his territory. It is thought that the defense of a territory by an individual, pair, or group of animals has the effect of limiting the population density of an area and conserving the availability of food and shelter. If an invader crosses into a territory that is too large for an individual or group to defend, he may settle. If, on the other hand, the population density is high, he will immediately be repulsed and forced to try another area. To conclude, populations seemingly can be regulated by the availability of food and shelter, territoriality, and perhaps social stress reactions.

SOCIAL HIERARCHY

In many animals territoriality and social hierarchy are closely related. In his study of rabbit territoriality, Myktowycz also showed a direct correlation between the amount of marker-gland secretion and the position of the individual in the social structure of the warren. The development and secretion of

Figure 5·49 Dr. Karl von Frisch, formerly of the University of Munich, Germany. His studies in the language of the bees are a classic work in animal behavior. (Courtesy of Ernst Bohm.)

these glands appears to be under the control of the sex hormones. A social structure or ranking can be found in nearly all animal groups. It is very evident among fish, birds, and domestic animals. Ring-necked doves exhibit a rather complex behavior under caged conditions. If the cage is large enough, each dove will settle into a specific territory although eating and drinking facilities are shared. The addition of more birds will eventually upset this balance and a rigorous *peck order* will result. Each bird will assume his place between those he literally can peck and those that peck him. Usually the largest and most aggressive bird becomes dominant and is not pecked by any other bird. This social order is maintained in the group, especially in feeding and roosting preferences. Although this social ranking is an obvious dictatorship, the result generally is a stable and efficient society.

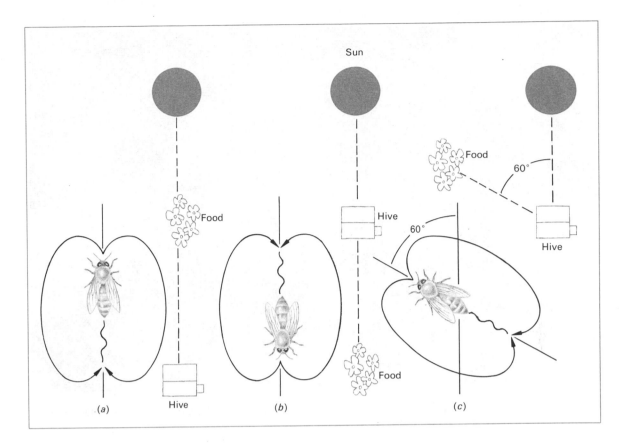

Figure 5·50 Three examples of bee-dance communication. (*a*) The source of food is in a straight path between the hive and the sun. (*b*) The food is directly away from the sun. (*c*) The food is toward the sun, but 60 degrees to the left. (After von Frisch.)

SOCIETY AND COMMUNICATION

A *society* may be defined as a group of animals living and working together for common benefit. It has long been recognized that certain species have evolved complex societies, but only recently have we begun to understand the nature of their languages and social structure. Other than man, the most highly developed societies are found in insects, principally bees, wasps, ants, and termites.

Bees and Communication

One of the best-studied examples of communication among animals is that of the honeybee. In the late 1940s, the Austrian biologist Karl von Frisch (Figure 5–49) reported several revolutionary theories based on his observations of bees. Von Frisch had demonstrated that a bee returning to its hive was capable of communicating the quality, direction, and distance of a food supply to the others. Soon most of the bees left the hive and flew directly to the food. Through careful observations, von Frisch learned that the messenger bee performed a specific dance on the vertical face of the honeycomb (Figure 5–50). The dance consisted of running around in a circular path but crossing the diameter in only one direction, or, more simply, two semicircular paths. As the bee crosses the diameter in a straight line, it waggles its abdomen (represented by the wavy line in Figure 5–50). Von Frisch studied the dance patterns very carefully and proposed the following interpretation. If the food source were on a line directly between the

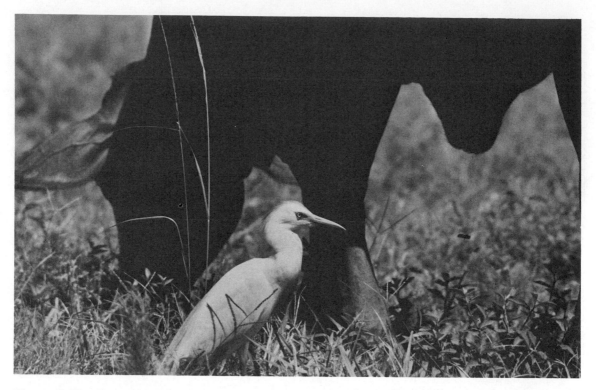

Figure 5·51 Commensalism. As insects are stirred up by grazing cattle, egrets follow and feed on the insects. (Photo by Walter Dawn, National Audubon Society.)

hive and the position of the sun, the straight crossruns are made straight up (↑). If the food were to be found on a line directly away from the sun, the crossruns were straight down (↓). In order to communicate the location of food that was not on a direct hive-sun line, the dancer angled its crossruns to correspond to the direction and angle from the hive (Figure 5–50c). For instance, a crossrun angle of 60 degrees to the left of the upward vertical axis meant that the food was on a path 60 degrees to the left of the sun-hive line (going toward the sun).

The "bee dance" has since been studied extensively with the aid of modern instrumentation. Harold Esch of the University of Notre Dame discovered that bees also emit sounds during their dance. Furthermore, he learned that "voiceless" bees could not stimulate others to leave the hive even though the dance was done repeatedly. Although the exact role of the bee sounds is not yet clear, it is probable that they are essential for interpretation by the bees inside the completely dark hive. In other experiments, Esch proved that the abdominal waggling time is the cue to the distance to the food; the longer the waggling time, the farther away the food. Von Frisch thought that this distance was conveyed by the number of crossruns per minute.

RELATIONSHIPS AMONG SPECIES

In most communities very close relationships may exist between two or more species. These intimate associations, *symbiosis* (living together), can be discussed under three categories: *commensalism, mutualism,* and *parasitism.*

Commensalism is a relationship between two organisms in which one member of the pair receives direct benefit while the other is neither benefited nor harmed (Figure 5–51). When

Figure 5·52 Mutualism. These small fish derive protection from predators by living among the tentacles of sea anemones. At the same time, the feeding fish benefit the anemone by cleaning small particles away. (Robert Ames, Photo Find, S.F.)

certain species of barnacles attach to whales, they are transported to new feeding grounds and are also geographically dispersed. In the tropics some plant species, such as orchids, grow on trees, gaining only a base for attachment. Another example is a tropical fish that lives in the intestine of a sea cucumber. Apparently, the sea cucumber is not affected but the fish gains a safe home.

Mutualism is the relationship in which two organisms benefit from each other (Figure 5–52). Many of these associations are found in nature and often the situation is not clear as to how much benefit each obtains. A lichen, for example, is made up of an alga and a fungus

living in a mutualistic relationship, wherein the alga produces food for both while the fungus obtains and holds water (Figure 5–53). Protozoans capable of digesting cellulose from wood live in the gut of termites. The termites provide shelter and food for the protozoans which assist the termite in the digestion of its food.

Parasitism is the relationship in which one member derives benefit while the other is harmed (Figure 5–54). Parasites that inhabit the outer surfaces of their hosts are ectoparasites; those that live within the host organism are endoparasites. External forms include fleas and ticks which suck blood from their hosts. Internal parasites, such as tapeworms or liver

155

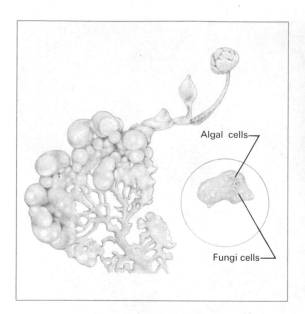

Figure 5·53 Mutualism in a lichen. The inset shows algae cells among the fungus filaments.

Algal cells

Fungi cells

Figure 5·54 An ectoparasite. A sea lamprey attached to a fish. (Courtesy of Ontario Dept. of Lands and Services.)

flukes, show interesting structural and physiological adaptations. The tapeworm, for example, has evolved attachment devices such as hooks and suckers on its anterior end to prevent dislocation from the host's intestine (Figure 5–55). During the course of the human tapeworm life cycle (Figure 5–56), a cow eats grass infected with tapeworm eggs from human feces. Upon entering the cow's intestine, the eggs rupture and release many six-hooked larvae. These larvae bore through the intestinal wall into the blood or lymph where they are carried to the skeletal muscles. Here they encyst in an inactive bladder until they are eaten by man. When man eats rare beef infested with these, the bladders turn inside out to expose the head which attaches by suckers to the intestinal wall. Sexual segments, known as proglottids, produced by the young worm mature and break off at the posterior end to release fertilized eggs which are distributed in feces. In this case man is the primary host since this is the phase of the life cycle where sexual reproduction occurs. The cow is the intermediate host which harbors

Figure 5·55 The anterior hooks and suckers of a mature dog tapeworm. These devices attach the tapeworm to the intestinal lining. (Courtesy of Carolina Biological Supply Co.)

Bladder worm called a cysticercus develops from each cyst

Onchospheres are released in cow's intestine, penetrate into the blood stream, and encyst in skeletal muscle

Man eats mature bladder worm in poorly cooked beef

Ripe proglottid

Egg containing six-hooked onchosphere

Cow ingests egg

Worm reaches sexual maturity and releases segments, called proglottids, in feces

Scolex evaginates in the intestine of man and attaches by means of suckers

Figure 5·56   Life cycle of a beef tapeworm, a parasite.

Figure 5·57   An example of a plant parasite: mistletoe growing on oak trees.

the larval forms. The Chinese liver fluke undergoes a more complicated life cycle in which the larvae develop in a snail and later encyst in fish muscle before becoming sexually mature adults in the human liver. Another parasitic adaptation of tapeworms and flukes is the capacity for laying large numbers of eggs.

There are also parasitic plants. Mistletoe, which lives on oak trees (Figure 5–57), is a common example of a plant parasite. It actually sends rootlike structures into the vascular tissue of the oak tree and taps its nutrient supply. In order for a parasite to be successful, however, the host must not be destroyed, and although well-adapted parasites may weaken their hosts, they seldom cause its immediate death.

The three symbiotic groups listed here are somewhat arbitrary and open to interpretation. Not all biologists agree on the placement of a particular association into a category. Perhaps one symbiotic relationship is evolving toward another type of relationship—a commensalistic toward a parasitic association. It is easy to visualize how a harmless commensal could eventually become a parasite. Perhaps the

157

mistletoe once used the oak tree only for an attachment, much like the commensalism between some tropical plants, but as parts evolved permitting complete penetration into the vascular system, a parasitic relationship was established.

EFFECT OF MAN ON NATURAL COMMUNITIES—CONSERVATION

Some of the biggest problems confronting the human species today involve the relationship of man to his environment and therefore are ecological in nature. These environmental problems result from two factors: (1) man's increasing population density which places a tremendous burden on the carrying capacity of the total world ecosystem (Figure 5–58), and (2) man's ability to control the ecology of other organisms and to intentionally alter the natural environment.

The first problem, the increasing human population, was pointed out in the discussion on population. Man's ability to ultimately provide adequate food and shelter and to withstand the psychological and sociological effects of overcrowding was questioned. Although these pose great dilemmas to man (especially

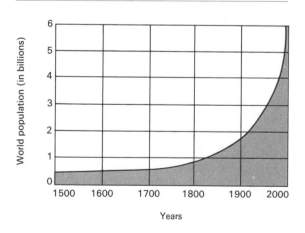

Figure 5·58 Graph showing human population growth from 1500 to present.

Figure 5·59 Downtown Los Angeles on a smoggy day in 1968. Heavy smog limits visibility so that mountains seen easily on clear days are completely invisible. (Courtesy of the Los Angeles County Air Pollution Control District.)

Figure 5·60 Detergent foam on the Mississippi River, an example of water pollution. (Photo by John H. Gerard from National Audubon Society.)

in underdeveloped countries), perhaps of even greater magnitude is the problem of pollution of the total environment. This problem has arisen mainly because of population increase. In the future the human race must be more concerned with adequate waste-disposal systems and control of air pollution (produced particularly by industry and automobiles), water pollution, and even noise pollution (Figures 5–59 and 5–60). In addition, each individual member of the population must assume a responsibility for a healthy environment to the point of a general concern for "littering" (Figures 5–61 and 5–62).

In most natural ecosystems a balance is generally achieved between the living populations and the environment, with certain limits providing the pivotal points for this balance. Although these balances can be upset and shifted by natural forces such as storms and

fires, they can also be disrupted by man. In fact, farming methods, and to a certain extent forest management, are based on a disturbance of natural conditions in which man clears the land and replants with his desired crop or uses the cleared land for grazing. Improper farming techniques or overgrazing may lead to a decrease in vegetational cover which in turn leads to erosion of the soil. A greater and uneven runoff of water usually flows from an eroded area, and this increase of water plus the added soil and rocks can affect aquatic ecosystems at some distance from the overgrazed site.

Of equal concern is the introduction of new plant and animal species into areas that are in relative balance. For example, the accidental introduction of the chestnut blight fungus from China virtually eliminated the American chestnut. In the early 1900s the Belgian hare

159

Figure 5·61 Careless disposal of wastes by man not only pollutes the environment but also distracts from the beauty of nature. (Photo by Dave Repp from National Audubon Society.)

Figure 5·62 Man's lack of concern for his environment results in water pollution and spoiled recreation areas as well as unfit habitats for many forms of aquatic life. (Courtesy of Ward's Natural Science Establishment, Inc., Rochester, N. Y.)

was introduced as a commercial enterprise on San Juan Island in Puget Sound. Many rabbits, however, escaped the breeding farm, reproduced rapidly, and soon overran the island. It was practically impossible to raise a home garden and the pea farms suffered severe damage during the cyclic peaks of the population. In 1962 the red fox was introduced as a predator and the rabbit population has dropped appreciably. A similar situation has occurred in Europe and parts of Asia where the American muskrat has been introduced and is spreading throughout these countries.

Earlier in this chapter the Kaibab deer story revealed how man can also upset an ecological balance through the removal of specific members from a community. Many serious problems have developed as a result of man's interference, either deliberately or accidentally, with natural, balanced ecosystems. The ecology of an area should be carefully studied and the relationships between all members of that area should be known before new species are added or existing ones removed.

The use of pesticides has been practiced extensively over the last 25 years in the United States in an attempt to protect crops from insects and fungi. Serious concern about the effects of these chemicals on other organisms has been expressed in the last ten years. For example, the unintended incorporation of DDT into the bodies of animals such as fish, birds, and mammals has recently alarmed many biologists. One such example is the effect of DDT on the reproductive capacity of ospreys. These birds feed on fish living in water which has been polluted by DDT. Essentially the DDT inhibits the natural mechanism that regulates the deposition of calcium in the egg shells. Embryos in the soft-shelled eggs have such a drastically reduced chance of survival that the osprey is now threatened with extinction. Rachel Carson, in her book *Silent Spring*, discusses the problem at great length and relates many instances in which pesticides used to control insects have also annihilated desirable organisms such as

birds, crops, and trees. The following quotation from her work indicates that mankind should certainly scrutinize this practice:

> For as long as man has dwelt on this planet, spring has been the season of rebirth, and the singing of birds. Now in some parts of America spring is strangely silent, for many of the birds are dead—incidental victims of our reckless attempt to control our environment by the use of chemicals that poison not only the insects against which they are directed but the birds in the air, the fish in the rivers, the earth which supplies our food, and, inevitably (to what degree is still unknown), man himself.[*]

The use of radioactive isotopes and the testing of nuclear weaponry is also a cause for concern. Although the total harm that radiation can produce in living organisms is still not known, we are aware of certain metabolic disorders and general genetic changes that it can produce. The increases in background radiation, to which organisms are susceptible, are due chiefly to fallout and, to some extent, to the disposal of radioactive waste materials.

Some aspects of human interference with natural ecosystems may not seem as important as the items just discussed—that is, they may not be considered "life or death" issues. These are aspects dealing with the preservation of natural areas and certain species such as the bison or American buffalo which are important to man's aesthetic and recreational needs.

Before mankind realized just how much he could influence natural systems and how much destruction he could produce through his interference, serious imbalances in nature occurred. Therefore man's imprudent exercise of his power, as well as his inability to efficiently use all natural resources, has caused many of the basic problems facing the human race. But many people now realize the importance of natural resources and the concept of *conservation*, the wise management of

*Rachel Carson, *Silent Spring*, Houghton Mifflin, New York, 1962, jacket copy.

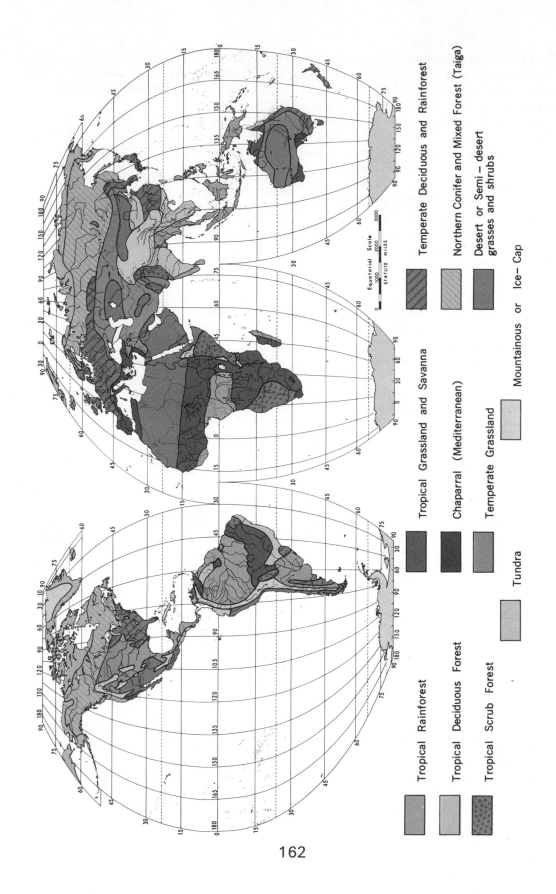

Figure 5·63 Map showing the major biomes of the world.

Tropical Rainforest

Tropical Deciduous Forest

Tropical Scrub Forest

Tropical Grassland and Savanna

Chaparral (Mediterranean)

Temperate Grassland

Tundra

Temperate Deciduous and Rainforest

Northern Conifer and Mixed Forest (Taiga)

Desert or Semi – desert grasses and shrubs

Mountainous or Ice– Cap

Equatorial Scale

STATUTE MILES

162

natural resources. In the United States, man's first conservational concern was for the forests that were heavily, and indiscriminately, logged in the 1800s. A relationship between logged-off lands, water runoff, and soil erosion was soon noted. Man cannot afford to exhaust resources such as soil and certain minerals which cannot be replaced. Although water and air are quantitatively inexhaustible, the quality of these resources must be guarded carefully. Man's success on this planet will be determined chiefly by the extent to which he is progressively concerned with his effect upon nature.

SUMMARIZING PRINCIPLES

All the organisms living and interacting within a particular area constitute a biotic community; when the nonliving components of an area are considered with the living, it is called an ecosystem.

The energy flow through a community is in one direction, from the producers to the consumers to the decomposers; and the materials, such as water, oxygen, carbon, nitrogen, and phosphorus, move in a cyclic pattern.

Every community undergoes a series of changes, succession, until a group of organisms, the climax, are established which can live and reproduce most successfully in that area; the major terrestrial regions of the earth are tundra, northern coniferous forest, deciduous forest, tropical forest, grassland, and desert.

The members of a particular species in a community form a population and only a limited number can be adequately supported by the environment, the carrying capacity of any area; certain regulating mechanisms exist in all populations such as predation, migration, territoriality, and social hierarchy.

In most communities very close relationships often exist between two or more species; these relationships are known as symbiosis.

Mankind faces many environmental problems because of his increasing population density and his interference with natural ecosystems; in the future, man must be vitally concerned with conservation, the wise management of natural resources.

REVIEW QUESTIONS

1   Define the terms ecology, biotic community, niche, habitat, population, ecosystem, producers, consumers, and decomposers.

2   Distinguish between autotrophs and heterotrophs and identify their roles in the energy flow of the ecosystem. What is meant by trophic levels?

3   Game laws in most states protect such birds as sea gulls, hawks and owls. Why is this important?

4   Control of hunting and predators has had little effect on the decreasing caribou population of British Columbia. Logging and forest fires, however, have proved to be the major causes of this population decline. From this information can you explain why this is happening?

5 Legumes such as peas and beans contain large amounts of protein even though they may grow on nitrogen-poor soil. Explain.

6 Construct a diagram that will show the interrelationship of the carbon and oxygen cycles.

7 Find out what the climax vegetation is in your area. Next, find a piece of land that has been cleared or altered by man. Describe the changes that will probably take place in reestablishing the climax.

8 On San Francisco Peaks near Flagstaff, Arizona, alpine fir grows at about 12,000 feet. In the Cascade Mountains of western Washington this same species may grow at 5000 feet. How can you explain this distribution difference?

9 What could be some of the consequences of a late summer "bloom" (explosive growth) of phytoplankton in a lake? Consider temperature, oxygen, and zooplankton interrelationships.

10 Compare the physical and biological characteristics of the benthic and intertidal oceanic zones.

11 In about 1830, when England was colonizing India, the Indian population, which had probably been stable for a long period of time, increased rapidly. Explain the reason for this population growth.

12 In the 1870s starlings were introduced to the United States from Europe and gradually spread throughout the country. Construct a population curve, based on your knowledge of population dynamics, that will predict the growth rate and survival of this species in the United States.

13 Certain crabs have large colonies of sponges on their backs. What do you think is the symbiotic relationship between these two organisms and give your reasons.

14 List five major environmental problems facing mankind today and suggest two solutions for each.

SUPPLEMENTARY READINGS

Bormann, F. H., and G. E. Likens, "The Nutrient Cycles of an Ecosystem," *Scientific American*, October, 1970.

Brower, Lincoln P., "Ecological Chemistry," *Scientific American*, February, 1969.

Carson, Rachel, *The Sea Around Us*, New York, Oxford University Press, 1951.

Carson, Rachel, *The Edge of the Sea*, Boston, Houghton Mifflin, 1955.

Carson, Rachel, *Silent Spring*, Boston, Houghton Mifflin, 1962.

Clark, John R., "Thermal Pollution and Aquatic Life," *Scientific American*, March, 1969.

Collias, Nicholas E., *Animal Language*, BSCS Pamphlet No. 20, American Institute of Biological Sciences, Boston, Heath, 1964.

Davis, David E., *Integral Animal Behavior*, New York, Macmillan, 1966.

Deevey, Jr., Edward S., "The Human Population," *Scientific American*, September, 1960.

Dethier, V. G., and E. Stellar, *Animal Behavior*, 2nd ed., Foundations of Modern Biology Series, Englewood Cliffs, N.J., Prentice-Hall, 1964.

Dewey, E. S., "Bogs," *Scientific American*, October, 1958.

Editors of Ramparts, *Eco-Catastrophe*, San Francisco, Canfield Press, 1970.

Ehrlich, Paul R., *The Population Bomb*, New York, Ballantine Books, 1968.

Esch, Harold, "The Evolution of Bee Language," *Scientific American*, April, 1967.

Frisch, Karl von, "Dialects in the Language of the Bees," *Scientific American*, August, 1962.

Hailman, Jack P., "How an Instinct Is Learned," *Scientific American*, December, 1969.

Isaacs, John D., "The Nature of Oceanic Life," *Scientific American*, September, 1969.

Johnsgard, Paul A., *Animal Behavior*, Dubuque, Iowa, Wm. C. Brown, 1967.

Kormandy, Edward J., ed., *Readings in Ecology*, Englewood Cliffs, N.J., Prentice-Hall, 1965.

Kormandy, Edward J., *Organisms, Populations, and Ecosystems*, Dubuque, Iowa, Wm. C. Brown, 1966.

Limbaugh, Conrad, "Cleaning Symbiosis," *Scientific American*, August, 1961.

Lorenz, Konrad, *King Solomon's Ring*, New York, Thomas Y. Crowell, 1952.

Lorenz, Konrad, "The Evolution of Behavior," *Scientific American*, December, 1958.

Marples, Mary J., "Life on the Human Skin," *Scientific American*, January, 1969.

Meyerriecks, Andrew J., *Courtship in Animals*, BSCS Pamphlet No. 3, American Institute of Biological Sciences, Boston, Heath, 1962.

Mudd, Stuart, *The Population Crisis and the Use of World Resources*, Bloomington, Indiana University Press, 1964.

Mykytowycz, Roman, "Territorial Marking by Rabbits," *Scientific American*, May, 1968.

Revelle, Roger, "The Ocean," *Scientific American*, September, 1969.

Storer, John H., *Man in the Web of Life*, New York, Signet Science Library, 1968.

Tinbergen, N., *The Study of Instinct*, New York, Oxford University Press, 1951.

Tinbergen, N., "The Curious Behavior of the Stickleback," *Scientific American*, December, 1952.

Tinbergen, N., "The Evolution of Behavior in Gulls," *Scientific American*, December, 1960.

Woodwell, George M., "Toxic Substances and Ecological Cycles," *Scientific American*, March, 1967.

Wynne-Edwards, V. C., "Population Control in Animals," *Scientific American*, August, 1964.

6

Energy

Most of us have learned at some time or another that the source of all energy on earth is radiant energy from the sun. This is true for the great majority of living things; certain bacteria, however, have evolved mechanisms by which they can utilize energy from inorganic substances such as iron and sulfur. In our discussion of the origin of life in Chapter 2, it was noted that all forms of life would probably have died if some organisms had not acquired the ability to transform energy from sunlight into food molecules such as glucose.

The ability of biological organisms to trap, store, and utilize energy from their environment is one of the most intriguing aspects of modern biology. The exact mechanisms of energy transfer from one compound to another, without the use of heat as an intermediate form, are yet unknown, but certain chemical relationships are known that can help us understand the basic process.

ATP AND HIGH-ENERGY BONDS

First of all, it has been discovered that one compound capable of storing large amounts of energy in its chemical bonds is found universally in living organisms. This chemical compound has been identified as ATP (adenosine triphosphate). The structure of ATP is very similar to that

Figure 6·1 Two types of phosphate ester linkages: (*a*) glucose-6-phosphate, an example of a low-energy phosphate; (*b*) ATP showing the pyrophosphate ester that contains more energy.

of the nucleotide subunits found in nucleic acids (DNA and RNA) and is composed of adenine (nitrogen base), ribose (sugar), and three phosphate groups with ester linkages. It differs from a nucleotide of nucleic acid only in that it contains two extra phosphates.

In organic compounds there are two major classes of phosphate ester groups (recall the ester linkage from Chapter 2): (1) simple phosphate esters and (2) *pyrophosphate esters*. These organic phosphate groups differ in the amount of energy released upon hydrolysis of the ester linkage. When glucose is phosphorylated on the sixth carbon to form glucose-6-phosphate, this simple ester contains a relatively small amount of energy. The pyrophosphate ester located on ATP, however, is easily hydrolyzed to release large amounts of energy (Figure 6–1).

It is interesting that the basic nucleotide structure which might have been important in the origin of life is involved not only with reproduction and heredity but also in storing and supplying energy. Alterations in the basic structure adapt the molecule for the different jobs to be accomplished within living organisms. This example of a fundamental compound serving different vital functions is one of several such versatile compounds that are encountered in the study of biology.

How does the ATP molecule trap and store energy? Experiments have demonstrated that the energy is trapped in the last two phosphate esters that make up the "tail" of the molecule. Once trapped, however, the energy is not equally distributed among the three phosphate groups—the last phosphate ester contains the greatest energy, the middle ester a lesser amount, and the third the least.

The last pyrophosphate group, which contains the greatest energy, may be designated with the symbol $O \sim P$ to show that it is a high-energy ester. Upon hydrolysis in the laboratory, this group will release as much as 15,000 calories (Figure 6–2). It is important to note that this energy is not a property of the $O \sim P$ bond alone but involves the entire structure of the pyrophosphate group. When the high-energy ($\sim$) bond of ATP is broken, only one phosphate ester is lost. The remaining portion of the molecule then becomes ADP (adenosine diphosphate). It is also possible to extract additional energy (somewhat more than that from a simple phosphate ester) from the middle phosphate ester. Thus ADP may be hydrolyzed to AMP (adenosine monophosphate) with the release of about 4000 calories.

We should now be concerned with the primary source of this energy which is located in the pyrophosphate group. The high energy of ATP is obtained indirectly from the poten-

168

Figure 6·2 Diagrammatic representation of the results of a typical laboratory hydrolysis of ATP.

tial energy of electrons which spin in energy shells around the nuclei of all atoms. Each electron contains a specific amount of energy which is relative to its distance from the attracting nucleus—the farther from the nucleus, the greater the potential energy. Just as a satellite requires rocket energy to lift it into space against gravitational forces, the electrons require energy to reach their characteristic orbits. If an electron at a specific energy level is raised to a higher, but unstable, energy level and then returns to its original level, energy may be released in the form of heat or light (Figure 6–3). It is not the release of energy that is biologically important, however; it is transfer, and that is the unique role

of ATP. It acts as an intermediary between higher and lower energy compounds.

OXIDATION AND REDUCTION

The two chemical processes that provide energy for all living systems are oxidation and reduction reactions. The taking of oxygen into the structure of a compound is termed *oxidation*; a classic example of this process is the rusting of iron. In a strict chemical sense, however, it is necessary to define oxidation and its counterpart, *reduction*, in terms of the electron structure of the atoms. A compound is *oxidized* when it *loses* electrons and *reduced* when it *gains* electrons. Therefore oxidation is the removal of electrons from a substance and usually involves oxygen but may involve other elements such as sodium. Oxidation-reduction reactions must occur simultaneously and therefore are called *coupled reactions*. One good example of the coupled reaction is that between calcium and zinc in which calcium loses electrons and zinc gains electrons (Figure 6–4). Calcium, then, is the electron

Figure 6·4 The simultaneous oxidation-reduction reaction between calcium and zinc. When two electrons are transferred from Ca^v to Zn^{++}, the Zn^{++} is reduced to $Zn°$ and $Ca°$ is oxidized to Ca^{++}. Although this reaction is not typical of biological systems, it serves to illustrate electron transfer.

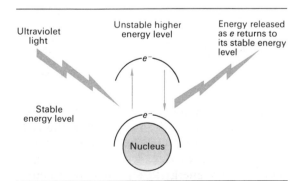

Figure 6·3 Diagram to illustrate how an electron can be excited by ultraviolet light to a higher energy level. Since the higher state is unstable, energy, in the form of light or heat, is released when the electron returns to its normal energy level.

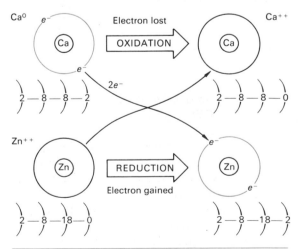

169

Figure 6·5 The structure of two hydrogen-transporting coenzymes—nicotinamide adenine dinucleotide phosphate (NADP) and flavin-adenine dinucleotide (FAD). The oxidized forms are shown on the left and the reduced forms are on the right. The reduced form of NADP is NADPH + H⁺ and will be referred to as NADP·2H.

donor and zinc is the electron acceptor. Organic oxidation-reduction reactions are somewhat more complex than this example. The electrons that we will be concerned with in our discussion of biological energy come from the carbon-carbon and carbon-hydrogen bonds produced in photosynthesis.

THE ROLE AND TRANSPORT OF HYDROGEN

In general, it is correct to equate the uptake of hydrogen with the uptake of an electron. Hydrogen will dissociate into its component proton and electron as $H \rightleftharpoons H^+ + e^-$ and the electron thus becomes a potential reducing agent. If the hydrogen-accepting dye, methylene blue, is exposed to hydrogen, it will take the electrons into its structure and turn colorless as shown in the following reaction:

Oxidized Form		Reduced Form
Methylene blue + 2H⁺ + 2e⁻	⟶	Methylene blue + 2H⁺
(blue color)		(colorless)

In the nutrition of an animal, certain foods must be digested and absorbed into the cells to provide energy. One exception to this is glucose (or dextrose), which is frequently called "quick energy." The quickness comes primarily because it does not require digestion and can be absorbed directly into the bloodstream to be transported to cells. The glucose molecule contains energy in its hydrogen bonds, and in every living cell there are special

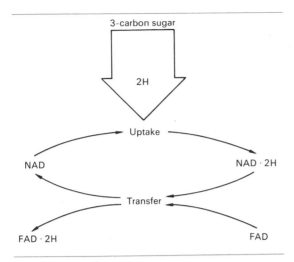

Figure 6·6 The oxidation-reduction reactions occurring between a three-carbon sugar and two coenzymes. Glucose is oxidized while NAD is being reduced. FAD is then reduced by hydrogen transfer from NAD·2H which then returns to its oxidized state. (The form of NAD here has one less phosphate group than NADP in Figure 6·5.)

enzyme systems to remove these hydrogens and make the released energy available for the production of ATP within the mitochondria. When hydrogen is removed by these *dehydrogenase* enzymes, it is passed on to a hydrogen-acceptor compound known as a *coenzyme*. The coenzyme may then transport the hydrogen to other compounds. Two coenzymes, very active in the uptake and transport of hydrogen, are NADP and FAD (Figure 6–5). The relationship between potential food energy, a three-carbon sugar, and the hydrogen-carrying coenzymes is summarized in Figure 6–6.

MITOCHONDRIA AND THE ELECTRON-TRANSPORT SERIES

In the description of the cell given in Chapter 3, the cytoplasmic organelles called mitochondria were introduced as the "powerhouses" of the cell. Biochemical research has demonstrated conclusively that ATP is actively produced in these bodies and made available for energy-requiring reactions throughout the organism.

In recent years, biochemists have succeeded in breaking the mitochondrion into small fragments. When enzymes and other compounds contained within the mitochondrion were identified, they were not surprised to find that many of the enzymes were actually attached to the cristae membranes. Thorough study of the fragments and their enzymes revealed that there was a definite pattern of hydrogen transfer through a series of alternate oxidation-reduction reactions. The first hydrogen acceptor is NAD which passes its 2H along to FAD as shown in Figure 6–6 and Figure 6–7(*a*).

Figure 6·7 The electron-transport series. Each segment is explained in the text. The compounds in (*a*) are coenzymes; (*b*) and (*c*) involve cytochromes *b*, *c*, *a*, and *a*₃.

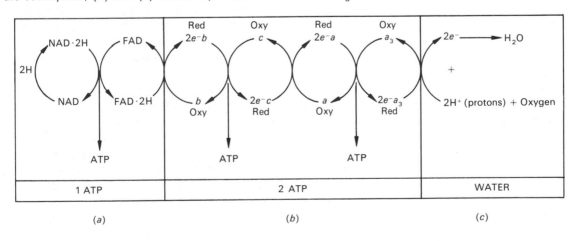

Cytochromes

The next compounds involved in the transfer of hydrogen are called *cytochromes*, Figure 6–7(*b*). Cytochromes are complex molecules that contain an atom of iron within a nitrogen ring structure (Figure 6–8). This nitrogen structure consists of carbon rings, known as pyrrol rings, and is called a *tetrapyrrol* compound. The name *cytochrome* (*cyto* = cell, *chrome* = color) refers to the fact that the basic tetrapyrrol ring structure is a colored compound or pigment found within the cell. The tetrapyrrol compound is an essential component of many important substances found throughout the living world. In fact, the chlorophyll pigment of green plants and the hemoglobin of blood are similar in structure to cytochromes.

The iron (Fe) is bonded to the nitrogens in such a manner that it can alternately pick up or lose electrons somewhat like the calcium in Figure 6–4. The cytochromes in this sequence, which have been studied primarily in beef heart muscle, are named *b*, *c*, *a*, and *a₃* (Figure 6–7). These cytochrome molecules differ only slightly in structure, and they all transport electrons along the folded inner membrane of the mitochondrion (Figure 6–9).

As electrons are passed along the *electron-transport series* (from $NAD \cdot 2H$ to cytochrome a_3), enabled by the action of enzymes known as reductases, enough energy is released at three points to complete the enzymatic phosphorylation of ADP to ATP. For every 2H made available to the transport series, three molecules of ATP are synthesized (Figure 6–7).

At the point where $FAD \cdot 2H$ gives up its hydrogens to the cytochromes (Figure 6–7, segment *b*) it is important to note that the protons ($2H^+$) are not directly transferred, since the iron accepts only the electrons. While the electrons are being transported along the cytochrome series, the protons are released in the mitochondrial fluid and, at the very end of the chain, protons are united with electrons with the help of cytochrome a_3

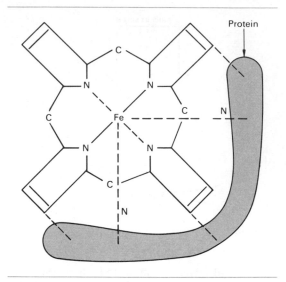

Figure 6·8   The general structure of a cytochrome molecule.

(Figure 6–7, segment *c*). At this time, cytochrome a_3 also catalyzes the addition of oxygen to the two hydrogen atoms to form the oxidation by-product, water. Oxygen thus acts as the final hydrogen acceptor and this is the vital role that oxygen plays in respiration.

HARNESSING AND RELEASING ENERGY

We have now formed a concept of biological energy, but it is still necessary to understand the *autotrophic* process by which energy from the sun is trapped to produce new organic molecules. When hydrogen is removed from these molecules in a stepwise process, energy is obtained for the synthesis of ATP. This process is called *cellular respiration*.

The processes of energy trapping and energy release can be illustrated as an "energy hill" in which the greatest potential energy is in the molecules at the summit (Figure 6–10). Note the cyclic movement of carbon dioxide and water. This schematic diagram summarizes the energy picture as we will discuss it—that is, the harnessing or trapping of

Figure 6·9 An electron micrograph of mitochondria from rat kidney tubule cells showing the inner cristae membranes; X 13,800. (Courtesy of J. D. Newstead.)

energy from the sunlight by *photosynthesis* and the subsequent release of this energy through the process of respiration in every living cell. Both photosynthesis and respiration are rigidly controlled and we need now to direct our attention to the detailed mechanics of these two processes.

PHOTOSYNTHESIS

"On this planet we are all guests of the green plants" is an expression used by some botanists to dramatize the fact that all organisms except some bacteria depend on photosynthesis as a

Figure 6·10 A summary of the energy concept showing the relationship between photosynthesis and respiration.

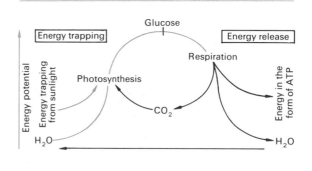

direct or indirect source of food. You may have experimented with goldfish or guppies and green aquarium plants to produce a "balanced aquarium." If you have, you may also have learned that it is a difficult task to "balance nature" in a closed container. In such a closed system many factors must be balanced between the plants and animals including gas exchange and assimilation of waste products. Three possible experimental approaches with some sprigs of *Elodea* and a goldfish are shown in Figure 6–11. Although this coexistence can actually persist for only a short period of time, because all aspects such as growth and reproduction rates have not been considered, it does illustrate the important interdependence of plants and animals.

Before proceeding with the details of this important process, we should consider some of the more important historical developments that led to man's present understanding of photosynthesis.

GAS EXCHANGE

The English scientist Joseph Priestley, in 1771, performed an experiment similar to our balanced aquarium in which he discovered that "plants purified the air for animals." Placing a green plant and a mouse in a sealed container, he observed that the organisms lived together much longer than either could exist alone (Figure 6–12). Although he did not understand the exact nature of the "purification" of air by plants, his experiments led ultimately to the discovery of the following interrelationship:

$$CO_2 + H_2O \xrightarrow[\text{Green plant}]{\text{Light}} \text{Organic molecules} + O_2$$

(from animal)   Green plant   (used by animals)

Our balanced aquarium was a simple example of gas exchange and food supply. It is neces-

Figure 6·11 The balanced-aquarium experiment.

Plant dies	Mouse dies	Plant and mouse live

Figure 6·12   Three experiments designed to show the interdependence of gas exchange between plants and animals.

sary to add, however, that the utilization of oxygen and release of CO_2 do not result only from the animal. Even though the green plant is capable of producing organic food, it must also oxidize this food to carbon dioxide, water, and ATP energy in order to continue its growth and function. Note the use of double arrows in Figure 6–13 to illustrate this respiration requirement.

RAW MATERIALS AND THE ROLE OF LIGHT

About 1450, Cardinal P. Nicolai Cusa was convinced that the mass of a green plant resulted from the interaction of water and sunlight and not from roots "eating" the soil as had been believed from the time of Aristotle. Much later, Jean-Baptiste Van Helmont reported in 1748 the results of an experiment that confirmed much of Cusa's thought. Van Helmont simply planted a five-pound willow shoot in 200 pounds of dried earth, watered this shoot for five years with rain water or distilled water, and finally weighed the two again. The willow had gained over 164 pounds while the soil had lost only two ounces. Van Helmont reasoned that 164 pounds of plant material had arisen from the water alone!

John Ingenhousz in 1779 recognized the role of light energy in photosynthesis. Ingenhousz wrote: "All plants possess a power of correcting, in a few hours, foul air unfit for respiration; but only in clear daylight, or in the sunshine." By 1804 advancements in chemistry allowed de Saussure to show that the photosynthetic process involved the uptake of carbon dioxide, the production of

Figure 6·13   A balanced aquarium illustrating the relationships of light, oxygen, and carbon dioxide.

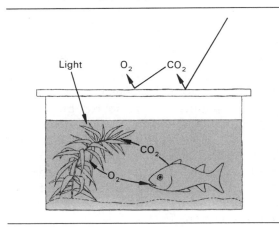

175

organic material, and the loss of oxygen. About this time Ingenhousz offered the incorrect theory that the carbon dioxide molecule was split by sunlight to provide carbon for the nourishment of the plant (and releasing the oxygen). If this were true, reasoned other scientists, the carbon must then be combined with the two hydrogens of water to form simple carbohydrates:

$$CO_2 + H_2O \xrightarrow{\text{Light}} \underset{\text{(carbohydrate)}}{CH_2O} + \underset{\text{(from } CO_2)}{O_2}$$

It was not until the 1930s that this idea was successfully refuted by C. B. Van Niel of Stanford University working with purple sulfur bacteria. Van Niel proposed that light somehow split (ionized) the water molecules and not the carbon dioxide molecules. Since Van Niel had found that these bacteria could photosynthesize without evolving oxygen, the splitting of carbon dioxide was seriously doubted. The new theory postulated that light energy split water into H^+ and OH^- radicals. The hydrogen could then be used to reduce CO_2 to carbohydrate (CH_2O) and the oxygen from the water could be given off as oxygen gas.

In 1939, a Cambridge University botanist, Robert Hill, published the results of a series of his experiments with isolated chloroplasts. In these classic experiments, dried leaves were ground with mortar and pestle and suspended in water. He then filtered this solution through glass wool to isolate the chloroplasts. By adding the known hydrogen acceptor ferric oxalate and the oxygen acceptor hemoglobin, Hill demonstrated that oxygen was liberated as iron was reduced. Hemoglobin, the oxygen-carrying pigment found in red blood cells, was a particularly good indicator since the oxyhemoglobin turns a bright red and could be easily distinguised in a colorimeter (Figure 6–14). Although Hill was not certain that the oxygen was being liberated from water, new techniques were soon to provide the answer to this question.

Figure 6·14 A representation of Hill's classic experiment. The chloroplasts were obtained from ground leaves and suspended in water. Hemoglobin was added as an oxygen acceptor. The chloroplasts reacted with the light to release oxygen from the water. When the hemoglobin accepted the oxygen, it turned bright red.

THE CONTRIBUTION OF OXYGEN-18

When isotopes of certain elements first became available in 1941, chemists at the University of California were able to incorporate oxygen-18 (heavy oxygen) into water to produce H_2O^{18}. Scientists were quick to recognize that oxygen-18 could be useful in clarifying the mystery surrounding the source of the oxygen liberated during photosynthesis. It should be explained here that oxygen-18 is not a typical radioactive element—that is, it does not emit radioactive waves or particles. With the use of a mass spectrograph, however, it can be identified by the difference in weight between it and oxygen-16. If the hypotheses of Van Niel and Hill were correct, green plants should take up this water and release oxygen-18 to the atmosphere. In experiments with the green alga *Chlorella*, it was determined not only that the oxygen released during photosynthesis contained oxygen-18 but also that no oxygen-18 could be detected in the plant carbohydrate. Although this experiment proved that oxygen was being released from ionized water, it did not prove that CO_2 was not contributing to the released oxygen. In order to confirm this, additional experiments were performed using $CO_2{}^{18}$ with the results that all the oxygen-18 was found incorporated into carbohydrate and no oxygen-18 was released. The experiments with oxygen-18 proved conclusively that the oxygen liberated in the Hill reaction was specifically that contained in the water molecule.

In nature water is always partially dissociated. As you recall from Chapter 2, most of the water on our planet is in the molecular form, but one liter of pure water contains 10^{-7} gram of hydrogen ion (H^+). This is a very small amount. If water is to contribute to the formation of organic fuel, there must be some mechanism for bringing about the permanent separation of the H^+ and OH^-. Essentially, this is the role of the light reaction often called *photolysis*. The light reaction then does not split the water molecule, but rather it brings about the permanent dissociation of the water molecule and makes protons and electrons available for the fuel-building process. This photolytic dissociation may be outlined as:

$$2H_2O \xrightarrow[\text{(in the chloroplast)}]{\text{Light}} 2H^+ + 2\,OH^-$$

(molecular state)   (in the chloroplast)   (ionized state)

THE CONTRIBUTION OF CARBON-14

Following the oxygen-18 experiments, many investigators became concerned with the chain of events in the photosynthetic process. Notable among these was Melvin Calvin (Figure 6–15) of the University of California at Berkeley who utilized carbon-14, a radioactive isotope of carbon, to trace the sequence

Figure 6·15 Dr. Melvin Calvin, noted for his work in tracing the pathway of carbon in photosynthesis for which he was awarded a Nobel Prize in 1961.(Courtesy of Lawrence Radiation Laboratory.)

of carbon compounds in the formation of glucose. Calvin was able to demonstrate the exact steps in this process by introducing $C^{14}O_2$ into green algae and determining the incorporation of C^{14} into the intermediate compounds produced during the synthesis of glucose. In this manner Calvin and his coworkers were able not only to identify the carbon compounds involved but also their sequence in the photosynthetic pathway.

In recent years many new schemes have been postulated to explain the actual mechanism of photosynthesis. These ideas have been formulated primarily through the use of modern biochemical techniques. The discovery and isolation of several new compounds in the chloroplast have led to the verification of their function in oxidation-reduction reactions. Most scientists now explain the process of photosynthesis in two interrelated stages: (1) the light reaction, in which radiant energy is trapped to ionize water and produce excited electrons from chlorophyll, and (2) the dark reaction, in which hydrogen is used to reduce carbon dioxide to simple sugars.

177

THE LIGHT REACTION

The physical problems of raising the electrons to sufficiently high-energy levels and transporting them into carbon compounds are only partially understood. As was stated earlier, some newly discovered electron-acceptor compounds are helping to clarify these problems.

There is now strong evidence to suggest that the light reaction consists of two phases called systems which work in tandem (Figure 6–16). In System I, chlorophyll *a* is excited by light energy causing electrons to be raised to a higher energy level. Since these activated electrons are now farther from the attracting

nucleus, they are easier to pull away from the chlorophyll molecule, but they also contain more potential energy. A very strong electron acceptor, an iron-containing protein called *ferredoxin*, now takes up the electrons from chlorophyll *a* leaving it in an oxidized state. In a subsequent transfer, ferredoxin passes the electrons to NADP (nicotine amide dinucleotide phosphate). In this reduced state NADP has the negative charges necessary to attract two protons (H^+) into its structure from ionized water. The final result of this phase of light reaction is the formation of the reduced coenzyme NADP·2H. It is also possible for the electrons captured by ferredoxin to be returned to chlorophyll *a* in a

Figure 6·16   A simplified diagram of the two steps (systems) of hydrogen transfer in photolysis. Note that electrons lost in System I are replaced by electrons gained from ionized water in System II. It should be noted that the electrons from ferredoxin may be passed to NADP to form hydrogen or be cycled back to plastoquinone, the cytochromes, and chlorophyll *a* to produce ATP.

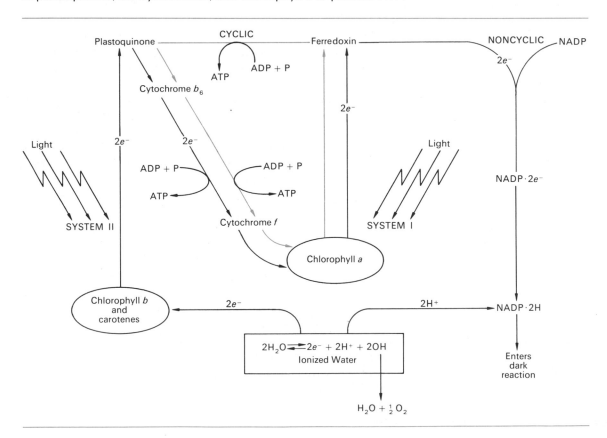

cyclic series of events. These reactions, often called *cyclic electron transfer*, yield the major portion of the ATP produced in the light reaction. This ATP can be used in the life activities of the plant the same as the ATP that results from respiration.

In the second phase of the light reaction, known as System II, excited electrons are passed from other pigments such as chlorophyll *b* and carotenes to a carbon-ring compound known as *plastoquinone*. Vitamin K, which has a similar structure, may also function at this energy level. The electrons are next passed to cytochromes b_6 and *f*. Since these electrons are passed to a lower energy level, electron energy may be used in this downhill reaction to phosphorylate ADP to ATP. The difference in potential energy between plastoquinone and cytochrome *f* supplies the energy which is utilized to produce ATP. This is another example of a coupled reaction in which the simultaneous release and uptake of energy occurs.

Figure 6·17 A diagram of the major steps involved in carbon fixation. The six PGAL molecules are produced by the enzymatic splitting of the three C_6 compounds. Five PGAL's are converted back to RDP while one PGAL represents the net gain.

| (higher energy level) | Plastoquinone | ADP + P | (lower energy level) |
| (lower energy level) | Cytochrome *f* | ATP | (higher energy level) |

$2e^-$

The electrons available from System II are finally passed to chlorophyll *a* to replace the electrons lost to ferredoxin. The electrons lost in System II are replaced from ionized water through the action of a yet unknown carrier substance.

Light reaction ends with the formation of NADP·2H and the release of oxygen. The process has taken hydrogen from ionized water and converted it to a usable form—that is, it may now be transferred to another compound by the coenzyme NADP·2H for the formation of carbohydrate.

THE DARK REACTION

Remember that the source of carbon for photosynthesis is atmospheric carbon dioxide. The conversion of CO_2 into carbohydrate is sometimes called "carbon fixation" and it occurs through a complicated series of enzymatic steps. For our purposes, we need to understand only the major steps involved at this point.

Calvin learned, by working with $C^{14}O_2$, that although carbon fixation occurred in systematic steps, it was not a true cycle, because some products were released as the reactions took place.

Since the dark reactions are somewhat cyclic, we must pick a point to begin our study. If we choose ribulose diphosphate (RDP), a five-carbon sugar having two phosphate groups, it can be shown how this substance is reformed (Figure 6–17).

Three molecules of the C5 compound, RDP, contain fifteen carbons. The addition of three CO_2 molecules will produce a total of eighteen carbons. When this is accomplished, three six-carbon double-phosphate molecules are formed.

$$3\,\text{P}—\boxed{\text{C5}}—\text{P} + 3\text{CO}_2 \longrightarrow 3\,\text{P}—\boxed{\text{C6}}—\text{P}$$

(18C) ... (18C)

This diphospho, six-carbon intermediate is very unstable and is quickly split into six C3 acids known as *phosphoglyceric acid*, abbreviated PGA. Calvin and his associates showed that PGA is a very important intermediate step in CO_2 fixation. At this point, NADP·2H reduces the PGA to the aldehyde form, *phosphoglyceraldehyde,* commonly known as PGAL.

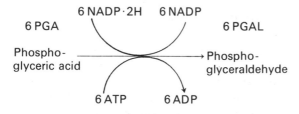

6 PGA   6 NADP·2H   6 NADP   6 PGAL

Phosphoglyceric acid → Phosphoglyceraldehyde

6 ATP   6 ADP

It should be noted that in the formation of PGAL, the light reaction and the dark reaction have merged to produce the end product of photosynthesis. We now know that photosynthesis ends with the formation of PGAL. In the case of RDP, five of the resulting six PGAL's must be phosphorylated and rearranged to replace the original three RDP's to keep the process going.

15C

$$5\,\boxed{\text{C3}}—\text{P} \xrightarrow[\text{ATP} \quad \text{ADP}]{} 3\,\text{P}—\boxed{\text{C5}}—\text{P}$$

PGAL   RDP   15C

This leaves only one PGAL as net product. If the cycle is repeated, enough carbon is produced to synthesize the organic compound glucose.

We will see in the next section of this chapter how the cell can burn PGAL directly for energy. If the immediate energy requirements are satisfied, then PGAL is synthesized into glucose and finally into starch which is stored. PGAL is also used in the synthesis of other compounds in the cell such as glycerin, fatty acids, and amino acids.

THE SITE OF PHOTOSYNTHESIS

Although most of us think of photosynthesis as occurring in the leaves of green plants, it is also accomplished in some of the protists such as bacteria and algae. The organisms making up green scum of ponds and lakes, for instance, and the minute pigmented organisms that form the plankton of the seas are extremely important in supplying nutrients on our planet. These photosynthetic organisms that form the basis for the food chains in the sea are primary producers of organic compounds and are presently under intensive study by biological oceanographers.

Until 1901, it was believed that the entire leaf was the organ of photosynthesis. Friedel refuted this concept by showing that suspensions of powdered leaves gave off oxygen when illuminated. Hill's work on isolated chloroplasts pinpointed the major source of photosynthetic activity. A schematic breakdown to show the relationship of the chloroplast to the gross leaf structure is presented in Figure 6–18.

Leaves, Chloroplasts, and Grana

A cross section of a green leaf has a functional arrangement of tissues (Figure 6–18). Apart from being necessary in the basic structure of the leaf, the palisade cells, which lie just beneath the upper epidermis, contain the functional photosynthetic units, the chloroplasts. Other leaf cells such as the spongy tissue and guard cells are also capable of photosynthesis.

The chloroplast is composed internally of a

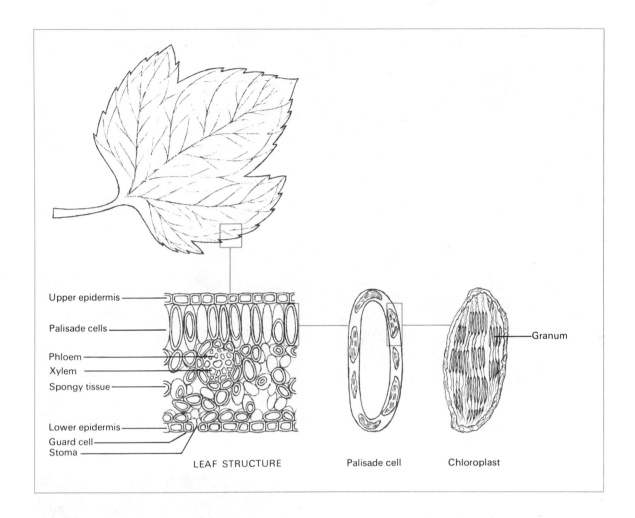

Upper epidermis
Palisade cells
Phloem
Xylem
Spongy tissue
Lower epidermis
Guard cell
Stoma

LEAF STRUCTURE

Palisade cell

Chloroplast

Granum

Figure 6·18   The site of photosynthesis.

parallel array of platelike membranes called *lamellae*. Electron micrographs show that the lamellae are not uniform in thickness (Figures 6–19 and 6–20). At various points along the plates, the membrane is expanded into thickened, disk-shaped areas. These disks are closely packed within the chloroplast, resembling a stack of poker chips, and are called a *granum*. These double protein-lipid membrane structures contain all the pigments and enzymes necessary for photosynthesis.

Many researchers have attempted to describe the internal arrangement of molecules within the grana disks. The present model indicates that the essential pigments and enzymes are situated in definite patterns along the inner membrane surfaces, similar to the arrangement of the cytochromes and related enzymes along the cristae of the mitochondrion (Figure 6–21). The importance of the membrane surface in the cell is again indicated as a site for chemical reactions. We know that the grana contain the pigments chlorophyll, carotene, and xanthophyll, and recent evidence shows the presence of small amounts of DNA. These simple strands of DNA are somewhat similar in structure and function to the DNA of mitochondria (discussed in Chapter 3).

181

Figure 6·19 An electron micrograph of a chloroplast from the leaf of *Peperomia*, an ornamental pepper; magnification X 72,000. The lamellar structure of the grana can be noted. Three large starch grains are visible. From *Plastids: Their Chemistry, Structure, Growth and Inheritance*, by J. T. Kirk and R. A. Tilney-Bassett, 1967. (Photo courtesy of Dr. B. E. Juniper.)

Pigments

Finally, we are led to the molecular level in our discussion of the site and structural elements involved in photosynthesis. The structure of chlorophyll was mentioned earlier in this chapter, and a diagram of the molecule is shown in Figure 6–22. Note particularly the similarities between the tetrapyrrol configuration of the main part of the molecule and the cytochromes. The metallic atom in the structure of chlorophyll, however, is magnesium rather than iron.

Figure 6·20 An electron micrograph of a granum from a chloroplast of a spinach leaf. The small subunits in the exposed area contain chlorophyll and are known as quantasomes. (Courtesy of Roderic B. Park.)

1000 Å

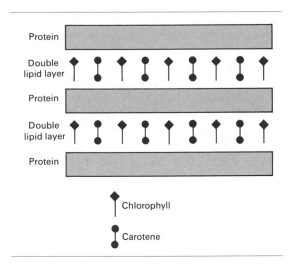

Protein

Double lipid layer

Protein

Double lipid layer

Protein

♦ Chlorophyll

● Carotene

Figure 6·21 Hypothetical arrangement of the photosynthetic pigments in the chloroplast membrane. Note that the chlorophyll and carotene lie in the double lipid layer of the granum.

The essential role of the chlorophylls and the other pigments located within the leaf is to trap light for the photosynthetic process. In Chapter 5 (Figure 5–3), it was indicated that visible light from the electromagnetic spectrum is the energy source for photosynthesis. The portions of the visible light spectrum that are absorbed by the photosynthetic pigments of green plants are shown in Figure 6–23a. Chlorophyll a has widely separated absorption peaks in the blue and red wavelengths, whereas chlorophyll b has highest absorbency in the blue-green and, to a lesser degree, red.

The characteristic action spectrum for photosynthesis, rate of photosynthesis plotted against wavelengths of light (Figure 6–23b), results from the combined absorption spectra for all three pigments. The excited electrons released from chlorophyll b and β-carotene are passed to chlorophyll a for the production of NADP·2H as outlined earlier in this chapter.

Figure 6·22 Molecular structure of chlorophyll a and b. Note the dashed lines representing the possible valence bonds of magnesium. Also note that chlorophyll b differs in having an additional

$$\overset{O}{\overset{\|}{-C}}-H$$ group.

Chlorophyll a

(a) ABSORPTION SPECTRUM

Ultraviolet | Violet | Blue | Green | Yellow | Red | Infrared

(b) ACTION SPECTRUM

Figure 6·23 (*a*) The relationship between the absorption of chlorophyll *a*, *b*, and *β*-carotene and the relative light absorption resulting from the light-trapping ability of these three pigments. Note the regions of the visible light spectrum which are most effective in photosynthesis. (*b*) The rate of photosynthesis plotted against the wavelengths of light effective in photosynthesis produce an action spectrum. This spectrum results from the combined absorption of all pigments involved in photosynthesis.

RESPIRATION

The story of the breakdown of organic molecules into usable energy is somewhat complex. All classes of foods, carbohydrates, fats, and proteins may be utilized for energy by most organisms. For example, the polysaccharide starch may be split into many glucose units by the action of several digestive enzymes. In vertebrates these enzymes are secreted in the mouth, pancreas, and small intestine. After the starch is hydrolyzed into glucose, the cells lining the intestine absorb the glucose into the blood where it is transported to all the cells of the body. Every living cell has the enzymes necessary to convert the potential energy of glucose into usable high-energy bonds in ATP.

The conversion of the energy in glucose into pyrophosphate bonds may be described as a stepwise process. Each step along the route is catalyzed by a specific enzyme and can be summarized as follows:

$$\text{Glucose} \xrightarrow{\text{enzyme}} \xrightarrow{\text{enzyme}} \xrightarrow{\text{enzyme}} \begin{array}{c} \nearrow CO_2 \\ \rightarrow \text{Energy in ATP} \\ \searrow H_2O \end{array}$$

This conversion of glucose into CO_2, water, and energy can be separated into two major phases: (1) the cytoplasmic phase and (2) the mitochondrial phase.

Both of these phases produce ATP, but the most energy by far is liberated in the mitochondrial phase. The enzyme action in the cytoplasm breaks the six-carbon glucose molecule into two three-carbon fragments called pyruvic acid. The biochemical term for the series of reactions that break down glucose or glycogen is *glycolysis*. Figure 6–24 should be consulted frequently in the study of the next section.

184

Figure 6·24 A summary of the chemical reactions in glycolysis.

GLYCOLYSIS

The first step in glycolysis involves getting glucose ready for the process, sometimes called a priming reaction. To accomplish this a phosphate group is placed on the sixth carbon by the enzymatic transfer of phosphate from ATP (the 6 in glucose-6-phosphate refers to the carbon on which the phosphate is attached).

In many enzyme reactions, an additional metallic ion is necessary; in the foregoing example this cofactor is the magnesium ion. (Cofactors should not be confused with coenzymes.)

Glycogen, the polysaccharide storage form of carbohydrates found in liver and muscle, can also enter the glycolytic pathway by the addition of a phosphate ester to one of its glucose units. It is interesting, however, that it does *not* require an ATP to accomplish this phosphorylation—instead, phosphoric acid (H_3PO_4) can be used. This is very economical for the cell because ATP is conserved:

The discovery that a phosphate was added to the glucose molecule in this process was one of the first indications of the importance of the phosphorylation mechanism. Glucose is now prepared for the second step, which involves a complete rearrangement of the carbon-ring structure. In this step, glucose is changed to form another type of sugar, fructose.

$$\text{Glucose-6-phosphate} \xrightarrow{\text{isomerase}} \text{Fructose-6-phosphate}$$

This newly formed fructose-6-phosphate is next phosphorylated on its first carbon by the expenditure of another ATP:

$$\text{Fructose-6-} \xrightarrow[\qquad\qquad]{\text{ATP} \quad \text{ADP}} \text{Fructose-1,6-}$$
$$\text{phosphate} \qquad\qquad\qquad \text{diphosphate}$$

We now have a six-carbon sugar with a phosphate group on each end. At this point, a very significant event occurs—the fructose-1,6-diphosphate is split into two molecules, each having three carbons and each bearing a phosphate group on one end. For our purposes here, these three-carbon compounds can be considered to be PGAL. (Remember that PGAL is also the end product in photosynthesis.)

$$\text{Fructose-1,6-diphosphate} \longrightarrow \text{2PGAL}$$

Actually, it is not possible to split fructose-1,6-diphosphate into two molecules of exactly the same structure, but it is not necessary to go into the chemical reactions that are required to convert the two compounds to PGAL's. At this point PGAL gives off hydrogen to the electron-transport series. When this happens PGAL becomes phosphoglyceric acid. It is important to note that this reaction, which is catalyzed by an enzyme called a dehydrogenase, involves the removal of hydrogen and is therefore an oxidation. Remember that oxidation is the loss of hydrogen and reduction is the gain of hydrogen. As the hydrogen is lost, an additional phosphate ester is attached to the number 1 carbon. Thus a glyceric acid molecule is formed with phosphorus at the one- and three-carbon positions. The overall reaction is:

$$\text{PGAL} \xrightarrow[\text{NAD}]{\text{H}_3\text{PO}_4} \begin{array}{l}\text{1,3-diphosphoglyceric} \\ \text{acid} \\ \text{NAD} \cdot 2\text{H}\end{array}$$

Two things are very important at this point: hydrogen has been given off to the electron-transport series and the 1,3-diphosphoglyceric acid now contains energy in the form of two high-energy phosphate ester groups. There is enough energy in this compound to allow the direct enzymatic conversion of ADP to ATP in essentially a two-step process.

1. $\text{P} \sim \text{PGA} \sim \text{P} \xrightarrow[\text{ADP} \quad \text{ATP}]{\qquad\qquad} \text{PGA} \sim \text{P}$

   1-3 diphospho-   3-phospho-
   glyceric acid   glyceric acid

2. $\text{PGA} \sim \text{P} \xrightarrow[\text{ADP} \quad \text{ATP}]{\qquad\qquad} \text{Pyruvic acid}$

In the foregoing dephosphorylations of diphosphoglyceric acid, two ATP's are formed from each three-carbon molecule; however, since we started with glucose (a six-carbon molecule), the ATP production will be doubled to four for each glucose molecule entering glycolysis.

Recall that if we started with glucose, two ATP molecules were used to prime the glycolysis process; one to phosphorylate glucose and one to produce fructose-1,6-diphosphate (refer to Figure 6–24). Since four ATP's are formed between 1,3-diphosphoglyceric acid and pyruvic acid and since the PGAL to PGA reaction yields six ATP's through the electron-transport series, the net gain is $10 - 2$ or eight ATP's. The cell is getting a good return for its original two-ATP investment.

Pyruvic Acid

When the pyruvic acid stage is reached, the phosphate bond energy is spent. All that is left is the potential energy of the C—C and C—H bonds, yet we will see that this constitutes a tremendous amount of energy. Pyruvic acid is a three-carbon compound that marks the end of anaerobic glycolysis. Anaerobic simply means that this process which produces pyruvic acid and energy *can* operate in the cytoplasm in the absence of oxygen. The further conversion of pyruvic acid into energy and carbon dioxide in the mitochondrion, however, requires oxygen and ceases to function if oxygen is not supplied. The final breakdown of pyruvic acid is accomplished through a cyclic series of reactions discovered by the Englishman Hans Krebs and named for him (Figure 6–25). The *Krebs cycle* (also called the citric-acid cycle) is summarized in Figure 6–27.

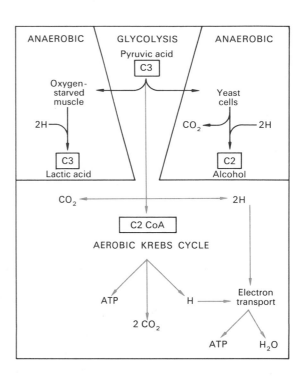

Figure 6·26 The three possible fates of pyruvic acid under anaerobic or aerobic conditions.

Figure 6·25 Dr. Hans Krebs outlined the series of chemical reactions involved in the oxidation of pyruvic acid in the citric-acid cycle, for which he was awarded a Nobel Prize in 1953.

Concerning the fate of pyruvic acid, we find that there are three possible routes for the breakdown of this compound in living organisms (Figure 6–26). If oxygen is available in the cell, the route is directly into the Krebs cycle and the electron-transport series to produce CO_2 and energy. If no oxygen is available, as might be the case in greatly exercised muscle cells, the electron-transport series cannot operate and lactic acid is formed. Note that it requires 2H to make this conversion from pyruvic acid to lactic acid. The result of this is a loss of six ATP's which would have been made under aerobic conditions because the hydrogen produced in the conversion of PGAL to PGA in glycolysis is now used to convert pyruvic acid to lactic acid. When lactic acid is formed in the oxygen-starved cells, most of it is carried by the blood to the liver and converted to glycogen when aerobic conditions return. This process,

Figure 6·27 A summary of the interrelated events of the Krebs cycle and the electron-transport series occurring in the mitochondrion. Water enters the cycle between D and E and F and G.

however, requires both time and energy and about 20 percent of the original energy value of pyruvic acid is lost. Thus the formation of lactic acid under anerobic conditions is very inefficient in energy production. The same thing is true in the yeast organism where alcohol and CO_2 are the end products.

THE KREBS CYCLE

Under aerobic conditions the pyruvic acid enters the Krebs cycle. For our purposes it is necessary only to note the names of the intermediate compounds in the Krebs cycle. It is very important, however, to keep track of the

loss of carbon dioxide as the three-carbon pyruvic acid molecule is completely converted to CO_2 and energy. The first step is to get pyruvic acid introduced into the cycle; to accomplish this, a sort of "key" compound is added. This key is a complicated coenzyme called *coenzyme A*, usually abbreviated CoA. With the loss of CO_2 and the addition of CoA, the molecule of pyruvic acid becomes a two-carbon structure known as acetyl CoA (Figure 6–27). In the next step, acetyl-CoA (or "active acetate" as it is sometimes called) is condensed with the four-carbon compound oxaloacetic acid (OAA) to form a six-carbon acid known as citric acid. It is important to see that the 2H

Segment			Lose	Gain
A–B	2 pyruvic acid	2 acetyl CoA	2 CO_2, 4H	6 ATP
B–C	2 acetyl CoA	2 citric acid	2 CoA	
C–D	2 citric acid	2 ketoglutaric acid	2 CO_2, 4H	6 ATP
D–E	2 ketoglutaric acid	2 succinic acid	2 CO_2, 4H	6 ATP 2 ATP
E–F	2 succinic acid	2 fumaric acid	4H to FAD	4 ATP
F–G	2 fumaric acid	2 malic acid		
G–H	2 malic acid	2 oxaloacetic acid	4H	6 ATP
			6 CO_2, 20H	30 ATP's

Figure 6·28 Table showing ATP energy released from one molecule of glucose oxidized in the Krebs or citric acid cycle. Note that the excess hydrogen and oxygen is from water molecules added in several enzyme steps. It should be remembered that eight additional ATP's were produced in glycolysis.

fragments are transported into the electron-transport series by the coenzymes NAD and FAD. At one point, between C_5 ketoglutaric acid and C_4 succinic acid, ADP is converted to ATP without the use of the cytochromes. The yield is, of course, only two ATP's per glucose molecule. Another unique reaction is the direct transfer of 2H to FAD between C_4 succinic acid and C_4 fumaric acid, with the result that the production of ATP between NAD and FAD is *skipped*, thus producing only four ATP's. The important events shown by the lettered segments in Figure 6–27 are summarized in Figure 6–28. The oxidative breakdown of one molecule of glucose into CO_2, energy, and water usually yields 38 molecules of ATP. One exception is with the compound glycogen where an additional ATP occurs as net gain from using phosphoric acid to produce glucose-6-phosphate.

So far we have been concerned only with the metabolism of carbohydrates. Can other foodstuffs enter into this scheme? The answer is yes, and such energy-rich compounds as glycerol, fatty acids, and amino acids may enter into the carbohydrate pathway at various steps and be oxidized as fuels (Figure 6–29).

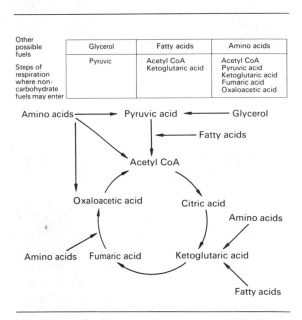

Other possible fuels	Glycerol	Fatty acids	Amino acids
Steps of respiration where non-carbohydrate fuels may enter	Pyruvic	Acetyl CoA Ketoglutaric acid	Acetyl CoA Pyruvic acid Ketoglutaric acid Fumaric acid Oxaloacetic acid

Figure 6·29 Key steps in respiration where non-carbohydrate substances may enter the respiration process (fuel breakdown).

At this stage you may wonder just what use can be made of all the ATP that is produced in cellular respiration. You will recall that ATP

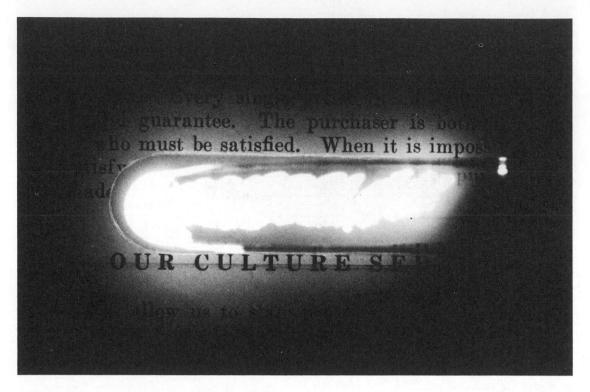

Figure 6·30   The utilization of ATP in the production of light by bioluminescent bacteria. The bacteria in this culture provided the necessary light for the photograph. (Courtesy of Carolina Biological Supply Co.)

is necessary in the dark-reaction stage of photosynthesis, and also that some ATP is used to "prime" the early stages of glycolysis. In addition to these requirements, all biological work, such as muscle movement, bioluminescence, and active transport, requires energy and in practically every case, ATP is the energy supplier (Figure 6–30). One of the first investigators to demonstrate that ATP is necessary for muscle contraction was Dr. Albert Szent-Györgyi (Figure 6–31).

The energy events discussed in this chapter are summarized in Figure 6–32.

Figure 6·31   Dr. Albert Szent-Györgyi was awarded the Nobel Prize in 1937 for his work with vitamin C. He is also a leading authority on muscle action. (Photo by C. Felker.)

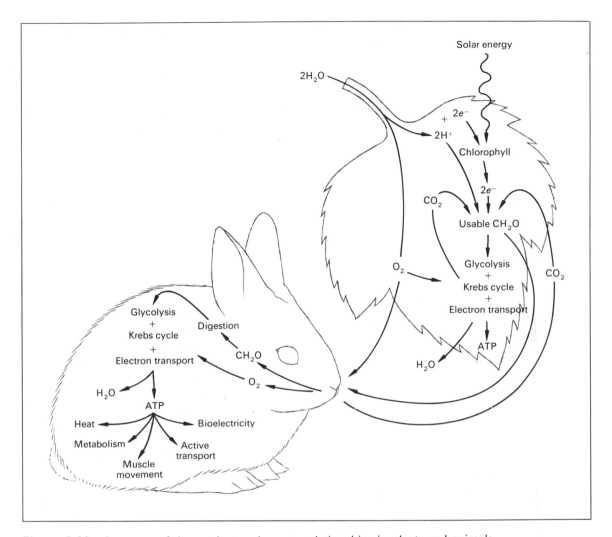

Figure 6·32 Summary of the nutrient and energy relationships in plants and animals.

SUMMARIZING PRINCIPLES

Energy is required to perform the chemical reactions necessary for life. The principal source of biological energy is the terminal phosphate ester of ATP; the unique role of ATP is as an intermediary between higher and lower energy compounds.

Most chemical reactions involve the breaking and reformation of chemical bonds; the electrons that participate in bonding therefore are exchanged in a reaction—uptake of electrons is reduction and release of electrons is oxidation.

The electron is the basic source of energy in all cells; the energy-making reactions in the cell trap the energy of the hydrogen electron for the production of ATP.

The ultimate source of energy for most organisms comes from the sun; the process of converting light energy to chemical energy in the form of carbohydrate (photosynthesis) is accomplished in plants with the aid of chlorophyll.

Photosynthesis can be considered as a two-step process: (1) the light reaction in which light and chlorophyll separate hydrogen from water and make it available in the form of reduced coenzyme NADP (NADP·2H); (2) the dark reaction or carbon fixation in which a five-carbon sugar, RDP, is combined with CO_2 and NADP·2H to form the usable fuel PGAL.

Respiration is the process occurring in all cells to release energy from the C—H bonds in organic molecules; this energy is transferred to ATP for use in biological work; the phases of respiration are glycolysis, which occurs in the cytoplasm, and the Krebs cycle and electron-transport series located in the mitochondria.

REVIEW QUESTIONS

1 Distinguish between a low-energy phosphate ester and a high-energy phosphate such as found in ATP. How is ATP used in the energy exchanges in living cells?

2 The action of cyanide poisoning is to inhibit cytochrome c from transferring electrons. Describe the effects that cyanide would have on energy production in the cell.

3 When organic materials are burned, the principal products are CO_2 and water, and energy is released. Sketch the chemical reaction that occurs between glucose and oxygen. Which compound is oxidized and which is reduced?

4 What are the roles of the following compounds in photosynthesis: ferredoxin, plastoquinone, NADP, and RDP?

5 How would you set up an experiment to demonstrate the source of the oxygen given off by green plants?

6 Explain the importance of PGAL in photosynthesis and respiration.

7 What is the role and importance of water in photosynthesis and respiration?

8 Essentially, what are the important chemical changes that occur in the Krebs cycle? What does this cycle accomplish?

9 Sometimes during strenuous exercise an individual cannot take in enough oxygen to meet his energy requirements. What happens in this case?

10 The burning or oxidation of glucose gives the same end products as the burning of any organic fuel such as wood or coal. How is this accomplished in the cell without the release of excessive amounts of heat?

11 Compare photosynthesis and respiration in terms of (a) raw materials, (b) end products, (c) site of occurrence, (d) energy relationships in the cell.

SUPPLEMENTARY READINGS

Ackley, M. E., and P. B. Whitford, *The Chemistry of Photosynthesis* (a programmed text), New York, Appleton-Century-Crofts, 1965.

Bassham, J. A., "The Path of Carbon in Photosynthesis," *Scientific American*, June, 1962.

Calvin, Melvin, and J. A. Bassham, *The Photosynthesis of Carbon Compounds*, New York, Benjamin, 1962.

Cheldelin, Vernon, and R. W. Newburgh, *The Chemistry of Some Life Processes*, New York, Reinhold, 1964.

Giese, Arthur C., "Energy Release and Utilization," in W. Johnson and W. Steere, eds., *This Is Life*, New York, Holt, Rinehart and Winston, 1962.

Goldsby, Richard A., *Cells and Energy*, New York, Macmillan, 1967.

Goodenough, U. W., and R. P. Levine, "The Genetic Activity of Mitochondria and Chloroplasts," *Scientific American*, November, 1970.

Lehninger, Albert L., "Energy Transformation in the Cell," *Scientific American*, May, 1960.

Levine, R. P., "The Mechanism of Photosynthesis," *Scientific American*, December, 1969.

McElroy, William D., *Cellular Physiology and Biochemistry*, Englewood Cliffs, N.J., Prentice-Hall, 1961.

McElroy, William D., and Howard H. Seliger, "Biological Luminescence," *Scientific American*, December, 1962.

Racker, Efraim, "The Membrane of the Mitochondrion," *Scientific American*, February, 1968.

Rosenberg, Jerome L., *Photosynthesis*, New York, Holt, Rinehart and Winston, 1965.

Siekevitz, P., "Powerhouse of the Cell," *Scientific American*, July, 1957.

Stumpf, Paul K., "ATP," *Scientific American*, April, 1953.

Tucker, Vance A., "The Energetics of Bird Flight," *Scientific American*, May, 1969.

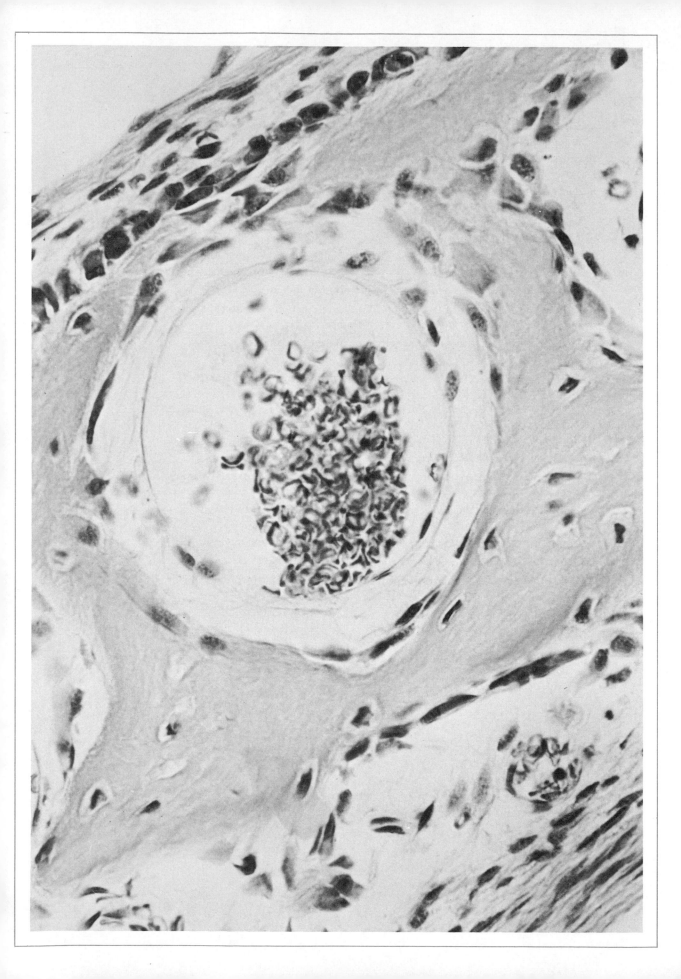

7

Supporting Processes of Life

The preceding chapter focused on the chemical energy pathways in cells—that is, the photosynthetic process and the various steps of respiration. To be sure, these are essential for life since organisms are powered by electron energy. But these are not the only chemical reactions that occur in living systems. For example, food must be broken down into small molecules that can enter cells and be used as fuels, gases must be exchanged with the external medium, and waste materials must be eliminated. The problems of transporting nutrients, gases, and other chemical compounds in a living organism must also be solved. We refer to these other necessary physical and chemical events as "supporting processes of life" since they essentially serve to facilitate energy production. All of these processes involve chemical reactions that are often summarized under the term *metabolism*. This chapter then concerns additional aspects of metabolism beyond those involved in the direct trapping and releasing of energy.

METABOLISM

FOOD AND CALORIES

The source of the raw materials for energy production is food. Basically, organic foodstuffs are composed of carbohydrates, fats, and proteins; the chemical structures of these were discussed in Chapter 2. Fats are the highest potential energy food because large amounts of hydrogen

AFTER COMBUSTION

BEFORE COMBUSTION

+ −

Mechanical stirrer

Thermometer

Air space

Water

Igniting wire

Bomb

Oxygen

Sample

Figure 7·1 Typical components of a bomb calorimeter. The resistance wire between the electrodes ignites the oxygen and combusts the sample in the sealed bomb. The temperature change is read from the thermometer.

are contained in fatty acids and glycerol. Recall the important role of hydrogen and its electron in energy production described in detail in Chapter 6.

The foods we consume contain specific numbers of *calories*, a term designating a unit of measurement defined as the amount of heat necessary to raise one milliliter of water one degree Celsius (centigrade). A special closed container called a bomb calorimeter is used to determine caloric content (Figure 7–1). It has been determined that, for example, one gram molecular weight of glucose (180 grams)

will yield 680,000 calories when completely oxidized. The sample to be combusted is placed in the inner chamber of the calorimeter. The chamber (or bomb) is then charged with oxygen, sealed, and the contents ignited with an electric current. The amount of heat produced in the combustion is read directly from the thermometer and converted to calories. A calorie may therefore be further defined as a heat equivalent in calculating the potential energy of foods. Calories are usually expressed as kilocalories (1000 calories), in which case the term "calories" is capitalized. For example, a slice of bread from a standard white loaf contains 63,000 calories (or 63 Calories) and one fried egg contains 77,000 calories (or 77 Calories).

In Chapter 6 we learned that one gram molecular weight of glucose (1 mole) oxidized through glycolysis and the Krebs cycle yields 38 moles of ATP. If we consider one mole of ATP to contain a potential energy of 10,000 calories, one gram molecular weight of glucose biologically oxidized would yield 380,000 calories. With this information we can now calculate the efficiency of the enzymatic energy production from glucose to be about 380,000/680,000 or approximately 56 percent. But when the high-energy bond of ATP is broken, only about 8000 calories of energy is usable. The remaining energy is released in the form of heat which helps to maintain body temperature. The total energy efficiency is therefore somewhat closer to 40 percent.

CALCULATION OF METABOLIC RATE

The caloric energy requirement may be calculated for any individual. This *basal metabolic rate* or BMR is a measure of the calories utilized by an organism that is awake and completely at rest. The caloric measurement is normally computed according to the amount of oxygen utilized and carbon dioxide released over a specific time interval. The amount of oxygen required and the amount of carbon dioxide released vary with the kinds of foods in an individual's diet. A normal human diet,

196

for example, consists of a mixture of carbohydrates, proteins, and fats with each of these classes of foodstuff requiring a characteristic amount of oxygen when burned. The specific amount of oxygen necessary to oxidize glucose to CO_2 and H_2O is:

$$C_6H_{12}O_6 + 6O_2 \longrightarrow 6CO_2 + 6H_2O + \text{energy}$$
$$\text{(input)} \qquad \text{(output)}$$

Therefore the ratio of carbon-dioxide output to oxygen input is 6/6 or 1.0. This mathematical relationship is called the *respiratory quotient* or R.Q. value. For proteins the value is about 0.9 and for fats, 0.7. The average R.Q. value for a balanced diet is approximately 0.86.

A generalized BMR for humans has been found to be about one Calorie per kilogram of body weight per hour. Significant variation from this normal relationship usually indicates an organic imbalance in hormone or enzyme production. For example, an individual whose BMR Calories are less than one per kilogram of body weight is likely to have a less than normal secretion of the hormone *thyroxin*. Basically, a *hormone* is a substance secreted in one part of an organism which has effects in other parts of the organism. Thyroxin, for instance, is secreted by the thyroid gland and this hormone helps to regulate carbohydrate metabolism.

In addition to weight, several other factors such as age, sex, and body surface area influence the basal metabolic rate. BMRs vary greatly among individuals. The basal metabolic rate for an eighteen-year-old male college student is calculated as follows:

Oxygen consumed in 1 hour = 18 liters

Body weight = 185 pounds ÷ 2.2 = 84 kilograms

It has been determined that one liter of O_2 will produce about 4.8 Calories from a mixed diet—18 liters O_2 × 4.8 Cal = 86.4 Cal.

Therefore the BMR relationship is:

86.4 Cal/84 kilograms/1 hr

1 Cal/1 kilogram/1 hr

THE LIVER AND METABOLISM

The largest and one of the most important organs for general metabolism in vertebrates is the liver. In adult humans the liver weighs between three and four pounds and performs a variety of functions. The liver, which is composed of four lobes, lies just below the diaphragm and above the stomach. The liver tissue cells are all similar and each one appears to be capable of all functions. Among the most important functions we should consider are synthesis, storage, regulation, and detoxification.

SYNTHESIS

The liver is the site of many chemical reactions. Some of the glucose molecules brought into the liver spaces from the small intestine are synthesized into the polysaccharide glycogen. The formation of glycogen from glucose molecules is termed *glycogenesis*. It is also possible for the liver cells to convert non-carbohydrate molecules such as amino acids and fats into glycogen, and this more complex process is called *glyconeogenesis*. The "neo" (meaning "new") indicates that glycogen was synthesized from molecules other than carbohydrates.

In the liver, amino acids may be converted into *keto* acids by the enzymatic removal of the amino group in a process known as *deamination*. The term keto refers to the structural group $C-\overset{\overset{\displaystyle O}{\|}}{C}-C$. Most amino acids can be transformed into different amino acids by the enzymatic exchange of an amino group between an amino acid and a keto or fatty acid in a *transamination* reaction. Transamination between glutamic acid and pyruvic acid, which yields alanine and α-ketoglutaric acid, is shown below.

pigments are derived from the hemoglobin from old red blood cells broken down in the spleen, liver, and bone marrow. Bile is released from the gallbladder into the small intestine

$$HO-\overset{O}{\underset{}{C}}-CH_2-CH_2-\overset{NH_2}{\underset{H}{C}}-COOH \;+\; CH_3-\overset{O}{\underset{}{C}}-COOH \xrightarrow{\text{transaminase}}$$

Glutamic acid
(5-carbon amino acid)

Pyruvic acid
(3-carbon keto acid)

$$CH_3-\overset{NH_2}{\underset{H}{C}}-COOH \;+\; HO-\overset{O}{\underset{}{C}}-CH_2-CH_2-\overset{O}{\underset{}{C}}-COOH$$

Alanine
(3-carbon amino acid)

α-ketoglutaric acid
(5-carbon keto acid)

In this manner the liver regulates the amino-acid balance of the body and quickly supplies required amino acids. The body does not store amino acids except in the form of protein. Any amino acid that cannot be synthesized or cannot be synthesized fast enough to satisfy the body demand is termed *essential*, that is, it must be obtained from the food supply. In man, 10 amino acids of a list of approximately 23 have been determined to be essential.

Most of the vitamins (to be discussed in the next chapter) are also essential. The synthesis of vitamin K, necessary for the normal clotting of blood, is accomplished by some intestinal bacteria. Vitamins are important to the normal functioning of the organism because they participate as coenzymes in many critical chemical reactions.

The synthesis of the yellow-green fluid known as *bile* occurs continuously in liver cells. The secreted fluid is collected by the bile ducts and transported to the gallbladder to be stored. Bile is a complex substance made up chiefly of pigments, salts, cholesterol, and water. Biliverdin (green) and bilirubin (yellow)

where it emulsifies fats. In the process of emulsification, large particles of fat are separated into smaller units which can be easily digested by enzymes.

STORAGE AND REGULATION

The cells and intercellular spaces of the liver, often called the "sugar bin" of the body, provide storage space for glycogen, fats, vitamins, iron, and bile. The liver is also important in maintaining the general balance of many chemical activities. Especially important is its regulation of carbohydrate metabolism. Glycogenesis is accelerated by the hormone *insulin* from specific cells (the beta cells) in the pancreas. Hormones from the adrenal cortex and anterior pituitary gland also help in glycogenesis. The breakdown of stored glycogen into blood sugar, called *glycogenolysis* (meaning to split glycogen), is enhanced by a second pancreatic hormone (from the alpha cells) called *glucagon*. The function of insulin and glucagon is a good example of the antagonistic action or check-and-balance system of hormonal control. The control of carbo-hydrate, protein, and fat metabolism occurring in the liver is illustrated in Figure 7–2.

DETOXIFICATION

Many organic compounds may be toxic to the organism if they accumulate in large amounts. Nitrogen in the compound ammonia, which is released in deamination, is extremely toxic. This toxicity results from the reaction of ammonia with water to produce a pH change to the alkaline range. We learn later in this chapter how the liver incorporates ammonia into less poisonous urea which may be safely excreted by the kidneys.

Large cells (macrophages) located in the liver capillaries actually engulf and digest small particles such as bacteria and parasitic pro-tozoa. These star-shaped cells move somewhat like amoebae in trapping and engulfing foreign material.

ENZYMATIC DIGESTION

The digestion of food is essentially the break-down of large molecules into smaller molecules that can be absorbed and utilized in the syn-thetic processes, energy metabolism, mainte-nance, and repair. The splitting of large molecules into smaller units is accomplished by the enzymatic addition of water at certain bonding sites. For digestion to take place water must be added, a process called *hy-drolytic cleavage*. This is the reverse of the

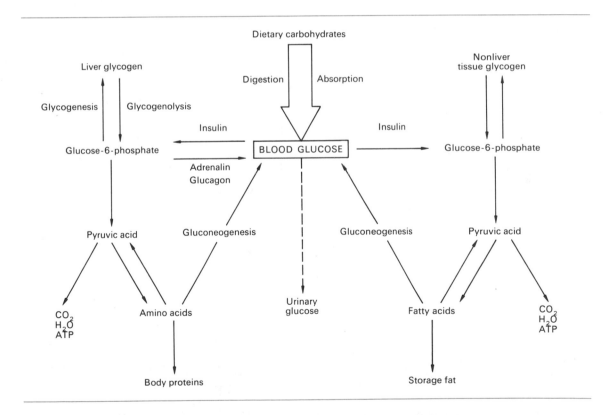

Figure 7·2 A schematic diagram of the possible fate of blood glucose. When blood glucose is high, insulin promotes the phosphorylation of glucose to produce glycogen; when blood sugar is low, glucagon and adrenalin initiate the conversion of glycogen to glucose.

199

synthesis of polysaccharides, proteins, and fats through the removal of water (dehydration synthesis).

Organisms which cannot synthesize their own food are termed *heterotrophic*. The photosynthetic autotrophs that were discussed in Chapter 6 do not require a complicated digestive system since the necessary nutrients are readily available to all cells. All heterotrophs, however, must possess a digestive mechanism that efficiently breaks nutrients down into absorbable products in a systematic process.

PROTIST AND ANIMAL EXAMPLES

The process of digestion in some protists and throughout the animal kingdom occurs in many different types of systems, some of which are described below and diagrammed in Figure 7–3. In many organisms digestion is entirely *intracellular* (within the cell). The amoeba, a protozoan, captures its food with a flowing pseudopod, whereas the *Paramecium* engulfs particles which are carried into a groovelike gullet by beating cilia. In either case the cell membrane surrounds the food which then is pinched off to form a food vacuole within the cell. Intracellular enzymes im-

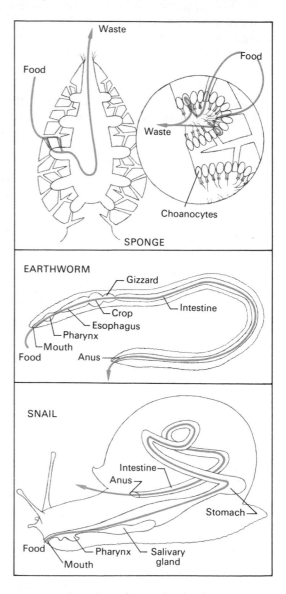

Figure 7·3 Some examples of how digestion occurs among selected protists and animals.

200

mediately begin to digest the food and the usable nutrients diffuse into the cytoplasm. In unicellular organisms such as these all of the processes of life must be accomplished in a single cell.

Sponges, considered to be at the cellular level of development, have a cavity which is lined with flagellated collar cells (choanocytes). Food particles brought in by the water current produced by the beating flagella are caught and engulfed by the cytoplasm in the collar that surrounds the flagellum. The digestion is again intracellular.

Even in the coelenterates such as hydra, jellyfish, and sea anemones, digestion is almost completely intracellular. Threadlike filaments, however, project from the thin layer of gastric cells lining the gastrovascular cavity and contact the food. These gastric filaments secrete enzymes which can actually initiate the digestive process outside the digestive cells. The one opening to the digestive area (the gastrovascular cavity) serves as both mouth and anus.

In the earthworm, phylum Annelida, a digestive tract with two openings, a mouth and an anus, is present. Along this tract are specialized regions for the digestion and absorption of food. These specialized areas are the crop, a thin-walled portion in which food is stored; the gizzard, a muscular region where food is ground; and the intestine, where digestive enzymes are added from the intestinal walls and digestion takes place. When digestion occurs outside of cells, in a cavity, it is known as extracellular digestion.

A variety of digestive processes are present among the mollusks. Certain aquatic snails digest most of their food within large digestive gland cells, whereas the octopus and the squid possess extracellular digestion almost entirely.

In general, digestive systems become more complex and extracellular digestion more predominant as one investigates the phylogenetic order from the kingdom Protista to the phylum Chordata. The fundamental enzymatic mechanisms of hydrolysis, however, are always similar.

THE VERTEBRATE PLAN

The digestive process as it occurs in man will be presented here as an example of digestion in vertebrates. The vertebrate digestive system, known as the *alimentary canal*, includes the mouth, esophagus, stomach, small intestine, large intestine, rectum, and anus. In addition, the liver, gallbladder, and pancreas serve as accessory digestive organs. Although foodstuffs do not pass through these organs, many hormones and enzymes are produced which are essential for digestion. The structure and function of vertebrate digestive systems vary in relationship to the foods eaten (Figure 7–4). For example, the herbivore digestive tract is generally longer and possesses one or more pouches for storage. During storage, special bacteria break down the tough, fibrous cellulose and provide nutrients for the host. The cow has a four-part stomach and the largest pouch, known as the rumen, is the site of extensive bacterial action.

Functionally, the digestive process may be separated into three phases: salivary, gastric, and intestinal.

SALIVARY PHASE OF DIGESTION

The mouth or buccal cavity contains the teeth and tongue which are necessary for the mechanical breakdown and transport of solid food. The permanent human teeth include four incisors, two canine, four premolars, and six molars. Incisors are used in biting, the canines are useful for ripping and tearing, and the molars are broadly ridged for chewing. The human teeth are efficient for masticating both flesh and vegetable matter, and man therefore is classified as an *omnivore* along with such animals as bears and pigs. The meat-eater or *carnivore*, represented by cats and dogs, have extremely sharp, needlelike teeth necessary for tearing and shredding flesh. *Herbivores*, such as cattle or beavers, which eat only vegetable matter, have flattened tooth surfaces for crushing and grinding (Figure 7–5).

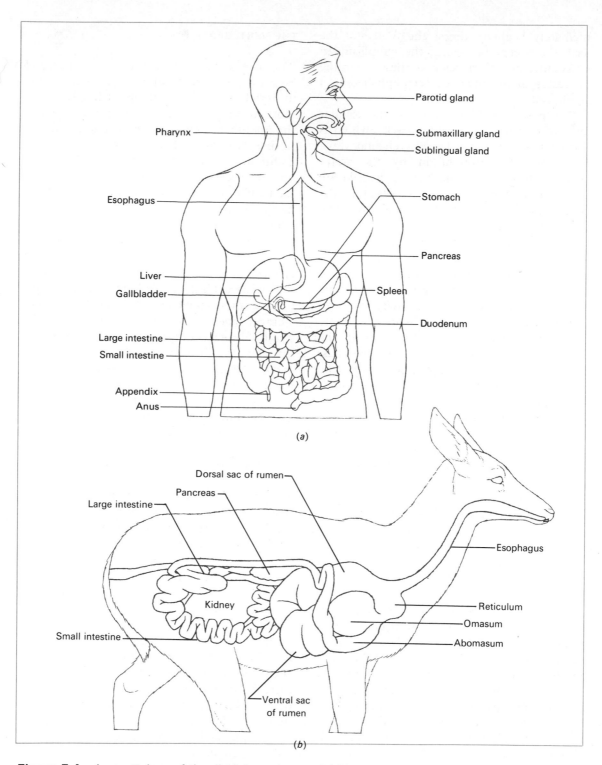

Figure 7·4 A comparison of the digestive systems of (*a*) man, (*b*) deer, and (*c*) cat. Note the large storage pouches in the deer, a herbivorous ruminant.

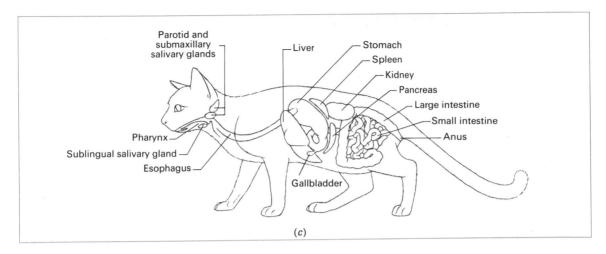

Parotid and submaxillary salivary glands

Liver

Stomach

Spleen

Kidney

Pancreas

Large intestine

Small intestine

Anus

Pharynx

Sublingual salivary gland

Esophagus

Gallbladder

(c)

Figure 7·4c

During mastication, three pairs of salivary glands, the *parotid* located just beneath each ear, the *submaxillary* near the angle of the jaw, and the *sublingual* which lie under the tongue, empty saliva into the mouth cavity. Saliva is a viscous liquid that contains water, salts, mucin, and a carbohydrate-splitting enzyme called salivary amylase. The functions of saliva include the breakdown of starches and the lubrication of food. In addition, it aids in speech and allows for the sensation of taste by liquifying dry foods. The flow of saliva may be activated by the presence of food in the mouth, the smell of food, or simply thinking about eating. The control of salivation is directed by the autonomic nervous system. This involuntary system will be discussed in the next chapter.

Salivary secretions contain two enzymes, *salivary amylase* or *ptyalin* and *maltase*. Salivary amylase hydrolyzes starches into smaller double-sugar units of maltose $(C_{12}H_{22}O_{11})$. Vertebrate amylases act only on the carbohydrate alpha linkages and have no digestive action on beta-linked cellulose molecules. These linkages were discussed in Chapter 2. Maltase cleaves the maltose into two glucose units through the catalytic addition of water. The pH of the mouth fluids is normally near 7 or neutrality. Experiments with human salivary amylase, using a starch substrate, indicate an optimum activity range of pH 6.5 to 7.5. The term *substrate* indicates a substance that is being acted upon by an enzyme. Glucose, as you learned in the previous chapter, is immediately available for energy metabolism when absorbed into the bloodstream. Total carbohydrate digestion, however, is usually not completed in the mouth. When the ball of food or *bolus* reaches the stomach, the high acid content of that organ ultimately inhibits the action of amylase. The final stages of starch digestion take place in the small intestine.

GASTRIC PHASE OF DIGESTION

The stomach, a muscular, J-shaped organ, lies just below the diaphragm. The esophagus, the tube leading from the mouth, enters the stomach through a constriction called the *cardiac valve*. The stomach is divided into three parts, the upper or *cardiac* portion which includes the saclike *fundus*, the *body*, and the lower region or *pylorus* where it joins with the small intestine. The wall of the stomach is composed of three layers of muscle—an outer longitudinal, a middle oblique, and an

(a)

(b)

(c)

internal circular. There is also a lining made up of distinct longitudinal ridges called *rugae*, and these rugae folds allow for expansion. The entrance to the small intestine from the stomach is guarded by a circular muscle called a *sphincter valve*. This valve keeps the food in the stomach for digestion and protects the relatively thin-walled intestine against large, abrasive chunks of food. The bolus to be digested is transported along the entire digestive tract by means of rhythmic waves of muscle contractions. This action, termed *peristalsis*, is controlled by the involuntary nervous system. Carbohydrate digestion has been arrested here because of the extreme acidity of the stomach which ranges from pH 2 to 5. The mixture of food in the stomach is termed *acid chyme*.

In invertebrates the stomach functions principally as a storage, grinding, or straining organ. In vertebrates, however, the stomach has a definite secretory role. The *parietal* cells secrete hydrochloric acid (HCl) and the *chief* cells secrete an inactive protein-splitting (proteolytic) enzyme called *pepsinogen*. Pepsinogen is acted on by HCl to form *pepsin* which in turn hydrolyzes protein into polypeptides, dipeptides, and amino acids (Figure 7–6). Hydrochloric acid also serves the important function of killing bacteria and breaking down the intercellular cement of fibrous plant and animal tissues. When food enters through the cardiac valve of the esophagus, the lining of the stomach secretes digestive juices. The presence of the food also activates the lining cells to release the hormone *gastrin* into the bloodstream which stimulates HCl and pepsinogen secretion. Due to nervous stimulation some gastric secretion may occur when food is taken into the mouth. In young mammals, a special milk-coagulating enzyme, *rennin*, causes the normally soluble casein protein of milk to unite with calcium and fat to form insoluble curds. As the individual ma-

Figure 7·5 Dentition of the upper jaws of three animals: (*a*) beaver (herbivore), (*b*) cat (carnivore), (*c*) bear (omnivore).

Chief cells → Pepsinogen (inactive) + Parietal cells ↓ HCl ⟶ Pepsin (active)

Figure 7·6 Pepsinogen secreted by the chief cells of the stomach is activated by HCl which is secreted by the parietal cells. Both of these cell types are located in the gastric mucosa.

tures, rennin production is greatly decreased or lost; the curdling role is adequately accomplished, however, by pepsin and HCl. The curds are finally digested by proteolytic and fat enzymes in the stomach and small intestine.

The occurrence of gastric ulcers illustrates the fact that gastric secretions are controlled primarily by the autonomic nervous system. An ulcer is an area of the alimentary canal that has been eroded away owing to the excessive action of peristalsis, HCl, and digestive enzymes. Anxiety and nervous tension can cause this condition. The stomach normally is lined with a glycoprotein coating known as *mucin* which protects the cells from self-digestion (autolysis). Excessive secretion and peristaltic action in the absence of food removes this protective coating. Ulcers are often painful and·may produce internal hemorrhages if the blood vessels lying below the lining are also eroded.

INTESTINAL PHASE OF DIGESTION

Peristaltic contractions force the acid chyme through the *pyloric valve* into the first portion of the small intestine. The first ten inches of the small intestine, called the *duodenum*, is the site of a number of digestive and absorptive functions. The duodenum contains numerous fingerlike projections or *villi* which extend into the lumen (center) of the tube. Functionally, these villi produce a greatly increased surface area for absorption. The fluids in the small intestine are generally alkaline in contrast to the stomach's acidic secretions. The pH ranges between 6.8 and 8.0 in the small intestine.

PANCREATIC ENZYMES

The presence of acid chyme in the duodenum stimulates the intestinal mucosa cells to secrete the hormone *secretin* which in turn causes the pancreas to secrete large amounts of sodium bicarbonate. It is this substance that maintains the duodenum in an alkaline condition. A second hormone produced by the duodenum, *pancreozymin*, stimulates the pancreas to release its digestive enzymes. Each day the pancreas produces 500 to 800 ml of fluid containing the various enzymes needed for the hydrolysis of all types of food. The specific enzymes produced by the pancreas and the types of food they hydrolyze are (1) *pancreatic amylase*—starch, (2) *pancreatic lipase*—fats, (3) *trypsin*—native protein (albumins, collagen), and (4) *carboxypeptidase*—peptide bonds which have a free-COOH group.

The action of pancreatic amylase on starches is very similar to that of ptyalin in the mouth. Pancreatic lipase cleaves fats at the ester bonds to release glycerol and fatty acids. Large globules of fat are emulsified by bile which enters the small intestine near the pancreatic duct via the common bile duct from the liver and the gallbladder. The bile lowers the surface tension surrounding the fat molecules and produces smaller droplets which exposes more surface area to the lipase enzyme. Thus bile is only an aid to fat digestion and not an enzyme. The presence of fats in the small intestine stimulates the intestinal lining (mucosa) to secrete the hormone *cholecystokinin* which enters the bloodstream and causes the gallbladder to release bile.

Trypsin, a protein-breaking enzyme, is comparable to gastric pepsin. It acts in an alkaline medium, however, and hydrolyzes complex proteins at a slower rate than does pepsin. Trypsin is secreted by the pancreas in an inactive form called *trypsinogen*. The conversion of trypsinogen to trypsin is accomplished by the action of a nondigestive enzyme secreted by the intestinal mucosa called *enterokinase*. It has been demonstrated that enterokinase removes a fragment from the trypsinogen molecule which permits it to become active. Since we know that an enzyme has a very specific geometry with important substrate-contact areas called "active sites," it is probable that the conversion process is simply an unmasking of the active sites (Figure 7–7).

Carboxypeptase, the remaining proteolytic enzyme supplied by the pancreas, serves a very specific function. It hydrolyzes the peptide linkages which are adjacent to free-carboxyl (acid) groups.

INTESTINAL ENZYMES

The small intestine is the site of final digestion and a number of digestive enzymes are secreted here. These enzymes are secreted by individual cells that lie at the base of the villi folds and also by the compound intestinal glands located in the submucosa layer. It is thought, however, that the intestinal glands primarily produce lubricating mucous. The flow of intestinal enzymes is initiated by the liberation of the hormone *enterocrinnin* in the intestinal mucosa. Again, the presence of acid chyme is the principal activator.

Intestinal lipase and amylase have functions similar to pancreatic enzymes already described. Dipeptidases split the small units of double amino acids into individual acids which can then be absorbed and utilized. *Aminopeptidase* is similar in action to carboxypeptidase and the two are compared in Figure 7–8. Most of the complex carbohydrates have been broken into twelve-carbon sugars by salivary and pancreatic amylases. The intestine produces not only an amylase but also three enzymes commonly classed as *disaccharases* which split disaccharides (twelve-carbon sugars). These three enzymes are: *maltase* (maltose → glucose + glucose), *sucrase* (sucrose → fructose + glucose), and *lactase* (lactose → galactose + glucose).

The digestion of foods is thus a stepwise process in which intermediate products are formed on the way to the end products. As noted in the preceding discussion, specific enzymes function at various steps along the way. For example, disaccharases function in the splitting of twelve-carbon sugar molecules to six-carbon sugar molecules. Dipeptidases are important for the hydrolysis of dipeptides into individual amino acids. A summary of

Figure 7·7 A diagrammatic model of the unmasking action of enterokinase on trypsinogen. The removal of the fragment frees the active site and trypsin becomes functional.

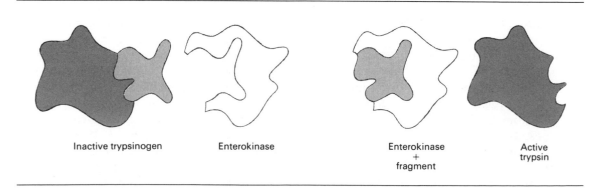

Inactive trypsinogen   Enterokinase   Enterokinase + fragment   Active trypsin

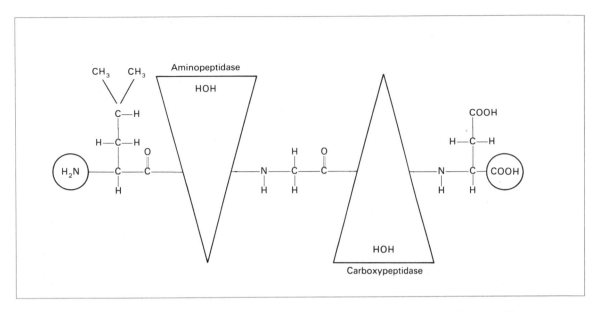

Figure 7·8 An example of the enzymatic action on peptide bonds of a polyeptide by either carboxy-peptidase (from the pancreas) or aminopeptidase in the small intestine.

the major steps in the digestion of the three classes of foods and the principal enzymes involved is shown in Figure 7–9.

ABSORPTION OF DIGESTIVE PRODUCTS

The duodenum is the first area of absorption of digested nutrients and absorption occurs along most of the small intestine. The cells lining the intestinal villi display selective absorption —that is, certain substances are absorbed faster than others. For example, the six-carbon sugar galactose is absorbed faster than glucose, and glucose is absorbed faster than fructose. The cells are also capable of absorbing substances against a *concentration gradient*.

Figure 7·9 A summary diagram showing the intermediate and end products resulting from the digestion of the three classes of foods. Some of the major enzymes that function at each step are noted.

Food	Enzyme Action	Intermediate Products	Enzyme Action	End Products
Carbohydrates	salivary pancreatic and intestinal amylase	Disaccharides	maltase, sucrase, lactase	Monosaccharides
Protein	pepsin, trypsin	Polypeptides and dipeptides	carboxypeptidase, dipeptidase, aminopeptidase	Amino acids
Fats (bile added)		Emulsified fat	lipase	Glycerol and fatty acids

In our earlier definition of diffusion we learned that particles tend to diffuse away from the greatest concentration. As absorption continues it is certain that each cell will collect a higher concentration of nutrients than is found in the intestinal juice. The movement of these substances into the cells and bloodstream thus is against the gradient and requires energy in the form of ATP. You might benefit by reviewing the section on active transport in Chapter 3 at this time.

Absorbed nutrients pass through the intestinal cells and enter the bloodstream. Each villus contains an arteriole and a venule connected by a capillary network. The venules finally form a larger vein called the *hepatic portal vein*. As a result of absorption, blood in this vein is highly concentrated with nutrients and passes directly to the capillary beds of the liver. This is interesting, because most veins lead directly to the heart. The term *portal* identifies any venous system that carries blood to an organ other than the heart. In frogs, for example, a special venous system carries blood from the legs to the capillaries of the kidneys, thus this vessel is termed the renal portal vein.

A third type of vessel called a *lacteal* is located in each villus. The lacteal vessels are part of an accessory venous system known as the *lymphatic system*. The lacteals absorb emulsified fats and route them away from the liver and into a larger lymphatic duct or *thoracic duct* which passes upward through the diaphragm and empties into the left subclavian vein above the heart. Perhaps it is now clear to you how excessive fat ingestion can cause fat deposition in the vessels near the heart.

The remaining part of the small intestine is separated into the *jejunum* (about eight feet) and the *ileum* (twelve feet). The villi are smaller in the jejunum and function in absorption of digestive products. The junction between the ileum and the ascending colon of the large intestine is controlled by the *ileocecal* valve which keeps nonabsorbed wastes from backing up in the system. The vermiform appendix (a vestigial organ in man) extends from the caecum or blind pouch of the ascending colon. The appendix apparently no longer serves vital function. The major organs and enzymes involved in digestion in man are summarized in Figure 7–10.

THE ROLE OF THE LARGE INTESTINE

The large intestine or colon functions primarily in water and ion absorption, concentration of feces, and defecation. Bacteria are common in the colon where residual polysaccharides and cellulose may be further broken down through the action of bacterial enzymes. In addition some bacteria produce vitamin K and some B vitamins. The colon averages about two and a half inches in width and is five to six feet long. The descending colon, in a long S shape, is often referred to as the sigmoid colon. The last eight to ten inches of the alimentary tract includes the rectum, anal canal, and anus.

CIRCULATION AND TRANSPORTATION

Organisms range in size from single cells of less than a micron to the 100-foot-long, 150-ton great blue whale. The world's largest plants are represented by the 300-foot giant redwoods of California. It is fairly clear to us how compounds enter, circulate, and leave small organisms by diffusion. It is somewhat more difficult, however, to understand the complex mechanism of circulation and transportation of materials in the whale or the giant redwoods.

Perhaps the most basic factor in circulation and transportation problems is the ratio between the volume of the organism to its external surface area. Most multicellular plants and animals which possess a high volume-to-surface-area ratio must also have special systems to facilitate nutrition, gas exchange, and excretion. This is necessary because most of the mass of the body of the organism is not directly exposed to the environment.

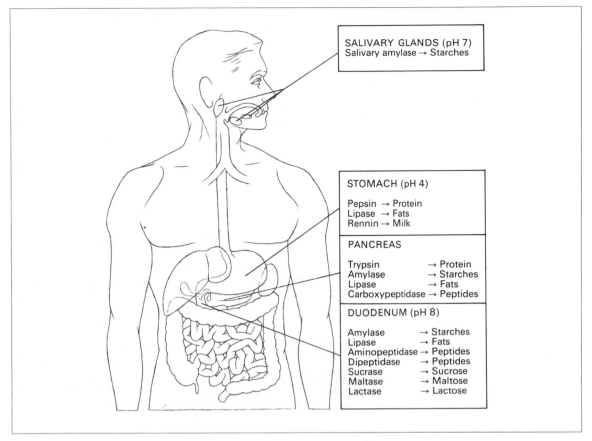

Figure 7·10 A summary of digestion in man. The enzymes and the foods they act on are shown for each area of digestion.

IN PLANTS

In Chapter 4 we learned that vascular plants contain special transport tissues. Xylem vessels carry water from the roots to all the branches and leaves. The fact that a redwood tree can effectively "lift" water over 300 feet against gravity is still an intriguing question to scientists. The most accepted theory to explain this has been presented by an English botanist, H. H. Dixon. Dixon demonstrated that molecules of water standing in slender tubes have very high cohesion—that is, they tend to stick together. As water is lost through *transpiration* (evaporation of water from stomates) or utilized in photosynthesis, new water molecules diffuse into the vessels at the root level. Roots generally possess high os-motic pressures owing to the presence of sugar-laden sap. High osmotic pressure permits water to move into the root cells from the soil—that is, from a region of greater concentration to a region of lesser concentration. This pressure alone, however, is not sufficient to account for the lifting of the water in the column. Transpiration creates a pulling effect on the unbroken column of water. These events are summarized in Figure 7–11.

The phloem vessels transport sugars from the leaves to other organs of the plant. The direction of this food flow is principally downward toward the roots. In the winter when food production is reduced, the flow may be upward from the storage areas in the roots. The movement of organic nutrients in the phloem is called *translocation*.

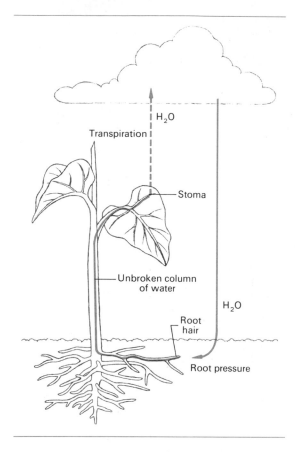

Figure 7·11 A diagrammatic representation of the movement of water from the roots to the leaves in trees. An unbroken column of water is essential between root pressure and transpirational pull.

and recirculation through the heart. A good example of the open system is found in the crayfish, an arthropod (Figure 7–12).

A *closed circulatory system* is present in earthworms (Annelida) and all vertebrates (Chordata). The closed system is composed of an artery–capillary bed–vein structure with which you are probably familiar (Figures 7–13 and 7–14). Exchange of gases, uptake of nutrients, and release of waste materials by the cells must occur across the capillary membranes in the capillary bed. Essentially, the function of the arteries and veins is to carry blood to and from the capillary beds. The higher pressure of the closed system greatly aids this process, as we shall see later in this chapter.

The closed system in man shows a separation of the respiratory function from the general circulation. All deoxygenated blood is collected in the right atrium, transfered into the right ventricle, and then pumped to the lungs through the pulmonary artery. This is the only artery that carries deoxygenated blood. The oxygenated blood is returned to the left atrium, passed into the left ventricle, and pumped into the general circulation. Note in Figure 7–14 that the liver not only receives arterial blood but also collects the venous blood from the digestive organs via the hepatic portal vein.

IN ANIMALS

Many small and parasitic forms, such as tapeworms and liver flukes, lack specific circulatory and respiratory systems. In general, however, two types of blood circulatory systems are found in animals—open and closed. In *open circulatory systems* the blood is pumped from a contractile heart into a main artery that supplies the body tissues. The blood collects in tissue sinuses (spaces), bathing each cell with nutrients and providing a medium for gas exchange. The blood then is collected in a large sinus or *hemocoel* before oxygenation

GAS EXCHANGE

Small aquatic organisms such as amoebae or even the flatworms can exchange gases with their environment by direct diffusion. The surface area of these organisms is large enough with respect to their volume so that special breathing organs are unnecessary. This large surface-area-to-volume ratio does not exist in vertebrates or most of the larger invertebrates, and some mechanism or organ system for breathing is necessary. Cellular respiration, discussed in Chapter 6, utilizes oxygen in the Krebs cycle and the electron-transport series. Carbon dioxide, which is given off in this pro-

210

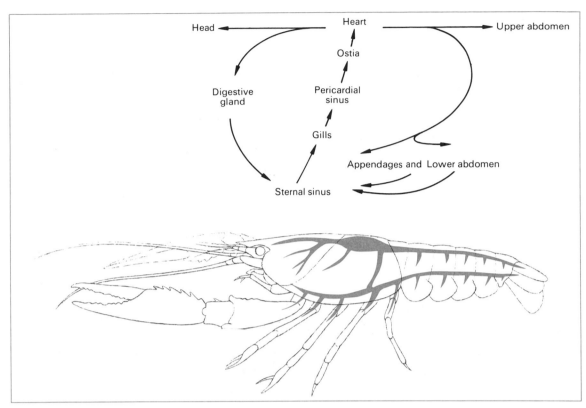

Figure 7·12 Generalized diagram of the open circulatory system of the crayfish (an arthropod). Note the sternal (hemocoel) and pericardial sinuses.

Figure 7·13 A simplified diagram of the closed blood flow in the earthworm. Each segment has a set of arteries that supply blood to the digestive tract, excretory organs, and muscles. All the arteries and veins are connected by capillary vessels. Oxygenation occurs by diffusion through the skin.

Figure 7·14 Circulatory system of man.

cess, must be carried away from the cell and eventually transported back to the environment. Keep in mind that although breathing or gas exchange is related to cellular respiration, it is not the same process.

Five basic breathing systems are known:

(1) direct diffusion (plants, protists, and some invertebrate animals such as planaria), (2) gills (crustaceans, some mollusks and fish), (3) positive-pressure lungs (reptiles and amphibians), (4) negative-pressure lungs (birds and mammals), and (5) tracheal tubes (insects).

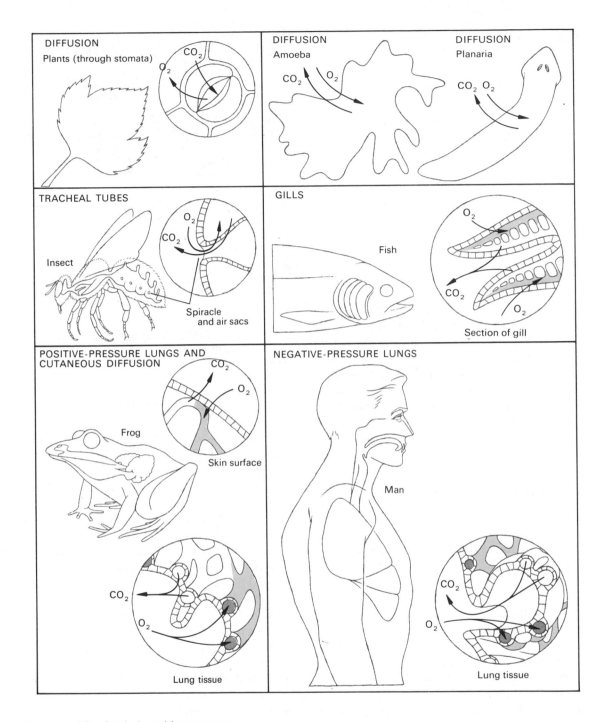

Figure 7·15 Basic breathing systems.

These five systems are illustrated in Figure 7–15 and discussed individually in the following sections. We should note that in all systems other than the direct diffusion of certain single-celled organisms and plants a thin, moist membrane is necessary for the exchange of gases.

213

DIRECT DIFFUSION

All aerobic (oxygen-requiring) protists exchange gases through body-surface diffusion. Since most of these organisms are aquatic and essentially unicellular, direct diffusion is an efficient mechanism. Sponges, coelenterates, and flatworms, although being larger and multicellular, require no special breathing organs or systems. In plants the exchange of gases occurs principally through small openings in the leaves called stomata (described in Chapter 4 in the section on plant tissues).

GILLS

Aquatic animals possessing many tissues and organs have evolved special organs known as gills to increase surface area for gas exchange. Very sluggish invertebrates such as tubeworms and snails have gills. Starfish have small projections from the skin which function as a type of gill. In more active animals, such as fish, water must be moved across the gills by swimming or, as with crayfish and other crustaceans, by special paddlelike appendages.

POSITIVE-PRESSURE LUNGS

The complications of the vertebrate body require a highly efficient gas-exchange and transport system. Amphibians, such as frogs, salamanders, and reptiles, possess lungs that open into the mouth cavity by a *trachea*. In order to inflate the lungs, these animals must close their mouths tightly and force air into the lungs by compressing the muscular floor of the mouth cavity. Amphibians that spend much of their time in moist habitats also "breathe" through their thin, moist skin, since the blood capillaries are very close to the skin surface. Frogs may accomplish at least one-third of their total respiration by this *cutaneous breathing*. Cutaneous diffusion is very important during winter hibernation at the bottom of ponds.

Figure 7·16 Photomicrograph of a cross section of human lung tissue. The alveolar sacs are composed of very thin squamous epithelium. (Courtesy of Eliott Weier.)

NEGATIVE-PRESSURE LUNGS

Mammals, including man, have structurally complex lungs. The tissue of the human lung is a good example of the thin, moist membranes needed for gas exchange. The tiny *alveolar sacs* are composed of extremely thin cells and are continuously bathed by tissue fluids (Figure 7–16). An average adult male inhales about 500 ml of air with each normal breath. The amount of air that can be forcibly exhaled (vital capacity) after maximum inhalation varies from 4500 to 7000 ml. At inhalation the dome-shaped, muscular diaphragm contracts and moves downward, away from the lungs, while the intercostal muscles of the ribs lift the chest cavity upward. These combined efforts cause a temporary decrease in pressure in the *thoracic cavity*, and permit air to rush in through the nose, mouth, and trachea to fill the lungs.

Birds are not equipped with a diaphragm even though they do have lungs. Birds in flight require a lot of energy and maintain very high metabolic rates. Gas exchange then becomes

214

a critical problem, and, since they do not gulp air as amphibians do, they must possess some unique mechanism. Bird lungs are small and compact and lie close to the body wall. Four pairs of lung sacs extend from the main lung into practically all parts of the body. The lungs and air sacs are filled when the muscular chest is expanded, and the trapped air in the air sacs is forced back into the lungs upon exhalation. Thus the main lung of a bird actually receives air at both inhalation and exhalation.

TRACHEAL TUBES

Gas exchange in insects takes place by the air circulating directly to the tissues. In the grasshopper or honey bee, for example, air enters the body through small openings called *spiracles*. The air then passes through a complex branched system of tiny tubules called *tracheae* and air sacs to all parts of the body. The tracheae are supported by tiny rings of *chitin* (the hard material found in the exoskeleton).

THE ROLE OF TRANSPORT FLUIDS

Once oxygen is taken in, it must be carried to the cells and the carbon-dioxide waste must be removed from the organism. In most organisms, this task is accomplished by body fluids. The water portion of blood (plasma) can transport oxygen, but this is not sufficient to meet the needs of most animals. Consequently, special molecules capable of transporting oxygen are often present. Since these molecules usually show color, we refer to them as respiratory pigments.

The earthworm has a rather complex circulatory system which contains plasma and small, colorless corpuscles. The blood is red due to the presence of the iron-containing pigment *hemoglobin* dissolved in the plasma. Although this pigment is not found in the corpuscles, it is very similar to the hemoglobin of human corpuscles and it does transport oxygen. The blood of arthropods is

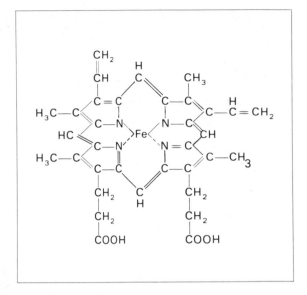

Figure 7·17 Structural formula of heme, the porphyrin part of the hemoglobin molecule.

generally colorless but certain crustaceans, such as crayfish, crabs, and lobsters, possess a bluish copper-containing pigment called *hemocyanin*. Hemocyanin is dissolved in the plasma and carries oxygen.

HEMOGLOBIN AND OXYGEN

The respiratory pigment of all vertebrates and some invertebrates is hemoglobin. The tetrapyrrol ring arrangement of hemoglobin (Figure 7–17) is very similar to the basic structure of the cytochromes and chlorophyll (see Figures 6–8 and 6–22). The iron-pyrrol complex is termed the *heme* group and the attached protein is called *globin* (Figure 7–18).

The primary function of hemoglobin is to combine with oxygen in the lungs and to transport this oxygen to the tissues of the organism. When hemoglobin picks up oxygen, a bright red complex known as oxyhemoglobin (often noted as HbO_2) is formed. The oxygenated arterial blood may be easily distinguished from the bluish venous blood which contains much less oxygen.

Chemically, the combination of oxygen with hemoglobin is quite loose since oxygen

Figure 7·18 Model of the hemoglobin molecule as deduced from X-ray diffraction studies. The light blocks represent α-polypeptide chains and the dark are β-polypeptide chains. The oxygen-binding sites are marked O₂. (Courtesy of M. F. Perutz.)

uptake and release must occur rapidly and easily. The uptake of oxygen in the lungs, or "loading" as it is sometimes called, takes place across the thin, moist alveolar membranes. The venous blood entering the lungs contains a low partial pressure of oxygen and a high partial pressure of carbon dioxide. In physical terms, the pressure of a mixture of gases is equal to the sum of the pressures of the individual gases. The pressure then of a specific gas in a mixture is known as the partial pressure of that gas. Partial pressures are generally stated in terms of millimeters of mercury (mmHg)—that is, the pressure required to support a column of mercury one centimeter in diameter at that height.

Since the oxygen pressure in the alveolar sacs is higher than in the blood, oxygen diffuses into the blood, whereas the high partial pressure of carbon dioxide in venous blood causes the CO_2 to diffuse into the alveolar air. When the red blood cells reach the tissue capillaries, the reverse occurs. The tissue cells have utilized oxygen and therefore have a low oxygen content. Due to the diffusion gradient across the capillary membrane, the hemoglobin immediately releases its oxygen to the cells. Since carbon dioxide was released to the environment through the lungs, the arterial blood has a comparatively low CO_2 pressure and this allows CO_2 to move from the tissues into the bloodstream. The general diffusion gradients and the diffusion of gases in the lungs and tissues is shown in Figure 7–19.

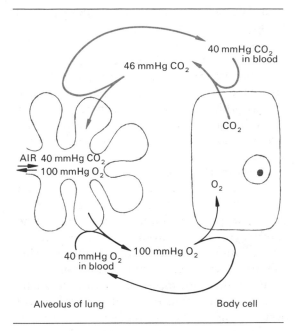

Figure 7·19 A simplified diagram of the gas exchange between the lungs and body cells showing the partial pressures that effect diffusion.

CARBONIC ANHYDRASE AND CARBON DIOXIDE

Although a small amount of CO_2 will combine with hemoglobin to form $HbCO_2$, most of the CO_2 is transported in another way. A special enzyme called *carbonic anhydrase* located within the red blood cells catalyzes the combination of CO_2 with H_2O to form carbonic acid, H_2CO_3. Carbonic acid dissociates into H^+ and HCO_3^-, and the bicarbonate ion (HCO_3^-) diffuses into the plasma. Therefore CO_2 is transported primarily to the lungs in the plasma as bicarbonate ions. In the lungs, the reaction in the red blood cells is reversed ($HCO_3^- + H^+ \rightarrow H_2O + CO_2$) and carbon dioxide is released.

When HCO_3^- leaves the red blood cells in the tissues, an imbalance of charges results. The ionic balance is restored when a chloride ion (Cl^-) moves into the cell. This exchange of negative-charged ions is called the *chloride shift* (Figure 7–20). A reverse exchange must

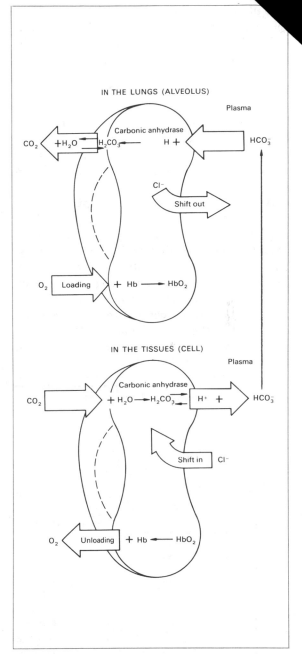

Figure 7·20 A diagram of the major gas exchange events occurring in the lungs and tissues. Note that CO_2 is carried in the plasma as the bicarbonate ion.

217

s when HCO_3^- is entering ... to produce CO_2. At this ... eave the red blood cells ... ionic balance.

...EATHING

The coordination centers for breathing are found in the medulla oblongata and pons of the human brain. The medulla contains the expiratory and inspiratory centers. A *pneumotaxic center* located in the pons has nervous connections with the expiratory and inspiratory centers and functions in relaying impulses and coordinating the breathing rhythm especially during labored breathing. The centers in the medulla, however, control the rate and depth of breathing during sleep and normal quiet breathing. Nerve pathways enter the breathing centers from the cerebral cortex and the hypothalamus. Because of these cerebral cortex associations, an individual

may consciously regulate his breathing or hold his breath for a short time.

Impulses are issued constantly from the inspiratory center and sent to the rib muscles and diaphragm to cause inspiration. At the same time impulses are sent to the pneumotaxic center, which activates the expiratory center to inhibit the inspiratory impulses. During this cessation of inspiratory impulses, a passive expiration occurs. An additional regulatory mechanism found in the lungs, are the tiny nerve endings, called *stretch receptors*, located in the alveoli. As the air sacs fill and stretch during inspiration, impulses are sent to the expiratory center through the vagus nerve. These impulses sufficiently inhibit the inspiratory center to permit expiration. This feedback mechanism, working with the pneumotaxic center, ensures that expiration will occur. This reflex mechanism between the alveoli and the expiratory center is known as the *Hering-Breuer reflex* (Figure 7–21).

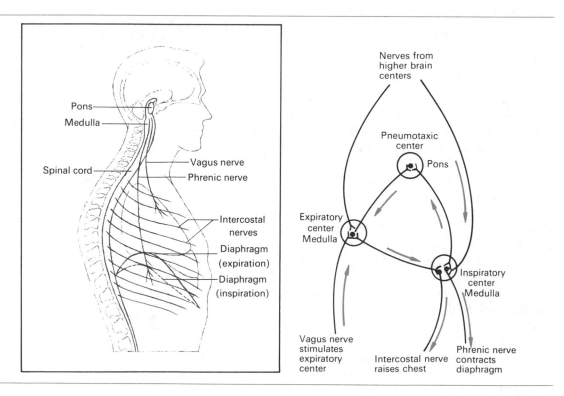

Figure 7·21   The nervous control of breathing.

218

The inspiratory center is sensitive to the amount of carbon dioxide in the blood. In fact, this is the primary stimulation for inspiration. In addition, oxygen- and CO_2-sensitive nerve receptors called *carotid bodies* are located in the carotid arteries and wall of the aorta. These bodies stimulate the inspiratory center and increase the rate and depth of breathing with any decrease in oxygen or increase in carbon dioxide in the blood.

EXCRETION OF METABOLIC WASTES AND WATER BALANCE

All organisms have the problem of ridding their bodies of metabolic wastes, some of which are extremely toxic even in small amounts. Plants, which lack excretory systems, have evolved a variety of mechanisms for the disposal of metabolic wastes. Some wastes are given off as diffusible gases and others are deposited in certain parts of the cell or on the external parts of the plant. Synthetic processes in plants can actually perform an excretory function when certain toxic nitrogen compounds are synthesized into nontoxic compounds. Caffeine and morphine are examples of these synthetic secretions.

As a result of the metabolism of amino acids and the breakdown of other nitrogen compounds in animal cells, especially in the cells of the liver in vertebrates, large amounts of nitrogen are released into the tissue fluids and blood. The waste nitrogen combines readily with water to form toxic ammonia. Small organisms living in an aqueous environment quickly discharge ammonia by diffusion. Most terrestrial animals, however, must conserve water and thus the nitrogenous wastes are held in the body longer. The cells of most animals have enzyme systems to detoxify the nitrogen compounds. The most common products of nitrogen detoxification are urea and uric acid. Since animals may excrete ammonia, urea, or uric acid as their nitrogenous waste products, they are sometimes classified by these products—that is, as *ammonotelic* (ammonia), *ureotelic* (urea) or *uricotelic* (uric acid). By comparison, ammonia is the most toxic followed by urea and the almost insoluble uric acid.

AMMONOTELIC, UREOTELIC, AND URICOTELIC EXCRETION

Most aquatic invertebrates are ammonotelic. This is easy to understand since they are relatively small and can easily diffuse waste compounds into the water. Freshwater bony fish also excrete ammonia through their gills. Earthworms excrete urea in the air and ammonia in water.

Urea is the major detoxification product of amphibians, sharks, and mammals. It is synthesized in the liver, released to the bloodstream, and filtered into the urine by the kidneys. When the intermediate compounds and enzymes of urea synthesis were worked out, it was learned that the process occurred in a cycle. Basically, ammonia and ornithine are finally returned to combine with more ammonia and carbon dioxide. A schematic diagram, Figure 7–22, shows the urea cycle. At (C) in this diagram, a specific amino acid, aspartic acid, enters which is essential to the completion of the cycle. Most of the aspartic acid molecule is lost, however, and can enter the citric-acid cycle to be oxidized (Chapter 6). One nitrogen atom from aspartic acid remains and becomes part of the released urea molecule.

Animals producing uric acid include some insects, birds, reptiles, and land snails. The white portion of bird droppings indicates the presence of uric acid. Uric acid, the least toxic compound, is synthesized by animals that must retain body water or produce land-type eggs. Reptile and bird embryos, for example, must develop inside eggs with little communication with the outside environment. Since toxic wastes must be stored inside the egg with the developing embryo the formation of insoluble uric acid is vital to the survival of the embryo. The ability of an organism to produce a proper detoxification product consistent with its environment is a good example of adaptation.

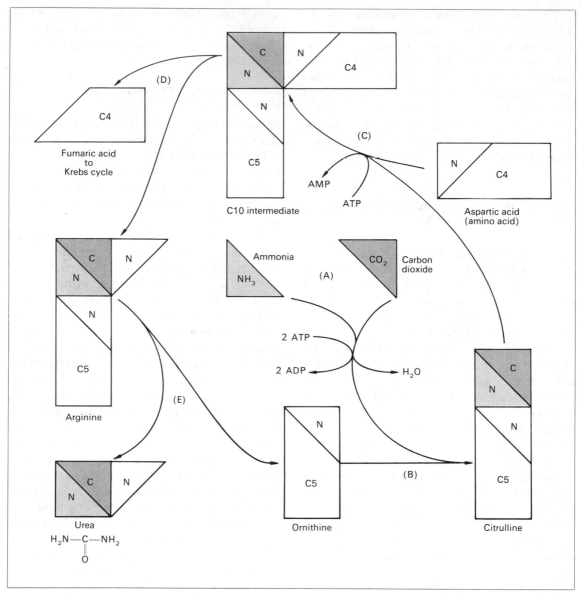

Figure 7·22 The urea or ornithine cycle. Begin the cycle at (A) and continue counterclockwise. Each lettered segment requires a specific enzyme. Excess amounts of nitrogen and carbon dioxide are removed in the liver through the formation of urea. The urea is removed from the blood and excreted by the kidneys.

EXCRETION IN THE INVERTEBRATES

Excretion mechanisms in invertebrates range from simple diffusion in unicellular organisms to the highly developed systems of arthropods. Some of these systems are shown in Figure 7–23. Although unicellular organisms excrete most waste by direct diffusion, in some cases entire vacuoles are expelled by reverse pinocytosis. In addition, a *contractile vacuole*, an excretory organelle (well developed in *Paramecium*) concerned primarily with regulating the water content of the organism, may also eliminate nitrogenous wastes.

220

Figure 7·23 Mechanisms of nitrogenous waste elimination in invertebrates.

In nonparasitic flatworms, such as *Planaria,* the excretory system is composed of two longitudinal ducts with a network of branching tubules connected to them. The ducts open to the outside through excretory pores. The tubules end in large *flame cells* that lie among the body cells. The specialized flame cells (so called because they resemble flames) have a central cavity with a tuft of cilia. When the cilia beat, body fluids containing metabolic wastes (including excess water) are carried into the tubules.

In earthworms each segment contains two excretory organs called *nephridia*. Each nephridium has a ciliated funnel that projects through the septum of the preceding segment and filters the body fluids into a collecting duct. In addition, a capillary network surrounds the collecting tubules allowing the absorption of waste products from the blood into the tubules. Near the end of each nephridium is a bladder from which wastes are discharged to the outside through a pore.

Crayfish, crabs, and lobsters have gills which are efficient organs of elimination in an aquatic environment. In addition, two organs, known as *green glands* because of their color, are found at the base of the large antennae. These glands, in the anterior portion of the blood sinus, remove metabolic wastes from the blood and pass them through a collecting tubule into a thin-walled bladder. A duct leads from the bladder to an opening at the base of the antenna. The collecting tubule, which is practically absent in saltwater forms, is probably functional in the reabsorption of salts in freshwater crayfish.

The excretory organs of insects consist of numerous, long tubules attached to the digestive tract between the stomach and intestine. These thin-walled tubules project into the body cavity and absorb nitrogenous wastes and salts from the blood. The tubules empty into the intestine. Malpighi, the famed Italian microscopist of the seventeenth century, described these organs and they still bear his name as *Malpighian tubules.*

EXCRETION IN THE VERTEBRATES— THE KIDNEY

The major organs of excretion among vertebrates are the *kidneys*. These paired, bean-shaped organs lie against the dorsal body wall on either side of the vertebral column. A rich supply of blood is received from the abdominal aorta and venous blood is returned to the inferior vena cava (Figure 7–24). The wastes are filtered from the blood in the cortex which, in the human kidney, contains about one million *nephron* units. The nephron is diagrammed in Figure 7–24c and the principal functions of each segment are identified in the legend.

Blood enters the capillary network, known as the *glomerulus*, at approximately 75 mmHg pressure. Since local capillary pressure in other tissues is only about 20 mmHg, filtration in the glomerulus is essentially by diffusion under pressure, sometimes termed *ultrafiltration*. The thin membrane of the glomerulus allows the filtration of glucose, vitamins, fatty acids, and amino acids, but normally

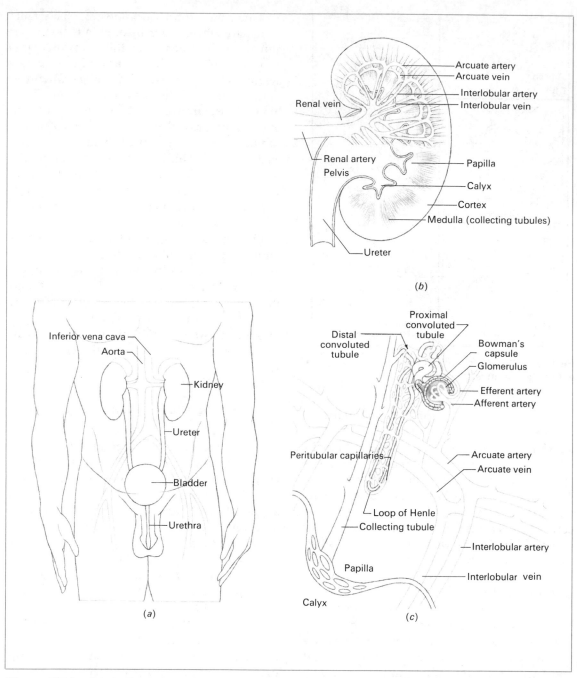

Figure 7·24 (*a*) A diagram of the urinary system in man. (*b*) A longitudinal section of the kidney showing the location of the major blood vessels. (*c*) The structure of the nephron unit of vertebrate kidneys. The principal functions of the segments are as follows. Proximal tubule: reabsorption of glucose, water, Na^+, K^+, and amino acids. Loop of Henle: reabsorption of Na^+, K^+, and Cl^-; obligatory water reabsorption. Distal tubule: reabsorption of Na^+ and K^+; secretion of H^+ and NH_3. Collecting tubule: reabsorption of water.

does not permit serum blood proteins to pass through. In cases of persistent or severe infection, such as pneumonia or middle-ear infection, the glomerular membranes may degenerate to such an extent that they allow large amounts of protein to enter the urine (Brights' disease). The loss of protein from the blood causes a decreased osmotic concentration in the plasma, and the tissues collect water bringing about edema (swelling).

The glomerular filtrate is collected in the *Bowman's capsule* and passed into the *proximal convoluted tubule* where substances required by the body are reabsorbed. For example, under normal conditions all the glucose filtered through the glomerulus is reabsorbed into surrounding capillaries, the *peritubular capillaries,* by diffusion and active transport. When the glucose level of the blood rises above 180 mg per 100 ml of blood, all the glucose cannot be reabsorbed and some glucose appears in the urine. The proximal convoluted tubules reabsorb Na^+, K^+, Cl^-, glucose, water, amino acids, and some urea and uric acid. The reabsorption of mineral ions is controlled, to some degree, by a group of hormones known as mineralocorticoids secreted by the cortex of the adrenal glands. It should be noted that when ions and molecules are transported from the tubules into the surrounding capillaries, an osmotic gradient is formed. Water must then move into the capillaries according to the gradient; this situation is *obligatory water reabsorption.* Osmotic reabsorption of water also occurs in the next segment of the nephron, the loop of Henle. This long tubule bends back upon itself to form a U-shaped loop. Na^+, K^+, and Cl^- may also be reabsorbed in this segment.

In the *distal convoluted tubule* and *collecting tubule,* water reabsorption is controlled by a hormone produced in the posterior lobe of the pituitary gland, the *antidiuretic hormone* (ADH). ADH increases the permeability of the tubule cells to water, thereby increasing water reabsorption. The urine thus is concentrated and body water is conserved. The distal convoluted tubule actively reabsorbs Na^+, K^+, Ca^{++}, and Mg^{++}, but in addition to its role in reabsorption, it can secrete ions from the blood and pass them into the urine. Large amounts of hydrogen ion (H^+) and ammonia (NH_3) are actively removed from the blood which helps to maintain a proper acid-base balance in the body. The distal tubule is more selective in reabsorption than the proximal tubule. The high hydrostatic pressure in the proximal tubule causes the diffusion of many substances into the peritubular capillaries. The composition of urine includes water (95 percent), urea, uric acid, ammonia, and creatinine (a product of amino-acid metabolism). Several ions, pigments, hormones, and vitamins may also be found in this waste product.

OSMOREGULATION

It is probably apparent that the kidney is not simply an organ for the elimination of toxic nitrogenous wastes. It is also involved in the balance of water, sugar, and ions within the organism. In fact, throughout the animal kingdom the processes of excretion of nitrogenous wastes and ion and water balance are closely related. The general term used to refer to the ability of an organism to control and regulate the fluid content of its body is *osmoregulation.*

In Terrestrial Animals

The essential problem facing land animals is the conservation of internal water. The most important defense against the dry environment is probably a thick epidermis. The presence of scales, hair, fur, or feathers add varying degrees of insulation. In addition to physical barriers against evaporation, most terrestrial animals also possess well-developed kidneys to provide for water and salt reabsorption. Animals surviving in extremely dry conditions eliminate very dry feces and highly concentrated urine. The small desert kangaroo rat (*Dipodomys*) shows a further adaptation in having no sweat glands. In addition, these tiny rodents live in an underground burrow and

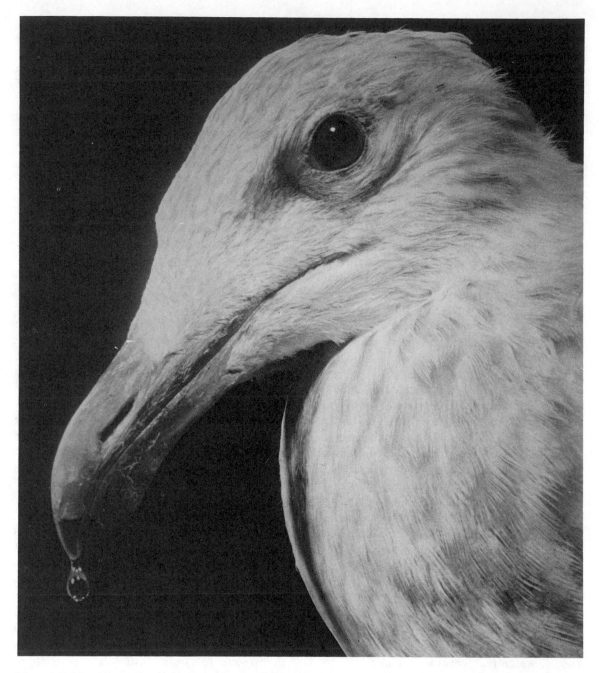

Figure 7·25 Marine birds, such as this sea gull, possess a salt-excreting gland. A highly concentrated salt solution flows into the nasal cavity and drips off the beak. (Courtesy Henry B. Kane.)

forage for food only at night. Under normal conditions, they never require a drink of water since the water from their food is sufficient.

In mammals water loss is most extensive through breathing and perspiration. Man, for instance, must maintain a body temperature of about 37°C and does so primarily through the evaporation of perspiration. Camels, on the other hand, are well adapted to desert conditions with their mat of insulating fur; furthermore, they do not begin to sweat until their body temperature rises to about 41°C.

One of the most interesting adaptations is found in marine birds. These birds feed on fish and apparently drink salt water. All marine birds possess special glands called salt glands above each eye which actively excrete sodium chloride when the bird's body fluids acquire excess salt (Figure 7–25).

In Aquatic Organisms

In aquatic organisms three conditions may exist. (1) The concentration of water and dissolved substances may be the same inside the organism as in the environment, and water is neither gained nor lost from the organism. This condition is called *isosmotic*. (2) The concentration of water may be lower and the concentration of dissolved substances higher inside the organism than in the environment which means water would move into the organism through osmosis. This condition is typical in freshwater organisms and is called *hyposmotic*. (3) The concentration of water may be higher and the concentration of dissolved substances lower inside the organism than in the environment, requiring the orga-

nism to rid itself of excess water. The term for this is *hyperosmotic*. These three conditions are shown in Figure 7–26.

Isosmotic conditions are found in many aquatic invertebrates that live in the sea. A simple example of hyposmotic conditions is displayed by *Paramecium*. The contractile vacuole of this freshwater protist has already been noted as a structure which can "bail out" the excessive amount of water that enters from the environment. Freshwater fish eliminate water by producing large amounts of a very dilute urine, but since salts also tend to be lost in this waste product, special cells in the gills must actively absorb salts from the water. The hyperosmotic condition of saltwater fish present the opposite problem of freshwater fish—that is, they are constantly losing water. These animals drink large amounts of sea water but produce a small amount of urine. The gills of these fish secrete excess salt back into the sea. Sharks and their relatives, which also live in a marine environment, have solved the balance problem in yet another way. Urea and other organic compounds normally excreted are maintained at higher levels in the blood. This raises the concentration of dissolved substances in the animals to a concentration equal to or greater than that in the sea and produces an almost isosmotic state of equilibrium. The conditions described here

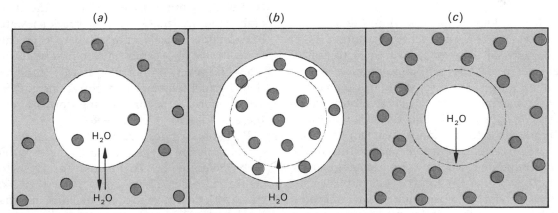

Figure 7·26 A diagram representing three possible osmotic conditions in aquatic organisms: (*a*) an isosmotic environment in which water moves in equal amounts into and out of the organisms producing no net gain nor loss of water; (*b*) a hyposmotic environment in which water is gained by the organism; (*c*) a hyperosmotic environment in which water is lost by the organism.

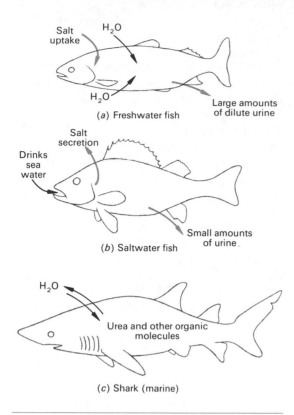

Salt uptake   H$_2$O

H$_2$O

Large amounts of dilute urine

(a) Freshwater fish

Salt secretion

Drinks sea water

Small amounts of urine.

(b) Saltwater fish

H$_2$O

Urea and other organic molecules

(c) Shark (marine)

Figure 7·27 Mechanisms for the maintenance of osmotic balance in (*a*) freshwater fish, (*b*) saltwater fish, and (*c*) shark.

Shore crab

Normal

Chinese mitten crab

Most marine invertebrates

Normal

Salt concentration in body fluids

Salt concentration of sea water

Figure 7·28 A graph showing the relationships of body fluid and salt concentrations against varying concentrations of sea water. The heavy line indicates equal concentrations (isosmotic) found in nonosmoregulating invertebrates.

for fish and sharks are shown in Figure 7–27.

Most marine invertebrates contain body fluid and salt concentrations equal to that of sea water. If the salt concentration of the water changes, the internal fluid also changes. These marine forms can survive only short-term changes slightly above or below normal. Organisms which cannot maintain their internal fluid concentrations against that of the environment are known as nonosmoregulators. The heavy line in Figure 7–28 indicates the survival range of these marine invertebrates, such as the spider crab, in varying seawater concentrations.

Many marine animals can move from their normal saltwater environment into more dilute or brackish water such as estuaries. Investigations by August Krogh and others on estuarine invertebrates have demonstrated that certain species of crabs can actively regulate their internal fluid and salt concentration by taking up salt through their gills. The green glands (a type of kidney) are also involved in this process and function primarily in the regulation of body water. One example is the shore crab which normally lives in brackish water but can move easily onto shore or even into fresh water in search of food. The shore crabs, however, do not fare as well in higher than normal saltwater concentrations and react similarly to nonregulating forms under these conditions (Figure 7–28).

Perhaps the most outstanding example of osmoregulation is that of the Chinese mitten crab (*Eriocheir*) which invades the rivers of central Europe. These crabs possess one of the most efficient regulatory mechanisms that has been studied and can live equally well in fresh and salt water. The mitten crab is capable of actively transporting salt from the blood into the water.

SUMMARIZING PRINCIPLES

The chemical reactions and physical processes not directly involved in energy production may be called *supporting processes*; they include digestion, absorption, circulation, gas exchange, and excretion. Metabolism is the total of all the chemical reactions occurring in an organism.

The vertebrate liver performs numerous functions essential to life; among these are synthesis, storage, regulation, and detoxification.

Large food molecules must be broken into smaller molecules that can be absorbed into the bloodstream and utilized by the cells; the process by which this is accomplished is enzymatic digestion.

In man and other mammals the digestive process and the enzymes involved can be organized into three phases—salivary, gastric, and intestinal; the pancreas is an important accessory gland that supplies enzymes for all classes of foods to the small intestine. The end products of digestion include simple sugars, fatty acids, glycerol, and amino acids.

The products of digestion are absorbed by the epithelial cells linning the small intestine; most of these nutrients are transported by the blood to the liver. The large intestine functions primarily in the control of water and ion balance.

Nutrients, gases, wastes, and other materials must be circulated and transported from one part of a living system to another; this is particularly important in large, multicellular organisms. In plants this is accomplished principally in vascular tissue—xylem and phloem. In animals a blood system composed of a heart and conducting vessels serves this purpose.

Gas exchange is accomplished in a variety of ways: direct diffusion (in plants, protists, and some invertebrates), gills (crustaceans, some mollusks, and fish), lungs (amphibians, reptiles, birds, and mammals), tracheal tubes (insects). Special gas-transporting pigments are utilized in many animals to increase gas-exchange efficiency.

Toxic substances, especially nitrogenous wastes, must be eliminated from all organisms; the excretion of metabolic wastes and the maintenance of water and ion balance are closely related processes.

The vertebrate organ involved in water balance, ion regulation, and the separation of nitrogenous wastes from the blood is the kidney; its excretion product, urine, contains water, urea and other organic products, and ions.

Osmoregulation is the ability of an organism to maintain constant concentrations of body fluids despite changing conditions in the environment.

REVIEW QUESTIONS

1   A person watching his weight is concerned with the number of calories taken into his body in a day. Why do we use heat units, such as calories, as reference units in weight control?

2 Some diets provide mainly proteins; how is it possible for the individual to get sufficient carbohydrates under these conditions?

3 What is the general scheme of carbohydrate metabolism regulation in the mammalian body? What effect does this control have on blood sugar?

4 The general pattern of food digestion in the mammalian body is:

large, nonabsorbable molecules + H_2O $\longrightarrow$ smaller, absorbable molecules

Use this scheme and note the specific molecules produced by carbohydrate, fat, and protein digestion.

5 What is the primary difference between an open and a closed circulatory system? What animals have open systems? Closed systems?

6 Some animals, such as salmon and certain crabs, are capable of moving from salt water to fresh water and vice versa. What are some of the mechanisms that make this osmoregulation possible?

7 Structurally, what do all animal breathing systems have in common? What is the relationship of a circulatory system to the gas-exchange process?

8 How does bicarbonate ion (HCO_3^-) function in both uptake and release of CO_2 in the red blood corpuscle?

9 Why does a human continue to breathe rhythmically while sleeping? Why is it impossible to hold one's breath indefinitely?

10 On many occasions marine turtles have been observed to "cry large tears" while depositing their eggs in the sand on the shore. Discounting the idea that egg-laying might be painful, can you offer an explanation for these salty tears?

11 If a human contracted a kidney disease that caused faulty distal tubules in his nephrons, what symptoms might he exhibit?

SUPPLEMENTARY READINGS

Bayliss, W. M., and E. H. Starling, "The Mechanism of Pancreatic Secretion," in M. L. Gabriel and S. Fogel, eds., *Great Experiments in Biology*, Englewood Cliffs, N.J., Prentice-Hall, 1955.

Biddulph, S., and O. Biddulph, "The Circulatory System of Plants," *Scientific American*, February, 1959.

Comroe, Jr., Julius H., "The Lung," *Scientific American*, February, 1966.

Fenn, W. O., "The Mechanism of Breathing," *Scientific American*, January, 1960.

Hammond, E. Cuyler, "The Effects of Smoking," *Scientific American*, July, 1962.

Kylstra, Johannes A., "Experiments in Water-Breathing," *Scientific American*, August, 1968.

Merrill, J. P., "The Artificial Kidney," *Scientific American* July, 1961.

Perutz, M. F., "The Hemoglobin Molecule," *Scientific American*, November, 1964.

Schmidt-Nielson, Knut, "Salt Glands," *Scientific American*, January, 1959.

Schmidt-Nielson, Knut, "The Physiology of the Camel," *Scientific American*, December, 1959.

Schmidt-Nielson, Knut, *Animal Physiology*, Englewood Cliffs, N.J., Prentice-Hall, 1960.

Scholander, P. F., "The Master Switch of Life," *Scientific American*, December, 1963.

Smith, Homer W., "The Kidney," *Scientific American*, January, 1953.

Solomon, Arthur K., "Pumps in the Living Cell," *Scientific American*, August, 1962.

Wiggers, Carl J., "The Heart," *Scientific American*, May, 1957.

Williams, C. M., "Insect Breathing," *Scientific American*, February, 1953.

Wolf, A. V., "Body Water," *Scientific American*, November, 1958.

Wooldridge, Dean E., *The Machinery of Life*, New York, McGraw-Hill, 1966.

Zimmermann, Martin H., "How Sap Moves in Trees," *Scientific American*, March, 1963.

8

Dynamic Equilibrium

Up to this point we have been discussing the many processes and chemical reactions that take place in all organisms. Since we know now that a myriad of chemical reactions must occur each second simply to keep an organism alive, we might wonder how these are coordinated and regulated within the cell and throughout the organism to prevent a state of disorder.

Internal conditions in all living systems are never static since materials are constantly entering and leaving the body of an organism. Moreover, external conditions also change the environment so that it is never exactly the same from minute to minute. Consider for a moment some of the factors that might influence you while you are reading this book. The gas content of the room— that is, the O_2/CO_2 ratio—will vary depending on whether the doors and windows are open or closed or whether you are in the room alone or with others. Your attitude or state of mind also may be determined by the poeple or other organisms in the room. Your ability to comprehend and understand the material you are reading may be influenced by the food you were served at your previous meal (or the thoughts you may be entertaining about the next meal) or a recent encounter with a fellow human being. Certainly the weather conditions can have a profound effect, especially if you are overly cold or warm. An organism must adjust to these and the many other changes that occur in the environment.

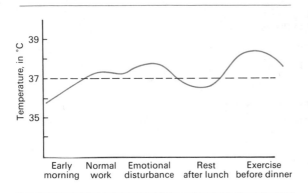

Figure 8·1 Body temperature in a human being plotted against a hypothetical portion of a normal day. Note that while the temperature varies, it always fluctuates about the 37°C line.

When we examine nature closely, we quickly see that the problems faced by organisms are due to change—changes produced internally by physical and chemical processes or externally by changes in the environment. The two phenomena are related since changes in the external environment can and do bring about internal changes. This chapter is concerned with the mechanisms employed by living systems in their constant struggle to prevent harmful internal change. Since the process of change is active and continuous, the internal medium will not always be in perfect equilibrium; we speak, therefore, of a *dynamic equilibrium.* The maintenance of this internal *steady state* is of paramount importance for, if this fails, illness or death results. Another term frequently used for this overall condition is *homeostasis.* Many biologists consider the continuous effort by living organisms to maintain a uniform internal environment to be the central theme of biology.

The human body temperature is usually given as 37°C (98.6°F). We know that exercise, emotions, sleep, the various metabolic activities, cold or hot weather, and so on, influence the body temperature and consequently it varies above and below 37°C. A hypothetical situation which could occur in the normal day of an individual is shown in Figure 8–1. The temperature in most humans fluctuates around 37°C because control mechanisms are attempting to maintain this temperature. What would happen if the temperature continued to rise and did not return to the 37°C base line? This does occur under certain conditions such as heat stroke when the temperature-control mechanisms in the body have ceased to function properly. If the controls cannot be put back into operation when this happens, death will result. Every acceleration must be followed by a deceleration and vice versa.

Another important variable that must be controlled is pH. The molecular mechanism for its control through a buffer system was described in Chapter 2. The average pH of the human body is 7.4, and we note that arterial blood usually has a pH of 7.45, whereas that of venous blood is usually 7.35.

When foreign proteins, known as *antigens,* enter a human body, *antibodies* are produced in an effort to combat the invading molecules. Hay fever and other allergies are examples of regulation and control since an "unnecessary" reaction occurs between the antigen and the antibody. This is a control mechanism, however, since the body is attempting to maintain a constant internal environment while coping with an invader from the outside. Cancer, on the other hand, is an example of an apparent complete breakdown of the control mechanisms, and certain cells continue to undergo uncontrolled cell division.

SOME PHYSICAL MODELS

Physical models can be used to illustrate the problem of maintaining internal stability in organisms against change. A series of three differently constructed water containers and the corresponding variations in water level that might be expected in each are shown in Figure 8–2. The first model is a closed and sealed container from which the water cannot escape and to which water cannot be added. The water level cannot fluctuate under these conditions and the straight line on the graph

232

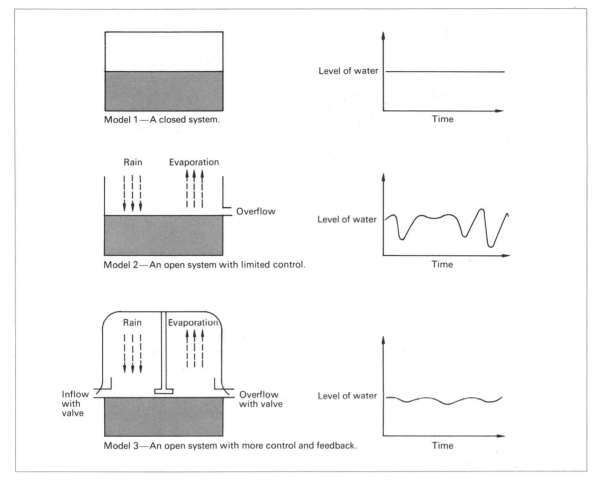

Figure 8·2 Three models to assist in understanding the problem of regulation in control in living organisms. See the text for complete explanation.

to the right of the container indicates this constant condition. If there were a corresponding system in organisms, there would, of course, be no problem in maintaining a homeostatic state. The second model represents an open tank provided with an overflow pipe. The tank can accumulate rain water and it is subject to the process of evaporation. The only control feature that can assist in maintaining a constant level is the overflow pipe, so great fluctuations can be expected as illustrated by the erratic wavy line on the graph. Any living system corresponding to this situation would be in a difficult position, since all the control is outside the system.

Several features could be added to an open tank to provide more uniform control, and model 3 of Figure 8–2 illustrates the basic mechanisms found in organisms. An inflow pipe connected to a reservoir of water provides a constant supply of water. Valves, attached to both the inflow and overflow pipes, regulate the amount of water entering and leaving the tank. A float, attached to the valves, rises and falls with the water level (similar to the tank of a toilet) to control the valve action. When the water level drops, the float drops, closing the overflow valve and simultaneously opening the inflow valve. The tank thus can fill to its original level, raising the float until both

233

valves are closed. A rise in water would produce the opposite reaction and the water level will fluctuate only slightly over a period of time. The water in the tank is moving and changing, yet the water level remains fairly stable.

To appreciate the similarities between the last model and a living system, four features of the model should be considered. *First*, it is a self-regulating system since the valves opened and closed automatically when certain limits were exceeded. *Second*, the element of *feedback* is part of the system—that is, both valves close automatically when the original level is reached and inflow and outflow action stop. *Third*, action is immediate when a change occurs in the tank so the water level does not undergo extreme changes in level. This is extremely important to living systems since they cannot withstand great changes from their normal range of operation. *Fourth*, more than one control element is utilized to regulate this process. In living things, most processes are multicontrolled. The value of this is simply that several control mechanisms offer a finer and more uniform level of control than only one mechanism.

Another important point to note is that the water level in the third model is not represented by a straight line. The level is shown as an undulating line which indicates what actually happened. Very soon after the water level drops, the inflow valve opens and the water level rises again. In other words, the inflow valve does not close at the exact moment the proper level is reached and a slight "overshooting" occurs. The outlet valve opens momentarily to drop the level to normal, but it again "overshoots" slightly. Thus an equilibrium is maintained—not a static equilibrium, but a dynamic equilibrium that requires continuous maintenance. Any graph, then, that represents metabolic activity in living organisms must show this variability (see Figure 8–1).

GENERAL SCHEME OF CONTROL

The homeostatic condition is so universal in living organisms that a general scheme is apparent, and all control activities seem to follow this pattern. Once again we can employ a model to explain and describe the general process. Both external and internal changes require regulation and action by an organism (Figure 8–3). Feedback must be built into the regulation to prevent excessive reaction (overshooting)—that is, the regulation machinery

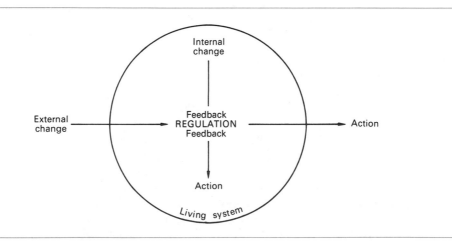

Figure 8·3 General scheme of steady-state control. Internal and external changes require regulation before action is accomplished. Feedback is part of the regulatory process which acts to prevent excessive "overshooting" by the process.

must *know* when enough action has been taken. Otherwise, the action might well continue, and this could be just as harmful to the organism as the original change that necessitated the action. In order for this process to work, a constant flow of information is needed along the various routes. For example, specific *receptors* are needed to pick up the stimulus caused by a change, and specific *effectors* are needed to carry out the action. A simple example of this flow may help show the complicated chain of events. A mosquito piercing a human's left arm and sucking blood presents a change to the individual. As the mosquito pierces the skin, touch receptors are stimulated and the individual is aware of the mosquito's presence. Almost simultaneously the person may look at his left arm and, by virtue of information stored in his brain, recognize a mosquito. Through the coordination afforded by another part of the brain and information traveling along nerves, action is taken in the form of a slap by the right arm. This either kills the mosquito or drives it away. Feedback prevents the continuation of the slapping since the mosquito is no longer present on the left arm. This sequence of events can be shown in the general scheme diagrammed in Figure 8–4.

The specific receptors and effectors are not always as clear cut as in this example, since receptor and effector activity may occur in the blood or body fluids with no external change. External changes can, of course, set off internal changes and the action that results in the internal medium can be quite complex. External forces, for instance, may cause an emotional disturbance which in turn can cause the heartbeat to increase, the face to flush, or perspiration to flow. We should turn now to some of the interesting specific control mechanisms employed by living forms and attempt to gain an understanding of how some of these work.

GENERAL METABOLIC REGULATION

ENZYMES

The role of enzymes in controlling and regulating vital chemical reactions of life was stressed in Chapter 2, so you have some knowledge about the basic and most important control mechanisms in a living system. When we recall that all enzymes are proteins and also recall the pattern of protein synthesis through the DNA-RNA system (Chapter 3), the

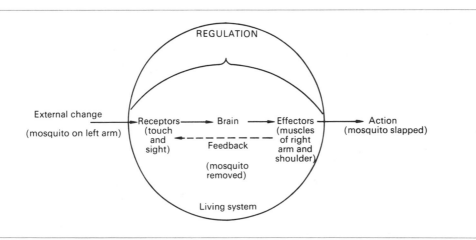

Figure 8·4 An example of regulation where specific receptors and effectors are utilized. A complete explanation is given in the text.

ultimate role of the gene as a control agent becomes apparent. In Chapter 2 we also showed a model explaining enzyme function on the basis of specific active sites on an enzyme molecule when it entered into loose chemical arrangements with the substrate molecules (see Figure 2–35).

Another problem related to enzyme activity is that of explaining how enzymes are "turned off" or stopped when enough of a particular product has been manufactured by the cell. Two theories, each supported by considerable experimental work, have been suggested to explain how enzyme action can be controlled by a feedback process. One theory holds that the enzyme stops when the manufacture of the product is completed. In other words, the product of the chemical reaction represses further synthesis of the enzyme. Such a series of reactions showing enzyme *repression* may be illustrated as follows:

Both theories explain how the end product of a chemical reaction can serve as a signal that its manufacture is no longer needed.

So far we have been discussing inhibitory or repressive feedback action. It is also known that some cellular products can have a positive or stimulatory effect on certain steps of a biochemical pathway. A series of reactions that provides energy for cells is familiar to you since it was studied in Chapter 6. We saw that the ultimate end products that trap the energy are the AMP-ADP-ATP system. These products can control the liberation of energy through glycolysis and the Krebs cycle by inhibitory and stimulatory effects. The places at which these products function and the manner in which they function is shown in the abbreviated diagram of the energy pathway in Figure 8–5. ATP apparently is an inhibitor of the enzyme that catalyzes the reaction to permit acetyl-CoA to enter the Krebs cycle.

Compound A $\xrightarrow{\text{enzyme a}}$ Compound B $\xrightarrow{\text{enzyme b}}$ Compound C $\xrightarrow{\text{enzyme c}}$ Compound D $\xrightarrow{\text{enzyme d}}$ Product

In this example the product interferes with the synthesis of enzyme c, which normally catalyzes the step from compound C to compound D. As the product gradually accumulates in this series of reactions and inhibits the synthesis of enzyme c, less product will be formed.

Another theory of how enzyme activity may be reduced is called *inhibition*. This means that the product interacts with the enzyme to inhibit its action. For instance, numerous experiments with bacteria have shown that the presence of the amino acid lysine can slow the action of an enzyme that is needed for the production of lysine. The pathway by which lysine is produced and the site of enzyme inhibition is:

As long as a high concentration of ATP is available, most of the acetyl-CoA will be used in other biochemical processes. AMP (adenosine monophosphate) exerts a stimulating effect on those enzymes that catalyze glycogen to glucose-6-phosphate and fructose-6-phosphate to fructose diphosphate. Thus when AMP is abundant in cells, energy metabolism is enhanced. The overall control picture is, of course, more complex than described here since other sites of stimulation and inhibition exist in the energy pathway.

MASS ACTION

The principle of mass action in chemical reactions was discussed in Chapter 2, but it

Aspartic acid + ATP $\xrightarrow{\text{enzyme a}}$ Intermediate product $\xrightarrow{\text{enzyme b}}$

Intermediate product $\xrightarrow{\text{enzyme c}}$ Intermediate product $\xrightarrow{\text{enzyme d}}$ Lysine

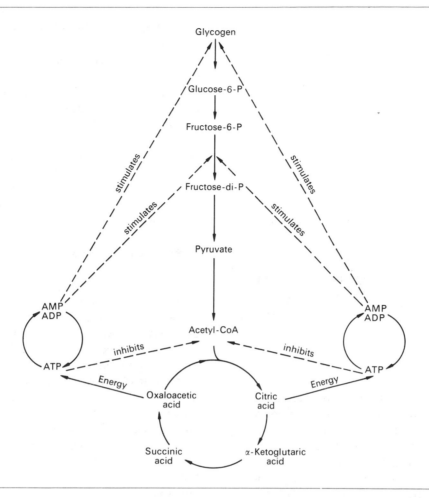

Figure 8·5 An example of feedback in energy metabolism. Some intermediate compounds are omitted from both the glycolytic pathway and the Krebs cycle in order to show a simplified diagram.

should be looked at again since the direction of chemical reactions can be determined, in part, by mass action. Recall the relationship between glycogen and glucose: glucose $\rightleftharpoons$ glycogen. Since this is a reversible reaction, it exists in somewhat of an equilibrium—that is, if a living system takes in more glucose, the reaction will increase to the right because of the mass-action effect of more glucose. Soon more glycogen is produced and the reaction will tend more to the left. If glucose is used up in an organism and little is being added, the reaction will shift strongly to the left. But

mass action is only one control mechanism on this particular reaction; other control agents, to be discussed later in this chapter, also influence the relationship.

pH

Another controlling effect in living cells is the concentration of the hydrogen ion (pH). You have already learned that the rates of chemical reactions often depend on the pH of the medium. For example, the enzyme salivary amylase is very effective in breaking starch

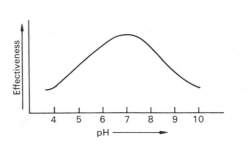

Figure 8·6 Relative function of salivary amylase at varying pH.

down to glucose at certain pH's, but it is almost ineffective at others (Figure 8–6). The chief influence of the pH on a chemical reaction is on the enzyme.

VITAMINS

A large and varied group of chemical compounds known as *vitamins* are also concerned with the control process in all organisms. The first discussions of vitamins developed when it was discovered that particular foods could prevent certain deficiency diseases such as scurvy and beriberi. Later, when analytical techniques were more refined, these substances could be isolated from the foods. Approximately thirty compounds so far have been isolated and classed as vitamins. In many instances it is still not known exactly what the vitamin does in the cell, and we merely know what will happen externally if the vitamin is not present. Knowledge is increasing quite rapidly, however, on the roles that vitamins play in cellular functions. For example, it has been clearly established that vitamin B_2, riboflavin, is the precursor of FAD, a component of the electron-transport system discussed in Chapter 6. In fact, most members of the large vitamin B group seem to be used as raw materials from which coenzymes, necessary for catalyzing vital func-

tions, are made. No wonder the symptoms are so evident when these are missing from the diet. Vitamin D, the only vitamin that humans can synthesize (the synthesis occurs in the skin under the stimulation of UV light), is known to be involved with calcium and phosphorus distribution, and a serious lack of vitamin D leads to rickets, a bone disease. Again, we know this by the results of a deficiency, and the actual cellular role of vitamin D in regulating calcium and phosphorus is still not known. A list of some of the vitamins with their roles and sources is given in Figure 8–7.

HORMONES—IN PLANTS

An extremely interesting and important group of control agents known as *hormones* are found in most organisms. Although a hormone may be concerned with a specific control function, its overall effect on the total organism is usually complex. Plants produce hormones that control growth, bending movements (*tropisms*), and flowering. The growth hormones, or *auxins*, as they are collectively known, are produced in all actively growing regions of plants, but they are especially concentrated in the stem and root tips. Perhaps the following discussion on auxins will clarify hormonal control.

Plant-growth studies were stimulated by observations of plant movements in response to external stimuli such as light (phototropism). Charles Darwin and his son Francis performed some of the first studies on plant movements in the 1870s and thus provided the groundwork and stimulation for further study in this field. Their studies on the coleoptile of grass seedlings, a sheathlike structure of only a few cells in thickness which covers the emerging shoot of grass, showed that when a coleoptile is exposed to light from one side, it will bend toward the light. This bending was prevented either by covering the tip or removing it (Figure 8–8). Since the actual bending occurred along the stem just below the tip, Darwin, in his book *The Power of*

238

Vitamin	Deficiency Symptoms	Cell Function	Source
Fat soluble			
Vitamin A	Night blindness; dry, scaly epithelial tissue; susceptibility to infection	Forms part of the molecules involved in the visual process	Yellow and green vegetables, fish oil, liver
Vitamin D	Rickets—abnormal bone development	Metabolism of calcium and phosphorus	Fish-liver oil, eggs, butter
Vitamin E	Muscle and nerve disorders; sterility	H transport in oxidation	Plant products, especially wheat-germ oil
Vitamin K	Slowed blood clotting	H transport in oxidation; synthesis of prothrombin	Most green plants
Water soluble			
Vitamin B_1 (thiamine)	Beriberi, nerve inflammation; muscle paralysis	Coenzyme to remove CO_2; for example, from pyruvic acid	Wheat germ, yeast, pork, eggs
Vitamin B_2 (riboflavin)	Lip lesions and inflamed eyes	Component of FAD, necessary for H transport	Milk products, green vegetables, liver, cereals
Vitamin B_6 (pyridoxine)	Dermatitis and reduced growth	Coenzymes for removal of CO_2 and trans-animation	Cereals, eggs, meat
Vitamin B_{12} (cyanocobalamin)	Pernicious anemia—reduced number of red blood cells	Coenzyme necessary for nucleic-acid metabolism	Meat, liver, egg yolk
Nicotinic acid (niacin)	Pellagra—diarrhea, mental disorder, dermatitis	Component of NAD and NADP, necessary for H transport	Meat, liver, milk, yeast
Pantothenic acid	None known in humans	Component of coenzyme A	Most foods
Biotin	Mouth lesions—rarely seen in humans	Part of an enzyme necessary for carboxylation (addition of CO_2)	Vegetables, liver, milk, meat
Folic acid	Anemia—reduced number of red blood cells	Nucleic-acid synthesis	Leafy vegetables and most foods
Vitamin C (ascorbic acid)	Scurvy	Aerobic H transport; synthesis of connective tissues	Citrus fruits and tomatoes

Figure 8·7 A summary of some of the important vitamins.

Movement in Plants (1881), suggested that the stimulus for growth passed from the tip to the stem.

Researchers have long since confirmed Darwin's hypothesis by performing various experiments on other plant-growth regions. One of the most widely used techniques has been to remove the stem tip, place it on an agar (gelatinlike) block and permit the auxins to diffuse onto the agar. Various concentrations of auxins can be accumulated in this manner, and the blocks of agar can then be used in experiments to determine the degree of bending and other variable factors (Figure 8–9).

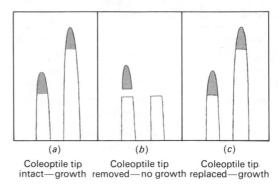

(a) Coleoptile tip intact—growth (b) Coleoptile tip removed—no growth (c) Coleoptile tip replaced—growth

Figure 8·8 Phototropisms in grass seedlings. The seedling with covered tip and the one with its tip removed do not bend toward the light.

In addition to these experiments, auxins have been isolated from plants and analyzed. We know that the principal growth hormone is indoleacetic acid and that it is found in most plants. The molecular structure of indoleacetic acid is:

Indole ring   Acetic acid

Coleoptile tip (d) removed and Placed on block of agar and auxin diffuses into block (e) Section placed on tipless coleoptile (f) Coleoptile bends in response to auxin

(g) 2 coleoptile tips removed and more auxin diffuses into block (h) Section placed on tipless coleoptile (i) Coleoptile bends in response to increased auxin

Figure 8·9 Experiments on grass coleoptiles.

The indole ring, with an attached acetic-acid molecule, then forms another structure basic to living systems.

It is also known that, if the uppermost bud, or apical bud, is pruned, the lateral buds lower on the stem will grow in many plants. This knowledge led to the theory that the apical bud exerts an inhibiting influence on the lower buds via its auxin supply. Some plants show strong apical dominance and grow tall and straight, whereas other plants, those that branch heavily and are bushy, show weak apical dominance (Figure 8–10).

Other interesting aspects of growth-hormone

240

Figure 8·10 Experiments to show apical dominance. (*a*) Apical bud inhibits lateral growth; (*b*) lateral buds develop when apical bud is removed; (*c*) lateral buds are inhibited if an agar block containing auxin is applied; (*d*) lateral buds continue to grow when agar block containing no auxin is applied.

control are the effects that auxins apparently have in the developing stem and root. When a seed germinates the root bends downward into the soil and the stem bends upward. The control of these behaviors is believed to be differential effects of auxin concentration on the two structures. When the embryonic parts emerge from the germinating seed (Figure 8–11), gravity forces concentration to

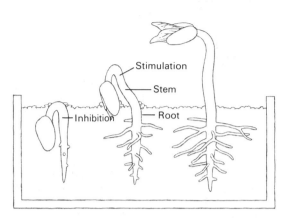

Figure 8·11 In the developing root, auxin is concentrated in the lower side because of gravity. It inhibits the elongation of the lower cells and permits the elongation of the upper cells, thus causing the root to grow downward. The concentration of auxin on the lower side of the stem, however, stimulates elongation of the lower cells and the stem turns upward.

be on the lower side of the structures. This apparently stimulates the cells of the stem in this region and they undergo a more rapid growth than the cells on the upper side. This uneven growth causes the stem to bend upward. On the other hand, the auxin concentration inhibits the growth of the cells in the lower part of the root and permits the upper cells to grow faster, thus causing the root to turn downward.

Everyone is familiar with the phenomenon of the bending of a whole plant toward the light. This unequal growth of the stem is attributed to an uneven auxin distribution. In other words, the auxin on the side of the stem toward the light migrates to the opposite side and this stimulates the cells away from the light to grow at a faster rate, producing the bending (Figure 8–12).

What does the auxin actually do to the cells to produce growth? At the present time, this is not known for sure, but one hypothesis suggests that auxins affect the cell wall and

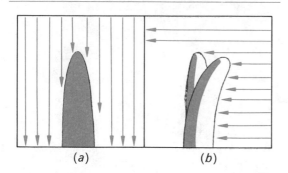

(a) (b)

Figure 8·12 Effect of light on auxin concentration and stem movement. (*a*) When the light strikes the stem from all directions, the auxin is evenly distributed. (*b*) When the light is predominantly from one direction, the auxin is more concentrated on the dark side, resulting in unequal growth and bending—thus exhibiting the phototropic response of plant stems.

permit the cell to take in more water, thereby increasing the size of the cell.

Another group of growth compounds are the *gibberellins*, discovered by Japanese bota-

Figure 8·13 The effect of gibberellic acid on plant growth. The tea rose plants on the left were treated with a 1-percent mixture of the acid. The plants on the right were untreated controls. (Courtesy of U. S. Department of Agriculture.)

nist E. Kurosawa in 1926. Gibberellins are produced by the fungus *Gibberella fujikuroi*, which causes the condition in rice known as "foolish-seedling disease." The chief symptom of this disease is exceptionally tall stem growth. Botanists have conducted many experiments with these compounds on other plants and, although other effects may result, the primary action of the gibberellins in all cases is to produce this rapid stem elongation. Gibberellins may prove to have economic value since typically biennial plants may be induced to complete their growth in only one year. Hormones similar to gibberellins are believed to be produced by most plants and to possibly interact with other hormones (auxins) in the control of stem growth and development. Recent studies indicate that the action of gibberellins results in increased enzyme synthesis and cell division (Figure 8–13).

Certain chemical compounds which are not normally synthesized in plants have hormone-like growth effects. One of the most familiar is 2,4-dichlorophenoxyacetic acid, commonly known as 2,4-D, a weed killer. At specific concentrations this compound produces abnormal growth and thus kills some broad-leaved plants such as dandelions and ragweed. At the same concentration, 2,4-D has no harmful effect on the narrow-leaf grasses and consequently is an effective weed killer on lawns.

The growth and development of ovaries into fruits normally follows the stimulation provided by fertilization. In the absence of fertilization, however, some plant ovaries can be forced into fruit development and made to grow through the use of synthetic hormone-like substances. Thus seedless fruits can be induced in such plants as watermelons, tomatoes, oranges, and cucumbers (Figure 8–14).

Flowering—Photoperiodism

Flowering does not occur in all plants at the same time of the year. Experiments conducted in the early 1900s by government biologists W. Garner and H. Allard have shown that

242

Figure 8·14 Seedless navel oranges grown in Florida. The seedless condition is the result of a natural mutation. (Photo by Robert Lamb from National Audubon Society.)

Figure 8·15 Photoperiodism in chrysanthemums. The plant on the right was subjected to one hour of light in the middle of the normal dark period. Blooming therefore was delayed in this plant. (Courtesy of U. S. Department of Agriculture.)

flowering is determined in some plants by the relative periods of light and darkness. For example, some plants, known as "short-day" plants, will not flower unless they are subjected to periods of short illumination normally represented by a period of short days. Others, which will not flower until exposed to long periods of light, are called "long-day" plants. A third group of plants, the "day-neutral" species, are reproductively insensitive to light and can bloom under varying light conditions. Asters, strawberries, cockleburs, and poinsettias are examples of short-day plants; corn, clover, lettuce, and beets represent long-day plants. Some day-neutral species are dandelions, tomatoes, sunflowers, and cucumbers. This effect of varying light periods upon flowering in certain plants is called *photoperiodism* (Figure 8–15).

It is believed that photoperiodism is determined by the presence of the hormone *florigen*, which has never been isolated, however. This theory is supported by the following observations. Since leaves must be present on a plant before it can respond to photoperiods and flower, the hormone is probably produced in the leaf and then transported to the flower bud. The critical period for short-day plants is the length of the dark period—that is, flowering will not occur unless these plants are subjected to dark periods of a specific duration. The critical period for long-day plants, on the other hand, is the length of the light period; this daylight length must be sufficient to produce flowering. Perhaps several intermediate compounds, whose syntheses depend on light and dark periods, are required for the production of florigen. In addition, other chemicals in the plant probably interact with florigen to produce the photoperiodic response.

HORMONES—IN ANIMALS

Some of the most remarkable examples of growth, metabolic control, and coordination

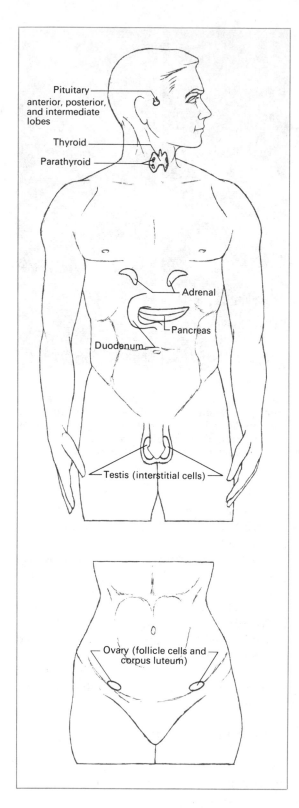

Pituitary
anterior, posterior, and intermediate lobes

Thyroid

Parathyroid

Adrenal

Pancreas

Duodenum

Testis (interstitial cells)

Ovary (follicle cells and corpus luteum)

are shown by the hormone systems of animals. In fact, many growth anomalies, mistakes, aberrant development, and behavior in humans are results of malfunctioning hormonal systems. Hormones have been discovered in a variety of animal groups including insects, crustaceans, mollusks, worms, and echinoderms. For example, the orderly *metamorphosis* process in insects is under hormonal control.

Much more is known about mammalian, especially human, hormonal systems than any other. Some of the hormones produced in humans can serve as examples since the intent here is to acquaint you with hormonal control. Human hormones are products of specific glands, known as *endocrine glands*, which have no ducts and secrete their hormones directly into the bloodstream. Although we speak of individual glands, we should keep in mind that strong interactions exist among the glands of the endocrine system, and they often operate together as a unit. A hormone from one gland may stimulate or inhibit another gland, or it may reinforce the action of another hormone. In most cases of endocrine malfunction, more than one gland is involved. The locations of the principal endocrine glands in humans are shown in Figure 8–16.

The Pancreas

Perhaps the best-known example of endocrine deficiency is *diabetes* (*diabetes mellitus* is the medical term) in which large amounts of sugar (glucose) are excreted in the urine. About 1890, two physicians experimenting with dogs discovered that the pancreas produces a substance that alleviates symptoms of diabetes. When the pancreas was removed surgically, an increased amount of sugar appeared in the urine. In 1922, two other researchers successfully isolated insulin from excised dog pancreases. It is common knowledge now that insulin injections will counteract a diabetic condition. It is also interesting to

Figure 8·16 The location of the principal endocrine glands in humans.

244

note that insulin, which is a protein, was the first protein to have its amino-acid sequence worked out (Figure 8–17). This was accomplished in 1954 after approximately ten years of research by Frederick Sanger of Cambridge University.

You have already studied the pancreas and therefore know something of its function in digestion. The pancreas contains two distinct types of tissue (Figure 8–18). The most abundant of these two tissues are the dark-staining tubule cells which secrete digestive enzymes. Scattered irregularly throughout this tissue are larger, lighter-staining cell groups that secrete hormones. These patches are called *islets of Langerhans*. Two types of cells (beta and alpha) are found in the islets and each produces a different hormone—the beta cells, insulin, and the alpha cells, glucagon.

We should now return to the relationship

Figure 8·18 Microscopic section of pancreas. The central mass is an islet of Langerhans. The surrounding tissue is exocrine in function and secretes digestive enzymes.

Figure 8·17 The molecular structure of insulin is shown below. The two amino-acid chains are connected by disulfide bridges. The amino acids represented are :

Ala	= alanine	Lys	= lysine
Pro	= proline	Thr	= threonine
Tyr	= tyrosine	Phe	= phenylalanine
Gly	= glycine	Arg	= arginine
Glu	= glutamic acid	Cys	= cystine
Val	= valine	Leu	= leucine
His	= histidine	Ser	= serine
Glu − NH$_2$	= glutamine	Asp − NH$_2$	= asparagine

between insulin and sugar in the urine. You will recall from Chapter 7 that digested carbohydrates in the form of glucose (blood sugar) are carried to the liver by the hepatic portal system. In the liver much of the glucose is converted to glycogen which can be stored. This conversion of glucose to glycogen can also take place in the muscles. Under normal conditions the blood retains about 80 to 120 mg of glucose per 100 ml of blood, and the remainder is converted to glycogen by the liver and muscles. Glycogen, however, can be converted back to glucose as you know and distributed to the blood to be carried to tissues for fuel. When the concentration of blood glucose reaches 180 mg per 100 ml of blood, glucose is excreted in the urine. This is where insulin comes into the picture. We know that glucose must either enter cells to be burned as a fuel or be converted to glycogen in the liver and muscle cells. We know that insulin does facilitate the conversion of glucose to glycogen. It is also believed that insulin increases membrane permeability in liver and muscle cells to permit glucose to enter these cells faster. In addition, insulin probably inhibits the liver from converting glycogen to glucose.

Several other control agents play important roles in maintaining proper levels of blood sugar. Glucagon has already been listed as another hormone produced by the pancreas. It seems to have the opposite effects of insulin —that is, it causes an increase in the blood-sugar level. The pancreas is one of the most interesting equilibrium-producing glands since it produces two hormones with opposite effects. Several other hormones also act as control agents for blood sugar. We know, for instance, that *epinephrine* (adrenalin) can increase blood-sugar level; this will be discussed further under adrenal glands. *ACTH*, a hormone secretion of the pituitary gland, stimulates the adrenal gland's cortex to produce *glucocorticoid* hormone which can also increase the level of blood sugar. One other hormone involved in the glucose-glycogen relationship is thyroxin, secreted by the thyroid gland, which controls the rate at which glucose is burned in glycolysis and the Krebs cycle. When thyroxin is increased in the blood, glucose is burned faster; thus, increasing thyroxin in the blood tends to decrease the blood-sugar level. These hormones are itemized in Figure 8–19 and glucose-glycogen metabolism is summarized in Figure 8–20.

In diabetes mellitus the harm to the patient is not caused by the sugar in the urine. The essential damage is produced when cells must burn fats and proteins for fuel rather than the number one fuel, glucose. In the oxidation of large amounts of fats, toxic products are given off and the body cannot cope with these. These products alter the body pH and can cause death. When diabetes is diagnosed the patient can supplement his faulty metabolism with insulin from other animals and live a normal life. A condition called *insulin shock* results when an overdose of insulin is administered. In such cases the blood-sugar level drops so low that the brain does not receive enough glucose, and unconsciousness or convulsions can result.

The Stomach and the Duodenum

Here are examples of organs that secrete hormones but whose primary function is the secretion of enzymes for the digestion of food. These have been discussed in Chapter 7 and

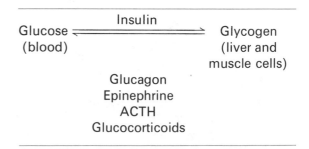

Figure 8·19 The various hormones that influence the glucose-glycogen relationship. If the hormones are present in normal levels, mass action also has an effect.

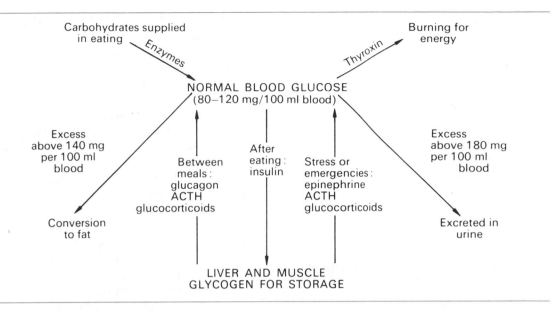

Figure 8·20 A summary of the factors involved in glucose-glycogen metabolism.

will be reviewed here with the other hormones. When partly digested food arrives in the stomach, it stimulates the mucosa layer of the pyloric region of the stomach to produce a hormone called *gastrin*. Gastrin travels through the circulatory system and returns to the stomach to stimulate the gastric glands to secrete gastric juices. Apparently this mechanism has evolved to ensure that adequate enzymes will be present for digestion in this organ.

A similar mechanism exists to stimulate the pancreas to produce pancreatic juice. Partly digested food in an acid medium moves into the duodenum from the stomach and triggers the release of two hormones from the intestinal mucosa—*secretin* and *pancreozymin*. Both hormones travel via the bloodstream to the pancreas stimulating its secretion of juices. Recent evidence indicates that secretin causes the pancreas to produce more sodium bicarbonate, whereas pancreozymin stimulates it to produce pancreatic enzymes which are released to the duodenum through the pancreatic duct.

Two additional hormones are produced in the duodenum itself. One of these is *entero-gastrone*, which inhibits the secretion of gastric juice; since its action is antagonistic to that of gastrin, it helps to produce a balanced effect in the stomach. Fats provide the stimulus for the release of enterogastrone by the mucosa of the duodenum so we can see why certain fats are advantageous in the diet of ulcer patients. The other hormone produced by the duodenum is *cholecystokinin* which allows the flow of bile from the gallbladder.

The Pituitary Gland

In any discussion of the human endocrine system considerable time must be devoted to the pituitary gland which lies beneath the midbrain above the roof of the mouth at the base of the skull. It is divided into three lobes—posterior, intermediate, and anterior (Figure 8–21). The posterior lobe is connected to the *hypothalamus* of the brain and thereby maintains a neural connection. This is important to remember since it has recently been shown

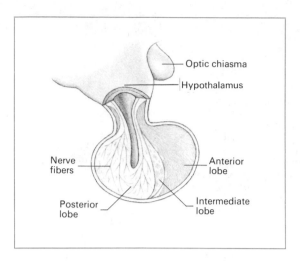

Figure 8·21   Diagram of a section of the pituitary gland.

that the nervous system can produce hormones also. In fact, the hormones secreted from the posterior lobe apparently are produced in the hypothalamus and transported to the posterior lobe. These two important coordinating and control systems, the nervous and the endocrine, show intimate connections at various places in the body. The two hormones secreted from the posterior lobe are *oxytocin*, which causes the muscles of the uterus to contract, and *vasopressin*, often called the "antidiuretic hormone" because it brings about reabsorption of water in the kidney tubules. Vasopressin also causes a constriction of the arterioles especially during hemorrhage to maintain blood pressure. The intermediate lobe secretes the hormone *intermedin* which controls the distribution of the pigmentation in the skin of certain amphibians.

The anterior lobe makes the pituitary gland one of the most remarkable of all endocrine glands, and it has often been called the "master gland" of the system. The reason for this name lies in the fact that it secretes *tropic* hormones which stimulate other glands to secrete. Probably the most familiar of anterior-lobe hormones is the growth hormone, *somatotropin*, which, along with thyroxin, controls the growth of the entire body. In-

creased amounts of this during the growing stage can lead to *giantism*, and a decreased amount below normal produces *dwarfism*. If oversecretion occurs later in life, only those bones will grow that are still capable of growth, such as some facial bones and the hands and feet. This condition is known as *acromegaly*.

Two very important examples of anterior-lobe hormones controlling other glands in the endocrine system are the *thyrotropic* hormone which stimulates the thyroid gland and *ACTH* (adrenocorticotropic hormone) which controls the adrenal gland. Apparently the anterior lobe is stimulated by the hypothalamus of the brain during periods of stress to produce ACTH even though there is no direct connection with the hypothalamus. Presumably this is done by neurohumors (not unlike hormones) carried in the blood through the venous capillary beds which supply these organs. Here we see another connection between the hormonal and nervous systems.

Two other pituitary hormones control the development and function of the gonads (ovaries and testes), and these are called *gonadotropic* (GTH) hormones. Specifically they are *FSH* (follicle-stimulating hormone) and *LH* (luteinizing hormone). One of the clearest examples of hormonal control is shown in the female where critical ratios of FSH and LH control ovulation. This will be discussed in more detail in Chapter 9 under reproduction. In the male, LH stimulates the interstitial cells of the testis to produce *testosterone*, the chief male hormone. FSH in the male stimulates the germinal epithelium to produce sperm.

The Thyroid Gland

The hormone from the thyroid gland, *thyroxin*, has already been mentioned in connection with the burning of fuel in the body. The relationship is a direct one—that is, the more thyroxin, the faster the food is oxidized. Thus people with an overactive thyroid show symptoms of weight loss, nervousness, and irritability. Opposite symptoms such as overweight and sluggishness are associated with an under-

248

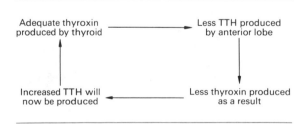

Figure 8·22 Structural formula of thyroxin. Note the four iodine atoms. If only two I atoms are present, the molecule exhibits only a fraction of normal activity.

active thyroid in the adult. If the thyroid undersecretes in early childhood, *cretinism* results in which the child's growth, sexual maturity, and mental development are retarded.

Chemically, thyroxin is an amino acid containing iodine (Figure 8–22). *Goiter*, which is overdevelopment of the thyroid gland, occurs when the thyroid cells lack enough iodine to make effective thyroxin. Hypothyroid goiter, as this type of goiter is known, is treated by the addition of iodine to the diet to increase the production of thyroxin. The excess thyroid tissue may then be removed by surgery. Hypothyroid goiter was once a common problem in inland areas such as the Alps in Switzerland and the Great Lakes region of the United States, but today iodized salt prevents this type of goiter in most areas. An oversecreting thyroid gland can also produce goiter due to the overactivity of the cells. This latter type of goiter, known as hyperthyroid goiter, is more serious and may increase metabolism by 50 percent above normal.

As we have said, the thyroid gland is stimulated to secrete thyroxin by the thyrotropic hormone (TTH) from the anterior lobe of the pituitary. Some feedback mechanism must exist to signal the anterior lobe when an adequate supply of thyroxin has been produced. This feedback is believed to work as follows: a high concentration of thyroxin inhibits the production of TTH; when the supply of TTH drops off, so does the amount of thyroxin since TTH is no longer stimulating the thyroid gland; when the concentration of thyroxin is reduced, TTH can again be secreted to stimulate the thyroid gland to produce thyroxin once more. This would provide a fairly constant level of thyroxin in the body (Figure 8–23).

In general thyroxin serves to stimulate most body functions. Addition of thyroxin, for example, increases the production of many enzymes, speeds up heart rate and circulation, and increases the excitability of the nervous system. For instance, metamorphic development in frogs is definitely under control of the thyroid gland. If the thyroid gland is removed from tadpoles, they cannot develop into adult frogs. Moreover, if thyroxin is added to the water of developing tadpoles, they metamorphose much earlier than those not receiving additional thyroxin.

Another hormone produced by the thyroid gland, *calcitonin*, is involved in the regulation of calcium balance. Recently it has been demonstrated that calcitonin acts to lower the concentration of blood calcium by inhibiting the release of calcium from bone to blood. This hormone has the opposite effect of the

Adequate thyroxin produced by thyroid ⟶ Less TTH produced by anterior lobe

Increased TTH will now be produced ⟵ Less thyroxin produced as a result

Figure 8·23 A diagram of the events involved in the control of thyroxin secretion. The feedback principle is evident in this cycle of events.

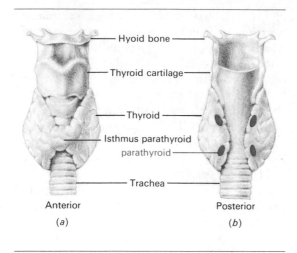

Figure 8·24   The human thyroid gland. (a) Front view showing the connecting isthmus over the trachea. (b) Back view illustrating the parathyroid glands embedded in the thyroid.

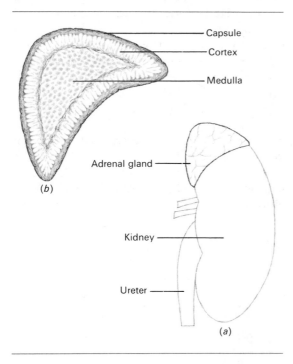

Figure 8·25   The adrenal gland. (a) The position of the adrenal gland on the superior surface of the kidney. (b) A cross section showing the cortex and medulla.

parathyroid hormone which we will consider next.

The Parathyroid Glands

When the four parathyroid glands, which are located near or in the thyroid (Figure 8–24), are surgically removed in experimental animals, muscle twitching and convulsions occur. Death results if injections of parathyroid hormone, known as *parathormone*, are not given to the animal. Physiologically, the calcium level in the blood drops when parathormone is not present, and rises when the hormone is added. Essentially, then, this gland is concerned with calcium metabolism and its constant circulation in the blood. An undersecretion of it produces a hyperirritability of these organs with slow reactions.

A second function of these glands is the control of the removal of phosphate from the body by the kidneys. Parathormone increases the concentration of calcium in the blood, but it decreases the concentration of phosphates. An undersecretion of the hormone, then, increases the phosphate level in the blood. Bones are partly composed of a calcium phosphate compound, so when calcium is released to the blood, the excess phosphate is removed from the body. Parathyroid hormone, along with the antagonistic action of calcitonin, from the thyroid, controls both of these activities.

The Adrenals and the Gonads

The adrenal glands lie on top of the kidneys and serve a variety of functions, some of which have already been mentioned. Each gland is divided into two distinct parts, each with distinct functions. An inner mass called the *medulla* is surrounded by an outside layer, the *cortex* (Figure 8–25). The cortex produces three different groups of hormones (there are also three layers to the cortex and it is tempting to suppose that each layer secretes a class of hormones). The *glucocorticoids* not only assist in controlling the conversion of glycogen to glucose (the opposite action to insulin) but are also concerned with fat and amino-acid metabolism. Part of the action is to convert these two groups of compounds to glucose. The second class of hormones secreted by the cortex are the *mineralocorticoids* and, as the name implies, these are concerned with salt and water balance. If these hormones are decreased for any reason, such as a diseased cortex, the sodium, chloride, and water concentrations of the body fluids drop while the potassium concentration increases. The hormones tend to increase kidney reabsorption of sodium and excretion of potassium. In Addison's disease, which is caused by a degeneration of the cortex, dehydration and changes in skin pigmentation occur and the sodium level decreases while the potassium level rises. Moreover, the patient has difficulty coping with mild disturbances and illnesses which are usually of minor consequence. An intact and normal cortex seems to be important to the organism in meeting stress situations. Here is another place where the connection between the nervous and the endocrine systems seems apparent. *Sex hormones* are also produced by the cortex; although these are predominantly male hormones (*androgens*), female hormones (*estrogens* and *progesterone*) are also secreted. Overactivity of the cortex at an early age can, and does on occasion, produce early and abnormal sexual maturity.

Do you remember that ACTH from the pituitary stimulates the cortex to produce its hormones? A faulty pituitary, therefore, can cause the cortex to over- or undersecrete. You should also note the structure of some of the hormones secreted by the cortex. Most of these are the basic steroid configuration with varying side chains (Figure 8–26).

The medulla of the adrenal gland produces the hormones *epinephrine* and *norepinephrine* which are commonly referred to as *adrenalin*. This has often been called the *emergency hormone* since it exerts the following effects: increases the blood-sugar level (the opposite of insulin), increases the heart rate and blood pressure, dilates the blood vessels in heart and skeletal muscle while at the same time con-

Cortisone, a glucocorticoid hormone

Aldosterone, a mineralocorticoid hormone

Figure 8·26 Two of the hormones secreted by the adrenal cortex.

stricting those vessels in smooth muscle, and causes erection of skin hairs to produce "goose bumps." You probably quickly recognize these characteristics as those that would enhance an individual's chances if he were faced with an emergency situation. The body resources are mobilized in emergencies and adrenalin seems to be the hormone that does it.

The ovaries in females and the testes in males produce hormones that bring about secondary sex characteristics and maintain the distinctiveness of the sex. In the male these hormones are called *androgens* (which include testosterone) and in the female, *estrogens*. Actually each sex produces both hormones but it is the relative amounts of each which determine sex. In the male therefore, more androgens than estrogens are produced whereas the opposite is true in the female. Remember that these organs are also

251

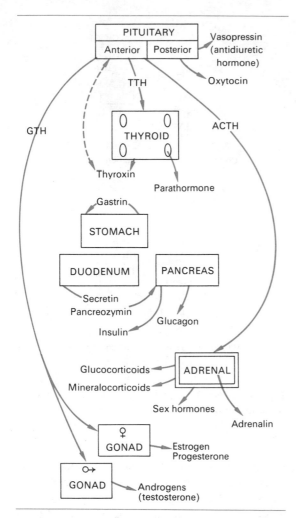

Figure 8·27 The principal endocrine glands and their secretions. One feedback flow is indicated by the broken line; other feedback mechanisms exist but are not shown.

stimulated by tropic hormones from the anterior lobe of the pituitary.

A summary of the principal endocrine glands and the major hormones they secrete is shown in Figure 8–27.

THE NERVOUS SYSTEM

Although the hormonal system may be slow in responding to change, taking perhaps minutes or days, the nervous system can react quickly and provide for immediate action—an action that may save an animal's life. A fly sitting on a table is aware of a sudden change in its environment should a destructive wave approach it because of receptors that can detect the change (a *stimulus*). Nerve impulses are then carried to *modulators* (the central nervous system) which in turn direct the impulse message to the appropriate effectors (wing muscles) which permit the animal to fly to safety. It is apparent, then, that special cells exist which provide for a two-way communication system between an animal and its environment and between parts of an animal. Neurons or nerve cells are irritable—that is, they will respond to a stimulus, but some nerve cells show a high degree of irritability and, in addition, conductivity. It is these neurons that provide for the rapid and often complicated activity that can be exhibited by animals. Although some plants such as the Venus's-flytrap respond to touch, there is no real counterpart here to neurons or the nervous system. Plants respond to stimuli in the manner described earlier under tropisms.

Most multicelled animals have some type of a nervous system to provide coordination and communication. This system may consist of nothing more than a group of connected neurons scattered throughout the animal's body to form a nerve net. In more advanced forms many neurons may come together to form a *ganglion* (a group or collection of nerve cell bodies) which can then act as a coordinating center. A series of connected ganglia may also form a nerve cord, which might be located either ventrally or dorsally, from which lateral nerves can emerge to distant parts of the body. Some of the various nervous systems found in the animal world are illustrated in Figure 8–28.

ANATOMY OF THE HUMAN NERVOUS SYSTEM

The most complex nervous system of all is found in vertebrate animals. We will use the human as our example here, but remember

252

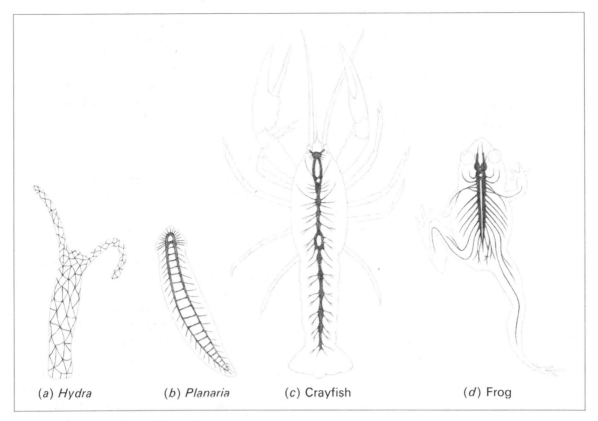

(a) *Hydra*   (b) *Planaria*   (c) Crayfish   (d) Frog

Figure 8·28 Various types of nervous systems found in the animal kingdom. (a) *Hydra*, nerve net; (b) *Planaria*, ladder-type nerve system; (c) crayfish, ventral nerve cord; (d) frog, dorsal nerve cord.

that all vertebrates possess similar structures differing only in size and number of various parts. For example, the cerebrum of the human brain shows considerably more development and complexity than any other vertebrate. The vertebrate nervous system can be considered to consist of two parts: the *central nervous system* (CNS) and the *peripheral nervous system* (PNS). The CNS is composed of the brain and spinal cord which contain the cell bodies, while the cranial and spinal nerves form the PNS. Information in the form of nerve impulses, to be discussed later in this chapter, can be carried to various parts of the body over the peripheral nerves from the brain and spinal cord. In the same manner, information can be transmitted to the CNS from various parts of the body. A nerve leading into the

CNS is called a *sensory* or *afferent pathway*. A nerve leading from the CNS is referred to as a *motor* or *efferent pathway*. Of the twelve pairs of cranial nerves emanating from the undersurface of the brain, some are motor, some are sensory, and some are mixed, that is, they contain both sensory and motor nerves. The thirty-one pairs of spinal nerves attached to the spinal cord are all mixed nerves. The cranial nerves serve mainly the head and neck regions, whereas the spinal nerves are distributed to the rest of the body supplying the skeletal muscles, skin, sweat glands, and blood vessels. In addition, from some spinal and cranial nerves, lateral ganglia arise which send nerve fibers to visceral organs. This part of the nervous system is not under voluntary control and is often referred to as the *autonomic*

253

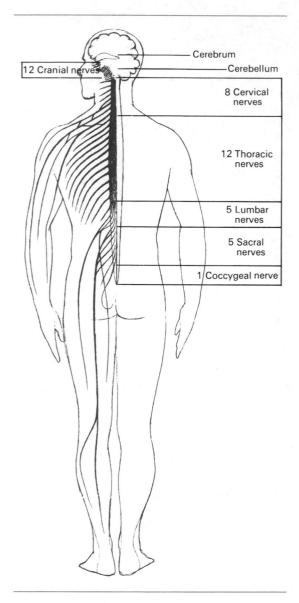

Figure 8·29 Diagram of the human nervous system. The 12 pairs of cranial and 31 pairs of spinal nerves are shown.

Labels on figure:
- Cerebrum
- Cerebellum
- 12 Cranial nerves
- 8 Cervical nerves
- 12 Thoracic nerves
- 5 Lumbar nerves
- 5 Sacral nerves
- 1 Coccygeal nerve

nervous system (ANS). The peripheral nervous system, therefore, consists of two parts: the *voluntary*, serving skeletal muscles, etc., and the *involuntary* (ANS), serving visceral organs. The diagram in Figure 8–29 should assist in understanding the anatomy of the human nervous system discussed to this point.

Each spinal nerve is connected to the spinal cord by two roots; one is dorsal and one is ventral. All of the nerves leading to the spinal cord (sensory) at this point enter the dorsal root, and those leaving the cord (motor) travel over the ventral root. These are shown more clearly in Figure 8–30 which illustrates reflex action.

Reflexes

A discussion of reflexes helps in understanding the detailed structure of some aspects of the nervous system. Moreover, it provides basic information on how the system functions. A *reflex* is considered to be a simple form of behavior wherein a stimulus evokes a specific response. One of the most familiar examples is the extension of the lower leg upon the stimulation (tapping) of the patellar (knee cap) tendon. The immediate withdrawal of the foot or hand upon touching a hot object is another familiar example. These actions occur instantaneously and involuntarily. A natural reflex can be modified by experience; this is often referred to as conditioning or a *conditioned reflex*. This can arise when the original sensory pathway of the reflex is replaced by a different sensory element. The response or the motor pathway remains the same. You are probably aware of Pavlov's famous experiments where the original stimulus (the sight of food) which produced the response of salivation could be replaced by a ringing bell and salivation would still occur.

A reflex results when a nerve impulse travels over a *reflex arc*. The spinal cord (or areas of the brain) is part of this reflex arc. The arc may consist of only two neurons or may involve three or more neurons. The neuron that picks up the stimulus and brings the information to the spinal cord is called the sensory or afferent pathway. The information (in the form of a nerve impulse) is then passed to a second neuron that carries the impulse out over a motor or efferent pathway to an effector which produces the response. In many reflexes other neurons called *internuncial* or connecting neurons are involved. These are

254

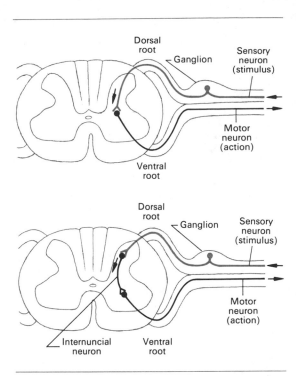

Figure 8·30 Reflex arcs. In the cross sections of the spinal cord, note that the cell body of the sensory neuron is in the ganglion of the dorsal root, whereas the cell body of the motor neuron lies in the spinal cord. The direction of the nerve impulse is indicated by the arrows. The H-shaped area of the spinal cord is the so-called gray region where the cell bodies lie; the white region of the cord is composed only of nerve fibers that carry impulses up and down the spinal cord, to and from the brain. (*a*) A reflex arc involving two neurons. The knee jerk exemplifies this type. (*b*) A reflex arc involving three neurons. Removing your hand from a hot stove exemplifies this type.

located in the spinal cord between the two pathways. Both of these examples are diagrammed in Figure 8–30. You should note that where two neurons meet, the axon of one is closely associated with the dendrite of the other. This association is called a synapse and the transmission of the nerve impulse across this region is accomplished by a chemical process.

It should also be noted how well the reflex arc illustrates the processes of control and regulation as described earlier in Figures 8–3 and 8–4. A reflex thus occurs as a result of a change which requires action from the living system; the regulating mechanism here is the nervous system employing sensory and motor neurons and the spinal cord.

The Brain

The CNS is considered to be the controller of nervous activity since it sends messages to all parts of the body through the PNS. The role of the spinal cord in this process was just discussed. The brain is the chief organ in this integration and it receives messages, transmitted upward through the spinal cord, sorts them out and relays the information to the appropriate part of the CNS for action. Many reflexes, therefore, may be modified as a result of brain action. Certainly all learned and intelligent behavior must involve the brain and certain parts of the brain should be discussed here (Figure 8–31).

The *cerebrum* contains the nerve centers that govern and integrate motor and sensory functions. In addition, the cerebrum is the site of the important functions of reasoning, intelligence, and memory. It is composed of two hemispheres and is by far the largest part of man's brain. The *corpus callosum* connects the two hemispheres of the cerebrum. The function of the *thalamus* can be summarized in two categories: (1) it relays sensory impulses to the cerebrum; and (2) it provides a low level of conscious recognition of sensations such as pain and temperature. The small area known as the *hypothalamus* is involved essentially with the control of involuntary or autonomic functions such as regulating appetite, sleep and waking states, water balance, body temperature, and stimulation of the pituitary gland. The *cerebellum* provides, or assists in providing, the coordination of muscular movements and the control of posture. The *medulla* contains many reflex centers for such functions as coughing, sneezing, and swallowing. More important, however, are the vital centers located in the medulla for the control of breathing and heart action.

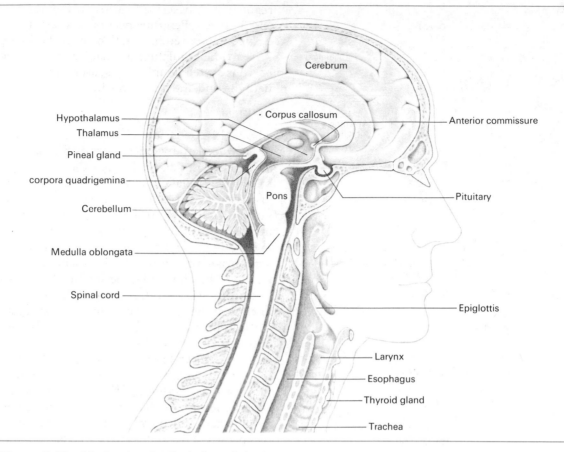

Figure 8·31   Median longitudinal view of the brain.

The Autonomic Nervous System

A division of the nervous system was mentioned earlier that is not under willful control and we called it the *autonomic nervous* system (ANS). Even though this part of the nervous system is "self-controlled," it is still connected to the rest of the nervous system through the spinal and cranial nerves. This connection with the spinal nerves is shown in the diagram in Figure 8–32. The ANS is divided into two divisions on the basis of function and anatomy (Figure 8–33). The *sympathetic* division arises from all of the spinal nerves in the thoracic region and the first three lumbar nerves. This division therefore is sometimes called the *thoracolumbar* portion of the ANS. The

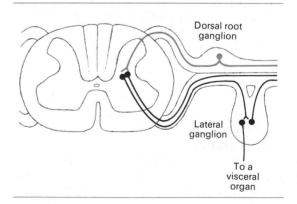

Figure 8·32   Diagram to show relationship between the ANS and the PNS. A lateral autonomic ganglion is shown arising from a spinal nerve.

256

parasympathetic division is composed of branches of the third, seventh, ninth, and tenth cranial nerves and the second, third, and fourth sacral spinal nerves. This division of the ANS is often referred to as the *craniosacral*.

These two divisions not only come from different regions of the CNS but also function entirely different—in fact, one division is antagonistic toward the other. (Remember that this is an involuntary system.) The sympathetic system accelerates the heartbeat, whereas the parasympathetic slows it down. The sympathetic system can produce dilation of the pupils of the eyes and the parasympathetic can bring about their constriction. The sympathetic system seems to be concerned with the mobilization of body resources for emergencies, whereas the parasympathetic returns the body to a more normal state after an emergency passes. The two divisions usually work together to provide a normal range of operation for the body through their accelerating and decelerating effects. The diagram in Figure 8–33 illustrates some of the effects of each system upon certain parts of the body.

THE NERVE IMPULSE

In preceding paragraphs we mentioned a nerve "message" traveling along a nerve. This message, possibly better termed a *nerve impulse*, occurs along an axon or dendrite when a nerve is stimulated. The process of nerve conduction has been studied by biologists for many years. In 1902, Bernstein, a German biologist, proposed a theory for the transmission of the nerve impulse, and experimental evidence in the 1930s and 1940s, especially by Hodgkin and Huxley, confirmed his theory. In fact, Bernstein's model, with slight modifications, is still used today to explain nerve-impulse transmission. The theory is based on the knowledge that the concentrations of specific ions are different inside the neurons from those outside. It is also known that the concentrations of some of these ions change instantaneously with the

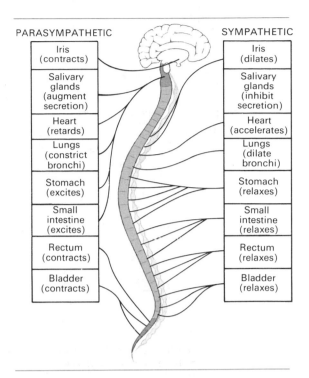

Figure 8·33 Diagram of the two components of the ANS and their actions on various organs. Note the opposing effects of the two divisions. Darker shades denote parasympathetic system; lighter shades denote sympathetic system.

passage of the nerve impulse. Therefore the process must be due to changes in ionic concentrations along the cell membrane.

In a nerve that is not conducting, more negative ions, mostly organic, are inside the cell than are outside. This produces a negatively charged region in comparison to the outside. The concentration of sodium ions (Na^+) is much greater outside the cell than inside, and more potassium ions (K^+) are found inside the cell. This uneven distribution of ions (more negative ions inside and more positive ions outside the cell) produces a potential across the membrane of living nerve cells of the magnitude of 50–70 millivolts. This is referred to as the *resting potential* and it establishes a definite polarity. When a nerve is stimulated the membrane becomes more permeable to sodium ions and they rush

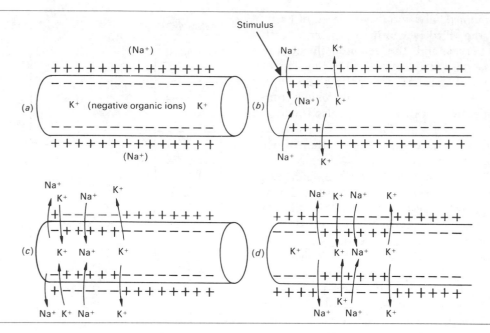

Figure 8·34   The series of events occurring during stimulation of a nerve and the subsequent conduction of the impulse. (*a*) Nonconducting nerve fiber. (*b*) Stimulus applied and Na⁺ flow in; very shortly thereafter, K⁺ move out. (*c*) The adjacent region becomes depolarized and the impulse is conducted along the nerve; note the region of the original stimulus is beginning to recover. Na⁺ is being transported out and K⁺ back in. (*d*) Conduction continues along the nerve to the right as recovery occurs at the left end of the fiber.

into the cell across the membrane. This reverses the polarity that previously existed and produces a temporary positive charge on the inside of the cell in relationship to the outside. When this depolarization occurs, we say that an *action potential* has developed. Immediately following the influx of sodium ions the membrane is highly permeable to potassium ions which flow through the membrane to the outside. At this point we must consider the restoration of the nerve cell to the state that existed before stimulation—that is, the original ionic balance with a greater concentration of sodium ions outside the cell and a greater concentration of potassium ions inside. If this should fail to occur, the neuron could not conduct nerve impulses again. It is known that a neuron normally can recover almost instantaneously, within thousandths of a second, and be ready to conduct once more.

For sodium ions to move outside the cell again and potassium ions to move inside would require the movement of these ions against a concentration gradient. The only way this can be done is by an active-transport mechanism such as that described in Chapter 3. In other words, sodium is actively transported to the outside while potassium is apparently moved back inside the cell. When this occurs the inside of the cell becomes negative again. The model proposed to account for these activities has been called the "sodium pump" or, more recently, the "sodium-potassium exchange pump." The latter mechanism postulates that the same system which transports sodium out of the cell also moves potassium back into the cell. Perhaps a carrier molecule, similar to that proposed for the transport of glucose in Figure 3–8, is operative in this process.

If the events described here account for the

Figure 8·35 (*a*) An oscilloscope—a type commonly used in experiments in college laboratory classes.

transmission of an impulse at one spot on the nerve, it is reasonable to assume this same process occurs for transmission along the entire length of the nerve. But how are the events set off in the region adjacent to the stimulated area and in succeeding regions? It was proposed by Bernstein, and others more recently, that the disturbance in membrane permeability which originally permitted the impulse to start upset the normal membrane permeability in the adjacent area. The impulse would then move to neighboring regions of the nerve until the impulse had traveled the length of the nerve. Thus a wave of depolarization moves along the nerve which is self-propagating and which is "powered" at each step along the way. This movement of the impulse along the nerve has been likened to a burning dynamite fuse that propagates itself by lowering the kindling temperature in the adjacent regions as the fuse burns. The series of events just described are summarized in Figure 8–34.

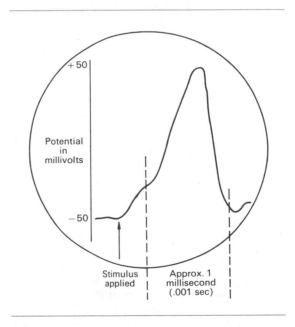

Figure 8·35 (*b*) The visible part of a nerve impulse (the "spike") as it would appear on an oscilloscope.

259

All nerve impulses are apparently the same whether the stimulus be touch or light or sound waves. That is, the impulse does not differ but receptors are different and they lead to different parts of the brain for interpretation. It should also be noted that a stimulus must be of a sufficient strength in order to initiate an impulse. This intensity is often referred to as a *threshold stimulus*.

The basic cause of the nerve impulse is electrochemical—that is, the ionic changes which occur along the membrane produce electrical events. Moreover, these events can be visualized and studied by the use of electronic instrumentation. When a nerve impulse is picked up between two points on a nerve it produces a "spike" (the action potential noted earlier) on an *oscilloscope*, an instrument that records a visual image of an electrical event on a fluorescent screen (Figure 8–35). We often refer to these electrochemical changes as *bioelectricity*, but it is entirely different from conventional electricity which travels through copper wiring. Common electricity results from electron movement along a wire, whereas bioelectricity is due to a separation of charged particles (ions) by a membrane (a process requiring active transport by the membrane). Electricity travels at the rate of 186,000 miles per second and is much faster than the nerve impulse which varies from 1 to 300 meters per second.

SUMMARIZING PRINCIPLES

All organisms must react to changing conditions in order to maintain a fairly constant internal environment. This internal balance (dynamic equilibrium) is accomplished through the active coordination and regulation of chemical and physical processes in the organism. Some of the factors involved in the maintenance of a steady state in organisms can be demonstrated by physical models. Four features are necessary: self-regulating mechanism, feedback, immediate response, and multicontrols.

General scheme of control: internal and external changes require regulation before action; feedback is necessary to prevent overreaction. These responses to change involve hormonal and nervous systems as well as certain ions, vitamins, and enzymes that may regulate specific chemical reactions.

Hormones produced by plants control growth, movement, and flowering. Animal hormones are usually secreted from endocrine glands and generally produce widespread effects. Examples of animal hormone action are: regulation of growth, development, metabolism, reproduction, digestion, and water and ion balance.

The nervous system is composed of neurons and nerve tracts; whereas hormonal control is often slow and generalized, the nervous system provides for fast, specific action. The nervous system of man may be considered in three functional divisions: the central, peripheral, and autonomic systems. CNS—the brain and spinal cord; PNS—the cranial and spinal nerves; ANS—an involuntary system consisting of two antagonistic divisions, the sympathetic and parasympathetic.

The reflex arc is a nerve pathway involving sensory, motor, and sometimes internuncial neurons. It occurs across the spinal cord from dorsal root to ventral root before the brain can modulate the sensory input. Some reflexes can be conditioned through training.

Nerve cells have the ability to pass a wave of excitation along their full length and transfer this excitation to other nerve cells. Electrochemical events involving ions (especially sodium and potassium) account for this wave of excitation.

REVIEW QUESTIONS

1   Review the Hering-Breuer reflex-control mechanism presented in Chapter 7 and place the events of this process in the "general scheme of control" as given in this chapter.

2   Describe the control or regulative reactions that would occur in the following situation: You are stepping from a curb into the street and suddenly you glimpse a fast approaching automobile about 25 feet away.

3   Can you explain the value of having both nervous and hormonal systems in animals? What are the advantages of each?

4   What evidence do we have that enzymes and genes act as control agents?

5   If a potato tuber is grown in a jar, the apical bud develops into a large and vigorous shoot and the lateral buds ("eyes") produce small shoots, if any. However, if the tuber is cut into five or six pieces, all "eyes" will develop sprouts of about the same size. Explain.

6   Land snails in the northwestern United States come into reproductive activity about May and June. What conditions must a researcher modify and control if he wants these snails to reproduce in the months of February and March?

7   What are some of the changes you would expect in a young rabbit that has been given periodic injections of pituitary extract?

8   What are some of the effects of an excessive growth of adrenal cortex tissue (a tumor). Consider the changes that might occur in a 5-year-old male and a 35-year-old male.

9   People with high blood pressure and a history of heart trouble are often advised not to attend exciting athletic contests. Explain.

10   Summarize the control mechanisms that interact to maintain normal blood-glucose metabolism.

11   Why would a physician test several specific reflexes on a patient following an accident that leaves the individual unconscious?

12   What effect would a severed ventral root of a spinal nerve have on a reflex arc?

13   Compare the effects of the sympathetic and parasympathetic divisions of the ANS on: digestion, heart rate, and blood pressure.

14   Explain why it is possible to start a nerve impulse along a nerve by applying electrical stimulation, pressure, or certain chemicals.

SUPPLEMENTARY READINGS

Baker, Peter F., "The Nerve Axon," *Scientific American*, March, 1966.

Benzinger, T. H., "The Human Thermostat," *Scientific American*, January, 1961.

Bonner, John T., "Hormones in Social Amoebae and Mammals," *Scientific American*, June, 1969.

Brown, Jr., Frank A., *Biological Clocks*, BSCS Pamphlet No. 2, American Institute of Biological Sciences, Boston, Heath, 1962.

Butler, W. L., and R. J. Downs, "Light and Plant Development," *Scientific American*, April, 1960.

Changeux, J. P., "The Control of Biochemical Reactions," *Scientific American*, April, 1965.

Di Cara, Leo V., "Learning in the Autonomic Nervous System," *Scientific American*, January, 1970.

Fieser, Louis F., "Steroids," *Scientific American*, January, 1955.

Katz, Bernhard, "The Nerve Impulse," *Scientific American*, November, 1952.

Keynes, Richard D., "The Nerve Impulse and the Squid," *Scientific American*, December, 1958.

Levine, Rachmiel, and M. S. Goldstein, "The Action of Insulin," *Scientific American*, May, 1958.

Li, Choh Hao, "The Pituitary," *Scientific American*, October, 1950.

Li, Choh Hao, "The ACTH Molecule," *Scientific American*, July, 1963.

"The Life-Giving Balancing Act," Part 5 in series on The Human Body, *Life Magazine*, November 8, 1963.

Loewenstein, Werner R., "Biological Transducers," *Scientific American*, August, 1960.

Mayr, Otto, "The Origins of Feedback Control," *Scientific American*, October, 1970.

McCashland, Benjamin W., *Animal Coordinating Mechanisms*, Dubuque, Iowa, Wm. C. Brown, 1968.

Overbeek, Johannes van, "The Control of Plant Growth," *Scientific American*, July, 1968.

Overmire, Thomas G., *Homeostatic Regulation*, BSCS Pamphlet No. 9, American Institute of Biological Sciences, Boston, Heath, 1963.

Rasmussen, Howard, "The Parathyroid Hormone," *Scientific American*, April, 1961.

Rasmussen, Howard, and M. M. Pechet, "Calcitonin," *Scientific American*, October, 1970.

Salisbury, Frank B., "Plant Growth Substances," *Scientific American*, April, 1957.

Salisbury, Frank B., "The Flowering Process," *Scientific American*, April, 1958.

Snider, R. S., "The Cerebellum," *Scientific American*, August, 1958.

Steward, F. C., "The Control of Growth in Plant Cells," *Scientific American*, October, 1963.

Suckling, E. E., *Bioelectricity*, BSCS Pamphlet No. 4, American Institute of Biological Sciences, Boston, Heath, 1962.

Thompson, E. O. P., "The Insulin Molecule," *Scientific American*, May, 1955.

Went, Frits W., "Plant Growth and Plant Hormones," in W. Johnson and W. Steere, eds., *This Is Life*, New York, Holt, Rinehart and Winston, 1962.

Zuckerman, Sir Solly, "Hormones," *Scientific American*, March, 1957.

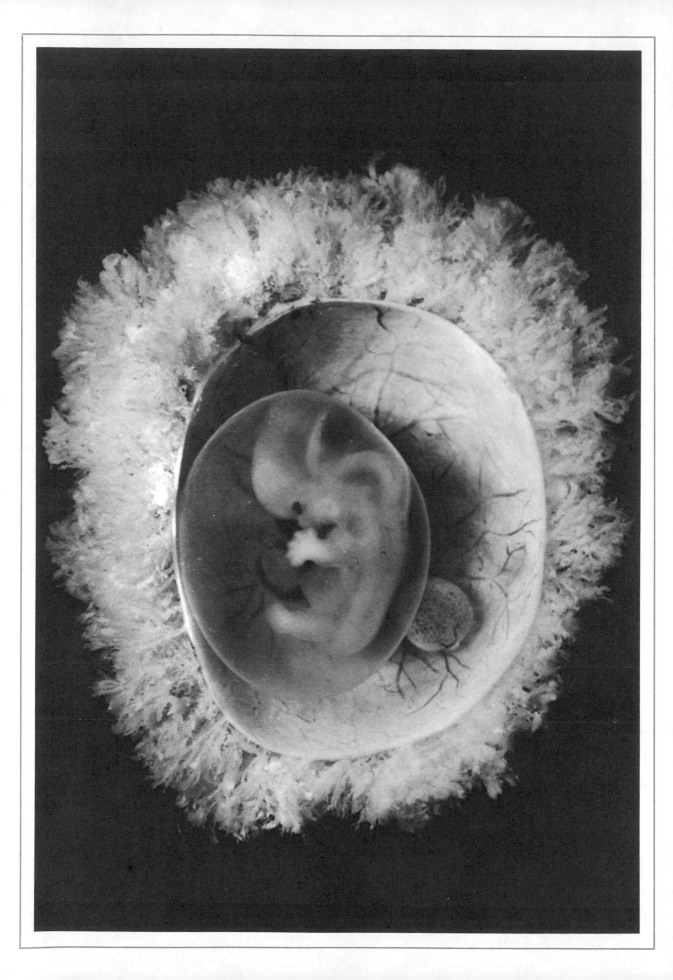

9

Reproduction and Development

The future of all species of plants and animals on this planet depends on their ability to produce offspring which in turn can reproduce. Although we know that some individual organisms can reproduce asexually, it has now been established that most living things are capable of sexual reproduction. Each type of reproduction has distinct characteristics. For example, asexual reproduction produces organisms exactly like the parent, whereas sexual reproduction gives offspring that are always different. Exactly how this variability comes about will be the subject of the next chapter which deals with heredity. The importance of variability to a given species will be stressed in the chapter on evolution. Before organisms can reproduce, cellular reproduction, an orderly series of events, must occur. And before cells can reproduce, molecular duplication must take place. Molecular reproduction in DNA has already been discussed in Chapter 2. In this chapter we will discuss the basic reproductive mechanisms at the cellular and organismal levels.

Closely associated with reproduction in organisms is the complicated process of development in which a fertilized egg undergoes a series of changes to produce all the adult tissues and organs. This developmental process must occur in all plants and animals. Perhaps you have wondered just how a tiny fertilized egg can possibly divide and change into a complete, functional,

265

multicellular organism. Certainly one important clue is the code in the DNA molecule (described in Chapter 3) which is essential since specific regions of the molecule direct the development of dividing cells. Development like cellular reproduction is also an orderly series of events. For example, what determines the future of a particular cell? Why does one cell become a muscle cell while a nearby cell develops into a connective-tissue cell? Why is a specific number of cells produced in one region of an organism? Why does development of one structure begin only after another structure is produced? Many experiments have been performed in attempts to answer these and other questions of development. We will first consider the reproductive process and then turn to some examples and studies in development.

CELLULAR REPRODUCTION

The nuclear events that occur during cell division were observed many years before any correlation between chromosomes and cell division was made. Cell division was observed in protozoa as early as 1744 by Trembley, even though he did not recognize them as cells. It was around 1824 that the process of dividing or cleaving frog eggs was finally recognized as multiplication by cell division. In 1888 Thedor Boveri published a classic paper on the division of fertilized *Ascaris* (roundworm) eggs in which he accurately diagrammed the distribution of nuclear material during cleavage.

Two types of cell division occur in most plants and animals: (1) *somatic* or body-cell division and (2) *gametic* or sex-cell division. More specifically the gametes are called *eggs* and *sperms*. Somatic division is known as *mitosis* and gametic division is called *meiosis*. In mitosis both the nucleus and the cytoplasm divide to form two daughter cells which contain the same number and types of chromosomes as the original cell. Meiosis, on the other hand, is a more complex process in

which the chromosome number in each gamete is halved in preparation for fertilization. Meiosis is necessary to maintain a constant chromosome number within a species. At fertilization each parent contributes, in its gamete, one-half the number of chromosomes characteristic of the species. In humans this number is 23, and this is called the *haploid* number, or simply *n*. The complete chromosome number of a body cell in man is, therefore, 46, and this is the *diploid* or 2*n* number.

MITOSIS

Before discussing the specific steps involved in mitotic cell division, it should be stressed that the chromosomes of a normal diploid cell occur in pairs. Each member of a chromosome pair is essentially similar in size, shape, and carry inheritance factors which influence similar traits. The term *homologous pairs* is often used to describe chromosomes that have these similar characteristics. In Chapter 10 you will learn more about the role of chromosomal DNA in the transmission of hereditary traits. Since the chromosomes contain DNA, they may be called the physical bearers of heredity, and for this reason the activities of the chromosomes during division are also of great interest to the geneticist.

Before a cell can divide, the chromosomes must duplicate. The DNA of each chromosome duplicates according to the base-pair specificity which was outlined in Chapter 2—adenine to thymine and guanine to cytosine. The generalized scheme for mitosis may be outlined as follows:

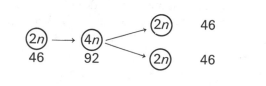

This diagram represents the mitotic duplication and division of the chromosomes in the formation of two daughter cells in man.

Figure 9·1   Diagram of interphase and the successive phases of mitosis in an animal cell.

The details of mitosis are somewhat easier to understand if we divide the process into a series of steps or phases. From beginning to end these phases are (1) *interphase*, (2) *prophase*, (3) *metaphase*, (4) *anaphase*, and (5) *telophase*. The significant nuclear and cytoplasmic events which occur in the successive mitotic phases are shown in Figure 9–1.

Mitosis in Animals

Interphase. Each diploid, body-cell nucleus generally contains two nucleoli composed mainly of RNA (see Chapter 3). The chromosomes within the nucleus are long and threadlike and, when stained with a nuclear dye, resemble a loose ball of yarn. Dense-staining areas called *chromomeres* appear at specific points along each chromosome. These thickened regions are concentrations of DNA produced by localized coiling. The nuclear membrane during this stage is intact and the centrioles are located in the cytoplasm near the nucleus.

For many years after the discovery of mitosis it was thought that the chromosomes duplicated about halfway through the division process (metaphase). When radioisotopes of phosphorus (P³²) and hydrogen (H³, tritium) became available, it was learned that the DNA rapidly incorporated new nitrogen bases into its structure immediately following the telophase. When radioactive thymidine (tritiated thymidine) was added to the medium of dividing cells, it was found that the thymidine bases were incorporated into the interphasic chromosomes. Chromosome duplication therefore occurs before the prophase step of mitosis.

Prophase. This early phase of mitosis involves several visible changes in the nucleus. The chromosomes which were long and threadlike begin to coil upon themselves much like the twisting of a rubber band. During this stage each chromosome becomes shorter, thicker, and more clearly visible. The nucleolus disappears and is not recognized again until the reorganization of the nuclei in the daughter cells. Near the end of prophase the nuclear membrane begins to break down and finally disappears. The centrioles form radiating protein fibers called *asters* and move slowly away from each other around the nucleus to form the opposite poles for the division.

Metaphase. When the centrioles have reached opposite positions across the nuclear area, protein fibers (*spindle fibers*) are synthesized between them. Some spindle fibers attach to specific regions on the chromosomes called

Figure 9·2 Dr. Daniel Mazia of the University of California, outstanding authority in cell division studies.

centromeres. Little is known about the mechanics of spindle-fiber attachment or the molecular structure of the centromere. We do know that each chromosome has one centromere which is always at the same spot on a specific chromosome. Some chromosomes have their centromere in the center and are called *metacentric,* while others have the centromere at the end and are known as *acrocentric.* The metacentric chromosomes typically are V-shaped and the acrocentric, rod-shaped. If the centromere is located between the center and one end, the chromosome is J-shaped and is called *submetacentric.* After the chromosomes have duplicated they appear double and each half is called a *chromatid.* This term will be used extensively in the discussion on meiosis.

During metaphase the chromosomes attached to the spindle fibers move about until they align on an equatorial plate which is oriented perpendicular to the centriole poles. The centrioles, spindle fibers, and chromosomes are collectively known as the *mitotic apparatus.* Daniel Mazia (Figure 9–2) of the

University of California has been successful in isolating this mitotic apparatus from dividing cells. By using a chemical to stop division at midpoint and breaking up the cell membranes with detergent, scientists can now remove the entire mitotic apparatus for analytical studies.

Anaphase. The spindle fibers that attach to the chromosomes are called *traction* or *chromosomal fibers.* It is thought that these fibers actually contract as the entire spindle elongates to pull the chromosomes to the poles. The separation of the duplicated chromosomes marks the beginning of nuclear division which is known as *karyokinesis.* By late anaphase, the entire cell begins to divide—that is, a cleavage furrow is formed at the center of the spindle which gradually deepens until the cell is completely constricted (or cleaved) into two cells (Figures 9–1, 9–3, and 9–4). The cleavage of the cell cytoplasm is called *cytokinesis.*

Telophase. The last phase of division is marked by the nearly complete cleavage of the cell into daughter cells. Usually, some of the spindle fibers are still visible between the cells. The tightly coiled chromosomes now begin to relax and uncoil. The nuclear membrane is reconstituted and the two nucleoli are formed. Each cell has received one centriole in the division process. The aster and spindle fibers disappear and the centriole duplicates itself in preparation for the next division, although in some cases duplication may not take place until early prophase. Remember that it is also at this time that the chromosomes duplicate by synthesizing new DNA.

Mitotic cell division in animals usually requires from thirty minutes to several hours. In mammalian cells the time is generally about one hour. In mouse-spleen cells in culture, prophase lasts 20–35 minutes, metaphase 6–15 minutes, anaphase 8–14 minutes, and telophase 9–26 minutes (from Hughes, *The Mitotic Cycle,* Academic Press, New York, 1952). Prophase and telophase in general take longer than metaphase or anaphase; in

(a)

(b)

(c)

(d)

Figure 9·3 Drawings of the mitotic phases of a fertilized ovum of *Ascaris megalocephala* (horse roundworm). (*a*) The sperm and egg nuclei in prophase; (*b*) side view of metaphase; (*c*) late anaphase; (*d*) telophase. Note that this subspecies (*univalens*) contains only one pair of chromosomes.

many cases anaphase may be extremely short (less than one minute).

Mitosis in Plants

One significant difference between plant and animal cells is, of course, the rigid plant cell wall. In the animal cell, cleavage of the flexible cell membrane permits the formation of two daughter cells. But how are new cell walls formed in plants? Small cell plates form in the mid-spindle region during anaphase and are believed to originate from the endo-

Figure 9·4 Mitotic phases in a developing egg of whitefish. Metaphase (lower right) and several anaphase figures. (Courtesy of General Biological Supply House.)

Figure 9·5 A section of onion root tip showing various stages of mitosis. Prophase, upper left; metaphase, lower left; anaphase, middle left; telophase, upper right. (Courtesy of Carolina Biological Supply Co.)

plasmic reticulum. These coalesce to form part of the new cell wall separating the daughter cells. Another interesting difference between the mitotic apparatus of plant and animal cells is the absence of astral fibers in plants. Furthermore, plant cells do not possess centriole organelles which are found in animal cells. The question of the formation and function of the spindle fibers in higher plants is still largely unanswered. The mitotic process in an onion root tip is shown in Figure 9–5.

MEIOSIS

The process of meiosis produces cells having a haploid chromosome number. The cell divisions that produce gametes (eggs and sperms) in diploid organisms reduce the chromosome number to one-half that of a normal body cell. As was noted earlier, if this did not occur the chromosome number would double in each species in each generation. Meiosis essentially includes two cell divisions with only one duplication of the chromosomes. In the first division (meiosis I) the duplicated chromosomes are separated into two diploid cells, whereas the second division (meiosis II) separates these two cells into four haploid cells (Figure 9–6). Prophase II and metaphase II are usually very brief. The chromosomes are observed to be double-stranded by about midway through a prolonged prophase I. Also at this stage homologous chromosomes pair—that is, each chromosome finds its homologous partner, and they attach along their full lengths. This process is called

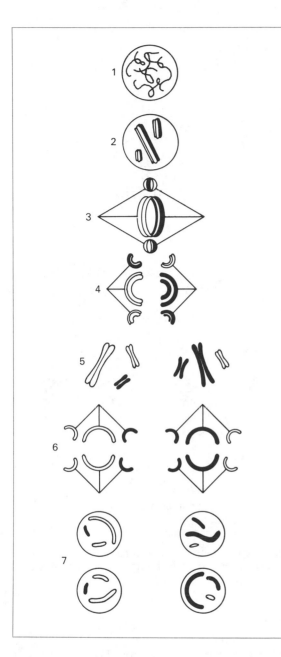

Figure 9·6 Meiosis in a nucleus containing three pairs of chromosomes. Meiosis I: (1) early prophase; (2) prophase with duplicated and synapsed homologous chromosomes (tetrad stage); (3) metaphase; (4) anaphase—bivalents separate; (5) two diploid nuclei containing one homologous chromosome of each pair and its duplicate. Meiosis II: (6) anaphase—chromatids separate; (7) four haploid nuclei each containing three chromosomes. (From Whaley.)

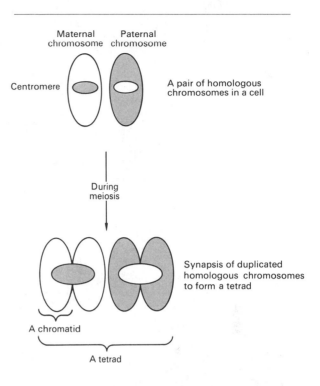

Figure 9·7 A diagram of a pair of homologous chromosomes in the early stages of meiosis.

synapsis and forms the basis for all subsequent meiotic events. Since one member of each chromosome pair in an individual comes from the mother and the other from the father, we speak of the pairing of maternal and paternal chromosomes. Each chromosome with its homologue is called a *bivalent*. The synapsed, duplicated chromosomes are also called a *tetrad* because the four chromatids (or two bivalents) are together, side by side (Figure 9–7). The centromeres apparently have not duplicated at this point, and each bivalent therefore shares only one centromere. It is at this point that a very significant event occurs. During synapsis, certain segments of the chromatids may *cross over*—that is, segments that contain genetic information can be exchanged. The results of one crossover in one

271

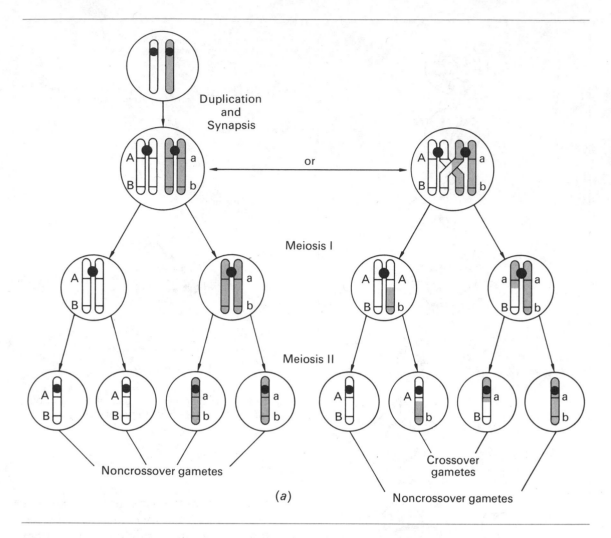

Duplication
and
Synapsis

or

Meiosis I

Meiosis II

Noncrossover gametes

Crossover
gametes

Noncrossover gametes

(a)

Figure 9·8 (a) A diagrammatic comparison of the chromosomal changes that occur in noncrossover and crossover during synapsis of homologous chromosomes. Crossover occurs in almost all chromosomes and is the rule rather than the exception.

pair of gametic chromosomes are shown in Figure 9–8. In the diagram, the letters represent units of heredity (commonly called *genes*). A comparison of crossover and noncrossover chromosomes illustrate how new combinations of genes may be formed in gametic chromosomes. Though the genetic significance of this process will be discussed in Chapter 10, it should be noted here that this

aspect of meiosis allows for the shuffling and recombination of the offspring's grandparental genes. The ability of an organism to adapt to its environment depends in part on crossover of chromosomes and recombination of genes. Crossovers can actually be observed in the chromosomes as they coil and shorten prior to metaphase I. Near the end of prophase, the chromosomes show interesting figures

Figure 9·8 (*b*) Crossovers in snail chromosomes as observed through the microscope. The areas where the chromatids cross are called *chiasmata* (meaning *cross*).

resembling crosses or chains. Crossovers in snail chromosomes, as they appear in a microscope, are shown in Figure 9–8*b*. Actually, *chiasmata* are the only visible evidence for the crossover events.

At metaphase I the chromosomes are aligned on the equatorial plane and will segregate at random; each half of each tetrad (or bivalent) has an equal chance of going to either daughter cell. The segregation possibilities for the chromosomes at anaphase I should be stressed. If two pairs of chromosomes are involved, four possible chromosomal combinations can result (Figure 9–9*a*). When three pairs of chromosomes are present, eight different combinations are possible (Figure 9–9*b*). In humans, with their 23 pairs of chromosomes, there are 8,388,608 possible combinations. The segregation possibilities for an organism can be readily computed by raising the base number 2 (the number of chromosomes in a pair) to an exponential

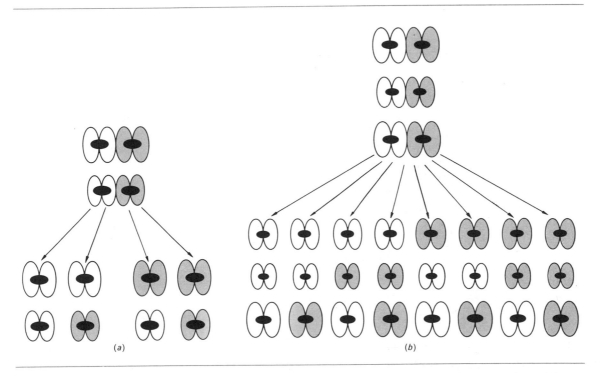

(a)

(b)

Figure 9·9 The possibilities of the chromosomal combinations that can result at anaphase I in an organism with (*a*) two pairs of chromosomes; or (*b*) three pairs of chromosomes.

273

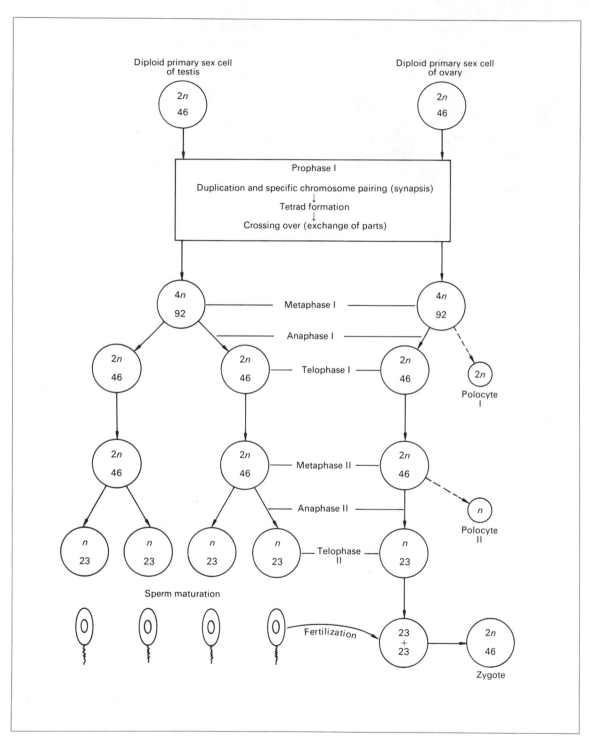

Figure 9·10 The process of meiosis as it occurs in human males, spermatogenesis, and in females, oögenesis. The fertilization of an egg by a sperm to form a zygote is also noted. The 4n stage refers to the number of chromatids.

power equal to the number of pairs of chromosomes in the species. For example:

$$2^2 = 4 \,;\; 2^3 = 8 \,;\; 2^{23} = 8{,}388{,}608$$

Again, it is strictly a matter of chance which bivalent of each tetrad will go to each daughter cell. We must assume, therefore, that each combination has an equal chance or probability of moving to either daughter cell. This point will be stressed again in the chapter on heredity, but it is necessary to understand this random segregation of chromosomes if we are to understand the fundamental principles of heredity.

In anaphase I, the tetrad separates between the synapsed chromosomes (Figures 9–6 and 9–9), and therefore an original chromosome with its duplicate (a bivalent of each tetrad) moves to each pole. The chromosome number has essentially been halved at this point since a maternal chromosome and its duplicate went to one daughter cell and a paternal chromosome and its duplicate went to the other daughter cell. Remember, however, that since crossovers have occurred some parts of the chromosomes have been exchanged. At anaphase II, the centromere of each bivalent divides and the original chromosome and its duplicate (a bivalent) are finally separated with each chromatid moving to a separate cell. Each gamete thus receives a chromosome from the original homologous pair. This is important because a fertilized egg would then contain a member of each homologous pair— one from the egg and one from the sperm.

The meiotic events that occur in males to produce sperm are called *spermatogenesis* and the production of eggs in females is known as *oögenesis* (Figure 9–10). Each stage of division is labeled in sequence for both meiosis I and meiosis II. In this diagram the chromosome number for man is used, but the *2n* and *n* may represent the specific number for any species. Note that prophase II may be very short or absent entirely. The major difference between spermatogenesis and oögenesis is the production of polar bodies (polocytes) in

oögenesis. A *polar body* is simply a packet of chromosomes extruded from the nucleus along with a very small amount of cytoplasm. This process conserves the egg cytoplasm and its protein-synthesizing ribosomes which will be essential to the developing embryo.

REPRODUCTION IN PROTISTS

A variety of reproductive processes occur in the protists including fragmentation, fission, spore production, and sexuality. Fragmentation reproduction occurs when a portion of an organism becomes separated from the main body and develops into a new organism. Fission, common in one-celled forms, is a process in which an organism splits into nearly equal halves. Spores are cells formed in an asexual process which are capable of giving rise to a new organism.

GREEN ALGAE

In the green alga *Ulothrix* (Figure 9–11), reproduction may be accomplished simply by the fragmentation of the filament; in this case, each piece continues to divide forming many new individuals. On the other hand, a cell may also divide several times within itself to produce swimming *zoöspores* which are released to reproduce new organisms. *Ulothrix* can also reproduce sexually. Vegetative cells divide internally many times to form motile gametes. When released through a pore in the cell wall, these gametes fuse with gametes from other filaments. The fusion of gametes from different filaments provides for the exchange of genetic information. Unlike typical sperm and egg gametes, these gametes (Figure 9–11c) are of equal size. This condition is called *isogamy* (*iso* meaning *same* or *equal*) as opposed to *heterogamy*, the condition where different-sized gametes are involved. The resulting *zygote* then undergoes meiosis to form four new haploid organisms (Figure 9–11c). The vegetative filament cells of *Ulothrix* are haploid and the gametes therefore can be

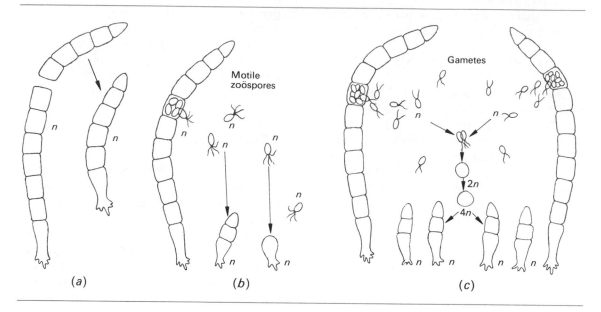

(a) (b) Motile zoöspores Gametes (c)

Figure 9·11 Three types of reproduction occurring in the green alga *Ulothrix* (Chlorophyta). (*a*) Fragmentation; (*b*) zoöspore formation; and (*c*) haplontic sexual. Note the production of isogametes.

produced by mitosis. The fusion of these haploid gametes produces a diploid zygote in which meiosis must occur. This pattern of sexual reproduction is called *haplontic* since the alga is haploid. You will note that the pattern is opposite to that of man and most plants.

A discussion of sexual reproduction in algae is not complete without a description of the sexual process in the green alga *Spirogyra*. An outstanding feature of this common pond scum is the spiral chloroplast in each cell and, like *Ulothrix*, the filament cells are normally haploid. Although no morphological distinction can be made as to the sex of a particular filament, two physiologically different "sexes," usually designated as + and −, pair up during the spring of the year and exchange nuclear material. This process is known as *conjugation* (Figure 9–12). Protoplasmic tubes emerge from each conjugating cell and fuse. The walls dissolve and the donor-cell contents

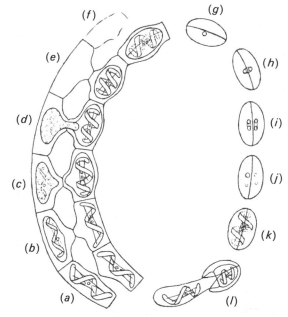

(a) (b) (c) (d) (e) (f) (g) (h) (i) (j) (k) (l)

Figure 9·12 Sexuality in *Spirogyra* (conjugation). Parts (*a*) through (*f*) show the formation and fusion of protoplasmic tubes between cells of adjacent filaments through which the contents of the donor cell flow into the recipient and form a zygote. Parts (*g*) through (*j*) represent the meiotic divisions that finally produce a single haploid nucleus. Parts (*k*) and (*l*) show the germination and production of a new filament by mitosis.

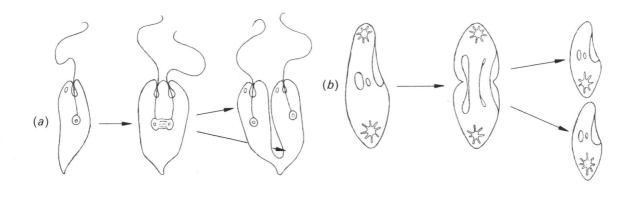

Figure 9·13 Examples of fission in Protozoa. (*a*) Longitudinal fission in *Euglena*; (*b*) transverse fission in *Paramecium*.

flow into the recipient. After fusion of the nuclei, the zygote divides by meiosis to form four haploid nuclei. Three of the haploid nuclei disintegrate leaving only one to develop. A tough shell forms around this haploid nucleus and it may lie dormant for some time. Upon germination the formation of a new haploid filament is by mitotic cell division.

FLAGELLATES AND PROTOZOANS

Euglena divides by reproducing its flagellum and nucleus and splitting longitudinally (Figure 9–13*a*). The ciliated *Paramecium* may either divide by transverse fission (Figure 9–13*b*) or undergo a specialized type of sexual reproduction in which nuclear material is exchanged between two individuals. This process is also known as conjugation even though it differs in many respects from that of *Spirogyra*. Two individuals come together along their oral grooves (Figure 9–14). Note that each *Paramecium* contains two types of nuclei, a large macronucleus and a micro-nucleus. The macronucleus of each organism disintegrates leaving only the micronucleus. The micronucleus next divides twice to produce four nuclei. Three of these disintegrate and the remaining nucleus divides un-

equally into macro and micro portions. At this point the micro portions (sometimes called male portions) are exchanged across the cell membranes and the micro portions now fuse with the macro portions. This marks the end of the conjugant phase and they move apart to complete their reproductive divisions (ex-conjugant stage). Following this fusion and separation three equal nuclear divisions occur. Of the eight nuclei formed in each *Paramecium*, four will become new macronuclei, three disappear, and one becomes the new micro-nucleus. In two divisions the macronuclei are distributed into four new individuals (the micronucleus divides each time). Thus two conjugating *Paramecia* can produce eight offspring following the exchange of genetic material (Figure 9–14).

REPRODUCTION IN PLANTS

Both asexual and sexual reproduction occur in the plant kingdom. Asexual reproduction is very common in plants, and new individuals frequently arise from bulbs, runners, cuttings, and in some cases even leaves. Sexual repro-duction in plants is part of a general life-cycle pattern which can be observed in all members

277

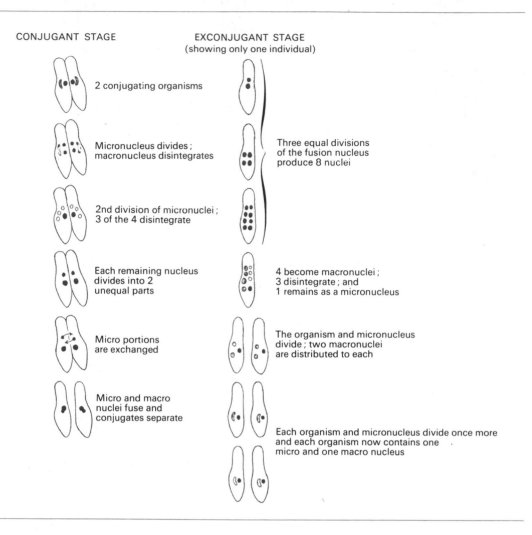

CONJUGANT STAGE

EXCONJUGANT STAGE
(showing only one individual)

2 conjugating organisms

Micronucleus divides;
macronucleus disintegrates

Three equal divisions
of the fusion nucleus
produce 8 nuclei

2nd division of micronuclei;
3 of the 4 disintegrate

Each remaining nucleus
divides into 2
unequal parts

4 become macronuclei;
3 disintegrate; and
1 remains as a micronucleus

Micro portions
are exchanged

The organism and micronucleus
divide; two macronuclei
are distributed to each

Micro and macro
nuclei fuse and
conjugates separate

Each organism and micronucleus divide once more
and each organism now contains one
micro and one macro nucleus

Figure 9·14 Conjugation in *Paramecium*. The conjugant stage is illustrated on the left and the exconjugant stage on the right. Note that only one exconjugant is diagrammed.

of the plant kingdom. This pattern involves the alternation of a spore-producing (asexual) stage with a gamete-producing (sexual) stage. Thus every plant undergoes a life cycle in which one phase of its existence is devoted to the production of spores and one phase involves the production of gametes. We speak of such a plan as an *alternation of generations*. The stage of the life cycle that produces spores is known as the *sporophyte*, a diploid plant, and that which produces gametes is

called the *gametophyte*, a haploid plant (Figure 9–15).

In the progression from simple plants (byrophytes, such as mosses) to more complex plants (seed plants), a greater development of the sporophyte occurs. In the byrophytes the dominant stage of the life cycle is the green, leafy gametophyte. The sporophyte, on the other hand, is usually unable to make its own food and is therefore dependent on the gametophyte. The ferns have a life cycle in

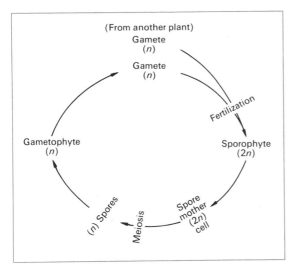

Figure 9·15 A simplified diagram of the stages in the life history of a plant.

however, the gametophyte generation is reduced to a structure retained on the sporophyte. The gametophyte here is often only a few cells in number. Figure 9–16 shows in a general way the relationships between the gametophyte and sporophyte generations of four of the major plant groups.

It should be noted that the process of alternation of generations between the gametophyte and sporophyte can also be observed in some protists. For example, similar life cycles can be found in the green algae but the dominant stage is the gametophyte. We should now discuss the life cycle of examples of each major plant group.

MOSSES (BRYOPHYTES)

When we examine the reproductive patterns of the nonvascular metaphytes such as liverworts and mosses, we find that the life cycle actually involves two plants—the green, leafy gametophyte and the stalklike sporophyte

which the gametophyte and sporophyte are both capable of making food even though the sporophyte is much larger. In the seed plants,

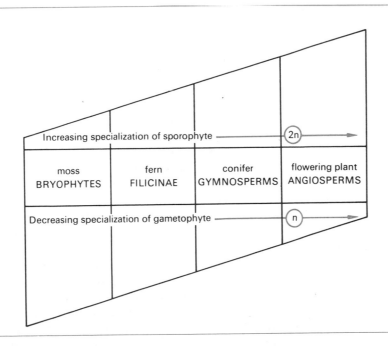

Figure 9·16 Highly generalized graph to illustrate the relationships between the gametophyte and the sporophyte generations of four plants.

279

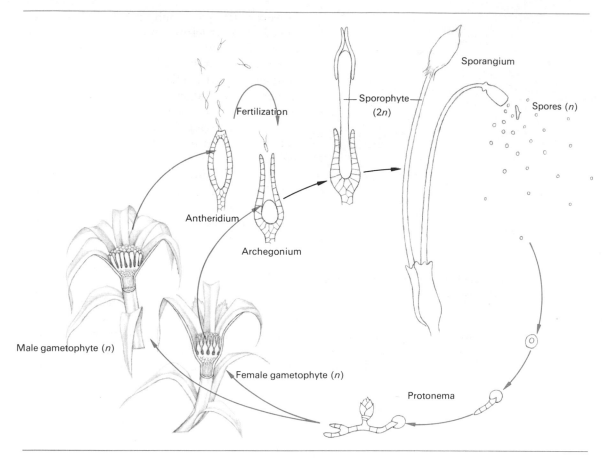

Figure 9·17 The life cycle of a moss. Spores are produced by meiosis in the sporangium and germinate as protonema. Gametes produced by the gametophytes fuse to form a sporophyte. Colored arrows represent haploid stages.

(Figure 9–17). There are both male and female gametophytes which have sex organs at the tips of their branches. The male sex organ is called the *antheridium* and produces motile sperms, whereas the female structure, an *archegonium*, produces eggs.

During a heavy dew or rain, the sperm move to the archegonium of a female plant and fertilize an egg. The resulting zygote divides to form a new 2n generation, the sporophyte. At the tip of the sporophyte a swollen organ known as the *sporangium* is produced. Usually, part of the old female archegonium is still present at the tip called the *calyptra*; this remnant soon dries out and gives the appear-

ance of a "hairy cap." Certain cells within the sporangium, called *spore mother cells*, divide by meiosis to produce many haploid spores. The spores are released at maturity when the top, or *operculum*, pops off. The spores germinate in the soil and develop into long threads called *protonema*. Buds develop from the protonema and produce new male or female gametophytes. Thus the complete life cycle of the moss requires two separate generations and the sporophyte and gameto-phyte generations are interdependent, al-though the gametophytes may spread by con-tinuous growth or produce asexual buds. The reproductive pattern in mosses is termed *haplodiplontic* and this is a completely workable process if both plants survive.

FERNS

The simplest of the vascular metaphytes are the ferns. The basic alternation of generation life cycle is similar to that of the moss (Figure 9–18). The familiar green frond represents the sporophyte generation. Spores are produced by meiosis in small sporangia located in brown clusters called *sori* on the underside of the frond. When the spores are mature, the sporangium dries, opens, and the spores are literally thrown to the winds. The heart-shaped gametophyte plants that develop from the spores are very small (only a few millimeters) and possess both male and female organs in archegonia and antheridia. Water is necessary in the ferns as in the moss for the transport of sperm to eggs. Since the predominant stage of the life cycle of the fern is

the diploid sporophyte, this pattern is termed *diplohaplontic*.

SEED PLANTS—GYMNOSPERMS AND ANGIOSPERMS

In gymnosperms such as pine, spruce, and fir, a period of two years generally is required to complete a reproductive cycle (Figure 9–19). Male or *staminate* cones and female or *ovulate* cones are present the first year. The staminate cones produce winged pollen grains that are carried by the wind to the larger, leafy pistillate cones. Each leaflike scale of the female cone develops two *ovules*, each of which contains a *megasporangium*. One megaspore cell divides by meiosis to produce multicelled female gametophytes (*n*) that produce several eggs in archegonia.

Each bractlike structure on the staminate cone, a microsporophyll, bears a pair of *microsporangia*. Each microspore mother cell,

Figure 9·18 The life cycle of a typical fern. The sporophyte (2*n*) is the predominant generation. In contrast to the moss, the gametophyte is much reduced in size. Colored arrows represent haploid stages.

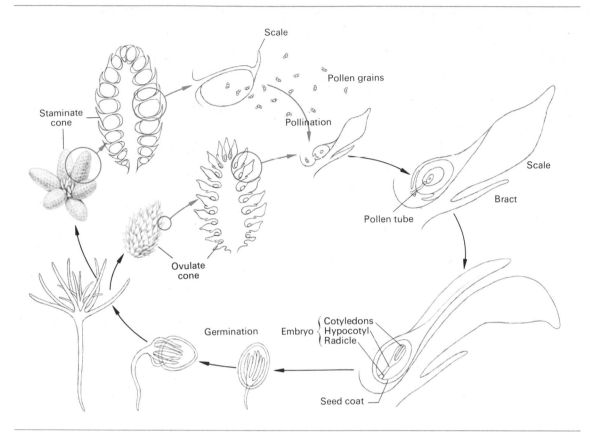

Scale

Pollen grains

Pollination

Staminate
cone

Scale

Bract

Pollen tube

Ovulate
cone

Cotyledons
Hypocotyl
Radicle

Germination   Embryo

Seed coat

Figure 9·19   A diagram of the life cycle of a typical conifer. Two years generally are required to produce a mature seed. Colored arrows represent haploid events.

produced within the microsporangia, undergoes meiosis to produce four haploid microspores. Each microspore will develop into a pollen grain. In this development two functional cells are produced, a generative cell and a tube cell, and two cells which soon degenerate. In addition, a thick coat develops around the outside of the pollen grain and two winglike structures form. At this point we should note that a pollen grain is actually a male gametophyte—a haploid structure, reduced to only a few cells in most gymnosperms.

In the process of pollination the pollen grains settle between the scales near the central axis of the female cone. The tube cell elongates and slowly grows into the female gametophyte. The generative cell at this time

divides into two sperms which enter the tube cell and migrate with the tube to the archegonium. This process may require approximately a year to complete. When an egg is reached, the pollen tube bursts to release the sperm. One sperm fertilizes the egg and a new sporophyte generation (*2n*) is formed. The tissue of the surrounding ovule develops into a hardened coat and the fertilized egg divides to produce a multicellular *embryo*. The developing embryo is nourished by the food stored in the cells of the old female gametophyte. The embryo with its associated food and the hardened coat is known as a *seed* (Figure 9–19). Such a structure has a distinct survival advantage. For example, if it is released from the plant under dry conditions, it can remain

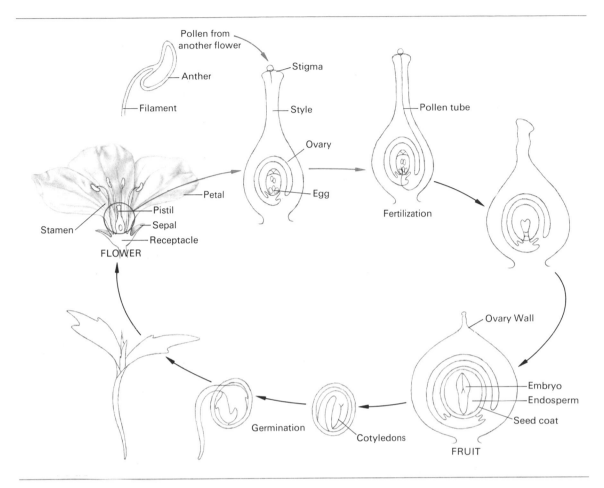

Figure 9·20 A longitudinal section through a typical perfect flower (containing both male and female organs). The fruit develops from the structures indicated. Colored arrows represent haploid events.

dormant until water is available for germination. Furthermore, a newly formed individual (an embryo) with a source of food and protective seed coat has a definite survival advantage in most environments over other plants. We do note that seed plants are the dominant plants on the earth today.

The female cone dries during the second year and the scales finally open to release the mature seeds. In many conifers, part of the seed coat extends into a thin wing which aids in dispersal. The mature embryo within the seed has several embryonic leaves known as *cotyledons* and an embryonic root, the *radicle*. The portion between these structures which

elongates to carry the cotyledons to the soil surface is called the *hypocotyl*.

Flowering plants, or angiosperms, are considered by most biologists to represent the most complex development in the plant kingdom and, as in gymnosperms, the sporophyte generation (diploid) has assumed complete dominance over the gametophyte. The gametes, as in other plants, are produced by gametophytes, but the gametophytes are reduced even more in the angiosperms than in the gymnosperms. Moreover, the gametophytes (and gametes) are produced in highly specialized structures, the *flowers*. Flowers which contain both staminate (male) and

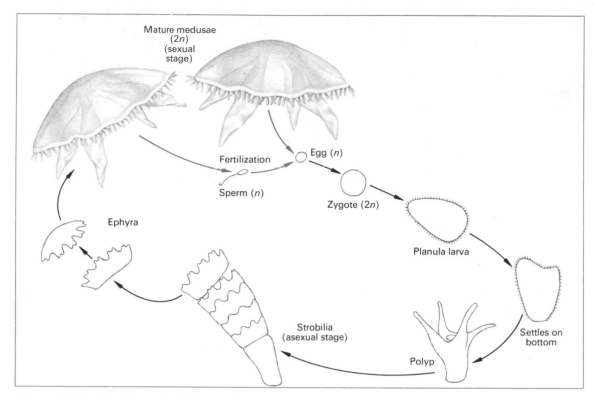

Figure 9·21 The life cycle of the scyphozoan jellyfish *Aurelia*. Colored arrows represent sexual stage.

pistillate (female) structures are termed *perfect* flowers; conversely, if the flower contains only staminate or pistillate organs, it is called *imperfect*. The major flower parts and the origin of angiosperm seed tissues are illustrated in Figure 9–20.

The small green *sepals* and the fragile, often brightly colored *petals* are attached to the flower base or *receptacle*. The female organ or *pistil* which contains the basal ovary may sit above the receptacle or actually be embedded within it (superior or inferior ovary). The apple is an example of a fruit developed from an inferior ovary. The outer flesh of the apple is formed from the ovary wall. *Stamens*, the male organs, develop *anthers* which form large numbers of pollen grains. Each pollen grain contains two haploid nuclei or sperms. At maturity, the pollen grains are released from the anther of one plant and carried to the pistil of another, usually by wind or insects,

where some land on the stigma. A long tube grows down through the style of the pistil and enters a small opening in the ovule (the organ that contains the egg). When the pollen tube reaches the ovule the sperms are released. One sperm unites with the egg nucleus to form a diploid zygote and the remaining sperm nucleus fuses with two haploid polar nuclei to form a $3n$ or triploid nucleus (Figure 9–20). This triploid nucleus is the beginning of the seed endosperm which will provide food for the developing embryo. In addition, the ovary wall usually develops into a thickened structure that may be hard or fleshy. The developed ovary wall with the seed or seeds inside is known as a *fruit*. The fruit may assist in dispersal of the seeds, for example, when animals eat fruits or when sticky fruits become attached to fur or clothing. The flower and the fruit, along with the enclosed seeds that contain nourishment for the developing embryo, provide a highly efficient method of reproduction for the angiosperms.

REPRODUCTION IN ANIMALS

Asexual reproduction is extremely limited in higher animals. It is true that many animals such as the starfish, crab, or lizard are capable of replacing lost or injured body parts through a process known as *regeneration*. An interesting exception here is the ability of a starfish arm to grow into a complete individual if the cut arm contains a portion of the central disc. The common brown *Planaria*, a small, free-living flatworm, may also undergo both regeneration and reproduction when cut into pieces. For example, if the worm is cut in half, the head end grows a new tail and the hind portion forms a new head. Sponges display a high degree of asexual reproduction. If a sponge is cut into very small pieces, each piece will develop into a new individual. Sponges may also reproduce by *budding*, a process in which the new individual grows directly as an outgrowth from the parent. In addition, special cells may form gametes to provide sexual reproduction. Throughout the animal kingdom, sexual reproduction is very similar in mechanism—that is, the union of a sperm with a larger egg to form a zygote.

Coelenterates (*Hydra,* jellyfish, and sea anemones) also reproduce by budding as well as sexually. The free-swimming jellyfish *Aurelia* is the sexual stage or *medusa* of an interesting life history. Although the jellyfish shows alternation of sexual and asexual stages, the body cells of both stages are diploid. After fertilization of gametes released into the water, the zygote develops into a flat, ciliated larva called a *planula*. The planula swims about for a time and finally attaches itself to a surface and begins to produce small buds asexually. These buds, known as *ephyrae*, look like a stack of saucers on the sessile *strobila* and develop into new medusae (Figure 9–21).

The sea anemone, which primarily reproduces sexually, adds a unique type of asexual reproduction to our discussion. The anemones

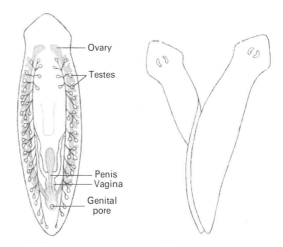

Figure 9·22 The internal fertilization process of *Planaria*. A reciprocal fertilization is accomplished in this manner.

normally are attached to rocks or some other solid objects beneath the water and may move very slowly on their broad attachment pedal disc. In some instances the foot may actually "walk away from itself" and split the animal down the center. Each half then repairs the damage and lives.

In most aquatic invertebrates fertilization occurs outside the body, requiring the release of tremendous numbers of gametes into the water. In the sea urchins which live in ocean tide pools, one animal releasing gametes into the water will "trigger" all the other urchins in the tide pool to release gametes. The eggs and sperms produce chemicals that keep the gametes together and ensure fertilization. Recent evidence indicates that the gelatinous egg coat contains a chemical which reacts with sperms causing them to gather in masses around the egg. Thus we see two mechanisms that aid in the success of external fertilization, synchronous gamete release and the production of chemicals to increase the probability of fertilization.

A few invertebrates and all land vertebrates with the exception of the amphibians utilize methods of direct internal fertilization. The flatworm *Planaria* has a penis through which sperms are transferred into the vagina of another worm (Figure 9–22). *Planaria* is

285

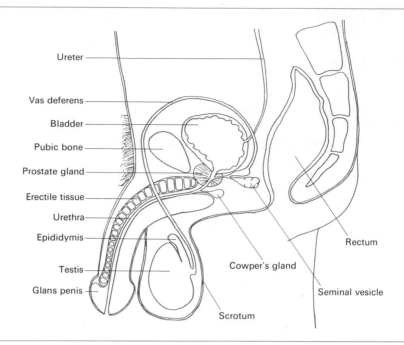

Ureter

Vas deferens

Bladder

Pubic bone

Prostate gland

Erectile tissue

Urethra

Epididymis

Testis

Glans penis

Rectum

Cowper's gland

Seminal vesicle

Scrotum

Figure 9·23   Human male reproductive system, side view.

monoecious or hermaphroditic, that is, each worm possesses both male and female organs. Monoecious means *one house*, which indicates that both sexes reside in one organism, whereas *dioecious* refers to separate sexes. Although both male and female organs are present in *Planaria*, self-fertilization does not occur.

Amphibians such as frogs and salamanders, which must return to water for reproduction, do not possess a penis. During mating, the male sits astride the back of the female and deposits sperms as the eggs are released. In these animals the urinary, intestinal, and reproductive tracts all come together to form a common canal called the *cloaca* from which the sperms and eggs are released. Birds and lizards also have a cloaca and, since there is no water carrier, fertilization must be accomplished by direct apposition of the cloacal openings of the male and female. In mammals and most reptiles, sperms are introduced through a penis.

MAMMALS

The reproductive structures and physiology of the human will be discussed as an example of mammalian reproduction. In the male (Figure 9–23) the sperm-producing tubules of each testis unite to form the epididymis which leaves the testis as the vas deferens. The vas deferens enters the abdominal cavity and unites with the urethra of the urinary system. Three pairs of accessory glands—seminal vesicles, prostate, and Cowper's—enter the system to provide lubricating and nutritional fluids. The seminal vesicles empty into each vas deferens, and the secretions of the prostate and Cowper's glands enter the urethra.

The major anatomical features of the female genital tract are diagrammed in Figure 9–24. The paired ovaries alternately discharge an ovum into the fallopian tube. At the junction of the fallopian tubes is a muscular organ, the uterus. The cellular lining of the uterus is called the *endometrium*, and following fertilization, the zygote is embedded in this lining which develops a rich blood supply. The females of most species of mammals undergo cyclic periods of egg production and sexual receptivity to the male called *estrus*. Mammals differ in the number of estrus cycles that may occur. The English fox, for example, is monoestrus and breeds only once each year. On the other hand, guinea pigs, rats, and rabbits are polyestrus, with estrus occurring every four to five days until conception occurs.

In the human female the sexual cycle, the *menstrual cycle*, differs from estrus in other animals in that there is no distinct period of male receptivity, and at the end of the monthly cycle, the cellular lining of the uterus is shed, accompanied by bleeding. If fertilization occurs the lining and the embyro are maintained for approximately nine months. The normal menstrual cycle, which requires approximately 28 days, is illustrated in Figure 9–25 and is summarized on the following page. The events that accompany fertilization and interrupt the menstrual cycle are also noted.

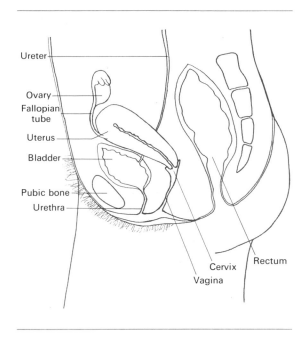

Figure 9·24 Human female reproductive system, side view.

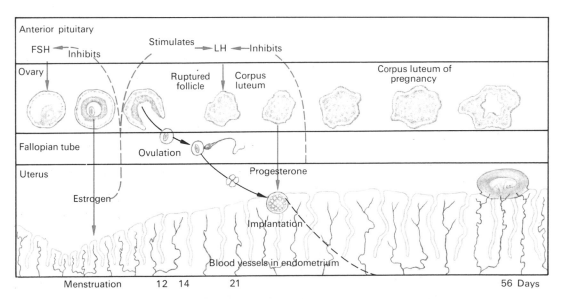

Figure 9·25 A diagram of the menstrual cycle in humans. The activities of four major areas are correlated: the anterior pituitary, ovary, fallopian tube, and uterus. If implantation does not occur, the corpus luteum degenerates and the uterine lining is shed after about 28 days as shown by the black dashed line. When fertilization and implantation occur, the lining is maintained to nourish the embryo until birth.

287

1 The ovary is stimulated by a follicle-stimulating hormone (FSH) from the anterior pituitary to produce a follicle which in turn produces an ovum (egg).

2 The Graafian follicle secretes the female hormone estrogen into the bloodstream which inhibits FSH and stimulates the production of luteinizing hormone (LH).

3 Estrogen stimulates the lining of the uterus to proliferate and vascularize in preparation for the implanting of the fertilized ovum.

4 After about twelve days the mature ovum is ejected from the follicle into the fallopian tube. This is called ovulation and occurs as the concentration of FSH is dropping and LH is increasing.

5 The anterior pituitary continues to secrete LH which acts to change the follicle into a yellow body known as the *corpus luteum*. LH inhibits the production of estrogen and stimulates the corpus luteum to secrete another hormone, *progesterone*, which maintains the uterine lining. Another hormone from the anterior pituitary, *luteotropic* (LTH), also stimulates the corpus luteum to produce progesterone as well as estrogens. During pregnancy LTH also causes the mammary glands to produce milk.

6 If fertilization does not occur, the corpus luteum degenerates, stops secreting progesterone, and the uterine lining is shed— a process known as *menstruation*. This phase of the cycle requires about four or five days.

7 If fertilization and implantation of the fertilized egg does occur, the corpus luteum continues to secrete progesterone which maintains the uterine lining, inhibits ovulation, and prevents the uterine muscles from contracting.

CYCLES AND REPRODUCTION

Most animal (and plant) reproduction occurs in a cyclic pattern—that is, it takes place during a definite breeding season each year. Moreover, a cycle of internal changes associated with the reproduction process occurs in each member of a species. Thus internal changes occur in organisms preparatory to the breeding period or season and these changes often can be correlated with changes in the external environment.

Our earth undergoes a variety of rhythmic changes that result from its relationship to other bodies in our solar system and its tilted rotational axis with respect to the sun. We therefore recognize the regular day-night cycles and the orderly progression through the seasons of a year, the yearly cycle. In addition, the moon revolves about the earth producing cyclic effects, often termed *lunar cycles*. As a result, rhythmic changes are observed in light, temperature, and the tides of the ocean. These physical cycles have definite and specific effects upon life's activities and metabolism such as feeding, behavior, and reproduction. The photoperiodic response of plants in reproduction was discussed in the last chapter and examples of rhythmic reproductive activity in animals will be presented here.

A type of periodicity related to the phases of the moon, lunar cycles, can be observed in the reproduction of several animals. The small grunion fish of the southern California coast swim onto the beaches during the high tides of the spring and summer months to lay their eggs in the sand (Figure 9–26). The females, which are five to eight inches long, bury their tails in the wet sand to deposit their eggs while male grunion lying nearby release sperms that fertilize the eggs. The fish then are carried back to sea by the next waves. The most intriguing aspect of this reproductive behavior is the grunion's unerring sense of the tidal cycle. The tides that bring the fish onto the beach are produced at the new moon and full moon. Since tides are influenced by the gravitational pull of the moon and sun, the higher water occurs during conjunction and opposition. Conjunction is when the moon is between the sun and the earth (new moon), whereas in opposition the earth is between the sun and the moon (full moon). In addition to sensing the exact time of the spring tides, the grunion must also deposit their eggs below the highest water. This will ensure that

Figure 9·26 Collecting grunion during a spawning run on a southern California beach. (Courtesy of Bill Beebe.)

the high water of the next tidal cycle will release the young from the sand and carry them back into the sea. Predictably, the grunion swim onto the sand on the nights following the peak of the spring tides.

Another case of animal reproduction related to lunar phases is that of the annelid Palolo worms of Samoa and the West Indies (Figure 9–27). These segmented worms live in burrows in the coral reefs and consist of two parts, an asexual anterior segment and a postanal, sexual portion. In the Samoan species the posterior sexual segments break away and swim to the surface during the early morning of the first and second days of the last quarter of the October-November moon. The sexual segments swim for several hours on the surface and finally burst, releasing gametes into the sea; by morning, the surface water is soupy with the gametes and the spent segments. The asexual segments remaining in the burrow produce new sexual segments. The Atlantic species on Bermuda, however, release their gametes in May and June. Thus

Figure 9·27 Palolo worm releasing gametes.

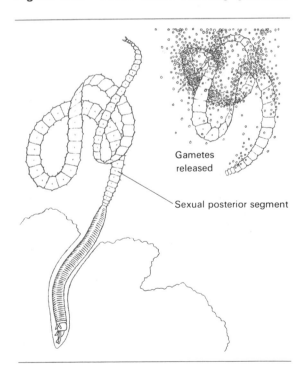

Gametes released

Sexual posterior segment

289

the monthly reproductive cycles of these two species are similar, yet the yearly time is different. Most investigators believe that the phase of the moon is simply one aspect of the reproductive regulatory mechanism; some correlations have also been found with regard to ocean turbidity and wave action.

Many birds and mammals breed either in the spring or the fall of the year. Deer and elk, for example, breed in the late fall while mating occurs in the varying hare in March or April. Charles Lyman of Harvard University has shown that the longer days of spring are responsible for estrus in the female hare and the development of the testes in the male. In certain breeds of sheep in the northern hemisphere, the shorter days of fall produce estrus in the females and increase sperm production in the males. In cases such as the hare and the sheep the length of day must act as a trigger mechanism to bring about internal changes which determine that reproduction will occur at a specific time each year. These internal timing devices, so important in the establishment of reproductive cycles, are known as *biological clocks*. Apparently these internal clocks "recognize" the duration of individual photoperiods which ultimately produce an accumulative effect—the breeding time.

Many activities and behavioral patterns other than reproduction occur in most organisms with a regular periodicity. Some of these rhythms, *circadian rhythms*, are on a 24-hour solar day cycle. The leaves of bean seedlings, for example, are elevated during the day and lowered at night. These "sleep movements" are characteristic of many plants. A person who ordinarily awakens at 7:00 A.M. each day on the West Coast flies to the East Coast and finds that he can quite easily sleep until 10:00 A.M. After several days on the East Coast his sleeping behavior will have adjusted to the change in time zones even though his internal clocks for other functions, such as the secretion of certain hormones, may not reset so easily. Since the normal sleeping habits persisted for several days in a new environment, it appears that the individual is not merely responding to the environment but has some internal timing mechanism. It has been demonstrated that bean seedlings will continue their normal day-night sleep movements even when kept under constant light and temperature. Moreover, sheep that are normally fall breeders in the northern hemisphere will continue to breed at the same time of the year when transported to the southern hemisphere even though it is spring. Biological clocks thus show a certain amount of stability which indicates that internal timing mechanisms have definitely been established within organisms. That internal clocks can be reset after some period of time also indicates the adaptability of these mechanisms since they assist organisms in adjusting to new environments. It seems then that the mechanisms which determine the time of periods in biological clocks are inherited and complex internal sequences of metabolic events that closely parallel environmental physical events.

Finally we might ask why are rhythmic and cyclic activities, especially in reproduction, important to organisms? Certainly when all members of a species are under the control of similar biological clocks and hence are capable of breeding at the same time, the probability of fertilization is greatly increased. For a particular species of plant, pollen and eggs would reach maturation at the same time. Animals such as worms or starfish living in the vast expanses of the ocean must produce their gametes at exactly the same time or the chance of fertilization is greatly reduced. For most vertebrates the cyclic events leading up to mating have a preparatory effect for the vital final event of fertilization. Courtship may even be a part of the reproductive cycles of some animals in which elaborate behavior may be used to attract a mate. Reproductive or breeding cycles therefore must be generally viewed as activities that ensure a greater probability of survival for organisms. The synchronization of internal mechanisms with rhythmic environmental phenomena such as light and temperature provides a common synchronization for all members of a particular species.

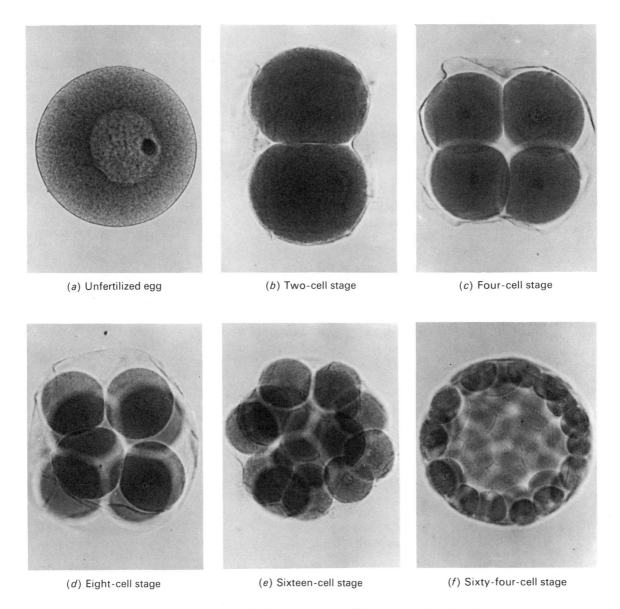

(a) Unfertilized egg   (b) Two-cell stage   (c) Four-cell stage

(d) Eight-cell stage   (e) Sixteen-cell stage   (f) Sixty-four-cell stage

Figure 9·28 Starfish development, early cleavage stages. (Courtesy of Carolina Biological Supply Co.)

ANIMAL DEVELOPMENT

The study of development, embryology, includes two major areas, *descriptive* and *experimental*. Descriptive studies deal with the visible changes that occur during the development of an organism. Experimental embryology, on the other hand, investigates the cellular mechanisms that cause or control these visible changes.

DESCRIPTIVE EMBRYOLOGY

We will first briefly outline the descriptive embryology of the starfish, frog, and human which represent three distinct patterns of

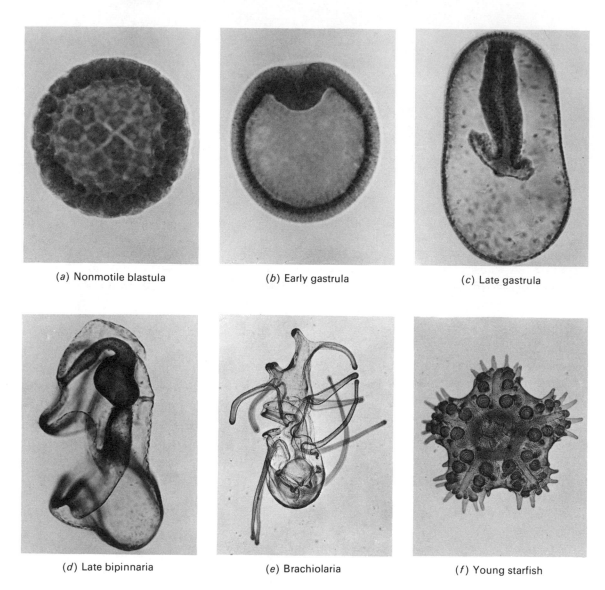

(*a*) Nonmotile blastula   (*b*) Early gastrula   (*c*) Late gastrula

(*d*) Late bipinnaria   (*e*) Brachiolaria   (*f*) Young starfish

Figure 9·29 Starfish development, blastula through young starfish. (Courtesy of Carolina Biological Supply Co.)

development. These will introduce most of the basic principles of embryological development.

The Starfish

A relatively uncomplicated example of the development of a fertilized egg into a multicellular organism is the starfish. The early cleavage of the starfish zygote is complete and equal—that is, the entire egg cleaves at each division. The first stage of development is characterized by a series of rapid mitotic divisions in which 2, 4, 8, 16, and 32 cells are produced (Figure 9–28). Soon a solid ball of cells, the *morula*, is formed. After many more divisions, this ball of ciliated cells develops a central cavity, the *blastocoel*, which is indicative of the "hollow ball" stage or *blastula* (Figure 9–29).

Shortly after this formation, an area of the blastula wall begins to push into the blastocoel, similar to the effect produced when one sticks his finger into a balloon or tennis ball. This invagination of cells is the beginning of the *gastrula* stage. The process of gastrulation produces a new cavity called the *archenteron* or primitive gut and leaves an opening in the wall, the *blastopore*. The old blastocoel is pushed ahead of this advancing invagination and gradually disappears. The two cellular layers produced by gastrulation are the *ectoderm* (outer layer) and *endoderm* (inner layer). A middle layer known as the *mesoderm* is next produced by a proliferation of cells from the ectoderm and endoderm. Animals showing this type of development are termed *triploblastic* and all tissues and organs of the adult animal will arise from these three primary germ layers. In general, the ectoderm gives rise to the epidermis and nervous system. Mesodermal structures include the skeleton, dermis of the skin, blood, muscles, connective tissues, and most of the excretory and reproductive systems. Endodermal derivatives constitute the lining of the digestive and respiratory tracts and the urinary bladder.

Following gastrulation, a primitive gut forms which has a mouth, stomach, and anus (the anus is formed in the region of the blastopore). At this point ciliated bands form on three pairs of lateral lobes and transform the embryo into a free-moving, feeding larva called a *bipinnaria*. Later, this bilateral bipinnaria larva develops long, ciliated lobes and is known as a *brachiolaria* larva. The brachiolaria finally develop into very small, radially symmetrical starfish (Figure 9–29).

The Frog

The frog is an *oviparous* animal which means that the fertilized egg develops outside of the body. Upon inspection of a fertilized frog egg, it can be observed that one-half is highly pigmented. This dark hemisphere is called the *animal pole* because the embryo will develop in this area. The white hemisphere, the *vegetal pole*, contains a heavy concentra-

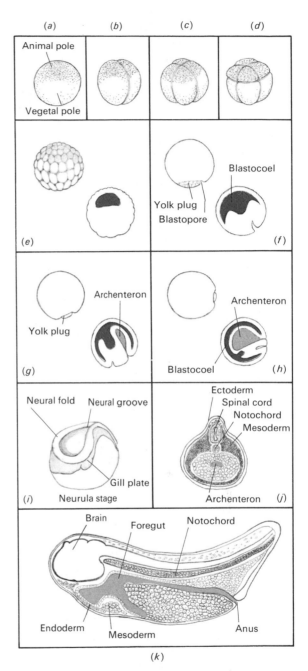

Figure 9·30 Early embryology of the frog. (*a*) Egg; (*b*) two-cell stage; (*c*) four-cell stage; (*d*) eight-cell stage; (*e*) blastula stage; (*f, g, h*) developing gastrula stages (cross sections are through the yolk plug); (*i*) neurula stage; (*j*) cross section of late neurula; (*k*) longitudinal section of early embryo.

tion of yolk nutrients. About one hour after fertilization the egg undergoes a mitotic cell division which constitutes the first cleavage. A second cleavage then occurs in the same plane at 90 degrees to the first (Figure 9–30). During subsequent cleavages the cells in the animal hemisphere divide more frequently than the yolk cells. It is important to note that this cleavage process has not increased the mass of the original egg.

The frog blastula is similar to that of the starfish except the blastocoel is relatively smaller and displaced toward the animal pole owing to the presence of the yolk and the unequal cleavage. The process of gastrulation, however, is different in the frog. At a point 180 degrees from the entrance of the sperm and the spot where the cells of the animal and vegetal portions merge, the cells of the animal pole turn inward and move into the blastocoel. In this process the animal cells actually overgrow the vegetal or yolk cells and turn inward forming a blastopore. The yolk cells fill the hole produced by gastrulation and form a yolk plug (Figure 9–30g). The position of the blastopore and its yolk plug marks the eventual orientation of the embryo since the blastopore is finally replaced by the anus and the head develops approximately 180 degrees from this spot.

Following gastrulation, the differentiation of primary germ layers into various organs begins and the first of these is the neural tube. The dorsal ectoderm sinks down to form a groove which closes at the top to form a single, hollow tube. The anterior portion of this tube will develop into the brain, and the remainder will form the spinal cord (Figure 9–30i). This stage of development is called the *neurula*.

In frogs and other chordates one of the most definitive structures that develops at this time is the mid-dorsal, elastic rod known as the *notochord* which is formed primarily of large, vacuolated mesodermal cells. In later development the notochord is replaced by the vertebrae of the spinal column. In the frog, the body cavity (the coelom) is formed by the splitting of two mesodermal sheets which have developed from the endodermal cells roofing the archenteron. One-half is attached to the external wall as a body lining and the other half surrounds the visceral organs (Figure 9–30j). By this time the embryo has elongated and a segmental series of paired mesodermal blocks, known as somites, have formed along the length of the organism. Three regions exist in each somite: an outer part that will form the dermis of the skin, an inner region from which the skeletal muscles will develop, and an upper part that will give rise to the vertebrae of the vertebral column. Internal organs and external gills develop next and, in ten to twelve days, depending on the particular kind of frog, the tadpole can be recognized. Limb buds and internal lungs develop, and the tail is reabsorbed so that in approximately ninety days after fertilization a young frog can be recognized.

Man

Fertilization and development is internal in mammals, and the female gives birth to well-developed young, a condition described as *viviparous*. In mammals, cleavage is complete and equal-sized cells are produced with each division because of the lack of large amounts of yolk material. The fertilized egg descends the fallopian tube and embeds in the highly vascularized uterine lining. During development a series of *extraembryonic* membranous sacs are formed of which the largest and outermost, the *chorion*, is directly attached to the uterine lining. Small fingerlike villi from the chorion interdigitate with the endometrium to form a *placenta*. The exchange of gases and the uptake of nutrients from the mother's blood takes place across these thin placental membranes. After about twelve weeks, when the human embryo reaches the *fetus* stage, a complete circulatory system and blood supply have developed. The placental attachment to the fetus, the *umbilical cord*, contains two arteries and a vein, and the fetus is enclosed by a fluid filled sac, the *amnion* (Figure 9–31).

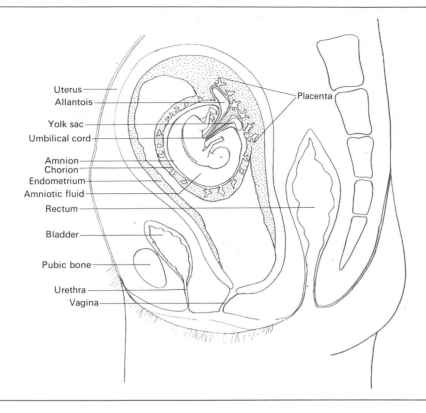

Labels on figure:
Uterus
Allantois
Yolk sac
Umbilical cord
Amnion
Chorion
Endometrium
Amniotic fluid
Rectum
Bladder
Pubic bone
Urethra
Vagina
Placenta

Figure 9·31   Diagram of the human uterus in pregnancy showing the extraembryonic membranes.

Two additional sacs, the *allantois* and the *yolk sac*, are greatly reduced in all mammals and form part of the umbilical cord.

In reptiles and birds, all of these extraembryonic sacs are essential since the young must develop inside a shelled egg. The highly vascularized chorion and allantois act as respiratory membranes and are pressed close to the egg shell. The allantois also serves as a depository for nitrogenous wastes, whereas the yolk sac contains the nutritive yolk material. Upon hatching, all the extraembryonic membranes dry up and are lost.

EXPERIMENTAL EMBRYOLOGY

Differentiation and Induction

One of the most fascinating and interesting areas of modern biology is the field of embry-ology that deals with the formation of different cell types in a developing organism. This process, in which unspecialized cells become specialized, is known as *differentiation* and represents a permanent change in cells during the course of development. Moreover, we can say that these changes result from an interaction with other cells or chemicals produced by cells or, sometimes, external influences.

Cell differentiation has been compared by C. H. Waddington of England, through the use of a "landscape" model, to a ball rolling down an inclined surface toward a series of valleys (Figure 9–32). As the ball rolls it commits itself to a particular region and, as it continues to roll, fewer opportunities are available. At certain stages there are alternative valleys but these become fewer and fewer until the ball ends up at the bottom of one valley. A

Figure 9·32 The "landscape model" proposed by Waddington which compares cellular differentiation to balls rolling down branched channels. Once a ball has entered a specific channel, it is committed to that line of differentiation. (Courtesy of Richard F. Trump.)

developing cell also becomes committed along its course of development and, just as the ball cannot roll back uphill, neither can the cell reverse its differentiation.

In 1891, Hans Driesch, a German embryologist, demonstrated that the cells resulting from the first and second cleavages in sea-urchin eggs could be separated and each would develop into a complete miniature embryo. It was learned, however, that complete development was impossible after the third cleavage. Evidently the cells had differentiated or lost their equal potential after two divisions. This gave rise to the idea that each cell in a developing embryo contained the information necessary to become a specific part of the organism and as development

proceeded, each cell became more and more specialized.

Later in the 1920s, Hans Spemann performed a very significant series of experiments with frog embryos. Working with the late gastrula stage, Spemann was able to reciprocally transplant a small piece of dorsal ectoderm (from the area of the presumptive neural tube) with a piece of potential belly ectoderm. The transplanted neural tube ectoderm differentiated into belly skin, and the graft from the belly region became part of the neural tube. Carrying his experiment one step further, Spemann transplanted a piece of the underlying notochord (beneath the neural tube) into the belly region. The result of this experiment was a double embryo attached

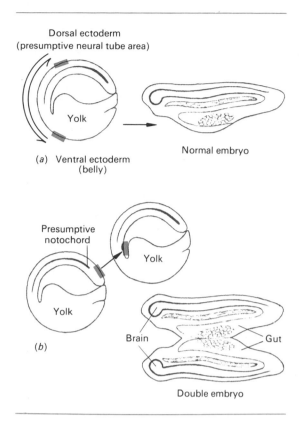

Dorsal ectoderm
(presumptive neural tube area)

Yolk

(a) Ventral ectoderm
(belly)

Normal embryo

Presumptive
notochord

Yolk

Yolk

(b)

Brain

Gut

Double embryo

Figure 9·33 A diagram of Spemann's germ-layer transplants which support the induction theory of embryonic differentiation. (*a*) Reciprocal transplant between dorsal ectoderm and ventral ectoderm at the gastrula stage results in a normal tadpole. (*b*) Transplant of section of notochord to the belly region results in a double embryo.

belly to belly (Figure 9–33). Obviously, something had been produced by the notochordal cells which altered the normal development of the embryonic tissues in the belly region. This information coupled with the fact that the ectodermal cells did not develop into self-determined structures gave support to the theory of *induction*, which implies that certain cells in an embryo can induce or control the development of other cells. In other words, the fate of a developing cell depends on the influence of neighboring cells or, simply, its position in the embryo. The exact molecular

mechanism of induction and the formation of "organizer areas" in the embryo is not completely understood, but many experiments have been performed in attempts to understand the process. Such experiments usually involve moving tissues from one region of an organism to another. In the formation of the vertebrate eye, for example, the optic vesicle that grows from the midbrain induces the ectoderm in the head region to form a lens. Other eye tissues are then formed and an eye results (Figure 9–34). If the optic vesicle is removed from a chicken embryo, a lens is not formed in the region of the ectoderm where it normally develops. Thus the optic vesicle can be considered an inducer for the development of a lens from the ectoderm.

THE ROLE OF THE NUCLEUS AND CHROMOSOMES

In 1963, a German cytologist named Hammerling performed a number of simple experiments with the green alga *Acetabularia* which is unique in several respects. It is composed of a base that contains the nucleus, a two-inch erect stalk, and a flaring umbrellalike cap

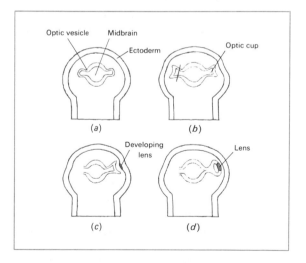

Figure 9·34 Diagrammatic sequence of events in the development of the lens of the eye from the ectoderm. If the optic vesicle is removed, as in (*b, c*), the lens does not form.

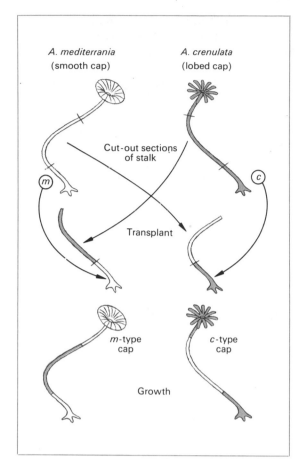

A. mediterrania
(smooth cap)

A. crenulata
(lobed cap)

Cut-out sections
of stalk

m

c

Transplant

m-type
cap

c-type
cap

Growth

Figure 9·35 A diagram showing the nuclear control of cap development in the unicellular alga *Acetabularia*.

(Figure 9–35). Hammerling noted that these algae possessed a high degree of regeneration, and if the cap was clipped off near the tip, a new cap was quickly reformed.

Closely related species of *Acetabularia* usually have characteristically different caps. By cutting a section of stalk out of two algae having different caps and transplanting them onto the opposite bases, Hammerling observed that the regenerated caps always resembled the nuclear type of the base to which it was transplanted. The cytoplasm, although essential to regeneration, appeared to be under the control of the new nucleus. Experiments with *Amoeba* and amphibians by other researchers have confirmed this theory of nuclear control.

We are already familiar with the controlling influence that nuclear DNA exerts in the cytoplasmic synthesis of cellular protein. It is likely, therefore, that the nucleus could produce specific enzymes at certain times during development which in turn could synthesize "organizer substances." Support for this hypothesis was given by Wolfgang Beermann in 1959 in a paper reporting the activities of giant chromosomes in differentiating cells of chironomid fly larvae (small flies related to the fruit fly, *Drosophila*). These chromosomes are over 10,000 times the size of regular chromosomes, because the DNA has duplicated many times without chromosome division (Figure 9–36). Beermann discovered that the giant chromosomes produce large puffs of thready DNA material which facilitates the synthesis of messenger RNA. Beermann and a coworker, Edstrom, were actually able to cut out several of these puffs and analyze the associated messenger RNA. Beermann studied the puffing patterns in several different embryonic cells and discovered that puffs form at certain locations and appear to parallel developmental changes in these cells. This evidence suggests that puffing is an expression of genetic action in the chromosome which could be directly related to protein synthesis and cellular differentiation.

Since the time of von Baer, the eminent German embryologist of the nineteenth century, much information has been accumulated which helps to explain many aspects of development. The use of new techniques in experimental situations has opened the door to understanding development as a directed physiochemical process. Certainly the genes on the chromosomes must control the developmental processes even though the exact mechanisms may not be understood at this time. In recent years, the correlation between DNA (the genes) and protein synthesis has been significant, and part of the next chapter deals with the function of the genes and how they control the development of an individual.

298

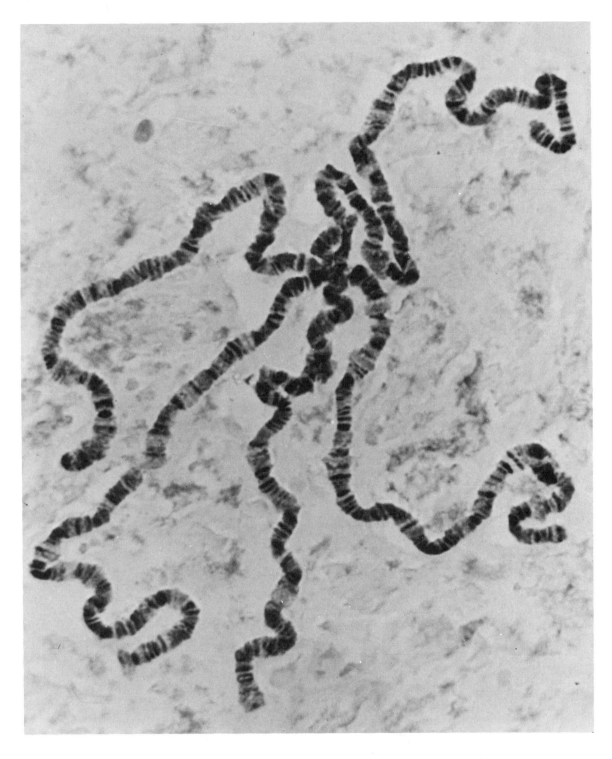

Figure 9·36 The giant chromosomes from the salivary gland of the fruit fly larva. The bands represent the sites of specific gene action. Magnified about X 1000. (Courtesy of Dr. B. P. Kaufmann.)

SUMMARIZING PRINCIPLES

Reproduction is essential to the success of all organisms. This includes, in addition to reproduction of the total organism, reproduction of molecules, cell parts, and cells. Moreover, multicellular organisms undergo a developmental process in which cells differentiate into specialized structures.

Mitosis is the process in which two daughter cells, identical to the parent cell, are produced. The orderly sequence of nuclear and cytoplasmic events are described in the following phases:

1 Interphase—chromosomes are extended and uncoiled; DNA is replicated.
2 Prophase—chromosomes shorten by coiling, centrioles move to the poles, asters form, nucleoli disappear, nuclear membrane breaks down.
3 Anaphase—chromosomes move to opposite poles; they appear to be pulled by spindle fibers.
4 Telophase—cell membrane constricts in animals, or cell wall develops in plants; daughter cells are formed; chromosomes and nucleus return to interphasic condition.

Meiosis, the process that reduces diploid cells to the haploid chromosome number, consists of two cell divisions with the chromosomes duplicated only once. The chromosomal events provide for the recombination of hereditary information between the maternal and paternal chromosomes; this occurs during prophase of meiosis I when the replicated homologous chromosomes synapse and undergo crossover. Meiotic production of gametes provides the basis for variation among sexually reproducing organisms and, consequently, successful adaptation.

Reproduction in protists includes the asexual processes of fragmentation, budding, fission, and spore production; sexuality involves the production and fusion of gametes. Examples of this sexuality are conjugation in *Paramecium* and *Spirogyra*.

In plants, reproduction involves life histories that include two separate phases, the gametophyte (haploid) and the sporophyte (diploid); generally one stage depends on the other for reproduction. In mosses, the gametophyte is the dominant phase (haplodiplontic pattern), whereas in ferns, the sporophyte is dominant (diplohaplontic). In seed plants, gymnosperms and angiosperms, the gametophyte is greatly reduced. A seed, which results from fertilization, consists of a dormant embryo, stored food, and a hardened coat. In addition to seeds, angiosperms produce fruit which are mature ovaries with enclosed seeds; fruits can be fleshy or dry.

Although some animals can reproduce asexually, most reproduce by sexual means. In mammals, sexual reproduction involves an estrus period of female sexual receptivity and egg production. In humans the cyclic production of eggs and preparation of the uterus is termed the menstrual cycle.

In many plants and animals reproductive cycles appear to be triggered by specific environmental conditions such as periods of light and dark, changes in temperature, seasons of the year, and phases of the moon. The reproductive success of a particular species depends on the synchronization of the production of gametes within the species.

Development is the complex series of stages from a fertilized egg to a multicellular organism in which certain cells differentiate into primary germ tissues (ectoderm, endoderm, mesoderm). These tissues give rise to the various organs and structures of the adult. The early developmental patterns among animals are strikingly similar—that is, from fertilized egg through gastrulation. The starfish, frog, and human represent three variations of development.

During development embryonic cells become more and more specialized until eventually they differentiate into specific tissues. In this process the course of development of these cells may be induced by neighboring cells.

The control of development is apparently under the direct influence of the chromosomes; they exert this control through the DNA-RNA-protein synthesis mechanism.

REVIEW QUESTIONS

1   What is the biological significance of synapsis and crossing over which occur in the first meiotic prophase?

2   The drug colchicine stops mitotic division at metaphase. What effect must the drug have on the mitotic spindle?

3   List at least one significant event involving each of the following structures at each stage of mitosis: (a) centrioles and spindle fibers, (b) chromosomes, (c) nuclear membrane.

4   Compare spermatogenesis with oögenesis. List the differences and similarities for each of the following stages: prophase I, anaphase I, telophase I, anaphase II, telophase II.

5   Many birth-control pills contain the hormone progesterone. How can progesterone prevent the formation of the ovum?

6   What does *Spirogyra* have in common with the gametophyte generation of mosses? How do the reproductive patterns differ?

7   Reptiles, birds, and mammals all possess four extraembryonic membranes—amnion, allantois, yolk sac, and chorion. Distinguish the functions of these membranes in each of these groups.

8   Consider the events of the menstrual cycle and correlate these with the general scheme of control presented in Chapter 8. Make specific references to feedback mechanisms.

9   There have been many examples of animals that have developed a third eye. From your knowledge of induction and differentiation, explain how this could occur.

10   Correlate the recent model of protein synthesis with the fact that giant salivary chromosomes of *Drosophila* show definite patterns of puffing at specific stages of development.

11   Many flowering plants may be propagated by either cuttings or seeds. What are the particular advantages of each method?

12   Explain why conjugation in *Paramecium* and *Spirogyra* is called a sexual process.

13 Compare the similarities and differences in the reproductive patterns of mosses and ferns.

14 List the advantages that seed-producing plants have over nonseed plants. Compare the seeds of angiosperms and gymnosperms.

15 It is possible to remove the nucleus from a frog egg and replace it with another nucleus. If an egg nucleus is replaced with a nucleus from a blastula cell, the egg will develop normally. If, however, an egg nucleus is replaced with a nucleus from a late gastrula cell, the egg will develop abnormally. Can you offer an explanation for these events?

SUPPLEMENTARY READINGS

Allen, R. D., "The Moment of Fertilization," *Scientific American*, July, 1959.

Balinski, B. I., *An Introduction to Embryology*, 2nd ed., Philadelphia, Saunders, 1965.

Barth, L. J., *Development*, Reading, Mass., Addison-Wesley, 1964.

Beermann, Wolfgang, and Ulrich Clever, "Chromosome Puffs," *Scientific American*, April, 1964.

Bell, Eugene, ed., *Molecular and Cellular Aspects of Development*, New York, Harper & Row, 1965.

Berrill, N. J., *Growth, Development, and Patterns*, San Francisco, Freeman, 1961.

Chase, H. B., *Sex: The Universal Fact*, New York, Dell, 1965.

Csapo, Arpad, "Progesterone," *Scientific American*, April, 1958.

Dreisch, Hans, "The Potency of the First Two Cleavage Cells in the Development of Echinoderms," in M. Gabriel and S. Fogel, eds., *Great Experiments in Biology*, Englewood Cliffs, N.J., Prentice-Hall, 1955.

Ebert, James D., "The First Heartbeats," *Scientific American*, March, 1959.

Etkin, William, "How a Tadpole Becomes a Frog," *Scientific American*, May, 1966.

Fischberg, M., and A. W. Blackler, "How Cells Specialize," *Scientific American*, September, 1961.

Gibor, Aharon, "Acetabularia: A Useful Giant Cell," *Scientific American*, November, 1966.

Gray, George W., "The Organizer," *Scientific American*, November, 1957.

Gurdon, J. B., "Transplanted Nuclei and Cell Differentiation," *Scientific American*, December, 1968.

Konigsberg, I. R., "The Embryological Origin of Muscle," *Scientific American*, August, 1964.

Mazia, Daniel, "How Cells Divide," *Scientific American*, September, 1961.

Moscona, A. A., "How Cells Associate," *Scientific American*, September, 1961.

Puck, T. T., "Single Human Cells in Vitro," *Scientific American*, August, 1957.

Spemann, H., *Embryonic Development and Induction*, New Haven, Conn., Yale University Press, 1938.

Spratt, Jr., Nelson, T., *Introduction to Cell Differentiation*, New York, Reinhold, 1964.

Waddington, C. H., "How Do Cells Differentiate?," *Scientific American*, September, 1953.

Wessels, Norman K., and William J. Rutter, "Phases in Cell Differentiation," *Scientific American*, March, 1969.

10

Similarity and Variation Through Heredity

Through the process of reproduction offspring are produced which, in multicellular organisms, follow a definite pattern of development. Although this developmental sequence of events is quite similar for closely related organisms, it is very specific for members of an individual species, and consequently all members of a given species resemble one another. Yet the offspring within a species, and even from the same parents, are always different. We can assume then that an information system which has a great amount of stability but which still permits some variation and change must be involved. We have already discussed DNA as the principal part of this information system; now the question of how the hereditary material is transmitted from generation to generation arises. Studies in peas, fruit flies, bacteria, and other organisms have revealed the existence of specific patterns in the distribution of hereditary characteristics, but just how is it that the hereditary substance (DNA) functions to produce these specific characteristics? We know that the fundamental unit of heredity is the *gene*, a small segment of a chromosome, and the study of the transmission and function of the hereditary material is known as *genetics*.

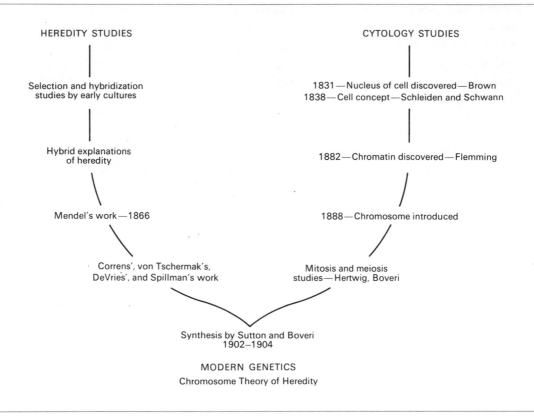

HEREDITY STUDIES

Selection and hybridization
studies by early cultures

Hybrid explanations
of heredity

Mendel's work—1866

Correns', von Tschermak's,
DeVries', and Spillman's work

CYTOLOGY STUDIES

1831—Nucleus of cell discovered—Brown
1838—Cell concept—Schleiden and Schwann

1882—Chromatin discovered—Flemming

1888—Chromosome introduced

Mitosis and meiosis
studies—Hertwig, Boveri

Synthesis by Sutton and Boveri
1902–1904

MODERN GENETICS
Chromosome Theory of Heredity

Figure 10·1   The general development of the fields of heredity and cytology and the beginning of modern genetics.

THE PHYSICAL BASIS OF HEREDITY

In the previous chapter the importance of chromosomes in cellular reproduction was pointed out and it was stressed that through sexuality chromosome complements could be changed and mixed. Fertilization provides for parts of two different chromosome groups to unite and form an individual with an entirely new chromosome makeup different from either parent. Meiosis is the key process here since it allows new combinations of chromosomes and genes through random assortment and crossing over. Chromosomal and gene changes can also contribute toward variation in offspring. The chromosome then is the structural unit asso-

ciated with reproduction, sexuality, heredity, and adaptation; it is the physical carrier of heredity. This relationship was only realized about the turn of the century following considerable experimentation. The question we should concern ourselves with is "How do we really know that heredity is carried in the chromosomes?"

Historical records indicate that early civilized cultures conducted breeding experiments to improve plants and animals. Man has continued these practices down through the ages as he attempts to obtain better domestic organisms. Although these were conscious efforts on the part of the breeders, they certainly did not understand the cellular mechanisms involved. The results obtained were often attributed to a process in which the characteristics of each parent blended together to produce observed effects in the offspring. In fact, many of the early explanations of heredity seem quite absurd and humorous to us today. For example, there were those who believed that all heredity was carried in either the sperm or the egg, and two schools of thought arose from this controversy—the spermists and the ovists. Others believed at one time that a camel and sparrow could cross and their characteristics would blend to produce an ostrich. Still others believed that heredity was carried by the blood. The *pangenesis* theory was a popular one held by some of the Greeks and later by Charles Darwin. This theory supposed that each structure in the body had tiny pangenes that moved into the gametes prior to fertilization. Thus each structure was represented by a pangene and if the structure changed, so would the pangene. This was obviously a mechanism that could explain the inheritance of acquired characteristics, another misconception of heredity. The theory of the inheritance of acquired characteristics is explained in chapter 11.

Some experimental studies were attempted but usually these were too ambitious since they involved many factors in one experiment or accurate reports were not kept. The first notable experiments in inheritance were conducted by Gregor Mendel and reported in 1866. Later, in the 1890s, Correns of Germany, DeVries of Holland, von Tschermak of Austria, and Spillman of the United States, working on several different organisms, obtained results similar to Mendel's. These studies presented a logical explanation of how traits might be passed from generation to generation and stimulated intense interest in genetics. Some of the most important cellular studies, as far as genetics was concerned, came

about in the 1880s and 1890s. Chromosomes were discovered and the details of mitosis and meiosis were worked out by some of the great German cytologists. So, at the same time as explanations were being sought for breeding and heredity experiments, cytological studies were advancing to the stage where they could supply some of the answers.

Perhaps it was only natural that sooner or later several investigators would see relationships between these two fields. At any rate, about 1902, Sutton from the United States and Boveri from Germany, in two notable works, stated the relationship between the fields of heredity and cytology. In effect they pointed out that the results of the inheritance experiments of Mendel and others could be explained by the behavior of the chromosomes in cells. The new field of modern genetics was thus born from this splendid synthesis and the "chromosome theory of heredity" was proposed (Figure 10–1).

At first this theory was not accepted by all biologists and many sought more definite proof. This involved associating a specific trait with the visible chromosome makeup in

Figure 10·2 T. H. Morgan (1866–1945), an outstanding American geneticist. (Courtesy of National Library of Medicine.)

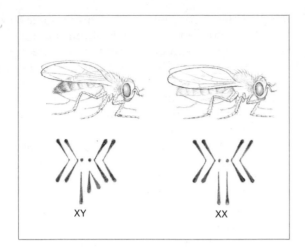

Figure 10·3 Male and female fruit flies (*Drosophila*) and their chromosomes. The male sex chromosomes are labeled *XY* and the female, *XX*.

the cells. Or, to state it another way, a definite chromosome change must be demonstrated for a physical change in an individual. This was made possible in the early 1900s by improved microscopy and a newly discovered experimental organism, the fruit fly (*Drosophila*). T. H. Morgan, an American geneticist (Figure 10–2), realized the possibilities for genetic studies that this small fly afforded. Populations can be kept in small bottles on a nutrient medium and a new generation can be produced in approximately ten days. The fruit fly has four pairs of chromosomes (Figure 10–3) and these can be readily studied under the microscope. Furthermore, considerable body variation exists which allows for various genetic crosses. The crucial evidence for the chromosome theory of heredity was provided by studies on *Drosophila* about 1914—this will be discussed later in this chapter after the basic laws of heredity have been presented. For now it will be sufficient to say that it is possible to correlate a specific trait with a change in chromosome composition not only in the fruit fly but also in other organisms, including man.

Included in the chromosome theory of heredity is the concept that each chromosome is composed of many genes. Each gene is now believed to determine or influence several traits and, furthermore, most traits are probably influenced by many genes. As you recall from the previous chapter, chromosomes occur in pairs in most organisms. Genes therefore must also occur in pairs and a specific trait may be affected by a specific pair of genes. It has been possible in *Drosophila*, where giant chromosomes occur in the larvae, to correlate a specific characteristic with a specific band or region on a chromosome. If we assume that these bands are genes, or groups of genes, then we can state that a specific characteristic is produced by these genes. To understand our explanation of how heredity is transmitted from one generation to the next, note that genes are distributed in the same pattern as chromosomes during meiosis.

TRANSMISSION GENETICS I

One aspect of genetics is the transmission of the physical material of heredity from generation to generation. This area of genetics, often called *transmission genetics*, seeks to explain how the chromosomes accomplish this process. These details must be understood before we can study the function of the genetic material. Any discussion of the principles of genetic transmission must begin with the work of the Austrian monk, Gregor Mendel (Figure 10–4).

MENDELIAN PRINCIPLES

Mendel, whose experiments extended over an eight-year period and were published in 1866, selected the garden pea as his experimental subject. This was a fortunate selection because this organism has many simple characteristics which are produced primarily by single pairs of genes. Also, owing to the structure of the pea flower, self-fertilization usually occurs and this process had produced many pure breeding plants. Pollen from another plant can be introduced, however, by an experimenter to

Figure 10·4 Gregor Mendel (1822–1884). (Courtesy of American Museum of Natural History.)

produce cross-fertilization. Mendel realized that simple experiments that contrasted only one of several characteristics at a time were necessary if the principles of inheritance were to be understood; he also realized the importance of keeping accurate records. Mendel selected seven pairs of contrasting characteristics on which he experimented, and his original paper, which is still available, is quite easy to understand. Two characteristics that Mendel observed in the pea were the shape of the seeds—they were either round or wrinkled —and the color of the embryonic leaf of the seed (the cotyledon), which was either yellow or green.

MONOHYBRID CROSS

Mendel noted that when pea plants that produced round seeds were self-pollinated, only round seeds resulted from the cross, and

that plants producing wrinkled seeds always bred true for wrinkled seeds. When a variety producing round seeds was crossed with a variety producing wrinkled seeds, all of the seeds were round. When the plants resulting from this cross were self-pollinated (constituting a self-cross), however, some of the plants produced round seeds while others produced wrinkled seeds. The wrinkled character therefore was not lost in the original cross and the ratio was approximately three round to one wrinkled. In this particular experiment, out of 7324 seeds obtained from 253 self-pollinated plants, 5474 were round and 1850 were wrinkled (Figure 10–5).

In considering Mendel's explanation of this experiment you should remember that Mendel was not aware of the process of meiosis. Since you studied meiosis in Chapter 9, you can see how closely his explanation of the events of this cross follows the details of meiosis. Mendel explained this cross as follows and the explanation is summarized in Figure 10–6. Each parent plant has two "units" for a given character. When gametes are produced, each gamete gets one unit and, therefore, individuals produced from a round-seed plant and a wrinkled-seed plant would contain one unit of each character. Two kinds of gametes can be formed from these parents and, when these plants are crossed, four fertilization combinations are possible. Approximately three-fourths of the resulting offspring would have received at least one unit for round seed (three-fourths also would have received at least a unit for wrinkled seed). Since approximately three-fourths of the offspring were round, we say that round seed is a *dominant* character and wrinkled seed is a *recessive* character. The similarity between Mendel's "units" and "genes," which were mentioned earlier, is quite obvious. In fact, if we were to place chromosomes in the scheme in Figure 10–6 and show the units or genes on the chromosomes, the illustration would then represent our modern explanation of the inheritance of this trait. Mendel pointed out that the units carrying these traits do segregate

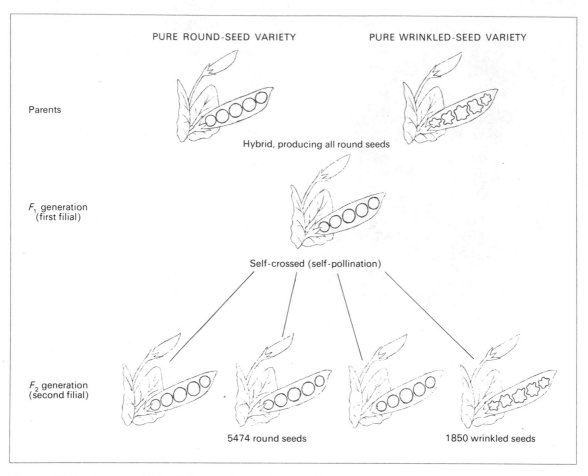

Parents

Hybrid, producing all round seeds

F_1 generation
(first filial)

Self-crossed (self-pollination)

F_2 generation
(second filial)

5474 round seeds   1850 wrinkled seeds

Figure 10·5 Results of Mendel's experimental cross of round-seed pea plants with wrinkled-seed pea plants. The exact ratio obtained here was 2.96 : 1.

as discrete factors at meiosis. This is known as *Mendel's Law of Segregation.*

It is important to remember here that each chromosome in a cell has a homologue. Since the genes are located on the chromosomes, there are two genes for each trait. We call these genes *alleles* and we define alleles as alternative or contrasting forms of genes which affect the same trait (*R* and *r*) and are located at the same position on homologous chromosomes. Alleles always line up beside each other at synapsis of meiosis. Individuals of the pure round-seed variety have the *RR* makeup and, since both

genes are the same, the term *homozygous* (meaning "same in the zygote") is used to describe the gene constitution with regard to round-wrinkled seed condition. Each gamete, however, carries only one-half of the chromosome complement, in this case *R*. When one of these gametes unites with a gamete from a pure wrinkled variety (carrying the allele *r*) in fertilization, a *hybrid, Rr,* is formed and we say that this hybrid is *heterozygous* (meaning "different in the zygote") with respect to the round-wrinkled seed condition. It appears round, however, due to the presence of the

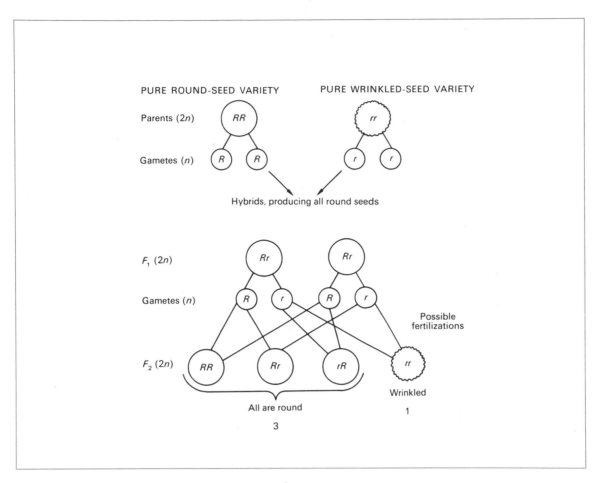

PURE ROUND-SEED VARIETY   PURE WRINKLED-SEED VARIETY

Parents (2n)   RR   rr

Gametes (n)   R   R   r   r

Hybrids, producing all round seeds

F_1 (2n)   Rr   Rr

Gametes (n)   R   r   R   r

Possible
fertilizations

F_2 (2n)   RR   Rr   rR   rr

Wrinkled
All are round   1
3

Figure 10·6 Mendel's explanation of the cross of round-seed pea plants with wrinkled-seed pea plants. R = a unit (gene) for round seed; r = a unit (gene) for wrinkled seed. This would explain the approximate 3:1 ratio that was obtained.

dominant gene R. The appearance of the individual is often referred to as the *phenotype* and the genetic makeup as the *genotype*. Thus the genotypes RR and Rr have the same phenotype, round seed. Although an Rr individual is round, the wrinkled gene r has not changed and it will probably show up in the next generation if two hybrids are crossed. In fact, you may have noted already that it has a 1 to 4 or 25 percent chance of showing up when two hybrids are crossed.

When the heterozygous or hybrid individual, Rr, undergoes meiosis, two kinds of gametes may be produced: R or r. If two hybrids are crossed, then we have the following possibilities for fertilization combinations which correspond to the F_2 zygotes in Figure 10–6:

♀ gametes	♂ gametes	
	R	r
R	RR	Rr
r	rR	rr

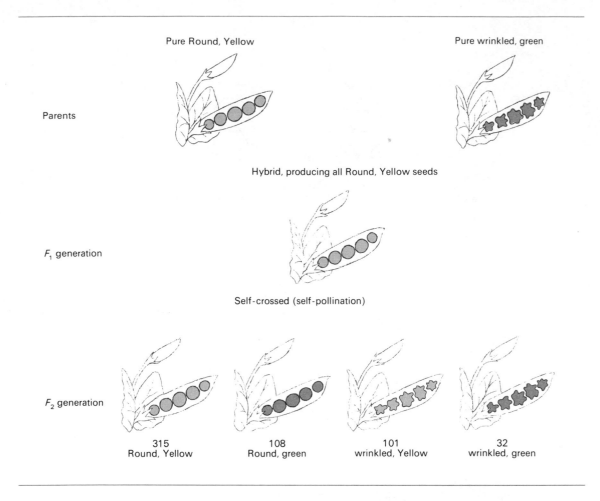

Parents   Pure Round, Yellow   Pure wrinkled, green

Hybrid, producing all Round, Yellow seeds

F_1 generation

Self-crossed (self-pollination)

F_2 generation

| 315 | 108 | 101 | 32 |
| Round, Yellow | Round, green | wrinkled, Yellow | wrinkled, green |

Figure 10·7   One of Mendel's experimental crosses involving two characteristics.

Note that the phenotype ratio (actual appearance) would be three round to one wrinkled, whereas the genotype ratio would be one *RR* to two *Rr* to one *rr*.

DIHYBRID CROSS

Mendel also made crosses involving two traits carried on separate chromosomes. One such cross was round-seed, yellow-seed coat plants with wrinkled-seed, green-seed coat plants (hereafter referred to as round, yellow seeds and wrinkled, green seeds). The results of this cross are shown in Figure 10–7 and the explanation for the results is given in Figure 10–8. The phenotype ratio resulting from this cross is:

<table>
<tr><td>9</td><td>:</td><td>3</td><td>:</td></tr>
<tr><td>round, yellow</td><td></td><td>round, green</td><td></td></tr>
<tr><td>3</td><td>:</td><td>1</td><td></td></tr>
<tr><td>wrinkled, yellow</td><td></td><td>wrinkled, green</td><td></td></tr>
</table>

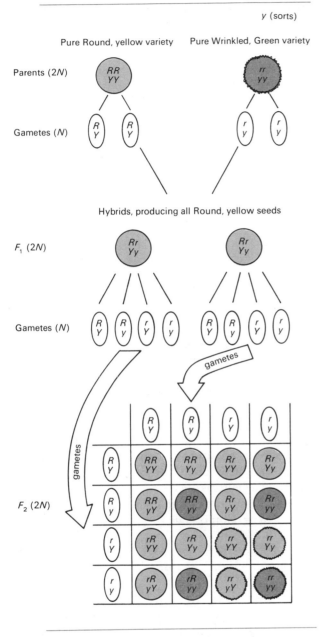

Figure 10·8 The explanation of Mendel's dihybrid cross.

Thus both dominant characteristics are present in $\frac{9}{16}$ of the offspring, one dominant trait in $\frac{3}{16}$, the other dominant trait in $\frac{3}{16}$, and both recessive traits appear in only $\frac{1}{16}$ of the offspring.

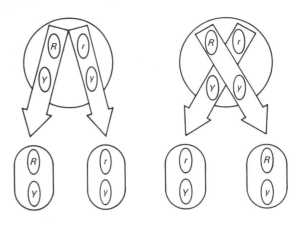

Figure 10·9 Independent assortment of two pairs of chromosomes at meiosis to produce four classes of gametes.

It should be stressed that the members of one pair of genes segregated independently of the other pair since they were on separate chromosomes. This is often known as *Mendel's Law of Independent Assortment.* Also note that when we are dealing with two pairs of genes on separate chromosomes, four kinds of gametes are possible. A review of the principles of meiosis at this point would show why this is true. Furthermore members of a pair of homologous chromosomes normally never go to the same gamete (an unusual exception will be given later). It should also be noted that whether the chromosome carrying R or the chromosome carrying r will segregate with the chromosome carrying Y or with the chromosome y is purely a matter of chance (Figure 10–9). If a large number of gametes is produced we would expect a 1:1:1:1 ratio of RY, Ry, rY, ry gametes.

At fertilization it is a matter of chance whether a male gamete carrying the RY constitution will unite with a female gamete carrying RY, Ry, rY, or ry. It is also chance that determines if one of the other three male gametes will unite with an RY or Ry or rY or ry gamete. When all the fertilization possibilities are considered, we note that a $\frac{9}{16}$ chance or probability exists for getting a round, yellow offspring from this cross. A probability of $\frac{3}{16}$ prevails for a round, green offspring; $\frac{3}{16}$ for a wrinkled, yellow, and $\frac{1}{16}$ for a wrinkled, green. It is possible therefore in certain genetic crosses to state a specific, theoretical probability for obtaining a particular phenotype.

PROBABILITY

The role of chance has been stressed in the independent assortment of chromosomes in producing different classes of gametes and in the union of gametes in fertilization. Since these events are a matter of chance, they are based on the laws of *probability*. In fact, many natural phenomena of chance occurrence (such as electron positions and even the weather) are often stated in terms of probability. Good examples of probability can also be found in dice, cards, and other games of chance from which the laws of probability were first derived many years ago.

Mathematical probability can be defined as the chance of the occurrence of any particular form of an event, stated as the ratio of the number of ways that form might occur to the total number of ways the event might occur in any form. Thus the probability of X event occurring is:

$$P(X) = \frac{f}{n}$$

where f equals the *number* of events in which X is found and n equals the total number of events that can occur.

Returning to Mendel's cross between round-seed and wrinkled-seed plants we note that the offspring would all be round-seeded but would be heterozygous (Rr). When crossing these F_1 hybrids (or allowing them to self-cross) we might inquire about the probability of obtaining a round-seeded offspring. Recalling the cross (Figure 10–6) we remember

that the gametes could have united at fertilization as follows:

	♂ gametes	
♀ gametes	R	r
R	RR	Rr
r	Rr	rr

The probability of a round-seeded offspring could then be computed as:

$$P \text{ (round seed)} = \frac{f}{n} = \frac{3}{4} = 75\%$$

where f = the number of events that will produce round seeds = RR, Rr, Rr

n = the total number of events that can occur = RR, Rr, Rr, rr

Albinism (a condition in which the hair and skin lack pigment) is produced in man by a recessive gene and, if two normal parents have an albino child, we could outline the series of events as:

where A = normal pigmentation gene

a = albino gene

Since the parents desire another child, they are concerned about the pigmentation of future offspring. Someone with a knowledge of genetics and probability could compute

314

for them the probability of having an albino child.

$$P \text{ (albino child)} = \frac{f}{n} = \frac{1}{4} = 25\%$$

It should be noted that *all* of the probabilities for any event should always add up to *one*. That is, the probability for having a normal child from these parents is:

$$P \text{ (normal pigmented child)} = \frac{f}{n} = \frac{3}{4} = 75\%$$

Seventy-five percent and 25 percent equal 1.

The parents may also wish to know the probability of having two albino children in a row. This could be calculated for them by applying another principle of probability, the principle governing two events occurring jointly or one directly after the other. This principle states: *the probability of two independent events occurring jointly is the product of the individual probabilities.* Therefore the probability of having two albino children in a row would be:

$$P \text{ (2 albino children)} =$$

$$\frac{f}{n} \times \frac{f}{n} = \frac{1}{4} \times \frac{1}{4} = \frac{1}{16}$$

Again, if we consider all of the possible combinations that might occur if this family had two children, these must add up to one.

P (albino and normal) $= \frac{1}{4} \times \frac{3}{4} = 3/16$

P (normal and albino) $= \frac{3}{4} \times \frac{1}{4} = 3/16$

P (normal and normal) $= \frac{3}{4} \times \frac{3}{4} = 9/16$

P (albino and albino) $= \frac{1}{4} \times \frac{1}{4} = \dfrac{1/16}{16/16} = 1$

It should be stressed that the probability of an albino child born to these parents is still $\frac{1}{4}$ for each occurrence. When we consider more than one birth in the family, however, the probability of the two similar events occurring in a row reduces the chance to $\frac{1}{16}$. This is like attempting to roll two 7s in a row in a game of dice and since there are six ways of making a seven with dice, the chance on a single roll is $\frac{6}{36}$ or $\frac{1}{6}$. The chance of rolling two 7s in a row, however, is $\frac{1}{6} \times \frac{1}{6}$ or only $\frac{1}{36}$.

The principles of probability are certainly of importance to plant and animal breeders. Whether or not to conduct a particular breeding program may be decided on the basis of the probability of obtaining the desired offspring.

TEST CROSS

In the cross between round (R) and wrinkled (r) seeds, you probably noted that the genotypes RR and Rr produced the same phenotype. In breeding experiments it is often important to know the exact genotype for a particular trait—that is, whether an individual is homozygous or heterozygous for the trait. This can be accomplished by a *test cross* (sometimes called a *back cross*), in which the organism under question is crossed with a pure recessive since the genotype of the pure recessive is known. The unknown genotype can then be determined by examining the resulting ratios. When RR is crossed with rr, all the offspring will show the dominant characteristic, that is, all offspring will be Rr. In a cross between Rr and rr, however, one-half of the progeny should show the recessive trait, rr (Figure 10–10). Therefore, if all offspring are round, the plant being tested is RR; if half the offspring are round and half wrinkled, the plant is Rr.

INCOMPLETE DOMINANCE

Up to this point we have considered only genes that are dominant or recessive; this has been done to explain the fundamental laws of heredity. It is extremely important, however, to realize that many pairs of genes (alleles)

This pea plant produces round seeds.
Is it homozygous (*RR*) or heterozygous (*Rr*)?

rr tester plant (wrinkled seeds) *RR* or *Rr*

Produces
only *r* gametes

Produces
only *R* gametes

Produces
R and *r* gametes

1st
possibility *rR* all offspring round

2nd
possibility *rR* *rr*

1/2 offspring Round 1/2 offspring wrinkled

Figure 10·10 The process of making a test cross and examining the results.

WHITE FLOWER RED FLOWER

Parents

Gametes

F₁ PINK FLOWER

Gametes

F₂

Red flower pink flower pink flower white flower
1 : 2 : 1

Figure 10·11 Inheritance of flower color in the four-o'clock family. This illustrates the principle of incomplete dominance of genes.

the result is a ratio of one red, two pink, and one white (1:2:1) (Figure 10–11). We will return to this principle of nondominance of genes to explain the inheritance of characteristics such as intelligence in man.

INTERACTION OF GENES

In some cases a pair of genes may be incapable of producing their effect because of the influence of another pair of genes. When a gene at one position on a chromosome suppresses the action of a gene at another position, it is called *epistasis* (meaning "standing above"). The example of coat color in mice illustrates this principle. The gray color (agouti) in mice is due to a dominant gene (*B*). The homozygous recessive condition (*bb*) produces a black coat. Another gene (*A*) is necessary, however, for any pigment to be produced, and in the homozygous recessive condition (*aa*) no pigment is present and an albino results. This is true regardless of whether the mouse

exist in which dominance does not occur. In these situations, since neither gene is dominant, an intermediate effect is produced in the hybrid. It should be understood that this effect is not produced by a "blending of the genes," since further crosses of these intermediate hybrids will produce offspring showing the original parental types. This principle of inheritance has been demonstrated by several classic experiments on flower color in a plant family commonly called the "four-o'clock" family. In one experiment a white flowering plant crossed with a red flowering plant will produce all plants with pink flowers. When two pink-flowered plants are crossed,

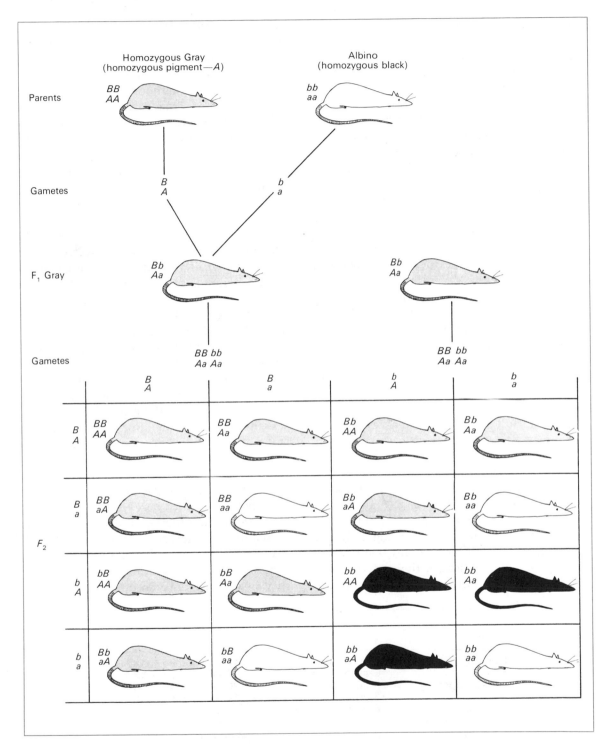

Figure 10·12   Gene interaction, epistasis, in mice coat color. The ratio 9 gray : 3 black : 4 albino is produced.

is *BB* or *Bb* or *bb*. Since two genes are involved here we might expect a typical dihybrid ratio from a cross of two F_1 hybrids. Because of the epistatic action of one gene pair on another, however, a modified ratio of 9:3:4 results (Figure 10–12).

A good example of epistasis in man is the Albino condition in a Negro where, even though dark pigmentation genes are present, they cannot function due to the lack of a dominant gene that permits their expression.

TRANSMISSION GENETICS II

In most organisms the members of one pair of chromosomes are different in the male than in the female. In the fruit fly, for example, the two homologous chromosomes labeled *X* are similar in the female, but the corresponding chromosomes in the male show only one *X* and a shorter homologue labeled *Y* (Figure 10–3). These chromosomes are called the *sex chromosomes*, whereas the other chromosomes in the cells are referred to as the *autosomes*. So far the traits we have been discussing in this chapter have been carried by genes on the autosomes. Genes on certain parts of the sex chromosomes may exhibit a different pattern of inheritance than those on the autosomes. This is true since all regions of the *X* and *Y* chromosomes are not homologous and an individual receiving only one *X* chromosome will receive only one allele of some genes. This changes the pattern of inheritance and we will see how in a few pages.

SEX DETERMINATION

The many differences between the sexes in all organisms are ultimately due to chromosomal differences although, in some species, there is no visible difference in the chromosome makeup of the two sexes. In others, however, such as the fruit fly, the chromosome difference between the sexes is quite apparent. In the early 1900s it was noted that in many species of insects the female had one more chromosome than the male, and for a while some people thought that this was the universal difference between sexes. Soon, however, the smaller *Y* chromosome was detected in the cells of the fruit fly and in many other organisms, including man. At first it was believed that the *X* chromosome carried genes for determining femaleness and the *Y* carried genes for maleness. This generalization was found to be untrue, and in many organisms, such as the fruit fly, the *Y* chromosome has very little to do with sex determination. From experiments on the fruit fly it is apparent that sex is determined by the ratio of autosomes to sex chromosomes, and this seems to be the situation generally in most organisms. In humans and presumably all mammals, however, the *Y* chromosome is necessary to produce the male characteristics.

It should be added here that the correlation between visible differences in organisms and chromosomal differences would certainly suggest proof for the "chromosome theory of heredity." If all individuals of a particular species with 22 chromosomes were females

Organism	Male	Female
Human	44 autosomes + *XY*	44 autosomes + *XX*
Fruit fly	6 autosomes + *XY*	6 autosomes + *XX*
Grasshopper	20 autosomes + *X*	20 autosomes + *XX*
Fowl	16 autosomes + *ZZ*	16 autosomes + *ZW*
Honeybee	16 chromosomes (*N*)	32 chromosomes (2*N*)

Figure 10·13 Different mechanisms of sex determination. Note that in fowl the sex chromosomes are different in the female and are designated *ZW* to avoid confusion with the *XY* type.

318

and all individuals with 21 chromosomes were males, the differences in sex would appear to be due to the chromosome composition. Various means of sex determination have evolved among the organisms and Figure 10–13 lists some of these mechanisms.

SEX-LINKED HEREDITY

In the late 1700s two examples of what we now know to be sex-linked heredity in humans were recorded—red-green color blindness and *hemophilia* (a disorder in which the blood-clotting mechanism functions improperly). In each case the trait is produced by a recessive gene carried on the X chromosome. Since females have two X chromosomes and males have only one, we would expect these traits to occur more often in males because it requires only one recessive gene to produce the disorder (Figure 10–14). Because both of these traits show the same inheritance pattern, only color blindness will be outlined (Figure 10–15). This pattern is often referred to as "crisscross" inheritance since an affected father can pass the gene to his daughter and the daughter can then transmit it to her sons.

Experiments with *Drosophila* have provided many explanations about the mechanisms of genetic transfer and we can turn to this organism again for another example of sex-linked heredity. The case of red–white eye color is diagrammed in Figure 10–16. You should note that red-eyed daughters of the F_1 generation were produced by a red-eyed father and, in the F_2 generation, the red-eyed females transmit the trait to one-half of their sons.

NONDISJUNCTION

The pattern of inheritance for red–white eye color in the fruit fly had been worked out early in the 1900s by T. H. Morgan and his students. However, one of his students, Calvin Bridges, noted some exceptions to the F_1 pattern (Figure 10–16). On very rare occasions white-eyed females and red-eyed males were produced from a cross between a white-eyed

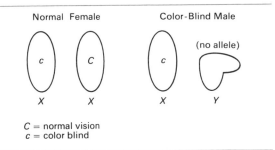

C = normal vision
c = color blind

Figure 10·14 Red-green color blindness as carried by the sex chromosomes. The female has the gene for color blindness but she has another X chromosome with the dominant normal gene. The male has the gene for color blindness but does not have another X chromosome on which a normal dominant could be present.

female and a red-eyed male. In order to explain this, Bridges postulated a phenomenon known as *nondisjunction* of chromosomes. Normally, homologous chromosomes will separate at meiosis with one member of each pair going to a gamete as illustrated below.

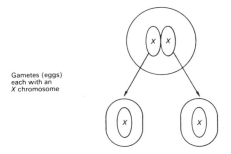

Gametes (eggs) each with an X chromosome

If the chromosomes failed to separate (nondisjunction), then the gametes may appear as below:

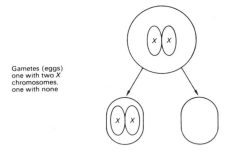

Gametes (eggs) one with two X chromosomes, one with none

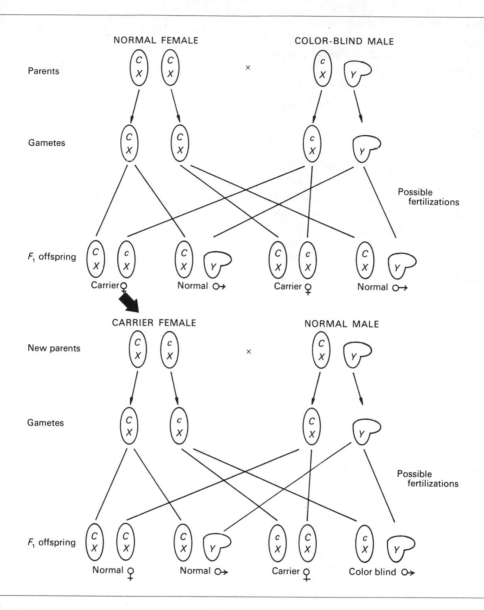

Figure 10·15 Sex-linked heredity in humans; the inheritance of red-green color blindness. Note how the daughter of a color-blind man can be a carrier. It can also be seen how she could pass this to her sons. Color blindness in females, though not impossible, is less likely to occur since both recessives are required.

A cross between a white-eyed female in which nondisjunction occurred and a red-eyed male is shown in Figure 10–17. Bridges was able to look at cells of the offspring from this cross under the microscope and verify the chromosome compositions he had predicted in these offspring. This was the proof that was needed for the chromosome theory of heredity.

Recently the occurrence of nondisjunction in the chromosomes of humans has also been

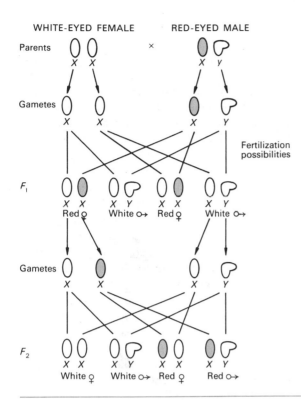

Figure 10·16 Sex-linked heredity in *Drosophila*: the inheritance of red-white eye color. Shaded *X* chromosomes indicate the presence of the gene for red eye; clear *X* chromosomes, the gene for white eye.

observed and several developmental anomalies such as *Turner's Syndrome* and *Klinefelter's Syndrome* have been traced to nondisjunction of the *X* chromosomes. Turner's Syndrome results from the union of an *O* egg with an *X*-carrying sperm to form *XO*. This individual is a sterile female and possesses many male characteristics such as heavy neck muscles and narrow hips. In the Klinefelter Syndrome, the nondisjunct *XX* unites with a *Y*-carrying sperm to produce a fundamentally male individual due to the presence of the *Y* chromosome. The male, however, possesses many female characteristics and, as in Turner's Syndrome, the sex organs do not reach maturity. Another anomaly, the mongoloid

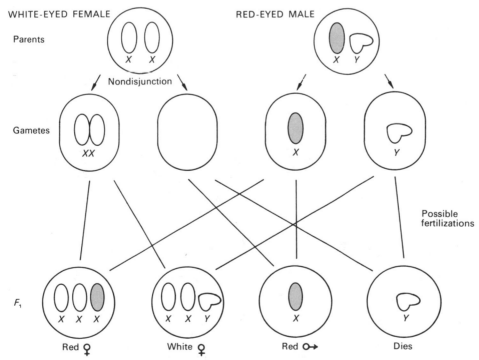

Figure 10·17 Bridges' explanation of the rare results obtained in this cross; nondisjunction.

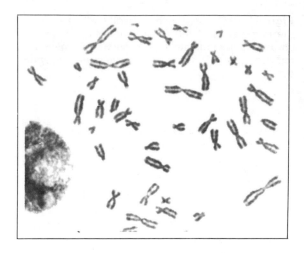

Figure 10·18 Human chromosomes. Normal male cell in metaphase. (Courtesy of Dr. J. I. Bryant.)

LINKAGE AND CROSSING OVER

It is believed that each species has thousands of genes controlling the numerous chemical processes and structures necessary for life. Thousands of chromosomes, however, are not found in most species and it follows then that each chromosome must contain many genes. We can further state that the genes on a particular chromosome are linked together in a group. For example, all of the known genes in the fruit fly fall into four *linkage groups*, a fact that Morgan and his students recognized early in their studies. If Mendel had chosen traits other than the seven he experimented with, perhaps he would have noted this principle in peas. Figure 10–20 illustrates the number 2 chromosome of the fruit fly showing the locations of some of the genes. The numbers on the left side of the diagram refer to the relative distances between genes. This type of diagram is called a *chromosome map* and fairly complete maps have now been made for all

or *Down's Syndrome,* is apparently produced by the presence of an extra chromosome (number 21) in the cells of mongoloid individuals (Figures 10–18 and 10–19).

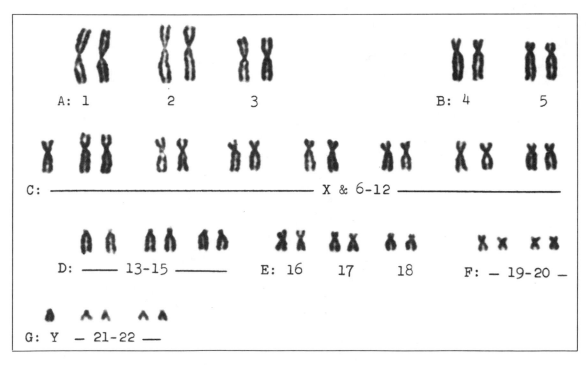

Figure 10·19 (*a*) Chromosomes from a normal human male. (Courtesy of Dr. J. I. Bryant)

322

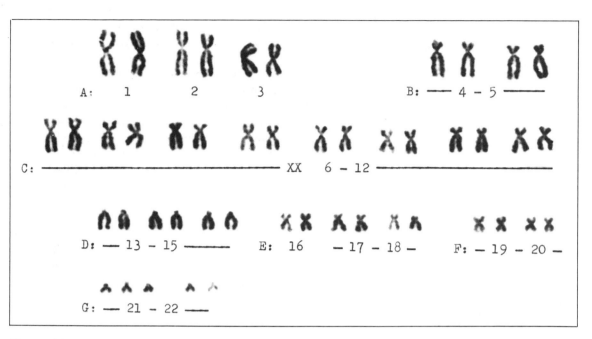

Figure 10·19 (b) Chromosomes from a female with Down's syndrome. Note the presence of an extra number 21 chromosome. (Courtesy of Dr. J. I. Bryant.)

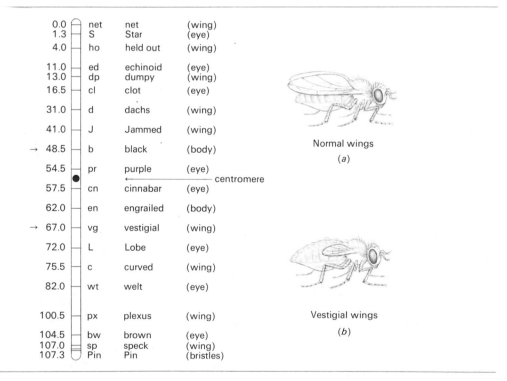

0.0	net	net	(wing)
1.3	S	Star	(eye)
4.0	ho	held out	(wing)
11.0	ed	echinoid	(eye)
13.0	dp	dumpy	(wing)
16.5	cl	clot	(eye)
31.0	d	dachs	(wing)
41.0	J	Jammed	(wing)
→ 48.5	b	black	(body)
54.5	pr	purple	(eye)
		←————— centromere	
57.5	cn	cinnabar	(eye)
62.0	en	engrailed	(body)
→ 67.0	vg	vestigial	(wing)
72.0	L	Lobe	(eye)
75.5	c	curved	(wing)
82.0	wt	welt	(eye)
100.5	px	plexus	(wing)
104.5	bw	brown	(eye)
107.0	sp	speck	(wing)
107.3	Pin	Pin	(bristles)

Normal wings
(a)

Vestigial wings
(b)

Figure 10·20 (a) Chromosome map for the second chromosome of *Drosophila*. (b) A sketch illustrating the appearance of vestigial wings.

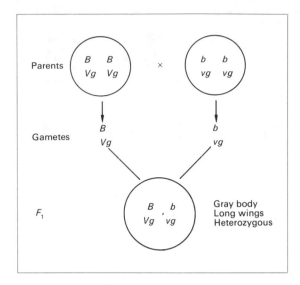

Figure 10·21 A cross in *Drosophila* between gray-body, long-wing flies, and black-body, vestigial-wing flies.

four of the fruit fly's chromosomes. Such maps have also been made for the chromosomes of corn and, to some degree, for some of the chromosomes of mice and humans. Perhaps the following discussion will help you understand how these maps are constructed.

In Figure 10–20 note the two genes, *b* for black body and *vg* for vestigial wings (arrows point to these). The normal allele for black body is gray body and is usually represented by *B*, whereas the normal allele for vestigial wing is long wing, represented by *Vg*. Thus gray body and long wings are dominant over black body and vestigial wings, a condition in which the wings are greatly reduced in size (Figure 10–20*b*). If we were to cross flies homozygous for gray bodies and normal wings with black-bodies, vestigial-winged flies, the *F₁* generation would all have gray bodies and long wings but would be heterozygous (Figure 10–21).

If these genes were on separate chromosomes they would assort independently according to Mendel's second law. (You may remember in the earlier discussion of the

dihybrid cross the point was made that the two traits considered were carried on separate chromosomes.) But since the genes are linked they should not assort at meiosis. Let us look at the results of an experimental cross between parents heterozygous for both of these traits (the *F₁* of Figure 10–21). It is possible to test-cross individuals from the *F₁* generation with individuals homozygous for black body and vestigial wings (double recessive). The "tester" flies can produce only one type of gamete, *b vg*, whether the genes for these traits are linked on one chromosome or are on separate chromosomes. If the genes are inseparably linked, the *F₁* individuals would produce two types of gametes, *B Vg* and *b vg*, and offspring from the test cross would be produced in a 1:1 ratio (Figure 10–22*a*). However, if the genes are not linked but are on separate chromosomes, four classes of gametes would be formed with equal frequencies: *B Vg*, *B vg*, *b Vg*, *b vg*. Four kinds of offspring would therefore be produced in a 1:1:1:1 ratio. Both possibilities (linked and not linked) are diagrammed in Figure 10–22.

As it turns out neither possibility provides the true answer. The results of the actual experiment are:*

Gray body, long wings	965
Black body, vestigial wings	944
Gray body, vestigial wings	185
Black body, long wings	206
	2300

All four types of offspring postulated in Figure 10–22*b* are present but *not* in a 1:1:1:1 ratio. Gray body, long wings and black body, vestigial wings, the two parental types, are present in almost a 1:1 ratio, but how can we account for the low numbers of the other two types of offspring? The answer lies in the fact that the genes are linked but crossing over occurred which exchanged the genes on the homologous chromosomes. The details of this process from a cytological viewpoint were discussed in Chapter 9 and an experimental

*A. M. Winchester, Genetics, 3rd ed., Houghton-Mifflin Co., Boston, 1966.

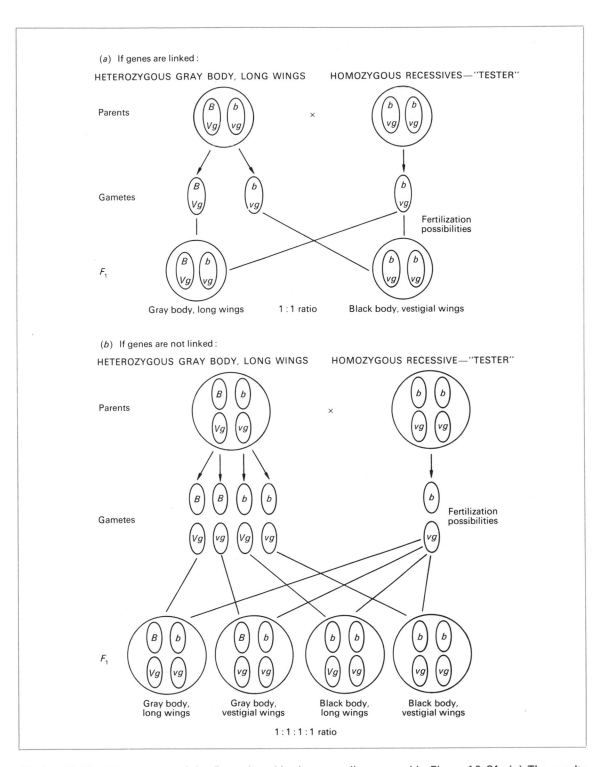

Figure 10·22 Test crosses of the F_1 produced in the cross diagrammed in Figure 10·21. (*a*) The results if the genes are linked on the same chromosome. (*b*) The results if the genes are on separate chromosomes.

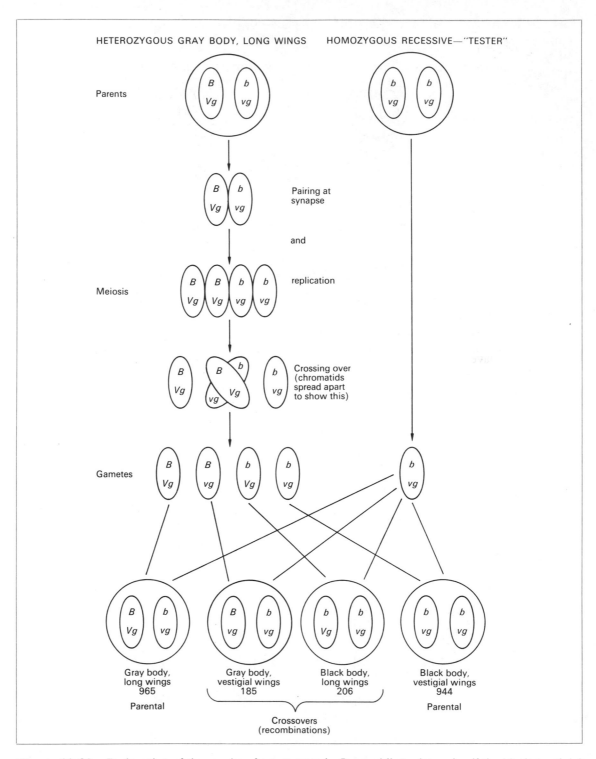

Figure 10-23 Explanation of the results of a test cross in *Drosophila* to determine if the black, vestigial genes are linked and, if so, the amount of crossing over that occurs.

cross, showing crossover, is diagrammed in Figure 10–23.

We further note that 391 total crossovers occurred (185 + 206) and this is about 17 percent of all the offspring produced (391 ÷ 2300). If this cross were conducted again and again (and it has been), the same percentage of crossovers, 17 percent, would occur. This has significance since the crossing-over frequency is directly related to the distance between these two genes on the chromosome. The closer two genes are, the lower the percent of crossing over; the farther apart they are, the greater the percent of crossing over. This principle will be more evident to you if you examine the chromosome map in Figure 10–20 again. One unit on chromosome maps represents one percent of crossing over.

From Figure 10–20 you should also note that the distance between the black-body gene and the vestigial-wing gene is 18.5 units (18.5 percent). We have stated the crossover frequency here as only 17 percent and the discrepancy should be explained. Crossing over occurs all along the chromosome and a *double crossover* between these two genes would return them to the original chromosome. Consequently, the actual percentage of crossing over between the two genes would be obscured. In comparing the crossover rates of the two genes discussed with other genes between the two, we note that the true distance is closer to 18.5 than 17, the difference accounted for by the double crossovers (Figure 10–24).

The actual mechanical processes that occur during crossing over are not completely understood. We can observe the chiasmata between the chromatids under the microscope (Figure 9–8b), and we can observe the resulting offspring which are products of the gametes. One proposed mechanism to account for recombination is the actual breaking and exchanging of parts of homologous chromosomes during meiosis which you may remember from Chapter 9.

MULTIPLE ALLELES

Up to this point we have treated a gene as though it could exist in only two forms—that is, as two alleles. Thus we spoke of the gene for body color on the second chromosome of the fruit fly as producing either a gray-body color (*B*) or a black-body color (*b*). The vestigial-wing gene, however, may have five different forms, whereas we noted only two alleles—normal wings and vestigial. Three other intermediate alleles seem to exist—nicked, notched, and strap—and any individual fruit fly could have only two of these alleles.

There is no particular reason why a gene must have only two varieties or forms. If we assume that the normal gene changed once we can also assume that it could change again. If the altered gene was successful in the environment, then it would be present in a definite frequency in the population. Some inheritance patterns can be explained only on the basis of several forms of a specific gene, *multiple alleles.*

Figure 10·24 Diagram to illustrate how double crossovers can return two genes to the same chromosome. The fact that crossing over occurred between these two genes could then be missed.

327

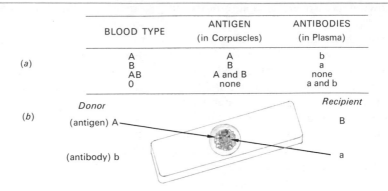

BLOOD TYPE	ANTIGEN (in Corpuscles)	ANTIBODIES (in Plasma)
A	A	b
B	B	a
AB	A and B	none
0	none	a and b

(a)

(b)

Donor

(antigen) A

(antibody) b

Recipient

B

a

Figure 10·25 (*a*) Human blood types showing distributions of antigens and antibodies. (*b*) The result of transfusing incompatible blood types. The antigen *A* in blood type A reacts with the antibody *a* in blood type B to produce clumping of the red blood corpuscles.

Coat color in rabbits apparently is due to four different alleles at one position (locus) on the chromosome. The wild-gray color (*C*) is dominant to all the others; chinchilla (c^{ch}) is dominant to the other two; himalayan (c^h) is dominant to albino; and albino (c^a) is recessive to all the other alleles. Any individual rabbit would have only two of these alleles and his coat color would be determined according to the hierarchial scheme listed.

The only way blood types in humans can be adequately explained is on the basis of multiple alleles (in this case, three). Humans are placed in one of the four blood groups, A, B, AB, or O, on the basis of *agglutination* (clumping of the red corpuscles) tests. This clumping occurs because of a reaction between a substance on the corpuscles known as an *antigen* and a substance in the plasma known as an *antibody*. Two different antigens, *A* and *B*, and two different antibodies, *a* and *b*, are known. The distribution of these in the various blood types is shown in Figure 10–25. A person with type A blood has antibodies (*b*) capable of agglutinating the red blood corpuscles of type B blood. In transfusions, therefore, care must be taken not to administer any blood that can be agglutinated by the antibodies of the recipient. Compatible and incompatible types can be recognized from Figures 10–25.

The following three alleles can account for the inheritance of blood type:

I^0—no antigen produced

I^A—antigen *A* produced

I^B—antigen *B* produced

The following genotypes would then explain the various blood groups:

I^A I^A or I^A I^0—type A

I^B I^B or I^B I^0—type B

I^A I^B —type AB

I^0 I^0 —type O

This information can be useful but not conclusive in cases of disputed parenthood. It would be possible, for example, to state only that a man could not possibly be the father of a specific baby, or that he possibly could be, on the basis of blood types.

QUANTITATIVE INHERITANCE

In previous examples we spoke of characteristics in a qualitative sense—that is, whether or not a given trait was present. Moreover, we have been attributing most of these traits to one gene. For example, Mendel's peas were

328

considered to have either round seeds or wrinkled seeds and the trait was due to two alleles. Two groups therefore would be present in the population, round and wrinkled seeded varieties. There are characteristics in organisms, however, that do not fit into discrete, contrasting groups. These characteristics show a continuous distribution in the population and are usually represented by the well-known normal distribution curve (Figure 10–26). Some of these traits are intelligence and body stature in humans, height in corn plants, and seed-coat color in wheat. Characteristics such as these can be explained only on the basis of several to many nondominant genes sorting independently but exerting a cumulative or additive effect on the particular trait. We have already considered the effect of one pair of nondominant alleles on a characteristic such as flower color (Figure 10–11). When two pink hybrids were crossed, the resulting phenotypic ratio was 1:2:1 and this ratio can be shown on a graph (Figure 10–27).

Let us now consider a trait that results when two pairs of alleles lacking dominance have a cumulative effect on that trait; the phenotypic ratio under these conditions would be 1:4:6:4:1 (Figure 10–28). If a trait were produced by three pairs of nondominant alleles, the ratio would be 1:6:15:20:15:6:1. Such a ratio would produce a much smoother curve than one for only two alleles. In humans it is estimated that skin color is produced by four to seven pairs of alleles.

EFFECT OF ENVIRONMENT

It must be remembered that we inherit genes not traits. When we say that a boy got his brown eyes from his dad, what we really mean is that he got the genes for brown eyes from his dad. Every gene must develop in an environment, and the environment determines to some extent how that gene will develop. In the case of vestigial wings in fruit flies (Figure 10–20), the vestigial-wing characteristic will develop if the flies are raised at room temperature. If the flies are reared at

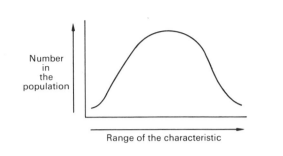

Figure 10·26 A normal distribution curve in the population for traits such as intelligence and body stature in humans.

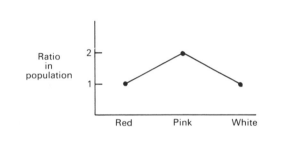

Figure 10·27 The results of the cross between two pink hybrid four-o'clock plants (see Figure 10·11).

about 92° F (33° C), however, the wings will be almost normal.

Identical twins reared apart will often show striking differences when compared later in life. The question often raised, "which is more important, heredity or environment?," is really a moot question with little practical meaning since both factors are necessary in the development of an individual organism.

GENE-ACTION GENETICS

While transmission genetics is concerned with the mechanical details of genes passed from

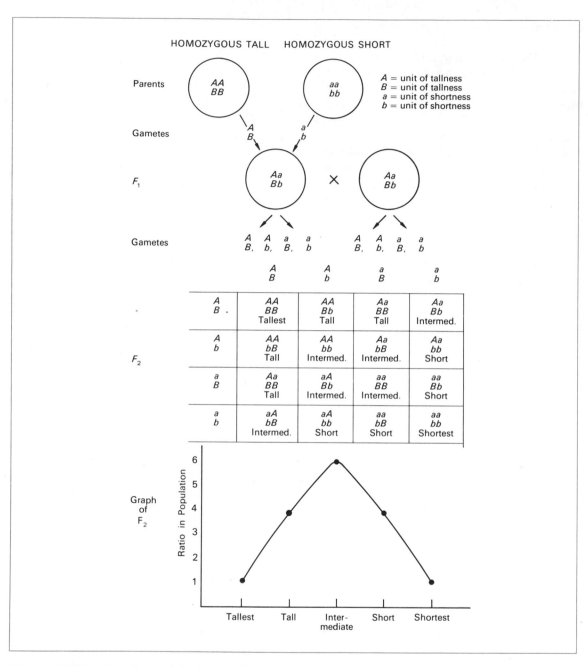

Figure 10·28 Quantitative inheritance of the trait of height in some organism assuming that the trait is produced by two pairs of cumulative, non-dominant alleles. The graph of the F_2 generation shows a normal curve.

generation to generation, gene action attempts to explain what the genes are actually doing to produce their effects. One of the most

active studies going on in modern biology is concerned with what happens between the gene on the chromosome and the visible

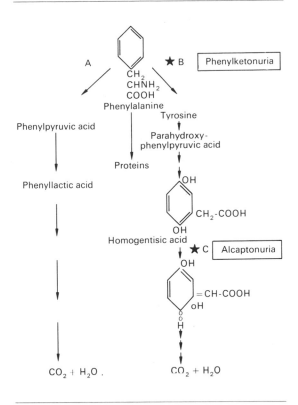

Figure 10·29 The partial metabolism of phenylalanine. It can be incorporated into proteins in the cell or converted to tyrosine or phenylpyruvic acid. If the enzyme is lacking at B, then most of the phenylalanine converts to phenylpyruvic acid, producing the serious disease *phenylketonuria*. If the enzyme is lacking (or is defective) at C, *alcaptonuria* results. Note that normally the ultimate products in these pathways are burned to $CO_2 + H_2O$ in the Krebs cycle. Many intermediate products are omitted here, thus the series of arrows in some places.

phenotype expressed by that gene. There are still problems to be answered in transmission genetics, but the greatest interest and activity in genetics today is in the field of gene action. How a gene produces its effect has already been indicated in Chapter 3 under the concept of protein synthesis. This basic scheme of DNA → RNA → protein forms the foundation for our discussion on gene action.

Perhaps the first notable discussion on gene action was published in 1908 by an English physician, Sir Archibald Garrod. In a book entitled *Inborn Errors of Metabolism,* he dealt with a group of congenital metabolic disorders. In tracing the inheritance pattern of these diseases, Garrod noted that they were apparently produced by the action of one gene. One of these "inborn errors" he studied was *alcaptonuria,* which has the symptoms of blackening of the urine upon exposure to air and the darkening of certain cartilages. The substance responsible for this is homogentisic acid, a carbon-ring compound that is normally split in the metabolism of an individual. Garrod believed that alcaptonuria was caused by the inability of afflicted individuals to split this ring compound due to the absence or inactivity of an enzyme. He further hypothesized that the lack of an effective enzyme was due to the absence of the normal form of a particular gene. Garrod was actually suggesting that a gene is responsible for the production of a specific enzyme and this idea was later developed as the *one gene—one enzyme* theory. It is interesting to note that in the 1930s it was discovered that individuals afflicted with alcaptonuria do lack the liver enzyme homogentisate oxidase which is essential for catalyzing the reaction that splits the ring compound, homogentisic acid. This series of chemical events is diagrammed in Figure 10–29.

A more serious "inborn error" is the disease *phenylketonuria,* which produces extreme mental retardation in children. This disorder results when phenylalanine cannot be converted to tyrosine, also due to the lack of an enzyme (Figure 10–29). When this occurs, phenylpyruvic acid accumulates and apparently affects brain development. It has been shown that this disease is the result of homozygosity for a recessive gene and only about one birth in 25,000 in the United States results in phenylketonuria (known also as PKU). Urine tests can determine at birth whether an individual is phenylketonuric and these tests

Figure 10-30 Dr. George Beadle, who was awarded the Nobel Prize in 1958 for his studies in gene action.

cycle in which the mold spends most of its life in the haploid state.

To summarize, *Neurospora* is well suited to genetic experiments for the following reasons:

1 It can be easily grown in the laboratory on a simple (called *minimal*) medium of sugar, inorganic salts, and biotin (a vitamin B).

2 The spores produced at meiosis are in a linear order (Figure 10-32) in a spore case and can be analyzed readily.

3 It can reproduce asexually (as well as sexually) so that different types can be propagated without genetic change.

4 It is haploid throughout most of its life cycle so that recessive genes cannot be masked by dominant alleles.

Beadle and Tatum knew that it was difficult to determine what a gene was doing if only the normal gene was available to study. However, they felt that if a gene could be changed so that it no longer performed normally then it should be possible to determine what the gene was doing. An analogous situation in an assembly line is described in Figure 10–33. Their objective then was to produce *mutations* in the genes and determine what related chemical changes occurred in the organism. By noting the specific chemical difference between the mutant and the normal molds, it should be possible to associate the normal chemical function with the normal gene.

The procedure used by Beadle and Tatum can be simply outlined as follows:

1 Asexual spores were x-rayed to produce mutations.

2 These spores then were crossed with another strain and ascospores produced.

3 The ascospores then were transferred to a complete medium that included minimal medium plus all the vitamins and amino acids; here they grew and produced colonies.

4 Portions of these colonies then were transferred to minimal medium and some could not grow here (remember that all normal

are mandatory in some states. If affected individuals are then placed on phenylalanine-free diets in the early years of their lives, most of the damage can be prevented.

NEUROSPORA STUDIES

If we want to know what a gene is doing in an organism, it is better to study haploid organisms (one set of chromosomes) than diploid organisms (two sets of chromosomes). The reason for this is that a mutant recessive gene can be masked by a dominant allele in a diploid form, whereas in a haploid organism the single gene, whether it is normal or mutated, must express itself. George Beadle (Figure 10–30) and Edward Tatum (who were later awarded the Nobel Prize along with Joshua Lederberg for their work in genetics) realized this and utilized the red mold *Neurospora* in their studies of gene action. The life cycle of this mold (Figure 10–31) displays a haplontic life

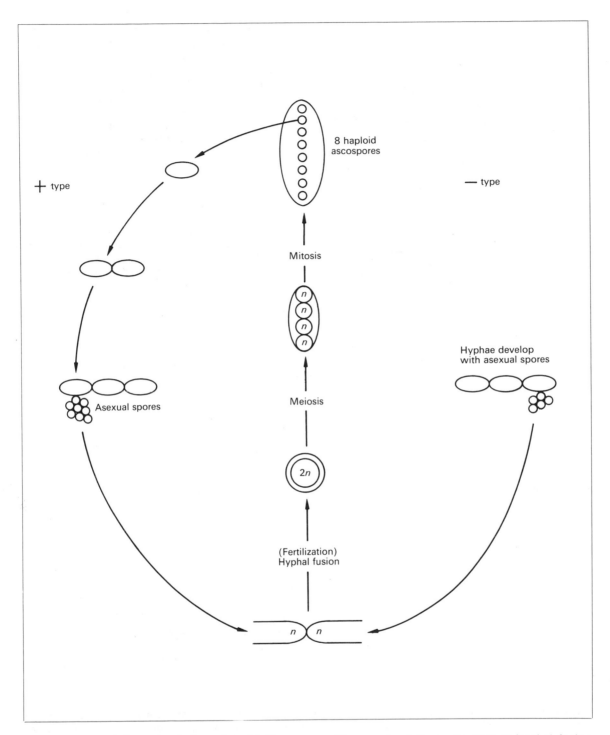

Figure 10·31 Life cycle of the red mold *Neurospora*. The events of the cycle start at hyphal-fusion stage (a hypha is a filamentous strand). Males and females are not produced in molds, and the situation is similar to that in *Spirogyra* where conjugation occurred. Thus we represent the combining forms as + and − types. Note that *Neurospora* can produce asexual spores also.

Neurospora can grow on minimal medium); those that could not grow here were evidently mutated.

5 Since Beadle and Tatum theorized that these mutated forms had lost the ability to synthesize necessary vitamins or amino acids, the next step was to transfer portions of colonies unable to grow on minimal medium to two different kinds of media: (*a*) minimal plus vitamins and (*b*) minimal

Figure 10-32 Appearance of the spore-containing structures (asci) produced when a wild-type strain of *Neurospora* is crossed with a mutant that exhibits delayed maturation. Dark spores are wild type while the lighter ones are mutant. Eight spores are produced in each ascus. When the spores are aligned with four dark and four light in an ascus, crossing-over did not occur at meiosis. Other spore distributions indicate crossing-over at meiosis. (Courtesy of Dr. David R. Stadler.)

Figure 10-33 A hypothetical sweater factory. Line I represents the normal assembly-line procedure. But when the normal assembly operation is changed or interrupted, the finished product is changed (Line II). If Worker B is missing, the factory piles up sweaters with no left sleeve, no collar, and no buttons. If Worker C is missing, sweaters accumulate having no collar and no buttons. Thus, by observing the factory on a day when B is missing and on another day when C is missing, we can deduce that B puts on left sleeves and that C puts on either collars or buttons, and that B handles the sweater before C.

plus amino acids. In this way it could be determined whether the mutation produced the inability to make a necessary vitamin or a necessary amino acid.

6 Those spores that grew on the minimal-plus-vitamin medium and died on the minimal-plus-amino-acid medium evidently had lost the ability to produce a particular vitamin; those that displayed opposite results on the two media could not make certain amino acids.

7 The next step was to determine which specific vitamin or amino acid the mold was unable to synthesize. This could be tested by placing portions of the colony of the mutant that lacked necessary vitamins on individual cultures which contained minimal medium plus one vitamin. If the mutant would then grow, for example, only on minimal medium plus vitamin B_1, the mutant had evidently lost the ability through a mutation to produce vitamin B_1. These steps are summarized in Figure 10-34.

Beadle and Tatum, who were familiar with Garrod's work, concluded that the mutant was unable to make vitamin B_1 because of the inability to produce a specific enzyme necessary for its synthesis. They further theorized that the inability to make the enzyme was due to a mutated gene. They were able to show through genetic crosses of the mutant strain with a normal strain that the inheritance of the mutant trait followed the pattern of Mendel's monohybrid cross. Beadle and Tatum's work thus strengthened the one gene–one enzyme theory of gene action.

Studies on *Neurospora* have been extremely helpful in the tracing of biochemical pathways in the synthesis of certain products, such as vitamins. Through the method of deductive reasoning, as noted in Figure 10–33, specific intermediate steps can be determined. As a result of these studies it has been possible to correlate many of the steps in these pathways with specific genes. Through these correlations we arrive at a better understanding of how genes act. For example, many of the steps in

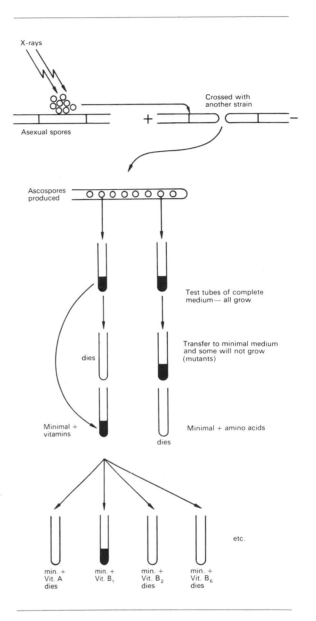

Figure 10·34 *Neurospora* experiment of Beadle and Tatum. Note the mutant ultimately grows on minimal medium plus vitamin B_1 only.

the synthesis of niacin (another B vitamin) from anthranilic acid in *Neurospora* are known, as well as the enzymes that control these steps. That specific genes are responsible for the production of specific enzymes in this sequence of events is also known (determined from genetic crosses). These general events can be illustrated as:

Ingram and his coworkers proceeded to analyze these two proteins (a complex chemical analysis which need not be presented here).

HEMOGLOBIN STUDIES

Another approach to the understanding of gene action was the study conducted by Vernon Ingram at the University of Cambridge. He reasoned that if genes do determine the synthesis of specific proteins, an examination of two different proteins, one produced by a normal gene and one produced by a mutant gene, should reveal how the genes produced these different proteins. Of the several forms of human hemoglobin known, perhaps the best known is the sickle-cell type, which produces sickle-cell anemia, a hereditary disease transmitted by a single gene. Therefore these two closely related proteins—normal hemoglobin and sickle-cell hemoglobin—can be studied and compared.

Each protein was separated into twenty-eight peptide groups and studied for differences. The peptides were exactly alike in the two proteins except for the number 4 peptide unit. In this peptide group, where normal hemoglobin has a glutamic-acid molecule, sickle-cell hemoglobin has a valine molecule. Thus the two proteins differ in only one amino acid out of 300. This may seem like an insignificant variation in the two molecules, and yet it determines how much oxygen will be transported by the two molecules.

In looking for the mechanism that produced these structural changes in the proteins,

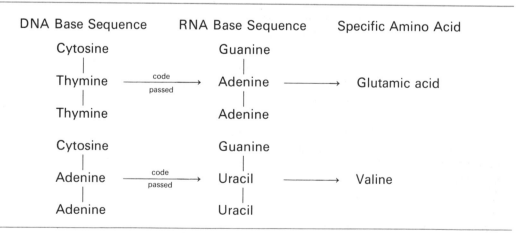

Figure 10·35 Proposed scheme for the coding of glutamic acid and valine into proteins. A slight change in one segment of the DNA base sequence could change the code in the RNA, hence a different amino acid would be incorporated into the protein.

Ingram proposed the concept discussed in Chapter 3 of the DNA providing a code for the construction of specific proteins. The gene would therefore be a segment of the DNA molecule in which the nucleotide sequence acts as a code to instruct the cell which protein to make (Figure 10–35).

BACTERIAL AND VIRAL GENETICS

It is extremely important to select organisms for experimental studies which are well suited for the investigation of a particular problem. We have seen how valuable the fruit fly has been to the field of transmission genetics, and that *Neurospora* had distinct advantages for gene-action studies. In studies on the fundamental substances of heredity, certain organisms have been helpful—such as bacteria which have all their genes in one chromosome, and viruses, composed only of protein and nucleic acids. Genetic studies on bacteria and viruses have suggested that the gene is far more complex than we originally thought. For example, it is now evident that crossing over and mutation can occur at many places within a gene.

In 1946 *conjugation*, or sexuality, in bacteria was discovered. In this process a bridge is formed between two bacteria of compatible strains and genetic material is passed from the donor to the recipient. It is also known that the amount of genetic material transferred can be controlled by varying the length of conjugation time.

One of the most interesting and informative genetic-transfer mechanisms in bacteria is *transformation*, the process wherein extracted DNA from one strain of bacteria is taken up by another strain of bacteria. This mechanism strongly suggests that DNA is the chief substance of heredity. For example, pneumococcus bacteria (producers of bacterial pneumonia) are typically enclosed in smooth capsules, but a mutation may produce bacteria that cannot make a capsule and consequently appear irregular and rough. DNA can be extracted from a colony of smooth, encapsulated bacteria and introduced into the culture medium of rough-coated bacteria. When this is done a low percentage (much higher than the mutation rate, however) of smooth colonies will appear among the rough colonies (Figure 10–36). It is believed that the DNA from the smooth bacteria is actually incorporated into the DNA of the rough strains. If the protein from the bacterial chromosome is placed in the culture, transformation does not occur. Since DNA is required to bring about transformation, it appears that DNA is the carrier of heredity.

A third type of genetic transfer in bacteria is *transduction*, in which viruses, known as *bacteriophages*, act as vectors and transport DNA from donor bacteria to recipient bacteria. After a virus enters a bacterial cell, the virus DNA can combine with the DNA of the host under certain conditions, and the viral DNA utilizes the protein-synthesis mechanism of the bacterium to reproduce itself. After the viruses reproduce and leave the bacterium, they can transfer part of the bacterium's DNA to another bacterium. Evidence from several studies indicates that only the DNA enters the bacterium cell while the protein jacket stays outside. This is one more bit of evidence that DNA is the genetic substance.

Viruses, as noted earlier, are extremely small noncellular structures composed of protein and nucleic acid which can parasitize plant, animal, and protist cells. Some viruses contain RNA as their nucleic acid while others have DNA, and genetic studies have been conducted on both types. We will only discuss here the DNA containing T2 and T4 viruses which infect *Escherichia coli*, the bacterium found in the colon of man (Figure 10–37). They are composed of a head, tail base or end plate with spikes, and tail fibers. The effects of bacteriophages (often shortened to *phage*) can be studied rather easily since they leave a clear area, known as a *plaque*, in a bacterial

337

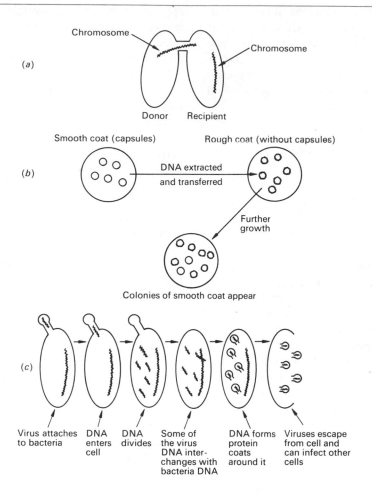

Figure 10·36 Types of genetic transfer in bacteria. (a) Conjugation; (b) transformation; (c) transduction.

culture where they have destroyed the bacterial cells. Many mutant forms of phages are known and these can be studied, and often identified, by the plaque, or type of plaque, that develops when they infect their hosts.

A T4 virus attaches itself to the bacterial surface of an *E. coli* cell by the tail fibers and spikes of the end plate. The tail then penetrates the cell wall and permits the DNA to pass into the cell from the head of the virus (Figure 10–38). Upon entering the cell the viral DNA begins to control the protein-synthesis mechanism of the bacterial cell and viral DNA and protein are made. About one-half hour after infection, approximately 200 new viruses have been produced and these are released from the destroyed bacterial cell in a process known as *lysis*. (Plaques thus form where lysis occurs.) A normal virus must be complete if it is to be infective—that is, the head, tail, end plate, etc. must be put together in an orderly manner. Over 40 genes are known in the T4 virus which control the normal development and construction of an individual

338

Figure 10·37 Electronmicrograph of T2 bacteriophages attached to a fragment of a bacterial cell wall, X 200,000. (Courtesy of Dr. R. W. Horne.)

phage, and more than 75 mutations are known which can interfere with normal development.

W. B. Wood and R. S. Edgar have recently studied the sequential steps involved in the normal assemblage of a T4 virus. They infected bacteria with various mutants, determined which parts of the virus had been constructed, and analyzed electron micrographs of the viral structures at various

Figure 10·38 (*Left*) Diagrammatic representation of a bacteriophage particle showing the six-sided "head" containing the strands of DNA, the "tail" with its central core, the "tail" plate and fibers. (*Right*) The same bacteriophage particle attached to the bacterial cell; the "tail" has contracted, the central core has penetrated the wall of the bacterium, and the DNA has passed down into the cell. (Courtesy of K. M. Smith in *Viruses*, Cambridge University Press.)

339

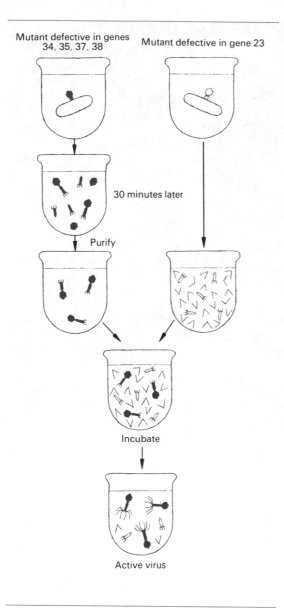

Mutant defective in genes 34, 35, 37, 38

Mutant defective in gene 23

30 minutes later

Purify

Incubate

Active virus

stages. One of their experiments is diagrammed in Figure 10–39. A partial genetic map of the T4 virus chromosome is shown in Figure 10–40 along with the way in which each mutant interferes with normal development. This study represents an attempt to discover how each gene functions in the development of a virus.

MUTATIONS

Mutations have already been introduced in this chapter and they were described as relatively permanent changes in the genetic material. The concept and term were first proposed by Hugo De Vries in 1901 to account for some sudden changes he observed in his experiments on the evening primrose. When we speak of a mutation we generally mean a gene mutation, although chromosomal mutations certainly do occur. Chromosomal mutations are structural alterations known as *deletions, translocations,* and *inversions,* and involve segments of one or more chromosomes.

Deletion occurs when any part of a chromosome breaks away during division and is lost in the cytoplasm. The result of deletion is usually the production of inviable gametes owing to the loss of genetic information. A deletion may occur at the end of a chromatid (one break) or in the middle of the arm (two breaks). In the second case, the broken ends may fuse to save the remainder of the chromosome. Several types of chromosome mutations are illustrated in Figure 10–41.

Translocation implies that some segment of a chromosome is shifted from its normal position and the broken piece may fuse with its homologue or even with a nonhomologue. Changes in chromosome number can occur by this process if simultaneous breaks occur near the centromeres of two chromosomes. Subsequent fusion may produce a large meta-centric chromosome (V-shaped) and this process reduces the chromosome number when it occurs in a cell.

Inversion, one of the most interesting aberrations, is the 180-degree reversal of a section

Figure 10·39 Tail fibers are attached to fiberless particles in the experiment diagrammed here. Cells are infected with a virus (black) bearing defective tail-fiber genes. The progeny particles are isolated with a centrifuge. A virus with a head-gene mutation (white) infects a second bacterial culture, providing an extract containing free tails and tail fibers. When the two preparations are mixed and incubated at 30°C, the fiberless particles are converted to infectious virus particles by the attachment of the free fibers. From "Building a Bacterial Virus" by William B. Wood and R. S. Edgar. Copyright © 1967 by *Scientific American, Inc.* All rights reserved.

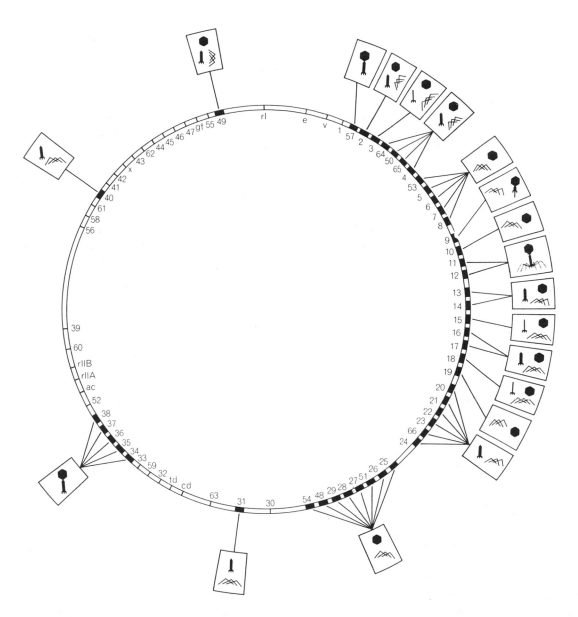

Figure 10·40 The genetic map of the T4 virus. The numbers represent the genes identified so far on the basis of mutations. The small diagrams radiating from each blackened gene area show the effect of that mutation. A mutation in gene 19, for example, would produce an incomplete virus, one without a collar and most of the tail. From "Building a Bacterial Virus" by William B. Wood and R. S. Edgar. Copyright © 1967 by *Scientific American, Inc.* All rights reserved.

of a chromosome. An inversion may occur in a terminal segment or involve two simultaneous breaks (Figures 10–41 and 10–42). When a chromosome with an inversion pairs with its homologue in prophase of meiosis, it must form a loop (inversion loop) to facilitate the gene-to-gene pairing. If a crossover occurs within the loop during duplication, very serious genetic consequences result (Figure 10–42). Not only are certain genes repeated or

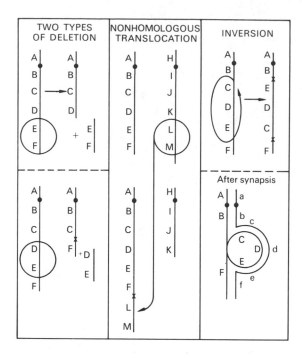

| TWO TYPES OF DELETION | NONHOMOLOGOUS TRANSLOCATION | INVERSION |

Figure 10·41 Three common types of chromosome aberrations: deletion, translocation, and inversion. Note the formation of the inversion loop during synapsis in the inversion. Refer to Figure 10·42 for the meiotic results.

deleted, but dicentric (having two centromeres) and acentric (without a centromere) chromosomes are produced. The dicentric chromosome is broken during division and the acentric is lost completely.

Gene mutations, on the other hand, are often called *point* mutations (or just mutations) and probably involve only one or a few nucleotides in the chromosome. We can also differentiate between spontaneous and induced mutations. Spontaneous mutations occur at random without known cause, and their rates vary considerably among organisms and among specific genes. It is difficult, therefore, to state a general spontaneous mutation rate although one in 100,000 to one in 1,000,000 cells is often given as the general frequency of their occurrence. The mutation rate for the gene that produces hemophilia is rather high, one in approximately every 40,000 gametes, where-

as the gene that produces aniridia in man (absence of an iris in the eye) mutates with a frequency of about one in every 200,000 gametes. Induced mutations, on the other hand, are the result of man's use of x-rays, certain chemicals and other means.

Mutations are certainly important to the evolutionary process, for they offer the only real source of raw material on which natural selection can work. New chromosome and gene combinations can be produced through meiosis, crossing over, and random fertilizations, but only mutations (chromosomal or gene) really offer new raw material to the process. Most mutations that we observe today are considered harmful. Since well-adapted organisms are the result of a long selection process, any change in their evolutionary development is more likely to be harmful than helpful. We should therefore expect useful mutations to the well-adapted organism to be quite rare. Whether a mutation is beneficial or detrimental may depend on the specific environment at the time it occurs. Moreover, if a mutation is to be passed on to the offspring, it must occur in the gametes. Mutations in the body cells are not transmitted to the next generation but often reveal themselves as patches of abnormal tissue, often forming mosaic patterns.

Mutations that may be harmful to a particular species are often selected by man for his benefit. A seedless orange (Figure 8–14) obviously can only be harmful to the species that produced it, but to man it represents a fruit that can be eaten conveniently. The Ancon breed of sheep, characterized by extremely short legs, arose from a single gene mutation that was first noted in 1791 in Massachusetts. For the sheep this is definitely a detrimental condition since it restricts their movement, but for man it is advantageous since lower fences are required to contain the sheep.

Some of the earliest experiments on the induction of mutations were performed with x-rays on *Drosophila* in 1927 by Herman J. Muller, who later won the Nobel Prize for his contributions. Since that time numerous

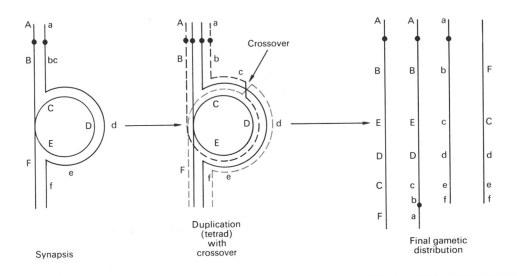

Figure 10·42 The meiotic results of a crossover occurring in a paracentric inversion (the centromeres are located outside the loop). Note that one chromosome contains two centromeres and that another has none.

experiments have shown many chemicals and radiations to be mutagenic. A variety of chemical agents such as formaldehyde, peroxide, caffeine, nicotine, nitrous oxide, 5-bromouracil, 2-aminopurine, and mustard gas can produce mutations. Furthermore heat, ultraviolet light, high-energy radiation such as x-rays, gamma rays, alpha and beta particles, and cosmic rays can all be mutagenic. Just how these many agents bring about mutations is the subject of much discussion among geneticists. The ultimate result must be a change in the coding of the DNA molecule, and this must involve a change in one or more base pairs in the normal sequence of nucleotides. Any mechanism that could open the DNA molecule or make it unstable, or substitute for some of the normal bases, could conceivably produce this effect. A group of compounds known as base analogues, represented by 5-bromouracil and 2-aminopurine mentioned above, are similar in structure to the normal purines and pyrimidines contained

in DNA. These are highly mutagenic and it could be that these replace normal bases in certain positions and then pair with a different normal base, thereby bringing about a change in the original nucleotide sequence. Such a process could bring about base-pair changes from thymine-adenine to cytosine-guanine, for example. When such a change occurs, T–A to C–G (or A–T to C–G or T–A to C–G, etc.), the code has been changed (Figure 10–43). This is the kind of change which produces the slight differences between proteins such as normal and sickle-cell hemoglobins where they differ in only one amino acid out of 300. Modern medicine utilizes base analogues, as well as x-rays and other radiation, to interfere with the mechanism of certain cells that are growing abnormally.

WHAT IS A GENE?

The word *gene* was first used in 1905 to indicate a single unit of heredity that occupied

343

a specific position in a chromosome. Experiments on *Drosophila* (fruit fly) added to an understanding of the gene in terms of recombinational (crossing over) and mutational units. *Neurospora* studies certainly shed much light on the gene as a functional unit—that is, what it actually does in the cell. The contribution of microbial genetics (bacteria and viruses) was really twofold: first, transformation and transduction experiments confirmed the fact that DNA is the hereditary substance and showed that a gene is a segment of the DNA molecule; second, studies on these simple forms of life, which contain less complex genetic material, have provided new concepts of the recombinational and mutational aspects of the gene.

In 1953, when geneticists working with bacteria and *Neurospora* were making significant contributions, a model that could account for the duplication, coding, and mutational features of DNA was proposed. Known as the Watson-Crick model, it suggested that the hereditary substance was composed of base pairs of nucleotides and that these bases spelled out a code to the cell's machinery. Since the one gene–one enzyme theory was strongly held, it seemed that the code was directing the cell to manufacture specific enzymes or proteins. Studies on the specific protein, hemoglobin, showed that the normal form differed from a mutant form by only one amino acid. A change in the coding mechanism, perhaps in only one nucleotide, could account for the substitution of the wrong amino acid. This then is how we defined a mutation, a change in the coding mechanism of the DNA molecule.

So we see that our concept of a gene has been modified considerably from the factors of Mendel to the nucleotides of the modern geneticist. Moreover, research in microbial genetics has shown that crossing over and mutation can occur within a gene. Perhaps a gene is not the same entity in more complex organisms that it is in the simple forms of life. A gene generally has been regarded in three different ways: as a unit of function, a

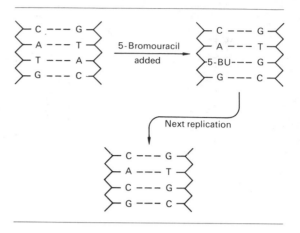

Figure 10·43 Hypothetical events that might produce a change in the code of the DNA molecule. 5-Bromouracil replaces thymine; during replication, 5-BU cannot pair with adenine but does pair with guanine. In the next replication, cytosine replaces 5-BU and combines with guanine. The ultimate effect is a change in a T–A base pair to C–G.

unit of recombination (crossing over), and a unit of mutation. In all these three roles it is still considered as a series of nucleotides along the DNA molecule. As it was pointed out earlier, however, microbial genetics show that these three functions can occur within sites formerly called genes and that these three functions have different boundaries. To account for this, three new terms have been designated and defined as: *recon*—the smallest unit of recombination and perhaps only one nucleotide in size; *muton*—the smallest unit of mutation and composed of one nucleotide; *cistron*—the smallest unit of function and probably many nucleotides in length.

Finally, in our consideration of the nature of the gene, we must remember that each gene is part of a functioning system. A certain gene that produces an enzyme to catalyze one step in the production of the vitamin thiamine could not really do its job if it were not for other genes producing other enzymes necessary for the total synthetic pathway. In fact, experimental evidence suggests that even the

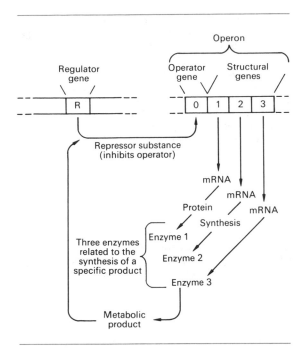

Figure 10·44 A diagram to show the functional relationships among structural, operator, and regulator genes. In this case the metabolic product apparently combines with the repressor substance produced by the regulator gene to inhibit the action of the operator gene.

position of the gene on the chromosome is vital to its function.

That genes function together has also been demonstrated by the discovery of *regulator* and *operator* genes. Recent studies by the French microbiologists Jacob and Monod (1961) have indicated that three different types of genes influence the synthesis of protein in the colon bacteria, *E. coli*. These are diagrammed in Figure 10–44 and summarized below:

1 *Structural genes*—These genes code messenger RNA for the synthesis of a specific protein or enzyme on the ribosomes. This is the gene discussed in Chapter 3 under protein synthesis.

2 *Operator gene*—This gene controls the function of a specific series of structural genes. It is always located adjacent to the genes it controls and turns the structural

genes on and off. The operator gene and its related structural genes has been termed an *operon*.

3 *Regulator genes*—These genes regulate the function of structural genes and act in a manner similar to that of operator genes. Regulator genes, however, may be located on different chromosomes. It is believed that the regulator genes produce a repressor substance which in some way affects the appropriate operator genes. Regulator genes in *E. coli* appear to be sensitive to metabolic substances and thus provide a feedback mechanism for enzyme synthesis.

As was stated earlier in this chapter, the true picture in most organisms is that a gene affects several to many traits and each trait in turn is produced by the action of many genes. Thus a balanced genetic system is the result.

POPULATION GENETICS

As we just noted, all of the genes in an individual contribute to its development and welfare through a process of interaction. This is also true for a population of individuals. That is, all of the genes in a population, known as the *gene pool*, are involved in the adaptation and survival of the total species. *Population genetics* is the discipline that deals with the heredity of a reproducing group of organisms (a population).

In 1908, Hardy, an English mathematician, and Weinberg, a physician from Germany, formulated a concept about the frequencies of genes in a population under certain conditions. This is now known as the *Hardy-Weinberg principle* and provides the basis for the study of population genetics. The principle essentially states that genotype frequencies will remain in a state of equilibrium (will not change) from generation to generation provided the population is large, mutations do not occur, migration in and out of the population is minimal, and mating is random. In other words, if one form of a gene does not have a selective advantage over another form of the

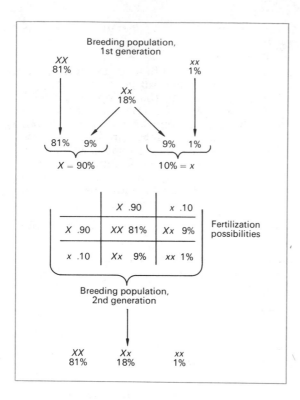

Breeding population,
1st generation

Figure 10-45 Hypothetical situation to illustrate the Hardy-Weinberg principle. The genotype *XX* has an 81% frequency in the population while the genotype *Xx* has an 18% frequency and the genotype *xx* has a 1% frequency. This means that the frequency of the *X* gene is 90% in the population (*XX* = 81% and 1/2 of the *Xx* genotype is *X*, therefore 1/2 of 18% = 9%; 81% and 9% = 90%). The frequency of *x* gene is 10% (*xx* = 1% and 1/2 of *Xx* genotype is *x*, therefore 1/2 of 18% = 9%; 1% and 9% = 10%). Assuming random mating (that each genotype has an equal chance to mate), no mutation of *X* → *x* or vice versa, a large population, and no migration into or out of the population, the frequency of each genotype will be exactly the same in the second generation. If for some reason, however, mating is not random and the *xx* genotypes do not mate as frequently as the other genotypes (this would represent selection against the *x* gene), then the frequency of the *x* gene would be less in the second generation.

gene in a population, the genotype frequencies will remain the same from generation to generation. A hypothetical situation to demonstrate this principle is shown in Figure 10–45.

We must hasten to add that the Hardy-Weinberg principle is essentially a theoretical concept and the conditions proposed by the principle are in reality never met in a natural breeding population. Breeding populations are often small, mutations do occur, migration occurs, and mating is never really random. But the Hardy-Weinberg principle is of value since it provides a theoretical basis with which we can compare the actual process occurring in nature. Gene frequencies do change in a population, and this is known as evolution. And the next chapter will deal with evolution—the gradual replacement of one genotype by another genotype as natural selection operates on the total gene pool of a population.

SUMMARIZING PRINCIPLES

Heredity and cytological studies laid the foundation for the science of modern genetics. It has been established that the chromosomes are the physical bearers of heredity.

Transmission genetics deals with the transfer and recombination of the genetic material from generation to generation. It involves Mendel's Law of Segregation and Law of Independent Assortment in monohybrid and dihybrid crosses and his concepts of dominance and recessiveness. Further aspects of transmission genetics are: sex-linked heredity, linkage and crossing over, multiple alleles, and quantitative inheritance.

Sex determination in most organisms can be correlated with a specific pair of chromosomes, the sex chromosomes.

The chance of the occurrence of a genetic event can be predicted through the use of the laws of probability. Therefore, if parental genotypes are known, the probability of certain traits occurring in the progeny may be determined.

Every gene must develop in a specific environment, and varying environmental factors can often affect the expression of a gene.

Various experiments have shown that genes direct the synthesis of enzymes. They apparently perform this action by serving as a code for protein synthesis. An alteration of a specific genetic code is a mutation.

Today the definition of a gene must be more than a simple unit of heredity. It must include the aspects of recombination, mutation, and function.

In arriving at a functional concept of the gene we may define several interacting types of genes: structural, operator, and regulator.

Genotype frequencies in natural populations generally do not remain the same from one generation to another because mutations, selection, and migration occur. The Hardy-Weinberg principle, which predicts stable gene frequencies, is useful in the study of population genetics.

REVIEW QUESTIONS

1   Correlate Mendel's Law of Segregation with the chromosomal distribution in meiosis.

2   What would be the distribution pattern of two different pairs of genes if: (a) they are on separate pairs of chromosomes or (b) they are on the same pair of chromosomes?

3   In any given roll of a pair of dice, what is the probability that one will throw a seven?

Solving genetics problems can be simplified by applying a systematic approach. Dominant traits are usually indicated by a capital letter and recessive traits by the lower-case letter of the dominant. For example, R is used to indicate the dominant trait, round seeds in peas, and r is used for the recessive condition, wrinkled seeds. Use this notation to list the genotypes of the parents in the following problems. Next, note the types of gametes produced by each parent. Then match the gametes of each parent against the gametes of the other parent, in a checkerboard pattern (similar to the ones used in this chapter to explain Mendel's work). The resulting genotypes of the cross can then be analyzed to determine the possible phenotypes produced from the cross; similar phenotypes can be tallied and a ratio stated. Often the probability of a specific genotype or phenotype is requested in a problem and this can be computed by using the approach just described. In each problem you should determine exactly what the problem asks you to do. The procedure may be modified according to the specific problem.

4   In tomatoes, red fruit color (R) is dominant over yellow (r). List the genotypes and phenotypes that could result from the following crosses:
(a) $Rr \times rr$ (b) $Rr \times RR$ (c) $rr \times RR$ (d) $Rr \times Rr$

5   Some species of plants have flowers that are red, pink, or white. Flower color in these species is due to a single pair of genes. In one experiment in which pink was crossed with pink, the following ratio was obtained: 25% red, 49% pink, and 26% white. How can you explain this ratio?

6   Glossy leaves in broccoli results from a recessive mutation and are susceptible to insects. Normally broccoli has dull leaves. A farmer desires to eliminate the glossy trait from his crops. In this process he would need to determine which plants were heterozygous and which were homozygous. How should he proceed?

7   In humans, free ear lobe (F) is dominant over attached (f) ear lobe, and the ability to taste phenylthiocarbamide, PTC (T) is dominant over the inability to taste PTC (t). A woman with free ear lobes who cannot taste PTC whose mother had attached lobes marries a man with attached lobes who can taste PTC but whose mother could not. What are the possible phenotypes of their children?

8   The polled or hornless (P) variety of cattle is dominant over horned (p). The heterozygous condition between red coat (R) and white coat (r) is roan. A polled, roan cow is mated to a horned, red bull. A horned, red offspring results. Show the genotypes of the parents and the offspring of this cross.

9   In fruit flies, long wings (V) are dominant to vestigial wings (v) and gray body color (B) is dominant over black body (b). A fly homozygous for both dominant traits is crossed with a fly showing both recessive traits. Diagram this cross, the F_1, and show the resulting genotypes. Now cross two of these and show all the genotypes and phenotypes of the F_2 generation.

10 A color-blind man marries a woman who has normal vision but whose father was color blind. Describe the possible genotypes and phenotypes of their children.

11 Summarize the evidence supporting the concept that DNA is the physical hereditary material.

12 What was the significance of Beadle's research on *Neurospora* for the field of genetics?

13 How does the modern concept of a gene correspond to the earlier notion that a gene was a structure on the chromosome?

14 Many characteristics in a natural, sexually breeding population have been observed to change over a long period of time. How can these changes be explained on the basis of the Hardy-Weinberg principle?

SUPPLEMENTARY READINGS

Auerbach, Charlotte, *The Science of Genetics,* New York, Harper & Row, 1961.

Barry, J. M., *Molecular Biology: Genes and the Chemical Control of Living Cells,* Englewood Cliffs, N.J., Prentice-Hall, 1964.

Beadle, George W., "The Genes of Men and Molds," *Scientific American,* September, 1948.

Beadle, George W., "Structure of the Genetic Material and the Concept of the Gene," in W. Johnson and W. Steere, eds., *This Is Life,* New York, Holt, Rinehart and Winston, 1962.

Beadle, George, and Muriel Beadle, *The Language of Life,* Garden City, N.Y., Doubleday, 1966.

Bearn, A. G., "The Chemistry of Hereditary Disease," *Scientific American*, December, 1956.

Bearn, A. G., and J. L. German III, "Chromosomes and Disease," *Scientific American*, November, 1961.

Benzer, Seymour, "The Fine Structure of the Gene," *Scientific American*, January, 1962.

Borek, Ernest, *The Code of Life*, New York, Columbia University Press, 1965.

Davidson, E. H., "Hormones and Genes," *Scientific American*, June, 1965.

Fraser, Alex, *Heredity: Genes and Chromosomes*, New York, McGraw-Hill, 1966.

Hartman, P. E., and S. R. Suskind, *Gene Action*, Englewood Cliffs, N.J., Prentice-Hall, 1965.

Hotchkiss, R. D., and E. Weiss, "Transformed Bacteria," *Scientific American*, November, 1956.

Ingram, Vernon M., "How Do Genes Act?," *Scientific American*, November, 1957.

Losick, Richard, and Phillips W. Robbins, "The Receptor Site for a Bacterial Virus," *Scientific American*, November, 1969.

Macalpine, Ida, and Richard Hunter, "Porphyria and King George III," *Scientific American*, July, 1969.

Mendel, G., *Experiments in Plant Hybridization*, Cambridge, Mass., Harvard University Press, 1948 (a description of his original work; translated from his paper of 1866).

Moody, Paul Amos, *Genetics of Man*, New York, Norton, 1967.

Muller, H. J., "Radiation and Human Mutation," *Scientific American*, November, 1955.

Peters, J. A., ed., *Classic Papers in Genetics*, Englewood Cliffs, N.J., Prentice-Hall, 1959.

Sager, Ruth, "Genes Outside the Chromosomes," *Scientific American*, January, 1965.

Sutton, H. Eldon, *Genes, Enzymes, and Inherited Diseases*, New York, Holt, Rinehart and Winston, 1962.

Tomasz, Alexander, "Cellular Factors in Genetic Transformation," *Scientific American*, January, 1969.

Wallace, Bruce, and T. Dobzhansky, *Radiation, Genes, and Man*, New York, Holt, Rinehart and Winston, 1959.

Whittinghill, Maurice, *Human Genetics and Its Foundations*, New York, Reinhold, 1965.

Wollman, E. L., and F. Jacob, "Sexuality in Bacteria," *Scientific American*, July, 1956.

Wood, William B., and R. S. Edgar, "Building a Bacterial Virus," *Scientific American*, July, 1967.

Yanofsky, Charles, "Gene Structure and Protein Structure," *Scientific American*, May, 1967.

Zinder, Norton D., "Transduction in Bacteria," *Scientific American*, November, 1958.

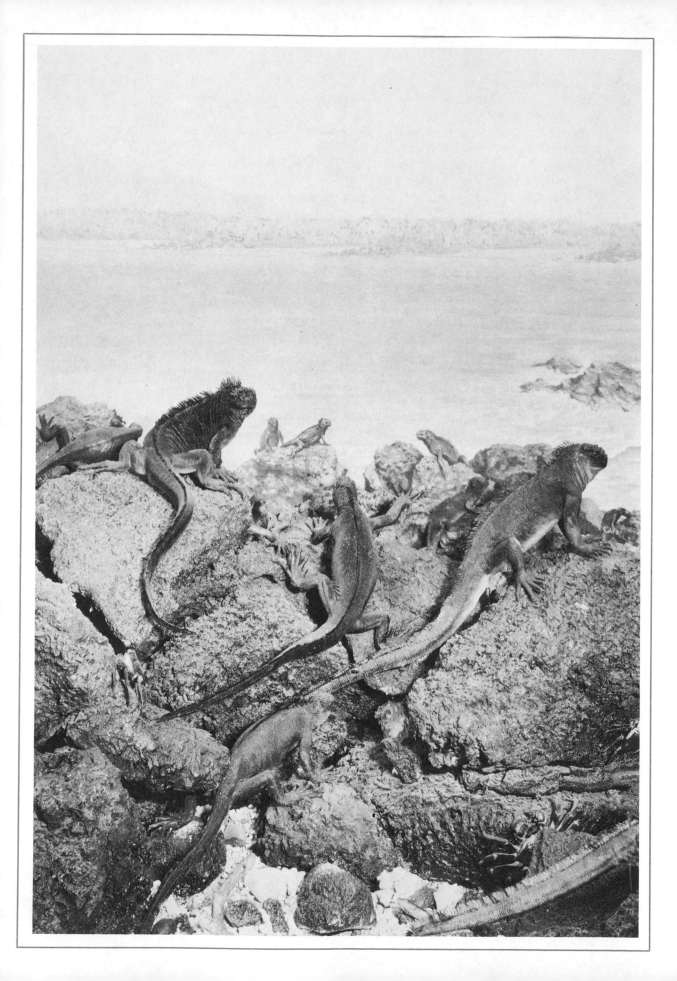

11

Evolution and Natural Selection

Overwhelming evidence indicates that during the course of time all species of organisms have changed. This can be demonstrated not only from the fossil record but with living populations under experimental and natural conditions. Evolution is often defined as the theory or concept dealing with the changes that occur in living organisms as a result of slight genetic variations through successive generations. This implies that present-day organisms have developed from preexisting forms and that the visible changes were produced by changes in genes and gene frequencies. Evolution, therefore, can be defined as a change in gene frequencies. The Hardy-Weinberg principle, discussed at the conclusion of the previous chapter, suggested how gene frequencies might change in a population under the influence of natural selection. Evolution is a generally accepted concept in society today and modern biology recognizes its foundation in genetic mechanisms. Moreover, evolution unifies the entire field of biology and helps to clarify the fundamental structural and functional relationships that exist among all organisms.

EVIDENCES OF EVOLUTION

FOSSILS

An excellent opportunity for reviewing the history of the development of life exists in the fossil record, and the *fossilization* process permits us to see the living forms that existed at various times in the history of the earth. Most fossils are formed when organisms containing hard,

Figure 11·1 The Grand Canyon from the South rim. (Photo by M. W. Williams, Courtesy of U. S. Dept. of Interior, National Park Service.)

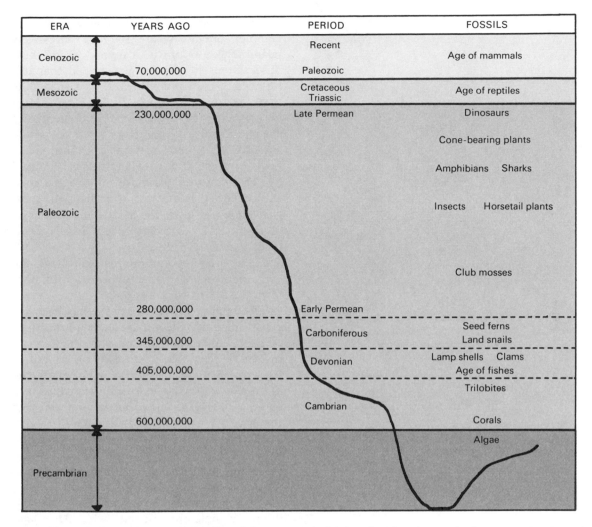

ERA	YEARS AGO	PERIOD	FOSSILS
Cenozoic		Recent	Age of mammals
	70,000,000	Paleozoic	
Mesozoic		Cretaceous Triassic	Age of reptiles
	230,000,000	Late Permean	Dinosaurs
			Cone-bearing plants
			Amphibians Sharks
Paleozoic			Insects Horsetail plants
			Club mosses
	280,000,000	Early Permean	
		Carboniferous	Seed ferns Land snails
	345,000,000		
		Devonian	Lamp shells Clams Age of fishes
	405,000,000		
		Cambrian	Trilobites
	600,000,000		Corals
			Algae
Precambrian			

Figure 11·2 Section through the Grand Canyon and vicinity showing the geologic eras and selected periods. Common names for some of the fossils are shown on the right.

mineralized parts are buried in mud or sand before they have decayed. After burial, decay stops and fossilization can occur in several ways. One type of fossil is the impression or mold that forms in the developing rock layers as the organismic parts are dissolved. Another type is formed when the original chemical compounds composing the hard parts of the organism, such as calcium carbonate, are preserved. A more common fossil, however, is formed by the replacement or recrystalization of the original minerals by another mineral.

Silicates and other minerals are present in the water associated with the sand or mud and can enter porous materials such as bone marrow or spaces left by the decay of softer parts.

If fossil-bearing rocks of approximate known dates are exposed, scientists can gain some knowledge of the plants and animals that existed in those times. Such a source is the Grand Canyon (Figure 11–1) where the Colorado River has exposed a series of rock layers a mile deep representing a two-billion-year period of time. Here we have a virtual

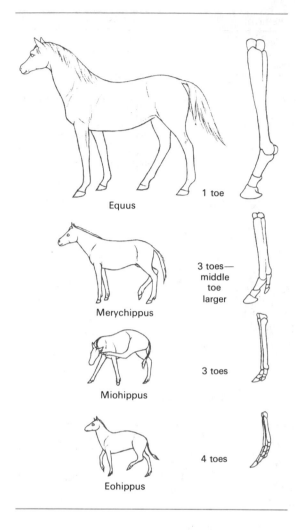

Equus

1 toe

Merychippus

3 toes—
middle
toe
larger

Miohippus

3 toes

Eohippus

4 toes

Figure 11·3 Part of the family tree of the horse. The forelegs are shown on the right. (From Manter and Miller.)

storybook of our earth and a record of some of the organisms that lived in the various eras over this period of time. The oldest rock is found at the bottom of the canyon, whereas the youngest rock occurs at the top. A diagrammatic cross section (Figure 11-2) shows the geologic eras and periods represented by the various layers. Representatives of each period are listed next to the layers in which they are found. As we might expect, the fossils of the most simple living forms are found near the bottom of the canyon and the fossils of more complex organisms are found progressively nearer the top of the canyon. From these observations it may be generalized that this represents the developmental pattern of life.

Another way in which the fossil record can be utilized is to trace the development of a specific family of plants or animals. From such studies general patterns of evolution can be determined. The excellent fossils produced by vertebrate animals make this group a good subject for such study, and perhaps the most well-known group is the horse family. Because of the extensive assemblage of fossils available, the horse family has been traced back approximately 55 million years although the early members of this family were far different from the horses we know today.

The family tree of the horse has been reconstructed by paleontologists (Figure 11-3). In this diagram one should note the increase in overall size, the increase in the length of legs, the increase in the size of the skull (the brain also increased in size and complexity), and the changes in the forefoot from four toes to one toe. We should not visualize a straight-line lineage beginning with *Eohippus*, changing to *Miohippus* and then to *Merychippus* and ultimately culminating in the modern horse, *Equus*. There were many lines (Figure 11-3), many experiments in nature, and *Eohippus* did not completely "die out" when *Miohippus* appeared, but its frequency in the population probably decreased. Thus the frequency of the genotype producing *Eohippus* became less in the population as the genotype that produced the horse *Miohippus* increased. This process of the gradual replacement of some genotypes for others in the populations occurred over the past 55 million years until the most successful genotype for our present environment, *Equus*, remained.

Considerable genetic variation exists within the modern horse family, and breeders have reported particularly great variations in size and foot structure. It is possible, therefore, through "backward breeding," or selection for primitive characteristics, to produce horses

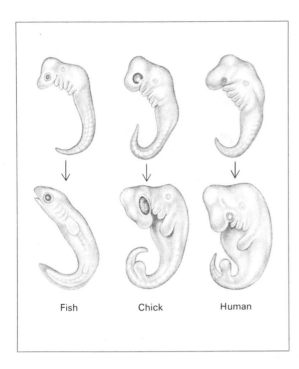

Figure 11·4 Sketches of the developing embryos of three vertebrates. Note how the embryos are quite similar in the early stage but how they change as development proceeds. Also note the gill arches and clefts in all embryos.

that resemble the forerunners of the modern horse. Through this process varieties have been developed that reach less than thirty inches in height and possess multiple toes.

EMBRYOLOGY

If we become more than a casual student of nature we feel compelled to go beyond the observational state and inquire about relationships. In fact, if we look closely at the natural environment, it is difficult to ignore some of the relationships and developmental patterns. For example, an observation of the developing embryos of vertebrate organisms reveals a remarkable similarity during early stages (Figure 11–4). A closer examination shows *pharyngeal gill slits* in all vertebrate embryos. These slitlike openings from the pharynx

(throat region) to the outside are present in all vertebrates (in fact, in all members of the phylum Chordata) and are similar in structure and appearance in the early embryo. As development progresses in the various vertebrates, however, these slits assume different functions. In the fish and fishlike animals, some of the gill slits develop into respiratory organs. Birds and mammals, however, occupy a different habitat where gills are unnecessary, but they face other problems such as transmission and detection of sound (sound is transmitted more readily in water than in air). Portions of the original gill slit and arch arrangement have been modified in birds and mammals into parts of the sound-producing and sound-detecting mechanisms. In man the auditory canal and the eustachian tube which connects the middle ear and the throat are remnants of gill slits. Here is an example of the opportunistic nature of the evolutionary process—a process that can take existing structures and modify them for a new environment. Modifications of some of the arches in various vertebrates are illustrated in Figure 11–5.

HOMOLOGY

Another observation on vertebrates reveals a basic similarity in the structure of the forelimbs. Although the forelimbs of man, whales, and birds appear to be different, there is a similarity of bone structure that apparently comes from similar embryonic development. Thus it would appear that the same basic plan was utilized for all vertebrate forelimbs, but modifications that occur are correlated with the different habits and habitats of these animals. This phenomenon of similarity in structure based on inheritance from a common ancestor is known as *homology* and the structures so derived are called *homologous*. Some of the comparative anatomists as early as the eighteenth and nineteenth centuries clearly saw these relationships in nature. Several variations from the generalized or ancestral-type vertebrate forelimb are shown in Figure

355

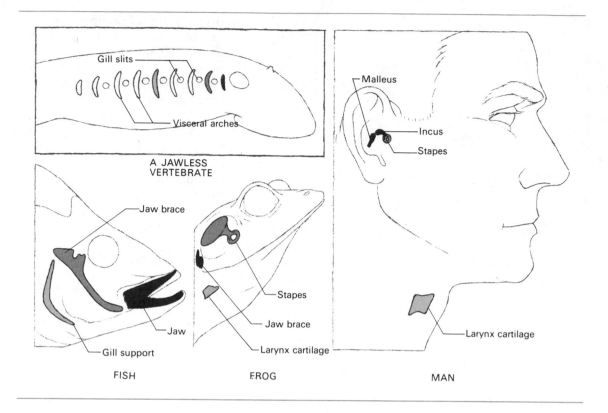

Gill slits

Visceral arches

A JAWLESS
VERTEBRATE

Jaw brace

Malleus

Incus

Stapes

Stapes

Jaw brace

Larynx cartilage

Jaw

Gill support

Larynx cartilage

FISH

FROG

MAN

Figure 11·5 Modification of pharyngeal slits and arches in selected vertebrates. Note that the first visceral arch forms the jaws in adult fish, jaw braces in the frog, and two of the middle-ear bones, incus and malleus, in man (for sound conduction). The second arch serves as jaw brace in fish; in the frog and in man it forms the stapes (bone for sound conduction). The fifth arch, which functions as support for the gills in fish, develops into part of the cartilage support for the larynx in the frog and man.

11–6. Functional comparisons between certain structures can also be made; for example, the wings of birds and insects have different origins although they serve the same function. Structures that are similar in function but different in evolutionary origin are termed *analogous*.

INTERMEDIATE FORMS AND "LIVING FOSSILS"

Classification schemes are simply attempts to group organisms according to similar characteristics and, as such, reflect man's interpretation of nature. (Actually classification schemes do vary and all biologists do not necessarily agree on one plan of classification.) Existing intermediate forms that actually violate man's classification schemes represent the popularly known "missing links" between classification groups. Perhaps the most classic example of a missing link is *Archaeopteryx*, an intermediate between the reptiles and the birds (Figure 11–7). It has so many reptilian characteristics that it could be considered as one of the flying reptiles except for one important feature —it had feathers, which can clearly be seen in some of the fossils. *Archaeopteryx*, then, is probably an intermediate form between these two large groups of animals.

An interesting little animal resembling a

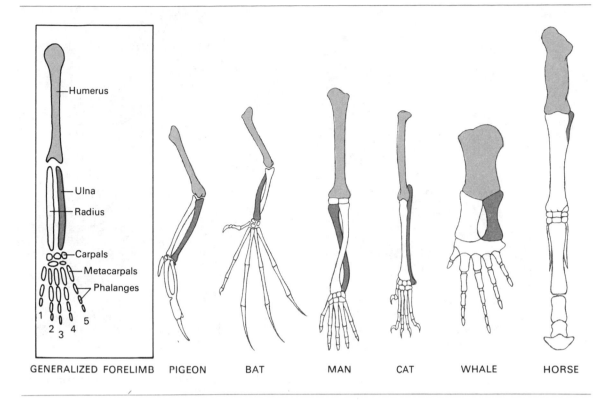

Figure 11·6 Homologous development of vertebrate forelimbs. The basic plan of organization is shown as a generalized forelimb. Variations of this plan can clearly be seen in the six examples of vertebrate forelimbs.

caterpillar is found in Africa, New Zealand, Australia, Central America, and other similar environments. *Peripatus*, which is about two inches long, lives an obscure life in damp places under bark and leaves (Figure 11–8). Its present discontinuous distribution indicates that it may have been more widespread in earlier times but is now nearing extinction. The importance of this group of animals (about seventy species) is that it has many characteristics of the Annelida (segmented worms) and the Arthropoda (insects, crustaceans, etc.). The respiratory system, blood system, and mouth parts are distinctly insect-like, whereas the excretory system, repro-

ductive ducts, and body wall resemble the earthworm group. Where should this organism be classified—in the Annelida or the Arthropoda? Most zoologists place it with the arthropods since this is a diverse phylum anyway, but it does have characteristics of another phylum. These missing links suggest strongly that organisms developed in a continuous fashion and were not "created" in large, discrete, and immutable groups.

On occasion living organisms have been found that were once known only as fossils. These "living fossils" provide biologists with a link to the past. An interesting example is that of *Metasequoia*, a deciduous, cone-bearing

Figure 11·7 Photo of Archaeopteryx. Cast of the fossil archaeopteryx (left) and a photo of a restoration (right). Photographs courtesy of the American Museum of Natural History.

tree, commonly known as the *dawn redwood* and closely related to the familiar redwood of the genus *Sequoia* (Figure 11–9). In 1941, a Japanese botanist proposed the genus name *Metasequoia* for fossil specimens of this tree which had been studied for some time. Then in the same year, after the Chinese had retreated from the Japanese armies into the interior of China, a forest survey disclosed the living *Metasequoia*. Later in the 1940s, after the close of World War II, United States botanists studied the plants in their natural habitat and shipped seeds all over the world. Today the tree has been moved back into areas such as the West Coast of the United States where fossils show that it once thrived.

One of the more exciting discoveries of a "living fossil" came in 1938 when a prehistoric-looking fish with lobed fins was taken by commercial fishermen in deep water off the coast of South Africa (Figure 11–10). This

fish, which was about five feet long, proved to be a coelacanth (the genus *Latimeria*) which was known widely in the fossil record from the Devonian period (about 400,000,000 years ago) through the Cretaceous (about 75,000,000 years ago). It had been considered extinct since the Cretaceous period.

Figure 11.8 *Peripatus.* An intermediate form which shows characteristics of two phyla, the Annelida and the Arthropoda. (Courtesy of Carolina Biological Supply Co.)

Figure 11·9 *Metasequoia*, the dawn redwood, and a close-up of a branch. (Photos by Lola B. Graham, National Audubon Society.)

Since 1952 more coelacanths have been taken off the coast of Madagascar near the Comoro Islands and subsequent studies of its anatomy have provided important information to students of animal evolutionary development. This animal is a direct relative of the group of fishes belonging to the order Crossopterygii, which gave rise to the amphibians. Thus the coelacanth is closely related to a group of organisms that lies in the direct line of descent of animals who made the transition from water to land.

VESTIGIAL STRUCTURES

In many plants and animals, structures are present which have no apparent function but are often homologous to specific parts of close relatives. Such apparently useless parts are called *vestigial structures*. The most probable

explanation for these structures is that, although they are no longer needed in some species, they are still carried along in the heredity of the entire group. They also represent a visible testimony to the relationships of the organisms possessing similar vestigial features. In some snakes, for example,

Figure 11·10 The lobe-finned coelacanth, *Latimeria*.

359

bones resembling a pelvic girdle (hip bones) are present, indicating a relationship to four-legged vertebrates. The small splint bones on the horse foreleg are interpreted as reduced toes homologous to the two outer toes of some of its three-toed fossil relatives. Man possesses many vestigial organs such as the appendix, the last several vertebrae (the coccyx), ear lobes, and "wisdom" teeth.

THE MECHANISM OF EVOLUTION

HISTORICAL DEVELOPMENT OF THE CONCEPT

In the preceding paragraphs the term *evolution* was defined and some evidence was presented to show that such a process does occur. We should now attempt to understand the mechanism that governs or controls this process. Man has attempted to do this in the past—in fact, long before conclusive evidence of evolution was available. In this discussion we will follow the sequence of man's thoughts and efforts leading to the development of a meaningful concept of evolution. Any suggestion of change to an established system usually meets resistance from certain segments of society and the theory of evolution is no exception. We will see, however, that man has been aware of relationships and development (even if he did not always use the word *evolution*) among living forms for some time. We should not be too critical of the investigators and observers of the past even though today their explanations and theories sound highly improbable (if not impossible). We must remember that we have the benefit of their contributions, whereas they often had very little information on the subject to assist them.

As soon as primitive man could care for his immediate needs he probably began to ponder his relationship to the natural world, his origin, and, no doubt, the "why" for his existence. Modern man is still thinking about these problems. We do not know exactly when man began this search or how the very

early cultures considered these problems, but we do know something of Greek thought concerning evolution. Anaximander, one of the Ionian philosophers who lived around 600 B.C., believed that life sprang from mud which had covered the earth. He thought that plants, animals, and human beings arose in that order, with the land-dwelling animals living first in water and then moving onto land. It was Aristotle who noted a consistent pattern in the living world and who organized the known living organisms into a "ladder of life" (scala naturae), beginning with simple forms and ending in more complex forms. Two of his statements are quite descriptive of his thought: "nature proceeds little by little from things lifeless to animal life" and "nature passes from lifeless objects to animals in such unbroken sequences, interposing between them beings which live and yet are not animals." In the works of Anaximander and Aristotle we see a recognition of the evolutionary process although there is little specific attempt at explaining the mechanism reponsible for it. Aristotle, however, proposed a "perfecting principle" which was inherent in the organism and which could produce change.

After Aristotle there was little discussion of change or development in the world. The concept of a static world without alterations, not only in the living forms but also in the physical world, became predominate. Several theories have been advanced to account for this, among them being the rise of Christianity and the indifference of the Romans to any pure scientific work. All of nature was considered to be inert; the mountains would never change, climates were forever true, and living forms were immutable. This was the prevailing attitude as mankind entered the seventeenth century—a time often designated as "The Intellectual Revolution" or the "Age of Enlightenment." Societal changes occurred in the 1600s and 1700s and existing political systems were challenged. The rights of the individual were stressed and the infallibility of the church was questioned. Along with changes in social structures came changes in the conceptual schemes in the physical sciences under the stimulation of such memorable scientists as Galileo and Sir Isaac Newton. It was this background that established the groundwork for changes in the geological and biological sciences.

The classification work of Linnaeus in the 1700s established a static and fixed concept about species. Although such a system of classification was desirable and necessary for the biological sciences, this particular system tended to reinforce the church's position on the static nature of the world. The idea of change and a dynamic environment had to be introduced if man were to understand and develop relationships about his natural world. The immutability of species was challenged almost immediately by the French natural historian Buffon (1707–1788), who believed, contrary to theological doctrine, that animals did change. He was impressed with similarity in structure in some organisms and how a "basic plan" often occurred in the structure of organs such as the vertebrate forelimb. It was evident to Buffon that "nature" had produced many organisms over long periods of time and that some forms had become extinct.

It was not only important to establish that the living world was in a process of change— if we were to know the mechanics, the relationships between time and change and development on our earth were also needed. It was long believed that the changes in the landscape of the earth were due to catastrophes— sudden disturbances. But geologist James Hutton, in his *Theory of the Earth*, published in 1788, proposed that the continuous processes of erosion, mountain building, and vulcanism have changed the earth's features and that these same forces are active today. He recognized the importance of time as a factor in the development of the earth, and this had not been appreciated before. Hutton appeared to understand the role of cyclical events in the history of the world and concluded the first chapter of his treatise with the phrase, "we find no vestige of a beginning—no prospect of an end."

Another geologist, William Smith (about 1790), through a bit of deductive reasoning, arrived at the simple conclusion that in beds of deposition, the older layers were on the bottom and the overlying strata were younger. Hence the fossils found in lower strata were older than those found in strata above, and that a comparison of these fossils would indicate the developmental pattern of life on our planet. Since a particular stratum had its own characteristic fossils and if the age of that stratum were known, any other layer bearing these fossils must be of the same relative age. Thus certain fossils could be used to determine the age of various strata. Smith had tied the fossil record to the development of life on earth in relationship to time. Somewhat later Charles Lyell published a revolutionary textbook, *Principles of Geology* (1830), in which he clearly presented the dynamic effect of physical forces, working through time, in shaping our planet. He actually paved the way for Charles Darwin's great work and probably influenced Darwin more than any other person. Lyell mentioned the creation of new species in his book and came very close to stating Darwin's theory. He had actually recognized natural selection but failed to see how it could be a creative force. Perhaps the most significant factor is that people were gradually becoming accustomed to the concept of change.

One of the most familiar (and sometimes considered the first) evolutionist was Jean Baptiste Lamarck (1744–1829). Although Lamarck recognized an evolutionary process in nature, his explanation of the mechanisms that produced this change and development was not correct, and is incompatible with modern biological knowledge. Lamarck's theory is often stated as "the theory of the *inheritance of acquired characteristics*," and it shows that, although he recognized the importance of the environment in evolution, Lamarck did not completely understand its role. He proposed that organisms moving to a new environment would require certain structural modifications. Because of this need,

Figure 11·11   Charles Darwin at 31. (Photo courtesy the American Museum of Natural History.)

employment of Lamarckism would be a case of white-skinned humans moving to tropical islands where the sun might not only tan their skins, but would cause the next generation to be born darker. We now know that this inheritance of acquired characteristics does not occur from changes in the body or somatic cells; only alterations in germinal or sex cells can be transmitted to the next generation.

CHARLES DARWIN'S CONTRIBUTIONS

The most important figure in the development of the theory of evolution was Charles Darwin (Figure 11–11). He was able to add to the concept of an evolutionary process and to propose a mechanism to account for it which was to gain almost universal acceptance. Born in 1809 in England, Darwin was the son of a physician and the grandson of a famous natural philosopher, Erasmus Darwin. His grandfather was also concerned with changes in living organisms and he accepted Lamarck's viewpoint of the inheritance of acquired characteristics to explain these changes. Young Darwin was interested in pursuing a medical career but soon dropped this program at Edinburgh and turned to theology at Cambridge. His real interests, however, were in geology and natural history and he was strongly influenced by the geologist Lyell. Another influence on Darwin was the *Essay on Population* written by Malthus, which stated the now well-known concept that populations increase at a geometric rate although resources for living are generally limited. Malthus believed that populations must be held in check or they would soon run out of subsistence, and this suggested to Darwin the idea of competition and a struggle for existence in populations.

changes in structure would result and the more a specific structure was used, the more highly it would be developed. As a result of this modification, other structures might not be used and these would tend to disappear. This part of Lamarck's theory is often referred to as the "use and disuse of parts." Thus a Lamarckian (one who accepts Lamarck's theory of evolution) would explain the reduction of the horse's lateral toes on the foreleg by stating that only the middle toe was used for running. Furthermore, Lamarck believed that a change in one generation, produced by the environment, would be passed on to the next generation through inheritance. An absurd example, if this theory were carried to its ultimate, would be the transmission of bulging biceps to his son by a father who had lifted weights during his lifetime. A more sophisticated example of the

That species could and did in fact change was a certainty to Darwin. The production of new varieties of domestic animals seemed to illustrate this point very well, and Darwin became extremely interested in animal breeding. In addition to familiarizing himself with many animal-breeding programs, Darwin conducted breeding experiments with various

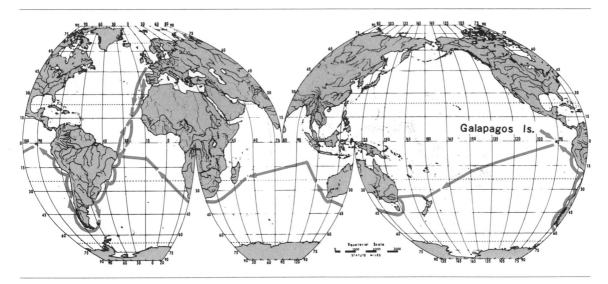

Figure 11·12 The voyage of the H.M.S. Beagle.

races of pigeons. He was acutely aware of the possibilities of obtaining desired traits in the offspring through the selection of characteristics in the parents. If man could produce varieties through controlled breeding experiments, why, wondered Darwin, cannot nature modify species in a similar manner through a selection process?

Perhaps the most important biological background for Charles Darwin was provided by a trip on the H.M.S. Beagle during the years 1831 to 1836 (Figure 11–12). Although the expedition was essentially for mapping and charting purposes, the value of having a naturalist was recognized and Darwin was selected for this job. As a result he was able to spend considerable time in the southern hemisphere, especially South America and the Galapagos Islands. Here Darwin observed native tribes and wild animals in an almost undisturbed state, and the results of this trip were described in a widely read publication entitled *The Voyage of the Beagle*. Darwin regarded this trip as the most important aspect of his education and preparation for the formulation of the theory of evolution.

The Galapagos Islands (Figure 11–13), located 650 miles west of Ecuador, are composed of volcanic peaks. Since some of the

peaks are high enough to produce local climatic differences, a variety of habitats exists, ranging from lava cliffs to cactus forests to moist, lush forests (Figure 11–14). Although located very near the equator, the small group of islands is washed by cool antarctic currents as well as tropical currents and the islands are separated from each other by great expanses (up to 60 miles) of deep water. All of these factors add up to a unique place and it is no wonder that this archipelago has been called a "living laboratory." Geologically the islands are considered to be rather young and the animal and plant life is American—that is, the inhabiting species probably came from the coast of South America. Seeds and spores, and possibly insects, could have been blown in by the wind. Additional plants and animals could have arrived on "rafts" from the mainland, while some birds could have flown the distance. Equally important, however, is the fact that the invading organisms had to find a suitable habitat if they were to survive in this environment. Here on these islands a unique and interesting fauna developed, numbering among its members the giant 400-pound tortoises, the prehistoric-looking iguana lizards, a small penquin species, flightless cormorants, boobies, and a variety of finches

363

Figure 11·13   The Galapagos Islands.

Figure 11·14   Sullivan Bay in the Galapagos Islands showing James Island in the distance. (Courtesy James Murray.)

364

Figure 11·15   (a) Marine iguanas from the Galapagos Islands. (Courtesy of the American Museum of Natural History.)

(Figure 11–15). Darwin studied all of these animals and particularly noted that the iguanas differed from island to island. But the animals in which he was most interested from the standpoint of the development of new species was the finch group. Through a detailed study of the fourteen species of finches in the Galapagos Islands, Darwin arrived at a theory to explain the evolution of new species.

He reasoned that a single finch species arriving from the mainland found a variety of habitats available to it. Since variation existed among the individual members of the species (and Darwin did not understand the source of this variability), it was possible for the species to exploit all of these available habitats which included barren ground, grasslands, shrubs, and trees. The fourteen species show a great variation in bill structure, and perhaps it was this anatomical feature more than any other that permitted the habitation of the various

Figure 11·15   (b) Flightless cormorants. (Courtesy California Academy of Sciences.)

365

niches. In Darwin's words, this is "a most singular group of finches, related to each other in the structure of their beaks, short tails, form of body, and plumage." He further summarized his feelings about this group by stating: "seeing this gradation and diversity of structure in one small, intimately related group of birds, one might really fancy that from an original paucity of birds in this archipelago, one species had been taken and modified for different ends." Actually this group of finches had filled the ecological roles of birds not found in this environment such as warblers, grosbeaks, blackbirds, woodpeckers, and nuthatches.

We can sense the value of these islands to science and to an understanding of the evolutionary process when we read Darwin's thoughts on this environment:

> Both in space and time, we seem to be brought somewhat near to that great fact—that mystery of mysteries—the first appearance of new beings on this earth. Reviewing the facts here given, one is astonished at the amount of creative force, if such an expression may be used, displayed on these small, barren, and rocky islands; and still more so, at its diverse yet analogous action on points so near each other. I have said that the Galapagos Archipelago might be called a satellite attached to America, but it should rather be called a group of satellites, physically similar, organically distinct, yet intimately related to each other, and all related in a marked, though much lesser degree, to the great American continent.

After assimilation of the material from the voyage of the Beagle and other studies, Darwin proposed his theory of evolution in 1859 in the now famous book entitled *On the Origin of Species by Means of Natural Selection*. The first printing was sold out almost instantly and its contents threw the world into a controversy over the mechanism of the development of life. The church and many biologists violently opposed it while many other biologists and some laymen applauded it. It is necessary to note here that another biologist, Alfred Wallace, had arrived at conclusions identical to Darwin's and had in fact sent Darwin a copy of his theory in 1858. Wallace had arrived at his concept independently of Darwin through his studies of the flora and fauna of Malaya. It was decided that they should publish their works simultaneously and thus most biologists speak of the *Darwin-Wallace theory*. Since Darwin's thesis was much better documented, the theory is often referred to as Darwinism. The Darwin-Wallace theory of how life has evolved to its present diversity can be briefly summarized as:

1   Variation exists among the members of a particular species (look about you at your fellow human beings).
2   Overproduction usually occurs in a population and more individuals are produced than can be supported in a particular environment (the species population remains relatively constant, however, because of the following factors).
3   Competition results from the population pressure on the environmental resources (a struggle for existence).
4   Certain individuals with favorable characteristics for the particular environment survive (*natural selection*).
5   A preservation of favored individuals occurs and these characteristics are passed on to their offspring (survival of the fittest).

As we have said, Darwin failed to recognize the source of the variation in organisms, and he looked to a modification of Lamarckism for the answer. He used a theory called "pangenesis" in which it was supposed that tiny units called "pangenes" pass from each part of the body into the gametes to determine what the offspring will inherit in the next generation. This was clearly a type of inheritance of acquired characteristics. But the essence of the Darwin-Wallace theory was the concept of natural selection—that is, the selective force of the environment.

THE MODERN CONCEPT—NEO-DARWINISM

Since the time of the Darwin-Wallace theory, discoveries in biology have contributed greatly to our knowledge of the process of evolution. Studies in sexuality, chromosomes, mutations, and genetics (the work of Mendel) have added to the basic theory proposed by Darwin. Therefore we cannot really credit the modern concept of evolution to any one man and must recognize that, as in most modern scientific theories, the labors and research of many are utilized in the formulation of a workable and probable concept to explain the development of life.

Modern biology attributes variation in living organisms to inheritable chromosomal units, called *genes*. Since the genes are on the chromosomes, variations are produced in the events of meiosis (crossovers and recombination) and mutation and are transmitted through fertilization. The role of the environment then is not to *produce* the variations but to *select* the variations. A particular environment acts as a "screen" permitting certain genotypes to inhabit it and "selecting out" other genotypes. Natural selection, as used by Darwin and most modern biologists, refers to the selecting role and function of the environment upon genotypes living in it. We speak of those organisms selected by a particular environment as being adapted to that habitat, and those characteristics they display, which are of value in that environment, as *adaptations*. Because heritable adaptations increase the probable success of a species, adaptive changes are beneficial. Many changes can occur in a species and all of these are evolutionary; all changes, however, are not necessarily adaptive.

Since better-adapted organisms in a particular environment reproduce at a higher rate than the less adapted, biologists currently

Birds, such as ducks, that have webs between their toes can swim better and faster than those without webbing. Swimming fast assists them in escaping enemies and obtaining food. LAMARCK would explain the development of webbing as:

Early ducks had no webs

As the feet were used for swimming, webs developed

Webbing continued to increase in subsequent generations

Finally, through continuous use in swimming, the webbed foot of modern ducks developed

DARWIN would explain this development as:

The first ducks showed variation in the structure of their feet; some had no webbing and others showed considerable webbing; he did not understand why this variation existed but it could be inherited by the offspring

Ducks with webbing survived through competition and natural selection; favored races were preserved; survival of the fittest

Finally, only ducks with webbed feet remained (there is still some slight variation in the webbing, however)

The MODERN CONCEPT explains this process as:
Ancestral ducks exhibited variation in the webbing of their feet and this variation was genetic in source, that is, it was due to gene and chromosomal differences which could be inherited

Those that had webbing were selected by the environment (natural selection) and their genotype frequencies increased in the population through differential reproduction

Finally, only those ducks with considerable webbing remained in the population

Figure 11·16 A comparison of Lamarckism, Darwinism, and neo-Darwinism. (Note the similarity in Darwin's concept and the modern interpretation.)

use the term *differential reproduction* to denote the success of favored forms rather than the term "survival of the fittest." As a result of differential reproduction, the frequency of certain genotypes increases in the population while the frequency of others decreases. If the environment should change, the overall frequency of genotypes could change and organisms of different appearance and function might result. It is quite correct then to treat evolution as a change in gene frequencies. Returning momentarily to the example of the horse used earlier, we see that horses with characteristics of the modern horse could better escape their predators, reproduce and increase their frequency in the horse population. A comparison of the Lamarckian, Darwinian, and *neo-Darwinian* concept of evolution is shown in Figure 11–16.

ADAPTATIONS

Adaptations have been described as those traits of an organism (or a species) that enhance its chances for survival and reproduction in a specific environment. Although the obvious adaptations to most of us are the variations in body structure, adaptive characteristics can also be physiological or behavioral. Some adaptations are for physical offensive and defensive purposes (such as claws, strong muscles, and teeth), others, such as *mimicry* and camouflage, are less physical but frequently a more effective means of protection (Figure 11–17). Many outdoorsmen are familiar with the adaptive coloration provided by the spots on fawns and many recognize the "broken wing" behavior of the female grouse as she limps through the brush diverting the intruder's attention from her brood hidden nearby. Everyone is also familiar with the pungent odor released by the skunk to deter his enemies. The whitish uric acid excreted by birds and reptiles is a physiological adaptation to provide for the release of nitrogenous wastes with little loss of water. And we could go on and on discussing adaptations, for these are essentially the story of biology—how organisms live, reproduce, and survive in their environments. Although the subject of adaptation has filled entire books, it is more important for us to understand the process, and for this

Figure 11·17 Examples of mimicry, a type of adaptation in which an animal blends with its surroundings. Here the insects resemble the leaves on which they are resting. (Courtesy of Dr. Asa C. Thoresen.)

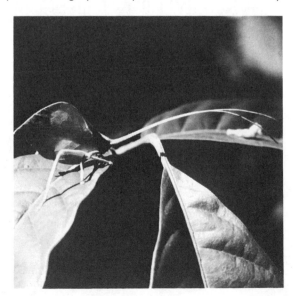

we will consider an example of a particular adaptation in a species over a definite period of time.

Most species of butterflies and moths display some variation in their coloration. In the British Isles many of the light-colored moth species have naturally occurring black mutants which represent a definite percentage of the population. About 1850, in the area of Manchester, England, the black form of the peppered moth, *Biston betularia,* represented only about 1 percent of the population (Figure 11–19). This rural area was characterized by a clear atmosphere and white, lichen-covered tree trunks. Thus the white variety of the moth blended into and could be camouflaged by the environment. The dark variety, however, was under heavy selection pressure from preying birds who could easily spot them and pick them off as they rested on trees in the daytime. As the Manchester area became industrialized, the environment changed, air pollution resulted, and the tree trunks were darkened from soot and the death of the lichen growth. By 1900 it was estimated that the black form made up over 99 percent of the population (Figure 11–18). To test the hypothesis that predation accounted for the change in gene frequencies in the population of *Biston betularia,* researchers released equal numbers

Figure 11·18 Map of the British Isles showing the relative distribution of the light and dark forms of *Biston betularia.* Industrial areas are designated by black circles. Large colored circles represent moth populations composed largely of light forms, whereas the shaded areas represent populations of predominantly dark forms. (Redrawn with permission of *Scientific American.*)

Figure 11·19 (*a*) The peppered moth, and its black form, *carboneria*, at rest on soot-covered oak trunk near Birmingham, England.

Figure 11·19 (*b*) The same two forms on a lichen-covered tree in an unpolluted area. (From the Experiments of Dr. H. B. D. Kettlewell, Oxford University.)

of black and light forms in a polluted area and in a natural area. Approximately twice as many black forms were recovered in the industrialized, polluted environment, whereas in the unpolluted area, many more of the lighter forms survived. It should be noted that the environmental changes did not produce the black mutant; it was always present in the population, and its frequency would have remained fairly constant had certain environmental changes not occurred. (Remember the Hardy-Weinberg principle.) When conditions in the environment which favored the light form changed, the black mutant was merely selected by the new environment. In other words, the light moth was adapted for one environment and the black moth for another. Variation is of definite survival value to a species since, as we have just noted, if the environment changes, certain variant members of the species may continue to exist.

With the enforcement of antipollution laws in the past decade tree trunks in England are returning to their lighter, natural state. It is significant that recent studies indicate an increase of the lighter form in the population. Thus it is apparent that the ratio of light to dark forms is again changing due to natural selection.

SPECIATION

Some biologists criticized Darwin and his theory of natural selection because they could not understand how the process could produce anything new. They frequently saw it acting in a destructive manner and, like Darwin himself, could not understand its creative possibilities. In the following discussion, emphasis will be placed on the creative aspects of natural selection.

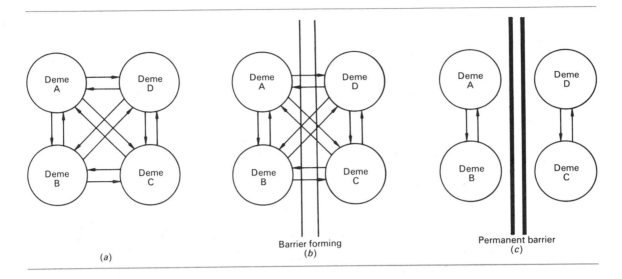

Barrier forming
(b)

(a)

Permanent barrier
(c)

Figure 11·20   The splitting of a population by a barrier. In (a) free mating among all demes occurs. In (c) the barrier restricts mating and two separate breeding groups are formed.

It is interesting to speculate what might happen if some members of a species were isolated from the others for a long period of time. Could the two populations change enough to produce two separate species?

Within a large breeding population, smaller breeding groups exist known as *demes* or gene pools. Demes are simply local breeding groups in which members are more likely to mate because they are closer together. The field mice in one field may form one deme and those a half mile away another. Figure 11–20 illustrates the breeding pattern among demes of a population; the arrows indicate that a free flow of genes is possible in the population. This population is also referred to as a "total gene pool." This figure also shows what will happen to the mating pattern if the population is split —that is, demes A and B can still mate and exchange hereditary material but they cannot mate with demes C and D. By splitting the population, we simply mean that the gene flow has been interrupted. Essentially, two new populations result.

Two questions need to be answered at this point: (1) what will happen under this new mating pattern to each of the new populations

and (2) what kinds of barriers can bring about situations such as this? In answer to the first question, gene and chromosomal mutations will continue on each side of the barrier, perhaps at the same rate and of the same kind or perhaps not. The environments on either side may be different or may change as a result of the barrier. Certain hereditary features may be incorporated into one population and not in the other through natural selection or through chance. If the two populations remain separated long enough, selection may incorporate different gene and chromosome mutations into the separate populations. If organisms from either population come together again, they may not be compatible; that is, they may not be able to produce fertile offspring. When this happens, two species exist where only one was present before and we say that speciation has taken place. The time required for this to occur has been estimated to be between 10,000 and 1,000,000 years. This large variation in time is due to the different rates of effective mutations and natural selection. The effect of a barrier on a population and the ultimate result are summarized in Figure 11–21.

371

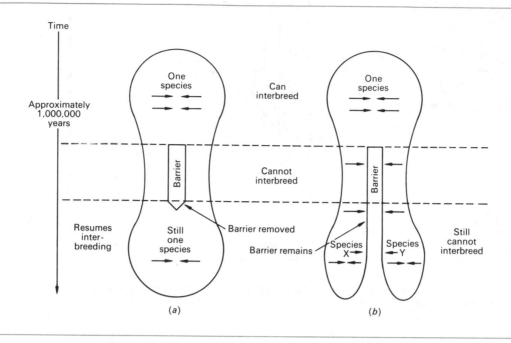

Figure 11·21 In diagram (*a*) a barrier occurs in a population of a species but it does not persist long enough to effect speciation. In diagram (*b*) the barrier is permanent and two species result.

Most barriers between populations are geographical, such as bodies of water or land masses. Barriers could be produced when a river cuts through land or when an earthquake dams up a river to change its course or form a lake. Mountain-building forces or earthquakes causing land slides could impose a land mass to separate a population. Any extensive, unsuitable habitat within the territory of a population will tend to isolate parts of that population. But before new species can be formed, a *biological barrier* or a biological isolating mechanism must occur which prevents the two groups from producing fertile offspring should they come together again. Such biological barriers can include the incompatibility of gametes, a difference in behavior, or a variation in breeding season. A type of biological isolation occurs between two closely related species of pine trees in California where interbreeding is prevented because the pollen of one species is mature in February and the pollen of the other is not ready until April. Differences in behavior may isolate two closely related species of fish that occupy the same stream. The male of one species of stickleback fish may construct its nest slightly different from the male of another species and the females of each species can recognize the difference. In the fiddler crab several species may occupy the same shore, but the courtship dance performed by the male differs in each species so that only the female of his species is attracted to him. The donkey and the horse came from similar ancestral stock and can be mated to produce a sterile mule. The isolating mechanism here is known as "hybrid inviability" and results from incompatible chromosomes that cannot synapse at meiosis. The mule cannot produce functional viable gametes and is therefore a sterile organism.

Both geographical and biological isolating mechanisms play a role in speciation. Most biologists believe that geographical or spatial isolation must occur first and after that some type of biological barrier develops to reproductively isolate the two groups of the original population. To summarize the speciation process we should note that two factors are important, namely: (1) genetic variability must exist in the population; and (2) the population must be split by isolating mechanisms known as barriers.

Earlier in this chapter we mentioned the Grand Canyon and its geologic time table. This area also provides us with a notable example of speciation. The Grand Canyon could certainly have acted as a geographical barrier to isolate two parts of any population that once occupied the entire area. This is believed to have happened in the case of the Kaibab squirrel on the north rim and the Abert squirrel of the south rim (Figure 11–22). These two squirrels have tufted ears and bushy tails and are very similar in appearance, yet they are generally considered to be two distinct species because they are effectively isolated by the canyon. Several other species apparently have undergone similar isolation and speciation in this area—for example, the pocket mouse, the antelope squirrel, and several plants.

DIVERGENCE AND ADAPTIVE RADIATION

The speciation process is an explanation of how species can be created and diverge from one another. Moreover, each new species may undergo further speciation at a later time. This further *divergence* leads to *adaptive radiation* wherein individuals of a particular species may move into different habitats and speciation continues. Eventually, a variety of organisms would be produced and this is the condition we see today. Classification systems reflect this divergence; when we denote the members of a classification category we are recognizing the subgroups that have diverged from a common ancestral group (Figure

Figure 11·22 The closely related Kaibab (top) and Abert (bottom) squirrels of the Grand Canyon. The Kaibab, from the north rim, has a distinctly larger and whiter tail. The Abert, on the other hand, has a white underside. (Kaibab courtesy of Dept. of Interior, Grand Canyon National Park; Abert courtesy of Dept. of Interior, National Park Service.)

373

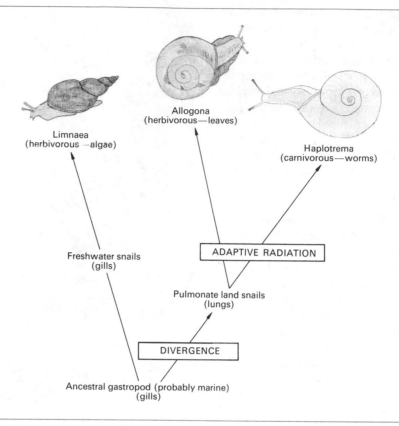

Figure 11·23 Evolutionary divergence in snails is illustrated by this diagram. Gills developed in these freshwater snails whereas lungs evolved in the land snails. Note that adaptive radiation occurred between the two closely related pulmonates.

11–23). Many major radiations have occurred in some of the large familiar groups of animals such as placental mammals, marsupial mammals, and the phylum Mollusca. But we will return to a group we have already discussed for our example, Darwin's finches (Figure 11–24). An ancestral finch arriving in the Galapagos Islands could have radiated into all of the habitats and ecological niches available to it. In fact, finches could even fill niches usually filled by woodpeckers and warblers because there was no competition. Some of the finches eat seeds whereas others feed on insects. Of the seed eaters, some eat cactus seeds specifically and others have adapted to large or small seeds of other plants. This speciation

and subsequent adaptive radiation was possible because the original species was able to disperse throughout the widely separated islands. Through this isolation, hereditary dissimilarities developed to a point where speciation could occur.

Darwin's finches can be divided into four categories based on their habitat and food-gathering characteristics:

1 *Ground finches*—six species that feed on seeds of varying sizes. The size of the seed eaten is related to the size of the bill. Competition for food therefore is avoided.

2 *Tree finches*—six species that live in moist forests and feed on insects in the trees.

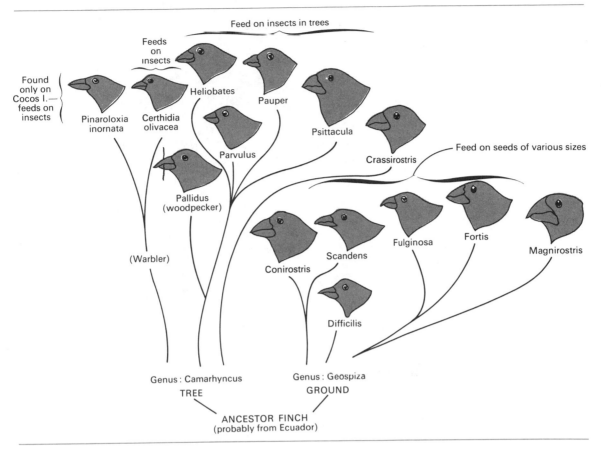

Found
only on
Cocos I.—
feeds on
insects

Feeds
on
insects

Feed on insects in trees

Pinaroloxia
inornata

Certhidia
olivacea

Heliobates

Pauper

Psittacula

Parvulus

Crassirostris

Feed on seeds of various sizes

Pallidus
(woodpecker)

Fulginosa

Fortis

Magnirostris

(Warbler)

Conirostris

Scandens

Difficilis

Genus : Camarhyncus
TREE

Genus : Geospiza
GROUND

ANCESTOR FINCH
(probably from Ecuador)

Figure 11·24 Adaptive radiation as shown by Darwin's finches. The first radiation was one of habitat: between ground and trees. Subsequent radiations were primarily on the basis of food.

One tree finch, *C. pallidus*, uses a cactus spine to probe insects from crevices. This represents a typical woodpecker niche. The use of tools by animals other than humans is quite rare and the spine-using finch is unique among birds.

3 *Warblerlike finch*—a single species that has found a habitat in the low bushes and feeds on insects.

4 *Cocos Island finch*—a single species that lives in a moist forest and feeds on insects. This bird is isolated from all the others since Cocos Island is several hundred miles to the northeast of the main group. It is thought that the Cocos Island species came directly from the mainland and is only indirectly related to the others.

CONVERGENCE AND PARALLELISM

Another evolutionary pattern occurs when two organisms (or groups) of different ancestry develop similar characteristics. Such a process is known as *convergence*. Figure 11–25 illustrates the convergent evolution that has occurred in marsupial and placental mammals. In placental mammals the embryo develops before birth inside the mother's uterus, attached by a placenta; marsupial embryos complete their development after an immature birth in an abdominal pouch on the mother. Placental mammals live extensively in all parts of the world. Although marsupial representatives are dispersed throughout various parts

375

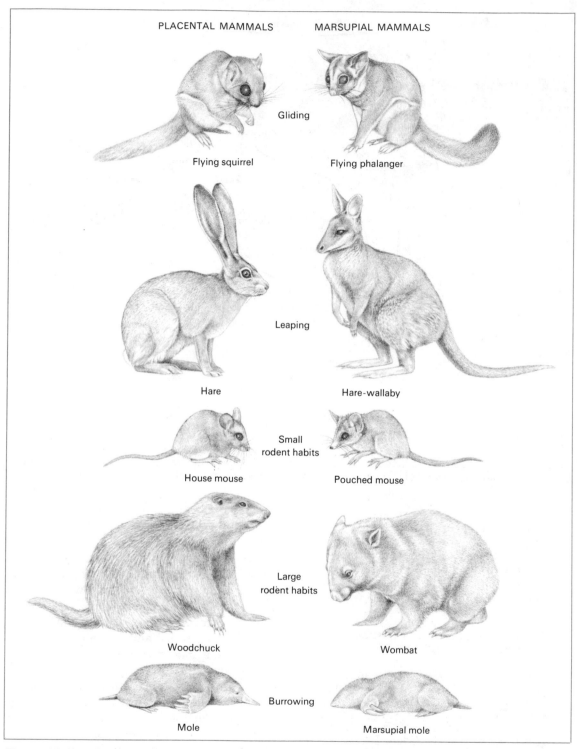

PLACENTAL MAMMALS   MARSUPIAL MAMMALS

Gliding

Flying squirrel   Flying phalanger

Leaping

Hare   Hare-wallaby

Small
rodent habits

House mouse   Pouched mouse

Large
rodent habits

Woodchuck   Wombat

Burrowing

Mole   Marsupial mole

Figure 11·25   Convergent evolution in the marsupial and placental mammals. (From *Zoology*, Cockrum and McCauley, Saunders.)

of the world, their primary development has been in Australia and they have radiated into almost every available niche. The principal reason for their extensive evolution on the continent of Australia was probably the absence of competition from placental mammals. When convergence occurs among fairly closely related organisms such as these, it is often termed *parallelism*. It is interesting that no marsupial has adapted to the flying niche represented by the bat in placentals. Some ecologists have proposed that the only reason this is true is that the flying niche in Australia may have been filled by bats from Asia and marsupials could not compete successfully. The principles of divergence and convergence are diagrammed in Figure 11–26.

THE MEANING OF EVOLUTION TO MAN

With the appearance of man a new type of evolution developed—cultural evolution—which is exclusive and unique to the human species. Through this process, man can transmit his knowledge and culture to future generations. Cultural evolution is possible because of man's large brain and his capacity for abstract thought and learning. Greater progress is thus possible when one generation can profit from the advances and mistakes of past generations. With the advent of man's large brain also came the ability to perceive ethics, moral relationships, concepts about the environment, and religions. All races of human beings therefore can concern themselves with more than simply acquiring food and shelter.

It is increasingly apparent that man has become an evolutionary agent who can modify, create, and destroy species through his interference with the normal environment. Practically every domestic plant or animal providing for man's subsistence has been artificially selected and bred for that role with man acting as the selective force. Human beings can also bring a species to extinction or near extinction as in the case of the passenger pigeon and the buffalo. Populations of wild animals such as deer can be regulated through

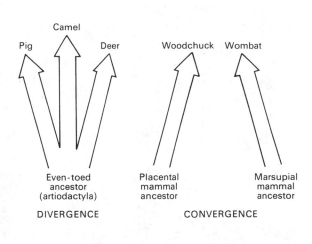

Figure 11·26 Examples of divergence and convergence among mammals.

game-management policies. In other words, nature is not the same since the human organism evolved and man can now control the evolutionary development of other species if he chooses. But can man control his own development and evolution? It seems that this could be possible since he understands the selective process and is learning more and more about the hereditary mechanism. The chief problem lies in the answer to the questions, how can man establish the principles to be used in the selection process in the human species, and which characteristics will be selected? At the present time there are certain traits that many people would agree are harmful to the human species, but the legal processes necessary to bring about selection against these traits would be too difficult to achieve. Many people fear the legal control of human heredity and behavior since its use obviously depends on who is in power. There are others, though, who believe that man will be forced to apply his knowledge of genetics and evolution to the human species if he is to survive and develop to his fullest capacities.

377

Figure 11·27 Theodosius Dobzhansky, outstanding investigator of the genetic basis of evolution. (Courtesy The Rockefeller Foundation.)

Many students of evolution have speculated on the appearance of the man of the future. These speculations range from very little change to a considerably different-appearing organism. Proponents of the "great change" hypothesis believe that, since man has changed so much in the short time that he has been on this planet (less than a million years), we can look for continued change in the future. One concept of change is in the direction of a larger cranium, to accommodate a slightly larger brain, and finer facial features. Another hypothesis holds that in the next 5000 years man will be slightly taller, have a skull that is more globular with the sensory organs more developed, have a more refined face with smaller teeth and fewer (the wisdom teeth missing), have less hair on his body, and have a slightly reduced appendix. That some changes will occur is almost certain, since we know that all species are mutable.

Perhaps of greater importance than man's future appearance is the problem of how an evolutionary concept is accepted by society. Conflicts between the modern concept of evolution and literal biblical interpretation have been frequent. However, this conflict is avoided by many religions today and evolution is accepted as the actual means for accomplishing the changes recorded in Genesis. As Theodosius Dobzhansky (Figure 11–27) has stated: "Evolution is the method whereby Creation is accomplished." The general feeling today is that a concept of evolution leads to a better understanding of our world and should be applied to other facets of our society, such as religion. Probably the greatest effect of the concept of evolution is that it provides a unifying framework for all of biology, and the great synthesis by Charles Darwin in 1859 provided all fields of biology with a central theme.

SUMMARIZING PRINCIPLES

Evolution is the concept that changes occurring in organisms result from slight genetic variations that are transmitted through successive generations. This orderly succession of change from preexisting species is a result of changes in genes and genotype frequencies.

Direct evidence for the existence of earlier forms of life may be obtained through the collection and dating of fossils. The well-preserved fossils of horses have provided an excellent reconstruction of the changes that have occurred in this family.

Numerous examples for illustrating evolution can be found in the development and structure of species living today, and many similarities exist in the embryology of closely related species. Several forms with characteristics intermediate between classification categories are known which strengthen the concept of gradual change.

The concept of organic evolution followed the realization that geological changes have occurred over periods of time. The statement of the theory of evolution and its probable mechanism through natural selection was made by Darwin and Wallace in 1858. Although Darwin accepted the Lamarckian theory of the inheritance of acquired characteristics, we now know that changes in species and subsequent natural selection are due to genetic changes with environmental selection for characteristics of adaptive value.

In order for new species to develop, it is generally accepted that an isolating mechanism must separate two parts of a population long enough for genotypes to become incompatible. In time further selection upon these two gene pools may give rise to other new species.

REVIEW QUESTIONS

1 List some of the historical contributions that led to the general acceptance of the concept of evolution.

2 Compare how Lamarck, Darwin, and modern biologists would explain the development of the long neck in giraffes.

3 Summarize the contribution of the Galapagos finches to Darwin's theory of natural selection.

4 A naturalist made the following observation: A species of field mice living in a wooded hillside and a field were studied; those in the forests had dark coats whereas those living in the field had light coats. What is the probable explanation for this?

5 Two marine organisms, the lampshell and horseshoe crab, appear relatively unchanged from their fossil ancestors dating back over 300,000,000 years, whereas the horse has changed radically in only 60,000,000 years. How can you account for these differences in rates of evolution?

379

6   Bacteria exposed to penicillin over a number of generations have been found to develop an immunity to this antibiotic. What is the probable explanation of this?

7   List as many examples as you can of convergent, divergent, and parallel evolution.

8   Show the relationship between the Hardy-Weinberg principle and the concept of natural selection.

9   If you were a researcher and desired a race of rats smaller than the normal, average size, how would you set up a breeding program to accomplish this? What problems might you encounter?

10 How has the concept of evolution influenced our thought in fields other than the biological sciences, such as political science, sociology, economics, and theology?

SUPPLEMENTARY READINGS

Allison, Anthony C., "Sickle Cells and Evolution," *Scientific American,* August, 1956.

Bitterman, M. E., "The Evolution of Intelligence," *Scientific American,* January, 1965.

Crow, James F., "Ionizing Radiation and Evolution," *Scientific American,* September, 1959.

Dayhoff, Margaret O., "Computer Analysis of Protein Evolution," *Scientific American,* July, 1969.

De Beer, Sir Gavin, *Charles Darwin,* Garden City, N.Y., Doubleday, 1967.

Dobzhansky, Theodosius, "The Genetic Basis of Evolution," *Scientific American,* January, 1950.

Dobzhansky, Theodosius, "The Present Evolution of Man," *Scientific American,* September, 1960.

Eiseley, Loren C., "Charles Darwin," *Scientific American,* February, 1956.

Eiseley, Loren C., "Charles Lyell," *Scientific American,* August, 1959.

Hardin, G., *Nature and Man's Fate,* New York, New American Library (Mentor Books), 1961.

Howells, William W., "Homo Erectus," *Scientific American,* November, 1966.

Kerkut, G. A., *The Implications of Evolution,* New York, Pergamon, 1960.

Kettlewell, H. B. D., "Darwin's Missing Evidence," *Scientific American,* March, 1959.

Lack, David, "Darwin's Finches," *Scientific American,* April, 1953.

Livingston, John, and Lister Sinclair, *Darwin and the Galapagos,* Canadian Broadcasting Corp., 1966.

Millot, Jacques, "The Coelacanth," *Scientific American,* December, 1955.

Napier, J., "The Evolution of the Hand," *Scientific American,* December, 1962.

Portmann, A., *Animal Camouflage,* Ann Arbor, University of Michigan Press, 1959.

Simons, Elwyn L., "The Early Relatives of Man," *Scientific American,* July, 1964.

Stebbins, G. L., *Processes of Organic Evolution,* Englewood Cliffs, N.J., Prentice-Hall, 1966.

Volpe, E. Peter, *Understanding Evolution,* Dubuque, Iowa, Wm. C. Brown, 1967.

Wallace, B., and A. M. Srb, *Adaptation,* 2nd ed., Englewood Cliffs, N.J., Prentice-Hall, 1964.

Washburn, Sherwood L., "Tools and Human Evolution," *Scientific American,* September, 1960.

Glossary

abiotic: denotes the nonliving aspects of the community.

acid: a compound that produces hydrogen ions in a solution.

acrocentric: describes the chromosome in which the centromere occurs at one end; the chromosome is rod-shaped at anaphase.

ACTH: *see* adrenocorticotropic hormone

action potential: the bioelectric potential that changes along a nerve membrane as a result of the propagation of an impulse.

activation energy: the amount of energy necessary to initiate a chemical reaction.

active sites: specific structural areas in the enzyme molecule which combine with specific reactant molecules.

active transport: the movement of materials across cell membranes against a concentration gradient, thus requiring the expenditure of energy.

adaptive radiation: the divergence of organisms into separate ecological niches where further adaptation and speciation occur.

adenosine triphosphate (ATP): an organic molecule composed of an adenine nucleotide that has three phosphate ester groups attached to the ribose; this molecule is the principal source of energy for all living organisms.

ADH: *see* vasopressin.

adrenocorticotropic hormone (ACTH): a hormone secreted by the anterior lobe of the pituitary which stimulates the adrenal cortex.

adrenalin: *see* epinephrine.

agglutination: the clumping or massing together of red blood cells under the influence of specific antibodies during incompatible transfusion.

albinism: a recessive genetic condition (*aa*) in which the organism cannot produce pigments.

alcaptonuria: a metabolic disease evidenced by the absence of homogentisate oxidase in the liver; apparently caused by the action of one gene.

alchemy: the early study of chemistry; alchemists frequently were preoccupied with the changing of iron or lead into gold.

alkali: *see* base.

allantois: an extraembryonic membrane with varying functions; in birds and reptiles it has a respiratory and excretory function, whereas in mammals it forms part of the blood vessel connection between embryo and mother.

alleles: alternative forms of a gene for a particular trait (for example, tall or dwarf are alleles for tallness in peas).

alveoli: the small air sacs of the lungs where gas exchange occurs.

amino acid: an organic acid containing a carboxyl and an amino group on the same carbon; there are approximately 23 amino acids.

aminopeptidase: an enzyme secreted by the intestine which breaks peptide bonds adjacent to free amino groups.

ammonotelic: describes the excretion of ammonia as the principal form of nitrogenous waste.

amnion: the fluid-filled sac surrounding the embryo.

analogous structures: structures having similar functions but different evolutionary origins.

anaphase: a stage of mitosis in which the chromosomes move to opposite poles; they appear to be pulled by spindle fibers.

androgen: a general term for male hormones (testosterone).

anther: the part of a flower that produces pollen; often called the male part.

antheridium: the sperm-producing organ of a gametophyte.

antibody: a specific substance produced by cells which reacts with a specific antigen.

antigen: a substance, usually a protein, foreign to an organism which stimulates the formation of specific antibodies in the organism.

archegonium: the egg-producing organ of a gametophyte.

archenteron: the cavity in the gastrula which later becomes the intestinal tract.

atom: the modern term for the basic unit of any element, proposed by John Dalton in 1808.

atomic number: a number equal to the number of protons in an atomic nucleus.

atomic weight: the sum of the number of protons and neutrons in an atomic nucleus.

atomos: the fundamental unit of all matter, unique and indivisible for each element, which was proposed by Democritus.

ATP: *see* adenosine triphosphate.

autonomic nervous system: an involuntary system closely associated with, but not under direct control of, the central nervous system; it controls secretions of various glands and smooth muscle contractions; it consists of two antagonistic divisions, the sympathetic and the parasympathetic.

autosomes: chromosomes other than the sex chromosomes.

autotrophic: describing an organism that can produce its own food from inorganic materials.

auxins: hormones that regulate the growth of roots and stems.

back cross: *see* test cross.

bacteriophage: a virus that parasitizes bacteria.

basal metabolic rate (BMR): the metabolic rate of an organism theoretically in a state of complete rest; usually expressed as Calories produced per kilogram of body weight per hour.

base (or alkali): in general, a compound in solution which can take up or accept hydrogen ions; often a substance that dissociates to release hydroxyl ions (OH^-).

base analogues: certain chemicals that can incorporate into nucleic acids, but are nonfunctional; they can cause mutation or death of the cell.

bilateral symmetry: a body plan that can be halved in only one plane so that each half is a mirror image of the other.

bile: a substance secreted by the liver which emulsifies fats for digestion.

biomes: the major terrestrial regions of the earth which are characterized by the dominant plant and animal life; these include tundra, northern coniferous forest, deciduous forest, tropical forest, grassland, and desert.

bivalents: the two chromatids of a duplicated chromosome, formed during meiosis.

blastula: the stage in animal development when a single layered ball of cells is formed; it is usually hollow, containing a blastocoel or blastula cavity.

blood: the fluid that circulates in the principal vascular system of man and other vertebrates, in man consisting of colloidal plasma in which cells and cell fragments are suspended; blood components function in gas exchange, ingestion of foreign substances, and blood clotting.

BMR: *see* basal metabolic rate

bolus: a swallowed ball of chewed food.

Bowman's capsule: the structure of a nephron in which the glomerulus or capillary network is contained; filtration products are collected here.

Brownian motion: the random movement of particles in liquid or gas due to molecular bombardment.

budding: a type of asexual reproduction whereby a complete, new individual grows from an organism.

buffer: a substance that removes excess hydrogen ions from a solution, thus preventing excessive pH changes.

calorie: the amount of heat necessary to raise one gram of pure water by one degree Celsius (centigrade).

capillary: the smallest vessel of the closed circulatory system which connects the arteries and veins.

carbohydrates: compounds composed primarily of carbon, oxygen, and hydrogen, such as sugars, starches, glycogen, and cellulose.

carbonic anhydrase: an enzyme found in the red blood cell which catalyzes the formation of H_2CO_3 and its breakdown into H_2O and CO_2.

carboxypeptidase: an enzyme that breaks peptide bonds adjacent to free carboxyl (acid) groups.

cardiac stomach: the upper portion of the stomach which receives the food from the esophagus and includes the fundus.

carnivore: an animal that eats a primarily meat diet; for example, cats and dogs.

carotenes: generally orange-red colored pigments closely associated with chlorophyll in the chloroplast.

carotid bodies: nerve receptors in the carotid arteries that are sensitive to increased levels of CO_2 and decreased levels of O_2; this causes an increase in respiratory rate.

carrying capacity: the number of species that a specific ecosystem can support; involves availability of food and shelter.

cell: all living organisms are composed of individual units called cells, which are divided into two main regions—the cytoplasm and the nucleus; the cytoplasm includes the cell membrane, centrioles, Golgi apparatus, mitochondria, endoplasmic reticulum, lysosomes, and ribosomes; nuclear cell parts are the nuclear membrane, chromosomes, and nucleolus.

cell membrane: the fat-protein structure between the cell and its environment.

cell wall: the outer, nonliving structure of a plant cell composed of cellulose, lignin, and pectin.

central nervous system (CNS): the brain and spinal cord.

centrioles: self-replicating bodies that form the spindle for cell division in animals and some protists.

centromere: the area of a chromosome to which the spindle fiber attaches at cell division.

cerebellum: connected hemispheres between the cerebrum and brain stem; functions in equilibrium and coordination of voluntary muscles.

cerebrum: the largest hemispheres of the brain; concerned with conscious, sensory, and motor functions.

chief cells: cells located in the stomach lining which secrete pepsinogen (inactive pepsin).

chitin: a tough carbohydrate-nitrogen substance found in the exoskeleton of insects and crustaceans.

chloride shift: the exchange of Cl^- for HCO_3^- and vice versa in the red blood cell in the transport of carbon dioxide; the shift maintains electrical balance.

cholecystokinin: a hormone released by the intestinal lining which activates the release of bile from the gallbladder.

chorion: the outermost extraembryonic membrane which forms part of the placenta in some mammals.

chromatid: each half of a duplicated chromosome.

chromomeres: areas of localized coiling on interphasic chromosomes; they stain heavily with nuclear dyes.

chromosome map: a diagram of the positions of genes along a chromosome based on the percent of crossover occurring among the genes.

chromosomes: long filaments in the cell nucleus composed primarily of DNA and protein.

chyme: the mixture of digestive juices and food in the stomach; highly acidic due to presence of HCl.

cilia: short, whiplike structures specialized for locomotion in some protists; cilia also occur on certain tissues of higher animals.

cistron: the individual functional units of a gene locus; perhaps involving many nucleotides.

climax: the final successional stage in an area which is stable and self-reproducing.

cloaca: the canal in some vertebrates where the digestive, excretory, and reproductive tracts come together.

closed circulatory system: a blood system composed of a continuous system of vessels— arteries, capillaries, and veins.

CNS: *see* central nervous system.

codon: a series of three nucleotides which code the position of a specific amino acid in a protein.

coelom: a body cavity in animals between the visceral organs and the body wall which is completely lined with mesoderm (this lining is called a peritoneum).

coenzyme A: a complex molecule containing the vitamin pantothenic acid which combines with pyruvic acid as it enters the Krebs cycle.

coenzymes: organic molecules that can transport intermediate products such as hydrogen in specific enzyme reactions.

cohesion: the attraction of like molecules for each other.

collenchyma: thick-walled cells that provide support in the stem region of plants.

colloid: the suspension of small particles (usually larger than molecules) in a medium; it can exist as a sol or a gel; in a cell the particles are protein and the medium is mainly water.

commensalism: two organisms living together in which one organism is benefited and the other is not harmed.

community: all the organisms living and interacting within a particular area.

compound: the chemical combination of two or more elements.

conditioned reflex: a reflex action developed through training.

conjugation: the process in which genetic material is exchanged between two protists.

connective tissue: provides intercellular support and cohesion among all types of tissues; cartilage and bone are dense connective tissues specially adapted for support.

consumers: organisms that feed on other species, either producers or other consumers.

contractile vacuole: a specialized organelle in some protozoans which functions in water balance and excretion.

convergence: the development of similar characteristics in two or more groups of organisms which are not closely related.

corpus callosum: a band of nerve fibers that interconnects the two cerebral hemispheres.

coupled reactions: two interrelated chemical reactions that occur simultaneously.

covalent bond: the bond formed when two atoms share a pair of electrons, such as the bond between carbon and hydrogen.

cretinism: a condition caused by lack of thyroxin during development; characterized by low mentality, retarded growth, and impish face.

crossover: the breaking and exchange between homologous chromatids during meiotic prophase (observed at tetrad stage); the microscopical observations are termed chiasmata.

cutaneous breathing: gas exchange that occurs across moist skin such as found in amphibians.

cytochrome: a tetrapyrrol ring molecule containing an atom of iron; the iron functions in the transport of electrons through alternate oxidation and reduction.

cytokinesis: division of the cell cytoplasm to form daughter cells.

cytology: study of cells.

Darwin-Wallace theory: the theory of evolution based on changes in species due to natural selection.

deamination: the removal of an amino group (NH_2) from an amino acid.

decomposers: bacteria and fungi that break large organic molecules of dead organisms into smaller reusable molecules.

deletions: parts of chromosomes that are lost.

deme: small breeding group within a population.

denaturation: a permanent structural change in a protein which alters its function in the cell.

denitrifying bacteria: bacteria that convert ammonia, nitrites, and nitrates into free nitrogen.

deoxyribonucleic acid (DNA): a nucleic acid containing deoxyribose, found chiefly in the nucleus of cells, that functions in the transference of genetic characteristics and in the synthesis of protein.

diaphragm: the muscular separation between the chest and abdominal cavities; functions in respiration and elimination.

differential reproduction: organisms better suited to their environment give rise to more and better adapted offspring than those less suited.

differentiation: a process of change in the developing organism in which nonspecialized cells become specialized.

diffusion: the movement of gas or solid particles from a region of high concentration to a region of low concentration.

dihybrid cross: a genetic cross involving two characteristics; for example, tallness and seed color in peas.

dioecious: the condition in which male and female or staminate and pistillate structures are in separate individuals.

dipeptidase: an enzyme that splits double amino acids into single amino acids.

diplohaplontic: a plant in which the perennial and most visible generation is the diploid (frond of fern).

diploid: the number of chromosomes formed by the union of two gametes ($2n$); 46 in humans.

diplontic: a life cycle with diploid adults; gametes produced by meiosis.

disaccharases: enzymes that split double sugars into simple sugars.

disaccharides: twelve-carbon sugars such as maltose.

dissociation constant: the numerical ratio between the ionized and non-ionized particles in a solution.

distal convoluted tubule: the region of the nephron where further reabsorption occurs, especially of water and some ions.

divergence: the development of different characteristics in two or more groups of closely related organisms.

DNA: *see* deoxyribonucleic acid.

dominant gene: a gene that always produces its characteristic when it is present.

double covalent bond: the sharing of two pairs of electrons between two atoms such as $C = C$ in benzene.

Down's syndrome: often called mongolism; evidenced by a third chromosome in pair 21.

duodenum: the first ten inches of the small intestine.

dynamic equilibrium: a balance due to the active coordination and regulation of all the chemical and physical interactions occurring in an organism.

ecology: the study of the relationships of organisms to one another and to the environment.

ecosystem: the living community and the physical environment associated with it.

ectoderm: the outside germ layer in the developing embryo; the skin and nervous system develop from this layer.

effectors: structures that react to stimuli to bring about a counterchange.

electrolytes: ionically bonded compounds that dissociate into charged particles in water and will conduct an electric current; for example, sodium chloride.

electron: a tiny particle located outside the atomic nucleus which possesses a negative charge.

electron-transport series: a series of reactions among electron-transfer compounds which serves to produce ATP and water; occurs in the mitochondrion; NAD, FAD, and cytochromes are important members of the series.

electrovalent (or ionic) bond: a bond formed by the transfer of one or more electrons from one atom to another; for example, sodium chloride.

element: a substance that contains atoms of only one type.

embryo: the multicellular beginnings of an organism before germination, hatching, or birth.

endergonic: describing chemical reactions that require energy.

endocrine glands: ductless glands that secrete hormones directly into the bloodstream.

endoderm: the inside germ layer (formed during gastrulation) in the developing embryo; forms the lining of the intestinal tract and the lining of several other internal organs.

endoplasmic reticulum: the membranous structure in the cytoplasm.

energy: energy may be defined as the ability to do work; in living organisms, energy is required to perform the chemical reactions necessary for life.

enterocoelom: a coelom formed in some animals by the outpouching of mesoderm from the developing gut.

enterokinase: a nondigestive enzyme secreted by the intestinal mucosa which activates trypsinogen to trypsin.

entropy: a measurement of the degree of disorganization in a chemical system.

enzyme: a protein molecule capable of bringing specific reactants together to speed up a biochemical reaction.

epidermal tissue: the protective tissue covering many plant parts; in the leaf, special guard cells surround openings (stomata) to permit gas exchange.

epilimnion: the region of a body of water above the thermocline.

epinephrine (adrenalin): a hormone secreted by the adrenal medulla which increases respiration, heartbeat, and blood sugar.

epistasis: the effect of one gene influencing the expression of another nonallelic gene.

epithelial tissue: tissue that covers or lines the organs of the animal body and sometimes forms glandular tissue; generally specialized for protection, absorption, or secretion; specific types include squamous, cuboidal, and columnar.

erepsin: a general term for a group of intestinal enzymes that hydrolyze polypeptides into amino acids.

estrogen: the female hormone produced by the egg follicle; responsible for female secondary sex characteristics.

estrus: a cycle of events in most female mammals in which the female is receptive to the male; the egg is released at this time.

eutrophic: describing a body of water that contains a large number of organisms and organic products.

evolution: the theory that all existing plants and animals were derived from preexisting forms; also includes the concept that the changes occurring in organisms are due to slight genetic variations through successive generations.

excretion: generally the release of waste products from a cell or an organism.

exergonic: describing chemical reactions that release energy.

experimental control: the standard or normal situation to which a test situation is compared in an experiment.

extracellular digestion: digestion that takes place outside the cells in a cavity such as the stomach or intestine.

extraembryonic membranes: a group of membranous sacs associated with the embryos of most reptiles, birds, and mammals; these membranes are the chorion, amnion, and allantois, and they function in protection, respiration, nutrition, and waste disposal.

FAD: *see* flavine adenine dinucleotide.

fats: compounds composed of glycerine and fatty acids.

feedback: a mechanism by which the output of a reaction may act to modify that reaction.

ferredoxin: an iron-containing protein that acts as an electron acceptor in system I of photosynthesis.

fetus: a stage of early development in man and other mammals; generally, in humans, from the third month of pregnancy until birth.

flagella: whiplike appendages similar to cilia in structure and function but much longer; flagella also occur as the locomotor organelles of sperm.

flame cells: specialized ciliated cells which function in excretion and water balance; for example, in flatworms.

flavine adenine dinucleotide (FAD): a hydrogen-transporting coenzyme.

follicle-stimulating hormone (FSH): a hormone secreted by the anterior lobe of the pituitary; it stimulates the production of an egg in the ovary.

food chain: the flow of energy from one trophic level to another based on which organisms eat other organisms.

food web: a complex of food chains involving many different species.

fossilization: the process of preserving the form or actual structures of an organism.

fruit: a mature ovary with seeds enclosed.

FSH: *see* follicle-stimulating hormone.

fundamental tissue: various kinds of cells which function in support, food making, or food storage; the three types are parenchyma, collenchyma, and sclerenchyma.

galaxy: a group of stars such as our own Milky Way.

gametophyte: the haploid generation of a plant which produces gametes.

ganglion: a collection of nerve cell bodies; for example, dorsal root ganglia.

gastrin: a hormone secreted by the stomach lining which causes the secretion of pepsin.

gastrovascular cavity: a cavity in some lower animals which serves the functions of both digestion and circulation (coelenterates).

gastrula: the stage in animal development when a two-layered (and later, three) structure is formed; a new cavity, which will become the intestinal tract, forms and replaces the blastocoel.

gene: the fundamental unit of heredity; a small segment of a chromosome defined according to its functional characteristics.

gene pool: the total possible genotypes in an interbreeding population.

genotype: the actual genetic composition of the alleles resulting from a cross.

gills: small membranous structures found in many aquatic animals which function in gas exchange.

glomerulus: the blood capillary network of a nephron.

glucagon: a hormone produced by the alpha cells of the islets of Langerhans which stimulates the conversion of glycogen into blood glucose.

glucocorticoids: a group of hormones secreted by the adrenal cortex which tend to increase blood glucose.

glycogenesis: the synthesis of glycogen from glucose.

glycogenolysis: the enzymatic hydrolysis of glycogen to glucose.

glycolysis: the breakdown of glucose or glycogen to pyruvic acid; this series of reactions occurs in the cell cytoplasm and involves the removal of hydrogen and the synthesis of ATP.

glyconeogenesis: the conversion of non-carbohydrate molecules into glycogen (amino acids and fats).

goiter: an overgrowth of thyroid gland tissue sometimes caused by inactive thyroxin due to iodine deficiency.

Golgi apparatus: smooth, membranous sacs in the cytoplasm which seem to function in the storage and transport of cellular secretions.

gonads: the male and female sex glands.

gram-atomic weight: the atomic weight of a substance expressed in grams.

granum: a structure composed of alternate layers of protein-lipid membrane in the chloroplast and containing all the pigments and enzymes necessary for photosynthesis.

green glands: excretory organs found in the head region of crayfish.

group: the vertical rows of the periodic chart in which all elements have the same number of electrons in their outer shell.

habitat: the specific physical area in which an organism lives.

haplodiplontic: a plant in which the perennial and most visible generation is the haploid (green gametophyte of moss).

haploid: the basic chromosome number for an organism abbreviated as (n); generally the number of chromosomes in gametic cells; 23 in humans.

haplontic: having only one set of chromosomes per cell in the adult organism; meiosis follows gamete fusion.

Hardy-Weinberg principle: in a biparental, sexually reproducing population, genotype frequencies will remain constant if the following conditions are met: no mutations, random mating, and a relatively large and isolated population.

hemocoel: a part of a body cavity which collects blood in open circulatory systems.

hemocyanin: a blue, copper-containing pigment found in the blood of some arthropods and molluscs.

hemoglobin: the respiratory pigment of man, other vertebrates, and some invertebrates; a complex of iron porphyrin and protein.

hemophilia: a sex-linked genetic disease in which the blood does not clot normally; commonly known as bleeder's disease.

hepatic portal vein: an accessory venous system which carries nutrient-laden blood from the intestines to the liver.

herbivore: an animal that eats a diet of only plant material; examples of herbivores are cow, sheep, and rabbit.

Hering-Breuer reflex: a nerve reflex that inhibits inspiration when the alveoli are filled with air.

heterogamy: gametes of different size, usually micro (male) and macro (female); gametic union occurs only between the two different forms; includes sperm and egg.

heterotrophs: organisms that cannot synthesize their own food (consumers).

heterozygous: describes the situation in which the alleles for a particular trait are different on homologous chromosomes (R,r).

histology: the study of tissues.

homeostasis (steady state): the concept that all processes in an organism must be controlled within certain limits or death will result.

homologous chromosomes: chromosomes occur as pairs following fertilization, one member of each pair coming from the mother and the other from the father; homologous chromosomes are similar in size, shape, and genetic content.

homologous structures: structures that have similar origins; for example, the forelimb bone structure of bird and man.

homozygous: describes the situation in which both alleles on homologous chromosomes are the same (RR or rr).

hormone: a chemical substance secreted by specific cells in one part of an organism and capable of stimulating cells in other regions.

hybrid: the offspring resulting from the crossing of two genetically different parents.

hydrogen bond: the attraction of the hydrogen proton for negatively charged chemical groups.

hydrogen ion: the positive ion produced when hydrogen is separated from its electron.

hydrolysis: a chemical process in which large molecules are split into smaller molecules; this usually involves the addition of water (hydrolytic cleavage).

hydroxyl ion: when a hydrogen ion is removed from water, the resulting charged radical is called a hydroxyl ion (OH^-).

hyperosmotic: a solution on one side of a membrane which has more dissolved particles (therefore a lesser water concentration) than the solution on the other side.

hypha: an individual, threadlike structure composing the body of a fungus.

hypolimnion: the region of a body of water below the thermocline.

hyposmotic: a solution on one side of a membrane which has fewer dissolved particles (therefore a higher water concentration) than the solution on the other side.

hypothalamus: the area of the brain beneath the thalamus; it is connected to the pituitary gland and regulates body temperature and some hormone secretion from the posterior pituitary.

hypothesis: an educated guess as to the explanation of an observed event.

iliocecal valve: the muscular constriction between the small and large intestine.

incomplete dominance: describes the situation in which one member of a pair of alleles is not dominant; each allele expresses itself and contributes to the phenotype.

independent assortment: genes on different chromosomes separate independently of one another during gamete formation; Mendel's second law.

induction: the developmental process in which a group of cells or tissues brings about the differentiation of neighboring cells; thus the position of cells in a developing organ is an important determiner of what they will become.

ingestion: the intake of materials into a cell or organism.

390

inhibition: a situation in which the product of an enzymatic reaction restrains or checks the action of an enzyme necessary for the formation of that product.

insulin: a hormone produced by the beta cells of the islets of Langerhans in the pancreas which converts glucose into glycogen.

intermedin: a hormone secreted by the intermediate lobe of the pituitary which controls pigmentation in some animals.

internuncial neuron: the intermediate neuron located in the gray matter of the spinal cord which shunts the impulse from the sensory to the motor tracts.

interphase: a stage of mitosis in which the chromosomes are extended and uncoiled; DNA is replicated.

intracellular digestion: digestion that occurs inside the cell.

inversion: an event in which a portion of a chromosome breaks and reunites on the same chromosome in such a way that the genetic order is reversed.

ion: a charged atom or group of atoms resulting from the gain or loss of electrons.

ionic bond: *see* electrovalent bond.

islets of Langerhans: isolated patches of endocrine tissue found throughout the pancreas.

isogamy: the fusion of gametes of similar size and shape to form a diploid cell.

isosmotic: refers to equal concentrations of water and dissolved substances on either side of a membrane.

isotope: any atom of an element which has a different number of neutrons and consequently a different atomic weight.

karyokinesis: division of the nuclear material; in some cases nuclear division occurs without cellular division.

kinetic theory: the theory that all matter is in constant motion in the universe.

kingdom: the most fundamental category for classification of the living world; examples of kingdoms are Protista, Metaphyta, and Metazoa.

Klinefelter's syndrome: a condition in humans in which the offspring receives a double X and a single Y chromosome because of nondisjunction.

Krebs cycle: a cyclic series of chemical reactions that occurs in the mitochondrion; pyruvic acid is oxidized to produce ATP, carbon dioxide, and water.

lactase: an enzyme that hydrolyzes lactose into glucose and galactose.

lacteals: small vessels found in the intestinal villi which absorb emulsified fat.

law: a theory which has a high degree of probability based on experimentation.

law of mass action: the rate of a chemical reaction is directly proportional to the concentration of the reactants.

LH: *see* luteinizing hormone.

linkage groups: genes on the same chromosome which are inherited as a group.

luteinizing hormone (LH): a hormone of the anterior pituitary which causes the formation of corpus luteum from the egg follicle after ovulation.

lymphatic system: a network of vessels that carries emulsified fat and lymph to the veins near the heart.

lysis: the dissolution or destruction of cells; a breaking down or decomposition.

lysosomes: membranous bags containing enzymes which digest proteins, fats, and nucleic acids.

Malpighian tubules: long, thin excretory structures connected to the digestive tract of insects.

maltase: an enzyme specifically for the hydrolysis of the double sugar maltose to two molecules of glucose.

mechanism: the concept that all natural phenomena can be explained in terms of physics and chemistry.

medulla oblongata: the anterior portion of the spinal cord which controls heartbeat and respiration; it is the origin of many spinal nerves.

medusa: the sexual jellyfish stage of certain coelenterates.

megasporangium: the structure that produces megaspores which will develop into female gametophytes.

meiosis: the process of gamete production in which the chromosome number is reduced from diploid to haploid.

391

meristematic tissue: cells responsible for growth in plants; these cells can form other tissue later.

mesentery: thin sheets of tissue which hold the internal organs together and to the body wall; composed primarily of connective tissue.

mesoderm: the middle germ layer (between ectoderm and endoderm) in the developing embryo; most parts of the animal body come from this layer—for example, muscles, bone, excretory system, and reproductive system.

messenger RNA (mRNA): soluble RNA synthesized by DNA in the nucleus into specific nucleotide sequences which convey information for protein synthesis to the cytoplasmic ribosomes.

metabolism: the total of all the chemical reactions occurring in an organism; the breakdown of food to produce the fuel molecules for energy is an important part of metabolism.

metacentric: describes the situation in which the centromere occurs at the center of a chromosome, producing arms of equal length; V-shaped at anaphase.

metamorphosis: the change in body form following embryonic development; often the changes from larva to adult.

metaphase: the stage of mitosis in which the chromosomes align on the equatorial plate prior to division.

Metaphyta: the kingdom name for plants.

Metazoa: the kingdom name for animals.

microsporangium: the structure that produces microspores which will develop into male gametophytes.

migration: the movement of species from one area into another.

mimicry: the imitation of one organism by another which serves for protection.

mineralocorticoids: steroid hormones secreted by the adrenal cortex which regulate the reabsorption of mineral ions by the kidneys.

mitochondria: membranous organelles in the cell cytoplasm that contain enzyme systems for energy production (Krebs cycle and the electron transport series).

mitosis: an orderly sequence of nuclear and cytoplasmic events which produce two daughter cells exactly like the parent cell.

models: generally synonymous with the term theory; models are formulated from existing evidence and subjected to more experimentation.

mole: the amount of a substance that is equal to its molecular weight in grams.

molecule: a group of atoms held together by mutual attractions called chemical bonds.

monoecious: the condition in which male and female or staminate and pistillate structures are present in the same individual.

monohybrid cross: a genetic cross involving only one characteristic—for example, tallness in peas.

monosaccharides: simple sugars such as glucose which may unite to form more complex carbohydrates.

motor (efferent) pathway: nerve tracts carrying impulses from the spinal cord to effect a response (muscle contraction).

mRNA: *see* messenger RNA.

mucin: a complex polysaccharide-protein which is the major constituent of mucus secreted along the digestive tract.

multiple alleles: describes the situation in which more than one set of alleles contribute to the expression of a particular trait.

mutation: any stable change in the genetic constitution of an organism.

muton: the smallest unit of genetic mutation; may correspond to a change in a single DNA nucleotide pair.

mutualism: two organisms living together in which both are mutually benefited.

mycelium: a collective mass of hyphae which forms the body of a fungus.

NADP: *see* nicotinamide dinucleotide phosphate.

natural selection: the effect of different reproductive rates in a population due to the influence of the environment upon the different genetic types in that population. A more classical definition is: a process in nature resulting in the survival and perpetuation of only those forms of plant and animal life having certain favorable characteristics that enable them to adapt to a specific environment.

neo-Darwinism: the modern development of

Darwin's theory of evolution which incorporates the theories of mutation and gene action.

nephridium: a tubular excretory organ found in some invertebrates such as the earthworm.

nephron: the individual, minute excretory unit of the vertebrate kidney.

nerve tissue: a tissue composed of cells specialized for the functions of irritability and conductivity; the fundamental nerve cell is called the neuron.

neutron: a component of the atomic nucleus which contributes one unit of mass but has no charge.

niche: the functional place of an organism in the community; sometimes called its "occupation."

nicotinamide dinucleotide phosphate (NADP): a coenzyme that transports hydrogen.

nitrogen fixing: the production of usable nitrate from atmospheric nitrogen by certain bacteria; $N_2 \rightarrow NO_2 \rightarrow NO_3$.

nondisjunction: a situation in which homologous chromosomes do not separate during meiosis II; one gamete receives an extra chromosome and one receives none.

nonelectrolytes: compounds that do not dissociate in water and do not conduct electricity; for example, covalent compounds like sucrose.

notochord: a supporting rodlike structure occurring at some stage of development in all chordates.

nucleic acids: macromolecules composed of long chains of nucleotides; the two types are RNA and DNA.

nucleotide: the basic unit of nucleic acids composed of a nitrogen base, a five-carbon sugar, and phosphoric acid.

nucleus: the structure in most cells that contains the chromosomes (carriers of heredity) and the nucleoli (storage centers for ribosomal RNA).

oligotrophic: a body of water that contains little organic material in ratio to the volume of water.

omnivore: an animal that eats both plant and animal material; for example, man, pig, and bear.

oögenesis: the meiotic process in the ovary which produces eggs.

open circulatory system: a blood system composed of a heart and main arteries (no veins or capillaries) found in arthropods and some mollusks.

operator gene: a gene that controls the function of a series of structural genes by turning the structural genes off or on.

operon: an operator gene and the associated structural genes that it controls.

organ: a group of tissues, united structurally, that performs a specific function in a multicellular organism.

organism: a living unit in nature.

ornithine cycle: *see* urea cycle.

oscilloscope: an electronic instrument somewhat similar to a television set which allows visualization of electrical events such as the movement of a nerve impulse.

osmoregulation: the ability to maintain constant concentrations of body fluids despite changing conditions in the environment.

osmosis: the movement of water across a semipermeable membrane from a region of high concentration of water to a region of low concentration of water.

oviparous: describes the development of an organism within an egg that has been laid outside the mother's body.

ovule: the structure of the seed plant in which the egg or ovum is contained.

oxidation: the addition of oxygen to a compound or the loss of electrons (removal of hydrogen).

oxytocin: a hormone secreted by the posterior lobe of the pituitary which stimulates contraction of smooth muscle.

pancreatic amylase: an enzyme produced in the pancreas which hydrolyzes complex carbohydrates in the small intestine.

pancreatic lipase: a pancreatic enzyme that hydrolyzes fats to glycerol and fatty acids in the small intestine.

pancreozymin: a hormone secreted by the intestinal lining which initiates the flow of pancreatic enzymes.

pangenesis: the theory that small "pangenes" were collected into the gametes from all parts of the body.

parallelism: the evolutionary development of

similar characteristics in two groups of organisms that are closely related.

parasitism: two organisms living together in which one is benefited but the other is harmed.

parathormone: the hormone secreted by the parathyroid glands which regulates the metabolism of calcium and phosphorus in the blood.

parenchyma: thin-walled cells that often contain chlorophyll and hence are sites of food making; they may also be sites for food storage in the stem or root.

parietal cells: cells in the stomach lining which secrete hydrochloric acid.

peck order: a social ranking system by which a definite hierarchy is established within a group; commonly observed in birds.

pepsin: an enzyme released into the stomach which breaks down complex proteins.

period: the horizontal rows of the periodic chart organized according to increasing atomic weight.

periodic chart: a table of all the known elements in which the elements are organized according to their chemical properties.

peripheral nervous system (PNS): a nerve network that includes the 12 pairs of cranial nerves and the 31 pairs of spinal nerves.

peristalsis: the rhythmic muscular contractions that move food along the digestive tract.

petals: the generally thin, leaflike, colored structures of the flower.

pH: *see* pH scale.

phagocytosis: the engulfment of solid particles into the cell.

pharyngeal gill slits: slitlike openings that appear in the pharynx of the embryonic stages of all chordates.

phenotype: the visible characteristics resulting from a genetic cross.

phenylketonuria (PKU): a metabolic disease that produces mental retardation and is caused by the inability of the organism to convert phenylalanine to tyrosine; phenylpyruvic acid is accumulated due to the absence of an enzyme.

phloem: food-conducting tissue of the plant that consists of sieve tubes and companion cells; it composes much of the bark of a tree.

photolysis: the separation of water into $[H^+ + e^- + OH]$ through the action of light and chlorophyll; sometimes called the light reaction of photosynthesis.

photosynthesis: the process of trapping light energy with the aid of chlorophyll to combine water and carbon dioxide to form carbohydrate.

pH scale: a numerical scale that indicates the relative amount of hydrogen ion in a solution; a pH value between 0 and 7 is acidic and between 7 and 14 is alkaline (7 represents neutral).

phylum: a major classification category of organisms with similar characteristics; phyla are subcategories within each kingdom.

pinocytosis: the engulfment of water into the cell.

pistil: the egg-producing portion of a flower, consisting of a stigma, style, and ovary; often called the female part.

pistillate: having a pistil or pistils, the egg- or ovule-producing structures in seed plants.

pituitary gland: the "master" endocrine gland attached by a short stalk to the hypothalamus of the brain; it is composed of three parts—a large anterior lobe, an intermediate lobe, and a posterior lobe.

PKU: *see* phenylketonuria.

placenta: the structural and functional connection between the mother and the embryo in most mammals; it is formed from parts of the chorion membrane and the lining of the uterus.

planet: a solid body of matter that orbits about a star and reflects light.

plankton: organisms that characteristically float with wind and tide; they provide food for larger consumers.

plastids: bodies found in the cytoplasm of plant and some protist cells; the three kinds are leucoplasts, chromoplasts, and chloroplasts.

plastoquinone: an organic compound that contains a carbon-ring structure which can take up and release electrons; it is important in photolysis of photosynthesis.

pneumotaxic center: the area in the medulla oblongata of the brain that functions in the nervous control of breathing.

PNS: *see* peripheral nervous system.

pollination: the process in which the pollen

grain comes in contact with an ovule and, ultimately, the egg.

polysaccharides: long chains of monosaccharide units; for example, starch, glycogen, and cellulose.

population: a group of one species of organisms.

population genetics: the genetics of a breeding group or population.

porphyrins: a class of compounds composed of four pyrrole rings and a metallic ion; the fundamental structure of chlorophyll, hemoglobin, and cytochromes.

predation: a relation between animals in which one species (predator) hunts down and kills another species (prey) for food.

probability: the chance, often expressed as a percentage, that a specific event will occur; a probability of 1 (or 100 percent) represents certainty.

producers: primarily the photosynthetic members of the ecosystem.

productivity: generally the amount of carbon (as glucose or starch) made available by producers.

progesterone: a hormone secreted by the corpus luteum which promotes the vascularization of the uterine lining prior to the implantation of the fertilized egg.

prophase: a stage of mitosis in which chromosomes shorten, centrioles move to poles, asters form, nucleoli disappear, and the nuclear membrane breaks down; in meiosis, homologous chromosomes synapse.

proteins: complex compounds composed of amino acids connected by peptide linkages.

Protista: the kingdom name for organisms that cannot be classified as either true plants or animals.

proton: a component of the nucleus of an atom which has one unit of mass and a positive charge.

protonema: the "first thread" or filament of a germinating moss spore.

proximal convoluted tubule: the region of the nephron near the glomerulus where reabsorption of glucose, water, and some ions occurs.

pseudocoelom: a body cavity incompletely lined with mesoderm.

ptyalin: *see* salivary amylase.

pyloric valve: the muscular constriction between the pyloric stomach and the small intestine.

pylorus: the lower portion of the stomach which passes digesting food into the small intestine.

pyrophosphate ester: the third or terminal phosphate ester of ATP which contains much more potential energy than a simple ester bond (8000 to 15,000 calories/mole).

quantitative inheritance: when more than one set of alleles appear to influence the expression of a trait; sometimes called additive inheritance.

radial symmetry: a circular body plan that can be halved in two or more planes so that each half is a mirror image of the other.

receptors: structures, often specialized, for the detection of chemical or physical changes both internal and external.

recessive gene: a gene that produces its characteristic only when two of the same type are present, that is, in the absence of a dominant gene.

recon: the unit of recombination; the distance between adjacent nucleotides in DNA.

reduction: the addition of electrons (or hydrogen) to a compound.

reflex arc: the reflex pathway that commonly involves sensory (afferent), internuncial, and motor (efferent) neurons; occurs across the spinal cord from dorsal root to ventral root.

regeneration: the process of producing a new structure to replace a lost part.

regulator gene: a gene that exerts a controlling action on other genes; probably acts on the operator gene.

rennin: an enzyme present in the stomach of young mammals which causes the curdling of milk.

repression: a situation in which the product of an enzymatic reaction interferes with the synthesis of an enzyme necessary for the formation of that product.

respiration: the release of energy in the form of ATP from organic fuel molecules which can be used by cells; hydrogen atoms are removed in a sequence of reactions with the liberation of carbon dioxide and water.

respiratory quotient (R.Q.): the ratio of carbon dioxide produced to oxygen used in the oxidation of foods (R.Q. = CO_2/O_2).

resting potential: the electrical potential between ions inside and outside a nonconducting nerve cell membrane.

ribonucleic acid (RNA): a nucleic acid that contains ribose, found chiefly in the cytoplasm of cells; in comparison to DNA, it is generally single stranded and contains the pyrimidine uracil; the genetic material of many viruses.

ribulose diphosphate: a five-carbon sugar $(C_5H_8O_7P_2)$ that combines with carbon dioxide in the first step of the dark reaction (carbon fixation) of photosynthesis.

RNA: *see* ribonucleic acid.

RQ: *see* respiratory quotient.

root pressure: the pressure produced by water moving into root hair cells which helps move water upward in the plant.

rugae: the ridgelike folds of the interior stomach wall.

salivary amylase (ptyalin): a salivary enzyme that hydrolyzes carbohydrate to double sugars.

salt: the product formed in the reaction between a strong acid and a strong base.

schizocoelom: a coelom formed in some animals by the splitting of a mesodermal sheet.

science: an organized study of the material universe; scientific methods involve procedures that provide an orderly and systematic approach to problems dealing with matter.

sclerenchyma: cells with thick, hardened walls which provide support and rigidity to plant stems.

secretin: a hormone secreted by the intestinal lining which stimulates the flow of sodium bicarbonate from the pancreas.

seed: an embryo with associated food and a hardened coat.

segregation: the random separation of genes during meiosis when each gamete receives a complete set of alleles; Mendel's first law.

sensory (afferent) pathway: the nerve tract bringing sensory impulses into the spinal cord.

sepals: the green, leaflike structures that protect the flower bud and are located at the base of an open flower.

sex chromosomes: a pair of chromosomes distinguishable from other chromosomes in the cell which are often different in male and female.

sickle-cell anemia: an anemia (impaired oxygen transport) caused by the production of an inefficient hemoglobin which is less soluble than normal hemoglobin; red blood cells assume elongated, sickle shapes.

somatotropin: a hormone secreted by the anterior lobe of the pituitary which stimulates growth and metabolism.

speciation: the process by which new species are formed; when sufficient changes have occurred in the genotypes of certain populations due to physical or biological barriers so that the organisms cannot interbreed, a new species is formed.

spermatogenesis: the meiotic process in the testes which produces sperm cells.

spindle: the mitotic spindle consists of long protein fibers between the two centrioles; each chromosome is attached to a spindle fiber.

spiracles: the small outside openings of the tracheal tube respiratory system in insects.

sporangium: the spore-producing structure of the sporophyte.

sporophyte: the diploid generation of a plant which produces spores.

stamen: the organ of a flower consisting of a pollen-producing anther and a supporting filament.

staminate: having a stamen or stamens, the pollen-producing structures in seed plants.

star: a self-luminescent collection of matter in the universe.

steady state: *see* homeostasis.

stimulus: any internal or external change that can cause a biological reaction.

structural gene: the gene that codes messenger RNA for the production of a specific protein.

submetacentric: describes the situation in which the centromere occurs nearer one end of a chromosome to produce a long and a short arm; J-shaped at anaphase.

succession: the progressive changes in vegetation in an area.

sucrase: an enzyme that hydrolyzes sucrose into glucose and fructose.

symbiosis: the living together of two dissimilar organisms, especially when the association is mutually beneficial.

synapse: the junction between two neurons.

synapsis: the pairing of homologous chromosomes in the first prophase of meiosis.

synthesis: a chemical process in which small molecules are joined to form larger molecules; this usually involves the loss of water (dehydration).

teleology: a philosophy which states that all things exist for a predestined purpose; events occurring under this philosophy are sometimes referred to as the "divine plan."

telophase: a stage of mitosis in which the cell membrane constricts (in animals) or cell wall develops (in plants) and daughter cells are formed; chromosomes and nucleus return to interphasic condition.

territoriality: the phenomenon whereby a specific number of animals mark and defend a particular area against intruding species.

test cross (back cross): a test for determining whether a parent is homozygous or heterozygous dominant; the doubtful genotype is crossed back to the recessive character.

testosterone: the male hormone secreted by the interstitial cells of the testis which is responsible for male secondary sex characteristics.

tetrad: the result of duplicated homologous chromosomes following synapsis (paired bivalents); it is thought that crossover occurs at this stage of meiosis.

thalamus: a portion of the forebrain beneath and posterior to each cerebral hemisphere; provides relay connections between spinal cord and cerebrum.

theory: an explanation of an observed event based on extensive experimentation or testing.

thermocline: a zone in a lake or ocean in which there is a rapid drop in temperature related to depth.

thoracic cavity: the chest cavity containing the heart and lungs.

thoracic duct: the large duct of the lymphatic system in mammals which transports fats and lymph from the lacteals to the superior vena cava.

thyroid gland: a bilobed endocrine gland located on each side of the trachea, the secretion of which regulates the rates of metabolism and body growth.

thyrotropic hormone (TTH): a hormone secreted by the anterior lobe of the pituitary which stimulates the thyroid gland to produce thyroxin.

thyroxin: the hormone secreted by the thyroid gland which contains iodine and increases metabolism.

trachea: the windpipe leading to the lungs.

tracheal tubes: a system of small tubules in insects which supply air directly to the tissues.

transamination: the exchange of an amino (NH_2) group between an amino acid and a keto acid or between two amino acids.

transduction: the result of the transfer of DNA from one bacterium into another through the agency of a bacterial virus.

transfer RNA (tRNA): a double-stranded RNA synthesized by DNA in the nucleus which has two areas of three unpaired bases—one area attaches to a specific amino acid and the other recognizes the mRNA code on the ribosomes.

transformation: the result of the direct transfer of DNA from one bacterium into another.

translocation: the movement of food materials in plants from the leaves to other areas for storage or respiration; also the breaking off of a segment of a chromosome followed by a reunion of that segment with a homologous or nonhomologous chromosome.

transmission genetics: the part of genetics that deals with the transfer and recombination of genetic traits between organisms.

transpiration: the release of water to the atmosphere from the leaves and stems of plants.

tRNA: *see* transfer RNA.

trophic levels: the various energy levels in an ecosystem beginning with the producers and ending with the decomposers.

tropism: the movement of plants in response to external stimuli.

trypsin: a pancreatic enzyme that hydrolyzes proteins into amino acids in the intestine.

TTH: *see* thyrotropic hormone.

Turner's syndrome: a human condition in which the offspring receives only a single X chromosome because of nondisjunction in the female; the single X chromosome comes from the male.

umbilical cord: the cord that contains blood vessels and connects the embryo to the placenta; the navel is the point of attachment on the embryo.

urea cycle (ornithine cycle): a cyclic series of chemical reactions that combine carbon dioxide and ammonia into urea.

ureotelic: describes the excretion of urea as the principal form of nitrogenous waste.

uricotelic: denotes the excretion of uric acid as the principal form of nitrogenous waste.

valence: the bonding potential of an atom; valence is determined by the number of electrons in the outer shell.

vasopressin (ADH): an antidiuretic hormone (ADH) secreted by the posterior lobe of the pituitary which causes constriction of blood vessels and reabsorption of water in the kidney tubules.

vestigial: describes anatomical structures that have been retained in an organism but are no longer of functional significance.

villi: fingerlike projections of the lining of the intestine; they greatly increase the absorptive surface area.

vitalism: a philosophy which holds that events of unknown cause are produced by supernatural forces.

vitamins: organic compounds necessary for the proper functioning of specific enzymes, usually forming a vital part of a coenzyme.

viviparous: indicates the development of an organism within the mother's body.

xylem: plant tissue that conducts water upward in the plant and consists mainly of tracheid and vessel cells and fibers; it forms the woody part of a tree.

yolk sac: the food source for embryos of reptiles and birds but practically nonfunctional in most mammals.

zoöspores: flagellated, motile spores that develop directly into new plants.

zygote: the result of the union of two gametes; a fertilized egg ($2n$).

Appendix
Classification of the Living World

The hierarchical levels of classification generally used are applied below to three different organisms.

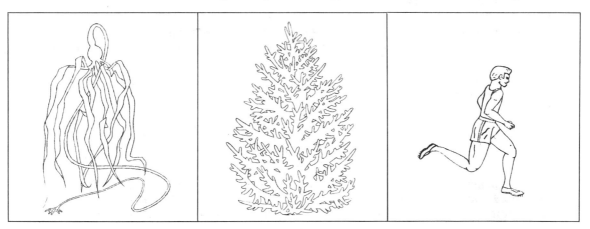

	Organism I	Organism II	Organism III
Kingdom	Protista	Metaphyta	Metazoa
Phylum	Phaeophyta	Tracheophyta	Chordata
Subphylum		Pteropsida	Vertebrata
Class	Heterogeneratae	Gymnospermae	Mammalia
Subclass	Polystichineae		
Order	Laminariales	Coniferales	Primates
Family	Lessoniaceae	Pinaceae	Hominidae
Genus	*nereocystis*	*pseudotsuga*	*homo*
Species	*luetkeana*	*menziesii*	*sapiens*
Common name	Kelp	Douglas fir	Man

Kingdom PROTISTA

Phylum SCHIZOPHYTA (bacteria):

1. Microscopic in size.
2. Nucleoprotein scattered in clumps through-out the cell; no organized nucleus.
3. Autotrophic by photosynthesis or chemo-synthesis.
4. Simple chromatophores similar to individual grana of a chloroplast.
5. Many produce toxins pathogenic to higher organisms.

Representative genera: *Bacillus, Streptococcus, Spirillum*

Streptococcus

Bacillus

Spirillum

Phylum CYANOPHYTA (blue-green algae):

1. Mostly aquatic and filamentous.
2. No organized nucleus.
3. May contain many pigments: green, blue, orange, yellow, or red.
4. Provide food for small aquatic animals and fish.
5. Large, empty heterocyst cells burst to cause fragmentation.

Representative genera: *Oscillatoria, Anabaena*

Heterocyst

Resting cell

Anabaena

Phylum CHLOROPHYTA (green algae):

1. Mostly aquatic or moist habitats.
2. Organized nucleus with membrane.
3. DNA present in distinct chromosomes.
4. Cell division by mitosis.
5. May form sexual gametes.
6. Possess complex chloroplasts.

Representative genera: *Pleurococcus, Ulothrix, Spirogyra*

Chloroplast

Nucleus

Spirogyra

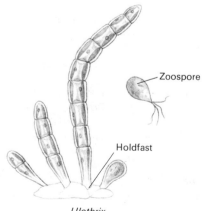

Zoospore

Holdfast

Ulothrix

400

Phylum CHRYSOPHYTA (diatoms):

1. Occur in both fresh water and marine.
2. Possess complex silicon—aluminum two-part "shells" or tests.
3. Contain yellow or brown pigments in addition to chlorophyll.

Representative genera: *Pinnularia, Staurastrum, Tabellaria*

4. Diatomaceous earth is important as a commercial abrasive.
5. Store oil as an energy source rather than starch.
6. First link in most aquatic food chains.

Tabellaria

Phylum PHAEOPHYTA (brown algae):

1. Contain chlorophyll and yellow or brown pigments.
2. Generally large, marine, leaflike forms.

3. Alternation of generation with diploid sporophytes.
4. Body differentiated into specific parts—holdfast, stipe, blade.

Representative genera: *Fucus, Laminaria, Macrocystis, Nereocystis*

Fucus

Nereocystis

Phylum RHODOPHYTA (red algae):

1. Contain chlorophyll and a red pigment, phycoerythrin.
2. Generally marine.
3. Alternation of generation with diploid sporophyte (some have three generations).
4. Feathery, filamentous, or leaflike.
5. Some deposit calcium on their cell walls.

Representative genera: *Polysiphonia, Corallina* (red-encrusting alga), *Grinnellia* (leafy red alga)

Grinnellia

Phylum MASTIGOPHORA (flagellates):

Class: Phytomastigina (autotrophic flagellates):

1. One to several flagella for locomotion.
2. Contain chloroplasts.
3. Store starch as food reserve.
4. Occur solitary or in colonies.

Representative genera: *Euglena, Volvox*

Euglena

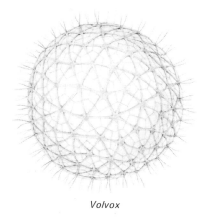

Volvox

Class: Dinoflagellata (dinoflagellates or fire algae):

1. Two flagella; one longitudinal and one transverse as a girdle.
2. May be armored with hard cellulose plates or naked.
3. Large blooms of these organisms in the sea are called *red tides.*
4. Contain chlorophyll.

Representative genera: *Ceratium, Gymnodinium, Gonyaulax*

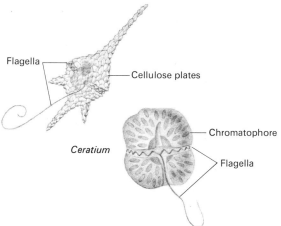

Ceratium

Gymnodinium

Class: Zoömastigina (heterotrophic flagellates):

1. Possess one to many flagella for locomotion.
2. Many are parasitic in the blood of animals and humans, such as sleeping sickness (*Trypanosoma*).
3. Some are commensal in the gut of termites where they digest cellulose (*Trichonympha*).

Representative genera: *Trypanosoma, Trichonympha*

Trypanosoma

Phylum MYXOMYCETES (slime molds):

1. Two stages in the life cycle: a multinucleate ameboid plasmodium and a stalked fruiting body which produces haploid spores.
2. Spores germinate into flagellated gametes. Two fuse to produce a new plasmodium stage.
3. Nutrition is phagotrophic. Ingest bacteria and decaying particles of organic matter.

Representative genera: *Physarum, Stemonitis*

Slime mold

Phylum EUMYCOPHYTA (fungi):

1. Most of body is made up of filaments called *hyphae*; a mass of hyphae is a *mycelium*.
2. Contain no photosynthetic pigments.
3. Nutrition is saprophytic on decaying organic matter.

Class: Phycomycetes (algal fungi):

1. Mostly aquatic fungi.
2. Long hyphae filaments.
3. Hyphae lack transverse walls.

Representative genus: *Rhizopus* (black bread mold)

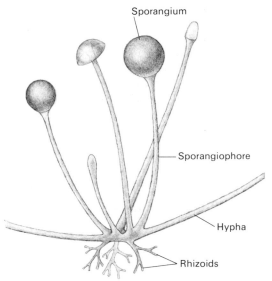

Rhizopus

Class: Ascomycetes (cup fungi):

1. Possess septate (transverse walls) hyphae.
2. Fruiting body is generally cup-shaped and called an *ascocarp*.
3. Includes the yeasts, molds, and mildews.
4. Many are pathogenic to plants.

Representative genera: *Saccharomyces, Penicillium, Aspergillus, Peziza*

Yeast cells
Saccaromyces

Peziza (cup fungus)

Class: Basidiomycetes (club fungi) :

1. Have septate hyphae.
2. Fruiting body of mycelium is large and characteristic (mushrooms, bracket fungi, and puffballs).
3. Spores are produced as buds from a club-shaped hyphal tip called a *basidium*.

Representative genera : *Amanita* (poisonous mushroom), *Fomes* (bracket fungus)

Phylum SARCODINA (amoebae) :

1. Move by extending pseudopods.
2. Ingest food by phagocytosis.
3. May produce tests of calcium carbonate or silicon or pick up bits of debris.

Representative genera : *Amoeba*, *Entamoeba histolytica* (causes amoebic dysentery), *Difflugia* (Testacea), *Globigerina* (Foraminifera), *Actinosphaerium* (Heliozoa), *Lychnocanium* (Radiolaria)

Amanita

Amoeba

Globigerina

Difflugia

Actinosphaerium

404

Phylum SPOROZOA (sporozoans):

1. All species are parasitic and bear spores at some stage of the life cycle.
2. Life cycle may involve a vector carrier such as the mosquito.
3. Possess no specialized organelles for locomotion.
4. Alternate stages of sexual and asexual reproduction.
5. Infest blood and tissues of animals and man.

Representative genera: *Plasmodium* (causes malaria), *Eimeria* (causes coccidiosis)

Plasmodium
(ring stage of malaria
parasite in red blood cell)

Phylum CILIOPHORA:

1. Have cilia or sucking tentacles.
2. Possess two types of nuclei.

Class: Ciliata (ciliates or infusoria):

1. Move by means of cilia throughout life.
2. Have definite body shape and a cell mouth and anus.
3. Possess stinging organelles (trichocysts) for protection and food capture.

Representative genera: *Paramecium* (slipper animal), *Stentor* (trumpet animal)

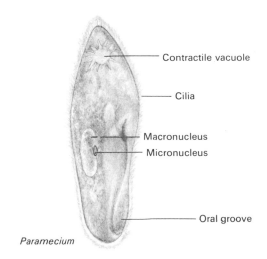

Paramecium

— Contractile vacuole

— Cilia

— Macronucleus
— Micronucleus

— Oral groove

Class: Suctoria (suctorians):

1. Cilia present only in motile young stages.
2. Mature adults lose cilia and generally become stalked and sessile.
3. Feed on protistans by piercing them with a sharp tentacle and sucking out the protoplasm.

Representative genera: *Podyphyra* (stalked), *Anarma* (no stalk)

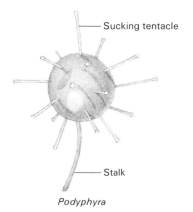

— Sucking tentacle

— Stalk

Podyphyra

Kingdom METAPHYTA

Phylum BRYOPHYTA:

1. Lack true roots, stems or leaves.
2. Possess multicellular reproductive organs.
3. Zygote develops within female gametophyte.
4. Produce multicellular embryos.
5. Undergo definite alternation of generation.
6. Gametophyte (haploid) generation is dominant.

Class: Hepaticae (liverworts) :

1. Flat leaflike gametophyte.
2. Produce stalked sex organs.
3. Form asexual buds called *gemmae.*

Representative genus : *Marchantia*

Class: Musci (mosses) :

1. Erect or trailing leafy gametophyte.
2. Produce asexual buds in "leaf" axils or stem bases.

Representative genera : *Polytrichum* (hairy cap), *Sphagnum* (peat bog moss)

Class: Anthocerotae (hornworts) :

1. Sex organs lie in cavities in the gametophyte thallus.
2. An erect sporophyte grows out of gameto-phyte.

Representative genus : *Anthoceros*

Marchantia

Polytrichum

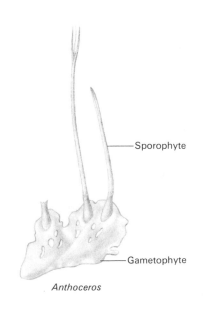

Anthoceros

Phylum TRACHEOPHYTA:

1. Possess conducting tissues, xylem, and phloem.
2. Have true roots, stems, and leaves.
3. Sporophyte is dominant generation.

Subphylum PSILOPSIDA:

1. Have small, scalelike leaves.
2. Stems produce capsulelike sporangia that form spores.
3. Tropical or subtropical distribution.
4. Only two living genera.

Representative genus: *Psilotum*

Subphylum LYCOPSIDA (club mosses):

1. Sporangia develop in conelike structures in leaf axils.
2. Asexual reproduction by buds called *bulbils.*

Representative genera: *Selaginella, Lycopodium* (ground pine)

Subphylum SPHENOPSIDA (horsetails):

1. Sporophytes are of two types, large sexual stalks bearing a conelike strobilus and a smaller, leafy vegetative stalk.
2. Narrow leaves are arranged in whorls or jointed stalks.
3. Strobilus is not composed of leaves but is a "new" structure—produces spores.

Representative genus: *Equisetum* (scouring rush or horsetail)

Sporangium

Psilotum

Strobilus

Selaginella

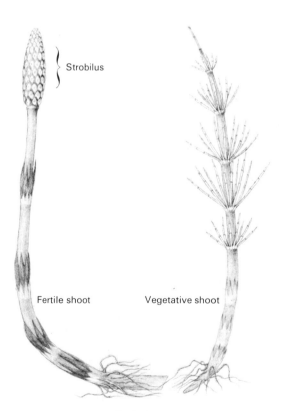

Strobilus

Fertile shoot   Vegetative shoot

Equisetum

Subphylum PTEROPSIDA:

1. Sporophyte generation dominant.
2. Possess large, complex leaves.
3. Produce seeds (except the ferns).
4. Conducting tissues are prominent.

Class: Filicinae (ferns) :

1. Fronds arise from a long underground stem called a *rhizome*.
2. Fronds bear clusters of sporangia called *sori* on underside.
3. Gametophyte known as a *prothallus* develops from a spore in the soil.

Representative genera : *Pteridium* (bracken), *Polypodium* (licorice), *Polystichum* (sword fern), *Adiantum* (maidenhair)

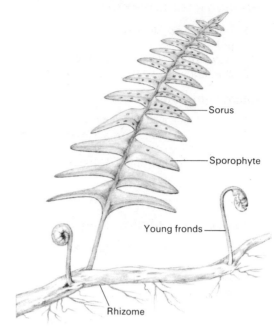

Polypodium

Class: Gymnospermae (cone-bearing seed plants) :

1. Seeds are exposed on scales of cones.
2. Seeds contain endosperm as starch food reserve.
3. Seeds develop on the sporophyte and are released for germination.

Order: Cycadales :

1. Mostly fossil plants—9 living genera.
2. Tropical and subtropical distribution—South America and Africa.
3. Many are known as tree ferns—grow over 50 feet tall and look like palm trees.

Representative genera : *Encephalartos* (large tree fern), *Dioon* (low plant)

Order: Coniferales (conifers) :

1. Usually trees with large branched stems.
2. Small, needle-like leaves.
3. Produce woody stem.

Representative genera : *Pinus* (pine), *Abies* (fir), *Larix* (larch), *Thuja* (western red cedar), *Tsuga* (hemlock), *Sequoia* (giant redwood)

Class: Angiospermae (covered-seed plants) :

Dioon

408

1. Seeds enclosed in a fleshy or dry fruit derived from ovary.
2. Bear flowers.
3. Produce herbaceous or woody stems.

Subclass: Monocotyledonae:

1. One embryonic leaf at germination.
2. Parallel veined leaves.
3. No cambium rings.
4. Vascular bundles scattered.
5. Flower parts in threes or multiples of three.

Representative genera: *Zea* (corn), *Lilium* (lily), *Triticum* (wheat)

Subclass: Dicotyledonae:

1. Two embryonic leaves at germination.
2. Net-veined leaves.
3. Distinct cambium present.
4. Vascular bundles in rings.
5. Flower parts in fours or fives or multiples.

Representative genera: *Acer* (maple tree), *Ranunculus* (buttercup)

Kingdom METAZOA

Phylum PORIFERA (sponges—porebearers):

1. Cellular level of organization.
2. Collect food by passing water currents through a porous body. There is usually a large internal cavity.
3. Water passages are lined with flagellate collar cells called choanocytes which produce water currents and digest food.
4. Body possesses skeletal spines called spicules among the cells.
5. Reproduction by asexual budding or sexual gametic fusion.

Class: Hexactinellida (glass sponges):

1. Silicon dioxide spicules.
2. Fine, lacelike structure.

Representative genus: *Euplectella* (Venus' flower-basket sponge)

Class: Calcarea (calcareous sponges):

1. Calcium carbonate spicules.

Representative genus: *Scypha* (the vase sponge)

Thuja

Lilium

Ranunculus

Euplectella

Class: Demospongiae (bath sponges) :

1. Silicon dioxide spicules.
2. Contain a fibrous protein called *spongin*.
3. Have very complex water passages.

Representative genus : *Spongia* (bath sponge)

Phylum COELENTERATA:

1. Tissue level of development (nerve tissue).
2. Mouth surrounded by tentacles containing stinging cells called *cnidocytes* (formerly called nematocysts).
3. Reproduction by asexual budding and sexual gamete fusion.
4. No anus.
5. Sessile polyp often alternating with a sexual medusa or jellyfish form.

Class: Hydrozoa (hydra-like animals) :

1. Solitary or colonial polyp predominant.
2. May produce sexually reproducing medusae.
3. Polyps may float on gas-filled bladders.

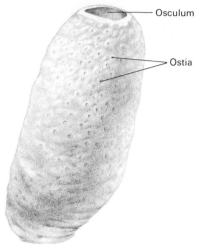

Sponge

Representative genera : *Hydra* (solitary—no medusa stage), *Obelia* (colonial, medusa stage), *Gonionemus* (conspicuous medusa stage), *Physalia* (Portuguese man-of-war ; colonial polyps on gas float)

Hydra

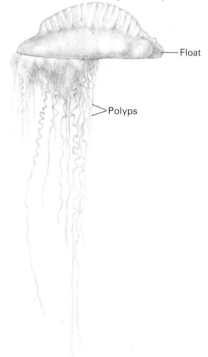

Physalia

Class: Scyphozoa (true jellyfish) :

1. Sexual medusa stage predominant.
2. Polyp produces asexual buds that develop into medusae.
3. Medusae possess balance organs at the edge of the bell.

Representative genera : *Aurelia, Cyanea*

Class: Anthozoa (flowerlike animals) :

1. Polyp stage predominant : solitary or colonial.
2. Reproduction by budding and gamete fusion.
3. Fairly well-developed nerve-net system with giant fibers for quick reactions.

Representative genera : *Metridium, Anthopleura, Lophelia* (coral)

Phylum PLATYHELMINTHES (flatworms):

1. Organ level of development.
2. Flattened dorsoventrally.
3. Incomplete digestive system or none.
4. Development of a head with "brain" and sense organs (cephalization) in free-living forms.
5. Most species are parasitic and follow complex life cycle.
6. No body cavity (acoelomate).

Class: Turbellaria (free-living flatworms) :

1. Digestive system with mouth but no anus.
2. Cellular epidermis.
3. High degree of regeneration.
4. Monoecious (possessing both male and female organs).

Representative genus : *Planaria*

Class: Trematoda (flukes) :

1. All parasitic.
2. Highly developed reproductive system — monoecious.
3. No digestive, respiratory, or circulatory systems.
4. Life cycle usually involves an intermediate host such as a snail.
5. Anterior and ventral suckers.
6. Body covered by protective cuticle.

Representative genera : *Fasciola* (sheep liver fluke), *Clonorchis* (human liver fluke), *Paragonimus* (lung fluke), *Schistosoma* (blood fluke)

Aurelia

Anthopleura

Planaria

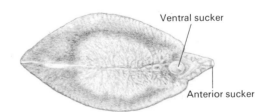

Fasciola

411

Class: Cestoda (tapeworms):

1. All parasitic.
2. Highly developed reproductive system—monoecious.
3. No digestive, respiratory, or circulatory systems.
4. Life cycle may involve intermediate host such as pig, dog, fish, or a copepod.
5. Body composed of head, neck, and proglottids (individual reproductive units).
6. Head (or scolex) may be armed with hooks or suckers for attachment to intestinal wall.

Representative genera: *Taenia saginata* (in beef), *Dibothrocephalus* (in fish)

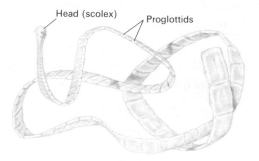

Taenia

Phylum ASCHELMINTHES (wormlike animals):

1. Organ-system level of development.
2. A false body cavity (pseudocoelom).
3. Complete digestive system with mouth and anus.
4. A varied group.

Class: Rotifera (wheel animals):

1. Aquatic.
2. Small—up to 1 mm.
3. Possess two ciliated food-collecting discs called a *corona*.
4. Elongated trunk usually has attachment "toes" with cement gland.

Representative genera: *Rotaria, Philodina, Keratella*

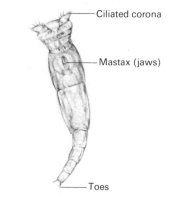

Philodina

Class: Nematoda (round worms):

1. Many are parasitic.
2. Cylindrical worms covered with a cuticle.
3. Well-developed nerve tracts.

Representative genera: *Turbatrix* (vinegar eels), *Ascaris* (in pig or horse intestine), *Trichinella* (in pig muscle), *Wuchereria* (filarial worm—elephantiasis)

Class: Nematomorpha (horsehair worms):

1. Larval stage is parasitic in an arthropod such as a grasshopper.
2. Free-living adults possess only a reproductive system and live only a short time.
3. Long, threadlike body.

Representative genus: *Gordius* (horsehair worm)

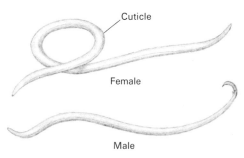

Ascaris

412

Phylum ECTOPROCTA (moss animals; sometimes called Bryozoa):

1. Mostly marine.
2. Live in colonies that resemble patches of moss.
3. Each animal lives in a shell-like cuticle.
4. Have a true body cavity, a coelom (lined on both sides with mesoderm).
5. Complete U-shaped digestive tract.
6. No respiratory or circulatory systems.
7. Possess a horseshoe-shaped band called a *lophophore* for food collection; the lophophore contains many ciliated tentacles.

Representative genera: *Bugula* (fuzzy ectoproct found on pilings), *Membranipora* (encrusting ectoproct)

Bugula

Phylum BRACHIOPODA (lamp shells):

1. Possess a true coelom.
2. All species marine.
3. Reside in hinged calcium carbonate shells. (Unlike a clam, the animal is oriented in a dorsoventral position; clams are laterally compressed.)
4. Collect food with a lophophore.
5. Have a complete circulatory system, heart, and blood vessels.
6. Attach to substratum by a fleshy stalk called a *peduncle*.

Representative genera: *Terebratulina, Magellania* (lamp shells)

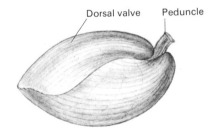

Magellania

Phylum MOLLUSCA (soft-bodied animals):

1. Possess a true coelom.
2. Freshwater, marine, or terrestrial.
3. All produce a fleshy mantle which may secrete a hard shell.
4. Possess all organ systems, respiration by gills, lungs, or mantle.
5. Many have a highly developed ventral muscular foot.

Class: Amphineura (chitons):

1. Marine.
2. Large muscular foot.
3. Eight dorsal calcium carbonate plates.
4. Reduced head.
5. Possess a radula for scraping up algae.

Representative genera: *Katharina* (black leather chitons), *Tonicella* (lined chiton), *Cryptochiton* (gum boot)

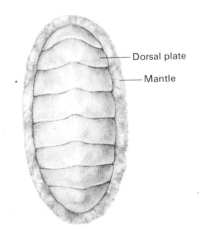

Tonicella

413

Class: Scaphopoda (tooth shells) :

1. Marine.
2. Small foot.
3. Live in open cylindrical shell.
4. No definite head.
5. Possess a radula and six grasping tentacles.

Representative genus : *Dentalium* (tooth shell)

Foot

Dentalium

Class: Gastropoda (stomach foot, snail-like) :

1. Freshwater, marine, and terrestrial types.
2. Large creeping foot.
3. Shell simple, coiled, or absent.
4. Well-developed head.

Representative genera : *Helix* (land snail), *Tegula* (turban snail), *Anisodoris* (sea lemon—nudibranch), *Hermissenda* (opalescent nudibranch)

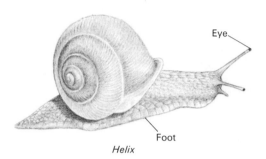

Eye

Foot

Helix

Class: Pelecypoda (hatchet foot) :

1. Bivalve, laterally compressed shells.
2. Dorsal hinge.
3. Foot modified for digging (or reduced as in sea mussels).
4. No definite head or radula.
5. Food is filtered from the water by the gills and passed to the mouth.

Representative genera : *Anodonta* (freshwater clam), *Siliqua* (razor clam), *Mytilus* (sea mussel), *Teredo* (ship borer), *Mya* (soft-shelled clam)

Hermissenda

Class: Cephalopoda (head foot) :

1. Shell reduced or absent.
2. Conspicuous head with well-developed camera-type eyes.
3. Foot represented by arms or tentacles.
4. Well-developed brain and nervous system.
5. Possess a radula and a horny beak.

Representative genera : *Loligo* (squid), *Octopus*, *Sepia* (cuttlefish), *Nautilus* (chambered nautilus)

Siphons

Umbo

Foot

Mya

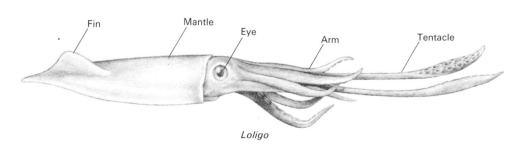

Fin   Mantle   Eye   Arm   Tentacle

Loligo

414

Phylum ANNELIDA (segmented worms):

1. Freshwater, marine, and terrestrial.
2. Body separated into segments.
3. High degree of cephalization in some species.
4. True coelom.
5. Respiration primarily through body surface.
6. Closed circulatory system with arteries, capillaries, and veins.
7. Special excretory organs called nephridia.

Class: Oligochaeta (worms with few hairs):

1. Reduced head with few sense organs.
2. Small bristles or setae on each segment.
3. Monoecious.

Representative genus: *Lumbricus* (earthworm)

Class: Polychaeta (many-haired worms):

1. Highly cephalized with eyes, sensory palps, and tentacles.
2. Each segment possesses a pair of flaplike appendages having long bristles.
3. Usually dioecious.

Representative genera: *Nereis* (marine clam worm), *Aphrodite* (sea mouse)

Class: Hirudinea (leeches):

1. Reduced head.
2. No bristles present.
3. Anterior and posterior suckers.
4. Blood-sucking forms possess three chitinous teeth.
5. All species are monoecious.

Representative genus: *Hirudo* (medicinal leech)

Phylum ARTHROPODA (joint-footed animals):

1. Segmented body has paired jointed appendages.
2. High degree of cephalization with many sense organs.
3. Possess a chitinous exoskeleton.
4. Body divided into head, thorax, and abdomen.
5. Circulatory system is open—has no capillaries.
6. Live in practically every world habitat.

Lumbricus

Nereis

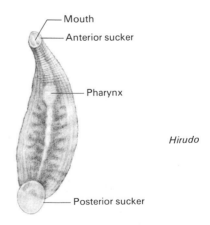

Hirudo

415

Subphylum: ONYCHOPHORA (claw bearers):

1. Internally segmented like annelid worms.
2. Possess nephridia like annelids.
3. Have small, clawed jointed appendages.
4. Respiration by tracheal tubes.
5. Characteristics place it phylogenetically between Annelida and Arthropoda.

Representative genus: *Peripatus*

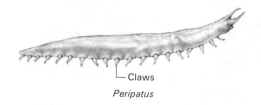

Claws

Peripatus

Subphylum: CHELICERATA (hard claws):

1. No jaws.
2. First pair of appendages have pincer claws for gathering food.
3. Head and thorax fused.
4. Respiration by book gills at base of abdominal appendages or gills or tracheae.

Representative genus: *Limulus* (horseshoe "crab")

Class: Merostomata:

1. Cephalothorax conspicuous.
2. Possess gills.
3. Two lateral compound eyes.

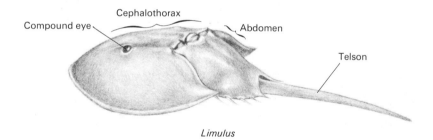

Cephalothorax

Compound eye

Abdomen

Telson

Limulus

Class: Arachnida (spiders, ticks, mites, and scorpions):

1. Four pairs of legs.
2. No antennae.
3. Respiration by tracheae, gills, or book lungs (spiders).

Representative genera: *Argiope* (garden spider), *Dermacentor* (tick), *Centrurus* (scorpion)

Subphylum: MANDIBULATA (possess jaws):

1. Possess mandibles (jaws).
2. Have antennae.

Mite   Dermacentor (atick)

Class: Crustacea (shelled) :

1. Mostly aquatic species, although some live in moist soil.
2. Respiration by gills.
3. Two pairs of antennae.

Representative genera : *Cambarus* (crayfish), *Homarus* (lobster), *Daphnia* (water flea), *Cyclops* (copepod), *Cancer* (edible crab), *Porcellio* (terrestrial sow bug)

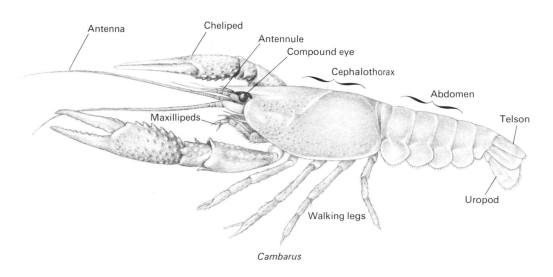

Cambarus

Class: Diplopoda :

1. Generally, two pairs of jointed appendages on each segment.
2. Cylindrical body.

Representative genus : *Spirobolus* (millipede)

Class: Chilopoda :

1. One pair of jointed appendages on each segment.
2. Dorsoventrally flattened.

Representative genus : *Scolopendra* (centipede)

Class: Insecta or Hexapoda (six-legged) :

1. Body divided into three distinct regions : head, thorax, and abdomen.
2. Three pairs of appendages on the thorax.
3. Thorax may possess one or two pairs of wings or none.
4. Respiration by tracheal tubes.
5. Open circulatory system.
6. High degree of cephalization, one pair of antennae, and compound and simple eyes.
7. As many as 700,000 species have been identified.

Scolopendra

Representative genera: *Dynastes* (rhinoceros beetle), *Musca* (housefly), *Speyeria* (fritillary butterfly), *Apis* (honeybee), *Romalea* (grasshopper)

Dynastes

Apis

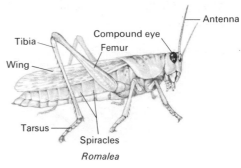

Romalea

Phylum ECHINODERMATA (spiny-skinned animals):

1. Endoskeleton of separate or fused calcareous plates (covered by epidermis).
2. Move by means of a water vascular system with tube feet.
3. Possess a true coelom derived from the same embryonic region as that of vertebrates.
4. Head absent.

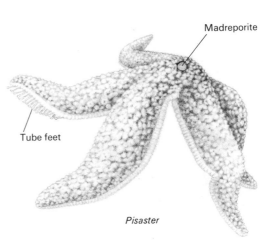

Pisaster

Class: Asteroidea (sea stars):

1. Oral, aboral flattening.
2. Five, six, twenty, or more radiating arms.
3. Two rows of tube feet in open groove under each arm.
4. Respiration by small dermal branchiae (gills) on aboral surface.

Representative genera: *Pisaster* (purple star), *Henricia* (blood star), *Leptasterias* (6-rayed star), *Solaster* (sun star)

Class: Ophiuroidea (serpent or brittle stars):

1. Small oral disc with no anus.
2. Long, slender arms.
3. Arm grooves closed or absent.

Representative genera: *Ophioderma* (brittle star), *Gorgonocephalus* (basket star)

Ophioderma

418

Class: Echinoidea (sea urchins, sand dollars, and sea biscuits) :

1. Calcareous plates fused to form a hollow test.
2. Possess movable calcareous spines.
3. Tube feet extend from small pores in the test.
4. Oral opening has a five-toothed structure for feeding (Aristotle's lantern).
5. Respire by dermal branchiae.

Representative genera: *Strongylocentrotus* (sea urchin), *Dendraster* (sand dollar), *Clypeaster* (sea biscuit)

Clypeaster

Class: Holothuroidea (sea cucumbers) :

1. Muscular body has extremely reduced plates.
2. Tube feet occur in five double rows along the soft cylindrical body.
3. Retractile tentacles surround the mouth.
4. Respire by internal, branching, anal trees.

Representative genus: *Cucumaria* (red sea cucumber)

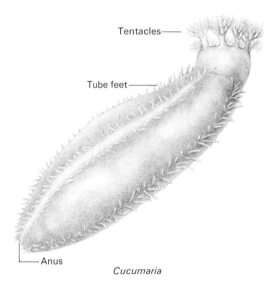

Tentacles

Tube feet

Anus

Cucumaria

Phylum CHORDATA:

1. Possess a notochord.
2. Pharyngeal gill slits at some stage of development.
3. Have a single, dorsal hollow nerve tube.

Subphylum: UROCHORDATA (tunicates):

1. Free-swimming larva possesses a notochord and segmental muscle.
2. Adult is solitary or colonial and sessile. Notochord is lost.
3. Surrounded by a tough cellulose tunic which contains incurrent and excurrent siphons.
4. All marine species.

Representative genera: *Molgula, Ciona* (sea squirts)

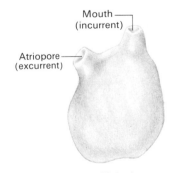

Mouth (incurrent)

Atriopore (excurrent)

Molgula

Subphylum: CEPHALOCHORDATA:

1. Fishlike animal with a head.
2. Notochord remains throughout life.
3. Segmental muscle and postanal tail.

Representative genus : *Branchiostoma* (lancelet or amphioxus)

Subphylum : VERTEBRATA :

1. Notochord replaced by cartilage or bone vertebral column.
2. Usually has paired appendages.

Class: Agnatha (jawless fishes) :
Representative genus : *Entosphenus* (lamprey eel)

Class: Chondrichthyes (cartilagenous fishes) :
Representative genus : *Squalus* (dogfish shark)

Class: Osteichthyes (bony fishes) :
Representative genus : *Perca* (perch), *Salmo* (trout).

Branchiostoma

Entosphenus

G. Curvier (tiger shark)

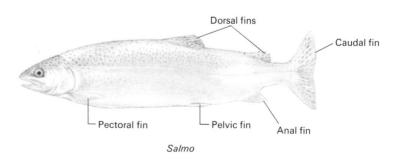

Salmo

420

Class: Amphibia (frogs, toads, and salamanders):

1. Thin, moist skin.
2. Four fleshy, jointed limbs.
3. Possess lungs.
4. Three-chambered heart.

Representative genera: *Hyla* (tree frog), *Taricha* (rough-skinned newt), *Ensatina, Bufo* (common toad)

Hyla

Ensatina

Bufo

Class: Reptilia (snakes, lizards, turtles, alligators, and crocodiles):

1. Possess clawed appendages (except snakes).
2. Body protected by scales.
3. Lay hard-shelled or leathery land-type eggs with functional allantois and yolk sac.
4. Three-chambered heart except crocodile which has four.

Lampropeltis

Representative genera: *Lampropeltis* (king snake), *Sceloporus* (Pacific swift lizard), *Caretta* (loggerhead turtle)

Caretta

Crocodylidac (American alligator)

Class: Aves (birds) :

1. Possess feathers.
2. May have wings with bone structure homologous to forelimb of tetrapods.
3. Four-chambered heart.
4. Warm-blooded (homeothermic).
5. Lay hard-shelled, land-type eggs.

Representative genera : *Turdus* (robin), *Larus* (herring gull), *Struthio* (ostrich)

Class: Mammalia (milk producers) :

1. Possess mammary glands.
2. Have external body hair.
3. Warm-blooded (homeothermic).
4. Four-chambered heart.
5. Embryo develops internally, attached to a placenta except in the egg-laying monotremes (*Platypus*).

Subclass: Prototheria :

Order: Monotremata (egg-laying mammals) :

1. Possess a horny beak as adults.
2. Lay small, leathery eggs.
3. Young nurse from small mammary glands distributed on the abdomen.

Representative genera : *Ornithorhynchus* (duck-billed platypus), *Echidna* (spiny anteater)

Subclass: Metatheria :

Order: Marsupialia (pouched mammals) :

1. Possess an abdominal pouch which contains mammary glands.
2. Immature young leave uterus, migrate to the pouch, and attach to nipples with their mouths.

Representative genera : *Didelphis* (American opossum), *Macropus* (kangaroo)

Larus

Ornithorhynchus

Didelphis

Subclass: Eutheria (placental mammals):

Representative orders:

Insectivora—small; insect eating; live in underground burrows; shrews, moles, and hedgehogs.

Sorex (shrew)

Chiroptera—possess membranous wings, enlarged ears, and sharp teeth; most feed on flying insects; bats.

Myotis (bat)

Lagomorpha—rabbitlike mammals; herbivorous; continuously growing incisors, no canine teeth, hind legs elongated for jumping; rabbits, hares, and pikas.

Sylvilagus

Rodentia—gnawing mammals; herbivorous; incisor
teeth grow continuously, no canine teeth; rats,
mice, beavers, squirrels, and porcupines.

Sciurus

Cetacea—aquatic; possess flippers, and dorsal nostrils or blow hole; whales, dolphins, and porpoises.

Tursiops (bottlenosed dolphin)

Carnivora—flesh eating; well-developed canine teeth, and sense organs; cats, dogs, foxes, raccoons,
bears, and aquatic forms such as seals and sea lions.

Vulpes (red fox)

424

Proboscidea—herbivorous ; large head and ears, elongated proboscis or trunk, upper incisors produce tusks ; pachyderms ; largest land mammals : African and Indian elephants.

Elephas

Perissodactyla—hoofed with odd number of toes; herbivorous; teeth with grinding ridges; horses, rhinoceroses, and tapirs.

Tapirus (Malayan tapir)

Artiodactyla—hoofed with even number of toes; herbivorous; four-part stomach; pigs, hippopotamuses, camels, cattle, moose, deer, and giraffes.

Alces

Primates—five digits on hands and feet, thumbs opposable to innermost toes permit grasping, head rotates on spine, well-developed brain, especially cerebrum ; lemurs, monkeys, apes, and man.

Cercopithecus (grass monkey)

Appendix II

Analysis, Presentation, and Interpretation of Data

THE USE OF MATHEMATICS

A vital aspect of any scientific endeavor involves the analysis and presentation of data. Only when data are properly presented can they be meaningfully interpreted. If possible it is best to present the results of an experiment in mathematical terms and most modern sciences utilize mathematics, since it provides a quantitative means in a universal language for analyzing, presenting, and interpreting data. The specific interpretation that an individual scientist gives to the results of an experiment may depend on the mathematical evaluation of the data. Standard statistical methods are available for analyzing data and arriving at a probability value. Thus the probability of a natural phenomenon occurring, or the probability of a solution to a problem being correct, can usually be stated in mathematical terms.

THE USE OF GRAPHS

Graphs are commonly used in all of the sciences to present data. They provide a means of readily visualizing and interpreting the findings of the particular study and perhaps of drawing some conclusions. Since graphs are such useful tools, we shall briefly consider their construction and meaning.

A graph is essentially a diagram that represents the variation of one variable in comparison with another. The first step in making a graph is to draw two axes at right angles to each other as shown below.

The vertical axis is termed the *ordinate* and the horizontal axis the *abscissa*. Suppose now we want to see the relationship between the number of students in a biology class and the grades they receive on a test. To portray this relationship graphically, we choose one of the axes, in this case the ordinate, and let it represent the number of students. The other axis, the abscissa, will then represent the grades received by the students. Next we lay off equal distances on the axes and assign specific values to them starting with zero at the origin, which is the intersection of the two axes. (Note that the scales of the two axes do not need to be identical.)

If we now draw vertical and horizontal lines from the abscissa and ordinate, respectively, these lines will intersect at some point in the plane of the diagram; this is called *plotting the*

data. These intersections have two values associated with them showing the relationship between the quantities plotted. If the points are then connected by a smooth curve, we can easily determine for any value of one variable the value of the second variable at any point. Such a graph is called a *line graph*. Data are often summarized in a table, from which the graph is then constructed. A summary table and a line graph are shown in Figure A-1.

Grades	A	B	C	D	E
Number of students	9	20	52	25	5

Figure A·1 A table and a line graph to show the relative frequency of the grades distributed over a class of 111 students on a biology test.

Another type of graph is the *histogram* or *bar graph*. Figure A-2 is a bar graph that represents the results of a study of the effect of different combinations of salts on the gill tissues of a saltwater mussel. One factor in the study was the variation of the combination of salts in which the tissues were placed. The other factor was the length of time the tissues remained alive. Mussel gill tissue possesses small whiplike structures called *cilia*. In the living tissue these cilia beat rhythmically, moving particles over the tissues. This movement may be easily observed with a compound microscope and "death" was established as the point at which the cilia stopped beating. Figure A-2 includes the table with the raw data and their graphical representation.

430

Solution	Length of Life of Tissues
Sodium chloride (NaCl) and calcium chloride ($CaCl_2$)	4 hr, 15 min
Sodium chloride (NaCl) and magnesium chloride ($MgCl_2$)	22 hr
Sodium chloride (NaCl), potassium chloride (KCl), and magnesium chloride ($MgCl_2$)	63 hr
Sodium chloride (NaCl), potassium chloride (KCl), calcium chloride ($CaCl_2$), magnesium chloride ($MgCl_2$)	72 hr
Sea water (control)	78 hr

Several conclusions can readily be drawn from a quick review of the graph. First, the tissues lived longest in the salt water in which they normally live. Second, the tissues lived longer in solutions containing combinations of many salts. Third, in solutions of only two salts the tissues expired much sooner than in combinations of three or more salts. This shows the summarizing characteristics of a graph.

A line graph could easily be constructed from this bar graph by drawing a line from the top and center of one bar to the next. Such a graph is shown in Figure A-3.

Figure A·3 A graph showing the length of time gill tissue remains alive in various salt solutions.

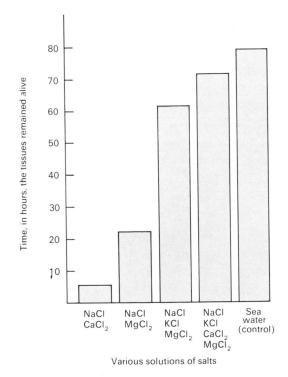

Figure A·2 A graph to show the length of time that gill tissue will remain alive in various solutions of salts. The table of data from which the graph was plotted is shown above.

Appendix III

The Major Fields of Biology

Biology includes many diverse areas of study that deal with all aspects of life. Usually biology is divided into *botany*, the study of plants, and *zoology*, the study of animals. Another common breakdown is based on *anatomy*, the study of structure, or *physiology*, function. Other specialized areas are:

Taxonomy
or Biosystematics—study of classification
Genetics —study of heredity
Evolution —study of variation and adaptation
Embryology —study of development of the individual
Pathology —study of diseases
Histology —study of tissues
Cytology —study of cells
Parasitology —study of parasites
Endocrinology —study of endocrine glands
Morphology —study of form
Ecology —study of the relationship of the
organism to its environment

Specific fields of biology that represent the various classification categories are often designated. Some of these are:

Bacteriology	—study of bacteria
Protozoology	—study of protozoans
Algology	—study of algae
Agrostology	—study of grasses
Mycology	—study of fungi
Entomology	—study of insects
Ornithology	—study of birds
Mammalogy	—study of mammals
Herpetology	—study of reptiles
Helminthology	—study of worms

Index

441

NOTES